Abortion Policy and Christian Social Ethics in the United States

Abortion Policy and Christian Social Ethics in the United States

Mako A. Nagasawa

WIPF & STOCK · Eugene, Oregon

ABORTION POLICY AND CHRISTIAN SOCIAL ETHICS
IN THE UNITED STATES

Copyright © 2021 Mako A. Nagasawa. All rights reserved. Except for brief quotations in critical publications or reviews, no part of this book may be reproduced in any manner without prior written permission from the publisher. Write: Permissions, Wipf and Stock Publishers, 199 W. 8th Ave., Suite 3, Eugene, OR 97401.

Wipf & Stock
An Imprint of Wipf and Stock Publishers
199 W. 8th Ave., Suite 3
Eugene, OR 97401

www.wipfandstock.com

PAPERBACK ISBN: 978-1-7252-7189-0
HARDCOVER ISBN: 978-1-7252-7190-6
EBOOK ISBN: 978-1-7252-7191-3

Unless otherwise noted, all Scripture is taken from the NEW AMERICAN STANDARD BIBLE®, copyright © 1960, 1962, 1963, 1968, 1971, 1972, 1973, 1975, 1977, 1995 by The Lockman Foundation. Used by permission.

01/04/21

For Ming, with hope.

For Gail, with gratitude.

Contents

List of Illustrations and Tables | ix

Introduction | xi

Part One: Abortion in the Context of the Bible

Chapter 1: Western Christianity and Abortion in the Last Century and a Half | 3

Chapter 2: The Bible and Abortion: Exodus 21 | 17

Chapter 3: Early Jewish and Christian Thought on Abortion and Exodus 21 | 33

Chapter 4: Science as a Friend in the Discernment of Fetal Life | 63

Part Two: Child-Raising and the Protection of Women

Chapter 5: Men and Male Power in Scripture and Church History | 85

Chapter 6: Holding Men More Responsible Today | 112

Chapter 7: God's Gift Economy and the Heretics' Reward Economy | 142

Chapter 8: How Christian Heresy Contributes to Economic Anxiety and Abortion | 164

Chapter 9: How Christian Heresy Contributes to Health Care Policies and Abortion | 181

Chapter 10: Contraception or Restrictive Abortion Laws? | 198

Chapter 11: Why Christians Fear Contraception | 230

Part Three: Abortion in the Context of the United States Constitution

Chapter 12: *Roe v. Wade* and the U.S. Constitution in Context | 255

Chapter 13: Abortion and the U.S. Constitution as It Could Be | 284

Chapter 14: Christianity and Liberalism: There Is Still Hope | 306

Bibliography | 325

Author Index | 359

Subject Index | 367

Ancient Near Eastern Documents Index | 375

Illustrations and Tables

Exodus 21:22–25 in the Hebrew Masoretic (NRSV) vs. Greek Septuagint (Brenton's) | 19

Chiastic Literary Structure: Example | 27

Chiastic Literary Structure: Exodus 21:2–36 | 27

Basil of Caesarea, *Epistle 188.2* in the Nicene and Post-Nicene Fathers vs. Cambridge Edition of Early Christian Writings | 43

Incomes as a Percentage of Poverty Level | 144

U.S. Housing Price Index Since 1900 | 169

White Median Household Wealth vs. Black Median Household Wealth, 2005 vs. 2009 | 170

Median Wealth by Race and Education, 2013 | 173

Abortions Per Year, U.S.: 2002–16 | 199

Abortions Per Year, Colorado: 2007–15 | 205

Abortions Per Year, Texas: 2002–16 | 212

Abortions Per Year, Texas: 2012–16 (Projections) | 213

Abortions Per Year by Age Group, Texas: 2011–16 | 215

Introduction

I THOUGHT I UNDERSTOOD abortion as an issue, until I started examining it more deeply. When I investigated how Christians have historically understood the moral worth of the unborn, and what their biblical foundations were, the issues became unclear. I suspect most readers will be surprised to find that the Bible itself has a range of possible views about the moral status of a fetus and that this uncertainty will impact the abortion debates. When I looked at how Christians translated their views into public policies, especially in the U.S., the issues became even more complicated. This book traces some important points along that journey.

It's an important moment to do so. Abortion is a hotly contested issue, so much so that some Christians have become single-issue voters. Nearly five decades after the famous Supreme Court rulings *Roe v. Wade*, and the lesser known *Doe v. Bolton*, Americans have learned a great deal about abortion-related policies. Yet maybe not enough. The Bible is more clear about how to organize communities and resources to encourage a mother and father to believe that bringing their child into the world will be a blessing to that child, to them, and to the world. Yet that clarity is largely ignored today.

My approach here is not to focus on abortion as an issue of personal ethics primarily, but to approach it in terms of social policies and via what some would call Christian "political theology." Christians in the U.S. *must* account for the social conditions and policies that influence abortion rates. Some conservative Christians, for example, say that women considering abortion should consider adoption. In the year ending September 30, 2016, Planned Parenthood reported performing 321,384 abortions and only 3,889 adoption referrals, so there is certainly room to grow on adoptions.[1] I am grateful for every household who wants to adopt a newborn, and for every

---

1. "Abortion or Adoption."

woman who chooses past the stigma and discomfort to carry her pregnancy to term and deliver that baby to an eager, adoptive home. But without diminishing the beauty of this picture and the courage needed to embody it, we need to face facts: it is unsustainable. If every woman considering abortion chooses to carry her pregnancy to term, generous adoptive families will be filled to capacity within two and a half years.[2] Those conservative Christians who suggest that every woman should choose adoption over abortion *as a way of ending abortion* are not thinking that far ahead.

Another recent article underscores the need to examine abortion from a social perspective, not just from a criminal justice one. What if most abortions happen because *motherhood is hard*? The Guttmacher Institute estimates that nearly 60 percent of women getting abortions today are already mothers.[3] According to the Centers for Disease Control, about 14 percent of all abortions are procured by *married* women.[4] Those are very significant indications that addressing social conditions, such as poverty and the ordinary challenges of childraising, must be part of any approach that calls itself broadly "pro-life." If being a parent is hard, then being a single parent is exponentially harder. Being a single mom trying to go back to school because you were eighteen years old when you got married, and your husband died in an accident, or in a case of police brutality? I cannot even fathom it. We must therefore address social conditions, including male accountability.

I was struck to learn that, from the 1930s to 1960s, the pro-life movement was anchored by Catholic New Deal Democrats who saw the federal government as an important component to promoting a culture of life. As such, they argued for anti-abortion policies but also social welfare spending and a pro-labor economic system. Roman Catholics stressed the "seamless garment of life" and, in the Catholic Social Teaching, took a more holistic approach to social policy through anti-poverty measures and advocating for everyone to receive more protection against predatory employers and banks.

When the pro-life movement became allied with evangelicals and the Republican Party in the 1970s, however, the social policies that we now associate with economic conservatism became joined to the pro-life cause. Historian Daniel K. Williams notes that "pro-lifers' alliance with the Republican Party was never a comfortable one, and it required them to make

---

2. "How Many Couples" estimates optimistically that there are 2 million families in the U.S. hoping to adopt a child. Meanwhile, Jones et al., "Abortion Incidence, 2017," estimates that abortion rates have just started to recently dip below 1 million per year; in 2017, they estimated 862,230 abortions were performed in that year alone.

3. "United States: Abortion."

4. Jatlaoui et al., "Abortion Surveillance."

compromises that distressed some members of their movement. As they became more narrowly focused on reversing *Roe*, pro-lifers began to lose interest in some of the earlier human rights causes, such as anti-poverty efforts, that had once been important to them."[5] This shift from Catholic Democrats to evangelical Republicans, and the nature of this more recent alliance, is vital to understand.

I wish to reexamine some of this history from the standpoint of how Christian theological positions, science, culture, law, and social policies interact. At times, I offer some tentative policy proposals, hopefully acknowledging where uncertainties exist. At other times, I speak especially to Christians, Christian ministers, and ethicists, or to those hoping to understand why Christians have taken the positions that they have, hoping for more meaningful conversations with them. In the end, I hope Christians can resume a much fuller and broader engagement with the issue of abortion, acknowledging the limits of our own knowledge and tools but still communicating the love of Jesus.

---

5. Williams, *Defenders*, 8–9.

Part One

Abortion in the Context of the Bible

1

Western Christianity and Abortion in the Last Century and a Half

Is Science the Adversary of Christian Faith?

THE INTENSITY OF THE debates about abortion sometimes means that people do not look deeply at the issue. Perhaps we worry that we will become frustrated, or convicted, or disgusted. As a result, many people assume that the Bible is crystal clear about abortion. We assume that Christians have always believed that human personhood begins when the sperm fertilizes the egg. We believe that, historically, Christians used the Bible alone, without help from science, to decide how to view the fetus and the ethics of abortion. We may believe that Christians at the time of the writing of the U.S. Constitution were firmly against abortion and indicated that in the Constitution itself. We may believe that Christians in the early U.S. were single-issue purists, who always took their position against abortion without being influenced by their views about immigrants or racial segregation. And we assume that the Christian approach to abortion policies has more or less resembled how the Republican Party and the conservative right have expressed it since *Roe v. Wade* was decided in 1973.

None of this is true.

The first time the Catholic Church officially declared that the fetus was ensouled and acquired human personhood at conception was in 1869. That should get our attention. What did Catholics believe before 1869? Prior to that, for over a millennium and a half, with the exception of one pope, Catholic leaders believed that ensoulment happened at "quickening," the moment when the mother felt the baby kick. That happened anywhere from 16 to 22 weeks of gestation. They rooted the older view of "quickening" in one manuscript type of Exodus 21:22–25 which said that there was a difference between a fetus that is "formed" versus one that is "unformed." There is a lot more to that story, and that passage, too, because Eastern Orthodox Christians believed *something else* about abortion, for different reasons. And the Jewish community used *different* ancient biblical manuscripts of Exodus to believe yet *something else*. The ancient Jewish community used both these biblical manuscript types before Jesus, and Jesus honored them both. There was a *range* of legitimate opinions on abortion based on disagreement between *biblical manuscripts*, the most foundational level.

Nevertheless, the Catholic Church raised the stakes. In 1870, just one year later, Vatican I declared the doctrine of papal infallibility. These two decisions—one about the Catholic Church's view of the fetus, and one about the pope's authority—were not coincidental. They reflected a similar character: a response to science, when conservative Catholics and Protestants alike believed the Christian faith was under threat because of science. Unfortunately, the pronouncements of 1869 and 1870 did not reflect the original meaning of the word "catholic," which referred to "that which has been believed everywhere, always, and by all." Neither of these two pronouncements expressed things that had been believed everywhere, always, and by all Christians from the start of the Christian movement. In fact, various Roman Catholic leaders voiced opposition to papal infallibility, and in 1909, Rev. W. J. Sparrow Simpson published the first English account of the "behind the scenes" record of the Vatican's decision.[1]

Regarding Christian faith and science, the relationship between them had been quite positive since the time of Jesus, contrary to some popular beliefs.[2] In fact, part of the reason why the Eastern Orthodox and the Roman Catholic churches went in different ways on their views of the fetus (which I will explain in chapter 3) is because Scripture is unclear about it, because there are two competing manuscripts on this very issue (which I will explain in chapter 2), and because they relied on different scientific accounts to develop their opinions. The Greek East depended on Hippocrates, the "father of medicine," and the Latin West depended on Aristotle, who had studied miscarriages and fetal formation. This point, about Christians drawing on both Scripture *and* science, is where we must eventually turn our attention (chapters 3 and 4). The early Christian witness is important as laying examples for Christians to keep drawing on both sources.

Before that, however, we must face a painful story about how Western Christianity, in both its Catholic and the fundamentalist-evangelical Protestant branches, adopted adversarial stances towards science since the mid-1800s. That adversarial stance has affected Catholic and Protestant views on

1. Simpson, *Roman Catholic Opposition*.
2. Hart, *Atheist Delusions*, gives a very readable account.

abortion for a century and a half. In order for Christians to carefully consider scientific data again, especially about the fetus, we must explore why Western Christianity has had a knee-jerk reaction against science, including recent discoveries about the first few days of fetal life.

By the mid-1800s, Catholics and Protestants felt like their faith was under attack from science. In the realm of philosophy and politics, "Enlightenment" thinkers as early as Voltaire praised scientists like Newton and Galileo for challenging the Catholic social order and cosmology, even though the popular portrayals exaggerated the conflict for dramatic effect.[3] Many scientists had been people of faith and had even been funded by the church. In the realm of biology, Charles Darwin published his *Origin of Species* in 1859, introducing the scientific hypothesis that organisms were not created instantly as they are, but evolved over the course of generations, through natural selection and mutation. Catholics were not as worried as fundamentalist Protestants would later become about Darwin, but in the realm of medicine, new discoveries were made about the fetus which challenged the "quickening" view. In the realm of literature, the "higher critical" approach to Scripture also gained popular recognition in the nineteenth and twentieth centuries. The higher critical scholars claimed to know what lay "behind" the biblical texts themselves in various ways, to know its human origins and sources, and to therefore know the Bible exhaustively in ways the church did not. Initially a movement of German scholars, these professors of literature—sometimes without any Christian faith, who were rightly or wrongly associated with German anti-Semitism—purported to dispense with church clergy as authoritative interpreters of Scripture. "Traditional Roman Catholic academics usually responded to the higher critics with suspicion and distaste. . . . In sharp and deepening opposition, conservative Roman Catholic, Protestant, and Jewish scholars wrote feverishly to counter the growing consensus of higher critics."[4] In the realm of economics, a "birth control movement" was launched in the 1800s by debates over economist Thomas Malthus's concerns about overpopulation and feminists arguing for education about contraception.[5] Condoms and diaphragms were mass-produced in the late 1800s,[6] which challenged the church's traditional teaching against contraception. A few decades later, the

---

3. Hart, *Atheist Delusions*, 56–74.

4. Stewart, "Higher Criticism."

5. The Malthusian League was formed in 1877 and engaged in political advocacy to eliminate penalties from birth control education. See Ledbetter, *History*.

6. Peel and Potts, *Textbook*.

mass-produced car was perceived (whether true or not) as giving young people an easy way to have sex.

This was the context in which the Catholic Church made its pronouncements in 1869 and 1870. They sought to protect human beings, including the unborn, to be sure, but also to respond to the claims and methods of science. They sought to have an intellectual consistency which had the appearance of engaging the physical sciences on its own terms. On the one hand, in 1869, they adjusted to the scientific view of the fetus by withdrawing the church's position beyond the reach of science, where it had not been placed before. Their decision in 1870 to declare that the pope was infallible placed "knowledge" of the faith on an authoritative level, perhaps to respond to the claims of science to "know" reality, at least as some perceived science.

Catholic theologians, however, were not *certain* that the fertilized egg in the first instance was a person. They used an argument from *moral probability*. There is a *probability* that the fetus was ensouled from fertilization and a full human person from that point. For clarification, the probability argument is not about one possible outcome resulting from an action (e.g., like smoking could result in cancer, or fossil fuel reduction could slow climate change), but the probability that the fetus itself has moral weight akin to a full human person.

Moral probability was not the only approach or option possible, however. Catholic philosophers Daniel Dombrowski and Robert Deltete, in their book *A Brief, Liberal, Catholic Defense of Abortion*, examine church history and the development of science to argue that a limited "pro-choice position is defensibly Catholic."[7] The *New Catholic Encyclopedia* also acknowledges:

> After a *certain stage* of intrauterine development it is perfectly evident that fetal life is fully human. Although some might speculate as to when that stage is reached, there is *no way* of arriving at this knowledge by any known criterion; and as long as it is *probable* that embryonic life is human from the first moment of its existence, the purposeful termination [is immoral].[8]

In 1974, in the Declaration on Procured Abortion, the Congregation for the Doctrine of the Faith added a footnote which explains why ensoulment from conception must be regarded as a *probability* among other probable points in time. The Declaration "expressly leaves aside the question of the moment

---

7. Dombrowski, *Defense*, 29.
8. O'Connell, "Abortion II," 29, col. 1. Italics mine.

when the spiritual soul is infused" because "there is not unanimous tradition on this point and the authors are as yet in disagreement."⁹

Another Catholic scholar, bioethicist Carol Tauer, noted in 1984:

> While the teaching of the magisterium is also supported by a variety of types of evidence (biological, philosophical, and theological), its position finally appears to rest on one line of argument. This argument, which is actually the crucial point in the magisterial presentation, has been largely ignored by theologians who have offered dissenting opinions. For it does not depend either on biological information or on metaphysical theories. Rather, it is based on a theory of practical decision-making which was developed within Catholic moral theology. This theory, which provides methods for attaining practical certainty in the face of moral doubt, has a long history within the Catholic tradition.¹⁰

Moral probability is an important consideration, but scientific knowledge about the first few days of early fetal life now requires us to speak of ensoulment and personhood from fertilization as moral *improbabilities*. While the moral probability argument might be sufficient reason for some people to not personally abort a fetus, or to use in-vitro fertilization because the process creates unused fertilized eggs, serious doubts can be raised about the use of moral probability for public policy like this in every instance. Not least, this particular proposal depends on assumptions which are open to question *from Scripture itself*. As I cover in the coming chapters, one point of uncertainty comes from whether the fetus acquires the status of human personhood at birth (in the Hebrew Masoretic Text) or at some point in fetal development (in the Greek Septuagint Text). The questions I am about to raise, and the range of possibilities I propose, may not satisfy those Christians and Orthodox Jews who believe ensoulment or personhood happens

---

9. "Declaration on Procured," n. 19 says, "This declaration expressly leaves aside the question of the moment when the spiritual soul is infused. There is not unanimous tradition on this point and the authors are as yet in disagreement. From some it dates from the first instant; for others it could not precede at least nidation [nestling in the mother's womb]. It is not within the competence of science to decide between these views, because the existence of an immortal soul is not a question in its field. It is a philosophical problem from which our moral affirmation remains independent for two reasons: 1) supposing a belated animation, there is still nothing less than a human life, preparing for and calling for a soul in which the nature received from the parents is completed; 2) on the other hand, it suffices that this presence of the soul be probable (and one can never prove the contrary) in order that the taking of life involve accepting the risk of killing."

10. Tauer, "Tradition of Probabilism," 4.

at fertilization based on the moral probability reasoning I noted above. But I believe they should still be considered because Scripture does not say the fertilized egg should be regarded as a full human person. The Bible even suggests something else, perhaps even for practical purposes, and our predecessors in church history engaged robustly with the scientific knowledge of their time, setting a precedent for later Christians to follow.

Meanwhile, conservative white Protestants in America had concerns about Scripture and science—including abortion, but in a very different way from Catholics—that were different from their Catholic peers. One might say they were unnecessarily defensive because they wedded themselves to unlikely interpretations of Scripture. The anti-Darwinian "young earth" theory was one. Other interpretations were directly political in nature. White Protestant fundamentalists in the nineteenth and early twentieth centuries were still defensive about white supremacy and sometimes chattel slavery, believing them to be biblically defensible, and even an aspect of the supposed "national covenant" with God, which in their minds made the United States so exceptional.[11] This idea dated back to the Puritans of New England and minister and governor John Winthrop, who "owned" three Pequot slaves. As they came to terms with the formal defeat of slavery in the Civil War, many interpreted abolition as the nation's rejection of authentic Christianity.[12] Conservative Protestants—who would later call themselves "fundamentalists"—were especially troubled by their "social gospel" liberal Protestant peers. As the North industrialized, they felt the threat of modernity and science especially as applied to the young vs. old earth theories, the literary criticism of the Bible, etc. Therefore, they located the doctrine of *biblical* infallibility (a parallel to *papal* infallibility) in the original autographs, which were well beyond the reach of verification.[13] In 1902, the American Bible League produced twelve pamphlets

---

11. Noll, *America's God*, 3–52, discusses the idea of the "national covenant" and its impossibility. See the discussion in chapter 11. To see the vigorous Christian defenses of slavery leading up to the Civil War, see Noll, *Civil War*, and an earlier book by Miller et al., *Religion and the American Civil War*.

12. Jemison, "Proslavery Christianity"; Wilson, *Baptized in Blood*; Baker, *Gospel according to the Klan*; Cho, "Two Machens," notes J. Gresham Machen's segregationist and white supremacist views. Machen (1881–1937) was a professor at Princeton Theological Seminary from 1906–29, and later founder of Westminster Theological Seminary in 1929 and the Orthodox Presbyterian Church denomination in 1933. Machen was fairly typical of white American conservative evangelicals in his views on race, and was also a radical libertarian politically. Cho also highlights B. B. Warfield (1851–1921), who was the lone voice for racial integration and equality at Princeton for some time.

13. Englehardt, *Foundations*, 212 n. 4, gives a concise summary of American evangelical fundamentalism.

called *The Fundamentals*, directed against higher criticism of the Bible. Historians both Christian and not acknowledge:

> Both movements [Catholic and Protestant] represent a synthesis of a theological position and an ideological-political stance against the erosion of traditional authorities. Both are antimodern and literalist.[14]

Nebraska politician William Jennings Bryan led a movement of populist Christian fundamentalism by advocating a literalistic interpretation of Scripture and opposing the theory of evolution, most famously in the Scopes trial of 1925. This is important to recall because:

> American evangelicalism has its roots in American fundamentalism, which emerged as a rejection of the "social gospel" movement in the late 19th century. The social gospel, popular among mainline Protestants, interpreted the Bible through a more critical lens and promoted the idea of social reform through government and public institutions. Fundamentalism emerged to defend the authority of the Bible as God's word, and as a reaction against the social gospel, it also rejected the idea of the idea of social improvement through government policy.[15]

Some government policies, though, were very important to the fundamentalists-evangelicals because they felt they were losing a "culture war." Many churches rallied around Anthony Comstock, a very devout conservative Protestant, against *contraception*. They managed to pass the Comstock Act of 1873 and the subsequent Comstock laws against contraception, among other things. The politics of reproduction, about women's bodies and one's own children and other people's children, had always been important in American life. Until then, contraception had been generally legal throughout the United States, *coitus interruptus* no doubt widely practiced, and lengthening the time of breastfeeding was already observed to reduce the likelihood of the next pregnancy.[16] But because science, technology, the social sciences, and political trends were perceived by these Christians to be *against* traditional Christian faith, matters of reproduction became part of the cultural and political battleground. Protestants came to later favor contraception in the early twentieth century because they wanted the large Catholic immigrant families from Ireland, Germany, and Italy to use it,

---

14. Kaplan, *Fundamentalism*, 84.

15. Christerson, "Why Do Christians." See also Marsden, *Fundamentalism*, 124–40 and FitzGerald, *Evangelicals*, 13–94.

16. Ryerson, "Medical Advice."

highlighting how reproduction—including abortion, as I will explore in chapters 12 and 13—regularly became enlisted by Protestant politics into larger concerns about immigrants and minorities. The Comstock Act of 1873 was finally ruled as unconstitutional in a series of Supreme Court decisions: *United States v. One Package of Japanese Pessaries* (1936) ruled that the federal government could not stop doctors from providing contraception to their patients; *Griswold v. Connecticut* (1965) ruled that a married couple could use contraception on the grounds of privacy; *Eisenstadt v. Baird* (1972) extended that to unmarried couples. Some still interpret those decisions as political and cultural defeats.

During the twentieth century, conservative Protestants' attitudes towards science can be illustrated by a few examples. After the 1925 Scopes Trial, Mississippi enacted a law *prohibiting* the teaching of Darwin's theory of evolution in their public schools. The bill easily passed both chambers of the state legislature. The law remained the state's official policy until the Mississippi Supreme Court invalidated it in 1971. The president of Mississippi College, a Baptist institution and the largest private university in the state, said that evolution was a "fad" which had "little support in Scripture."[17] In the mid-1960s, the Christian intellectual critic of secular humanism named Francis Schaeffer "attacked biological evolution and modern geology on the grounds that the theories were weak and the facts probably wrong."[18] His books were bestsellers and he was a sought-after speaker. In 1980, Republican presidential candidate Ronald Reagan spoke to the Religious Roundtable, which filled Reunion Arena's 17,000 seats—among them, 2,500 pastors from around the country. Just prior to making his address, he told journalists that he believed "the biblical story of creation [should] be taught in the public schools as an alternative to evolution."[19] In 2012, Georgia Congressman Paul Broun (R-GA), who is also an MD and a licensed physician, dismissed the theory of evolution, the big bang, the long ages of the universe and earth, and the field of embryology as "lies straight from the pit of hell." He made those comments while speaking at Liberty Baptist Church Sportsman's Banquet in Georgia on September 27, 2012 while running for reelection, which he won.[20] Broun served in Congress from 2007–2015 and sat on the House Science Committee. Clearly, the fundamentalists and evangelicals were uneasy with science and felt they had to defend what they understood as the Christian faith. This anti-science bent is concerning when we discuss

---

17. Dupont, *Mississippi*, 25–26.
18. FitzGerald, *Evangelicals*, 354.
19. FitzGerald, *Evangelicals*, 313.
20. Pearce, "Paul Broun."

abortion and find that, also in 2012, Missouri Congressman Todd Akin (R-MO) justified his opposition to the "morning after pill" by saying, "If it's a legitimate rape, the female body has ways to try to shut that whole thing down"; therefore pregnancy by rape was "really rare." Akin apologized for his statement, then retracted his apology on the grounds he believed the physical and psychological stress of "legitimate rape" would prevent pregnancy.[21] It is not clear what Akin would say to the study of over four thousand women that found that 5 percent of all rapes resulted in a pregnancy, even when the rapist used a condom.[22] Akin earned a master of divinity degree from Covenant Theological Seminary, a denominational seminary of the Presbyterian Church of America (PCA), in 1984[23] and, at the time he made his remarks, sat on the House Science Committee as well. All this suggests that conservative Protestants, especially on the popular level, continue to feel in varying degrees that science is not an ally because they have wedded themselves to unlikely interpretations of Scripture.

Catholics, Protestants, Scripture, and Abortion in the Pro-Life Movement

Until the *late* 1970s, most Protestants—liberal mainliners and conservative evangelicals alike—did not see abortion as a pressing matter because they thought Scripture was fundamentally unclear about it. Especially during the 1800s, Protestants in the U.S. embraced different views about abortion, not because of biblical reasons, but because of political and scientific reasons, which I will discuss in chapters 12 and 13.

Therefore, the pro-life movement has only *recently* been tied to an economically conservative platform. From the 1930s, and largely encouraged by the example set by FDR, Catholic New Deal Democrats believed that they could use the liberal welfare state to protect the vulnerable. The unborn were vulnerable, as were the poor, the laborer, etc. This concern for all the vulnerable was reflected in the Catholic Social Teaching.[24] That fact might

---

21. Haberkorn, "Abortion, Rape." Palmer and Parti, "Akin Un-Apologizes," notes that although Akin apologized for his comments, he then retracted his apology by saying he meant that the stress due to rape would likely make a rape victim infertile.

22. Holmes et al., "Rape-Related Pregnancy."

23. McCrummen and Fahrenthold, "Akin's Legacy." To see Protestant congressional representatives' anti-science views related to climate change, see Klein, "Todd Akin."

24. Piux XI, *Casti Connubi* (1930), and Paul VI, *Humanae Vitae* (1968), taught on abortion and contraception. Leo XIII, *Rerum Novarum* (1891), taught on capital and labor. Piux XI, *Quadragesimo Anno* (1931), aimed at the entire social order. John XXIII, *Mater et Magistra* (1961), presented Christian faith and the Christian church as the

also surprise people today, who again assume that Republican moral and economic conservatives have always carried the pro-life cause. We will have much more to say about social policies affecting abortion rates. However, the Catholic bishops took a stance which was too challenging for the general American public, including Protestants. Complicating the Catholic stance further was the fact that many Catholic bishops and doctors stood against abortion *even when the mother's life was at stake*, as well as in cases of rape, incest, and severe fetal deformities. When better surgical and medical techniques were developed in the mid-twentieth century, the conflict between mother and fetus became rare in practice. But Jews and Protestants believed that the mother's life should be given more weight, arguing for instance that if a pregnant woman died, leaving behind three grieving children and a bereaved husband, and possibly a newborn baby who is in the NICU on the edge of death, by what criteria would that be a moral choice? But Catholics had a particular style of reasoning that was not readily accessible by, or attractive to, others. Catholics also linked their anti-abortion stance with their anti-contraception stance. In their view, sex was for marriage, and sex within marriage was for childbearing. Therefore, every act of sex had to be theoretically open to conception, with only natural family planning as a guide to minimize that possibility.

Conservative Protestants, by comparison, did not join Catholics in their view that human personhood began at conception precisely because they could not find that view supported with certainty *in Scripture itself*. Historian Daniel K. Williams says:

> Evangelicals remained on the sidelines because they were suspicious of Catholics and because they lacked a clear theology of when human life began. Although the vast majority of evangelicals favored retaining most restrictions on abortion, many also thought that the Catholic Church's insistence that human life began at conception *lacked clear biblical support*.[25]

After Vatican II from 1962–1965, the Catholic church relaxed its openly political stance against contraception. This shift first attracted liberal Protestants who were also anti-war and anti-poverty, into an alliance with some Catholics. Conservative Protestants remained aloof, however. In 1968, *Christianity Today* published an article criticizing Pope Paul VI's encyclical

---

driver of meaningful social progress.

25. Williams, *Defenders*, 67. Williams further notes, "One could find at least a few evangelical scholars and leading pastors at all points along the spectrum, but a general consensus emerged: in favor of abortion in limited circumstances, but opposed to 'abortion on demand.'"

Humanae Vitae, which was about contraception and abortion, as "alien to biblical revelation."[26] The symposium of twenty-five prominent evangelical medical doctors and theologians which led up to the publication was coordinated by Harold Ockenga and Harold Lindsell, evangelical leaders. Lindsell had recently become editor of the magazine. Respected biblical scholar Bruce Waltke, then of Dallas Theological Seminary, expressed the general consensus that the Bible does express care to protect the fetus. "While the Old Testament does not equate the fetus with a living person, it places great value upon it." But there were other factors to consider. He took note of Exodus 21, saying:

> God does not regard the fetus as a soul, no matter how far gestation has progressed. The Law plainly exacts: "If a man kills any human life he will be put to death" (Lev 4:17). But according to Exodus 21:22–24, the destruction of the fetus is not a capital offense. . . . Clearly, then, in contrast to the mother, the fetus is not reckoned as a soul.[27]

Waltke's observations support the majority Jewish opinion on the fetus and abortion, which viewed the mother's life as more important than the fetus's in cases of direct conflict. About this, Waltke says, "In the absence of any biblical text forbidding abortion," we must compare the Sinai covenant laws with other Near Eastern laws. Noting that ancient Assyria punished the procuring of abortions, Waltke commented, "The fact that God did not set forth a similar law becomes even more significant when one realizes that in sexual matters the Mosaic Code is normally more extensive and more severe than other codes."[28] Scripture's relative silence deserved careful consideration. Historian Frances FitzGerald, in her study of evangelicals in America, says of the gathering:

> The participants expressed a variety of opinions in their papers, but the final document showed consensus on certain points, among them that *the Bible did not explicitly prohibit contraception or abortion*; that contraception was not in itself sinful; and that abortion, while possibly sinful, was necessary and permissible when it served to safeguard "greater values sanctioned by the Scriptures" such as individual health, family welfare, and the social good." The document, "A Protestant Affirmation on the Control of Human Reproduction," located personhood at *birth* and spoke with approval of the changes in state laws [towards

26. Williams, *Defenders*, 146.
27. Stetzer, "Morning Roundup," and Galli, "Evangelicals."
28. Carter, "Bible."

formal permission of abortion in cases of rape, incest, and risk to the mother's life].[29]

Daniel Williams concurs:

> The "human fetus" was either "an actual human life or at the least, a potential and developing human life," they declared, so physicians should "exercise great caution when prescribing an abortion" and should do so "only to safeguard greater values sanctioned by Scripture." Their approach echoed editorials that were appearing in evangelical magazines such as *Christian Life, Eternity,* and *Christianity Today,* which cautiously endorsed abortion legalization for a narrow range of cases: medically necessitated abortions or instances of rape or incest. This stance positioned evangelicals to the right of legalizers, but well to the left of pro-life Catholics. Hardly any evangelical Protestants joined Catholics in lobbying against the abortion law reform efforts of the late 1960s.[30]

Gradually, in the years following Vatican II, Catholic activists repositioned their anti-abortion stance in a single-issue "right to life" framework, which conservative evangelicals found more palatable for many reasons which we will explore in this book. These groups countenanced what we now consider to be the typical exceptions: rape, incest, and risk to the mother's life. In the early 1970s, evangelicals began to join the pro-life cause. In May 1971, *Christianity Today* encouraged evangelicals to join pro-life groups.[31] Meanwhile, also in 1971, another evangelical magazine, *Eternity,* devoted an entire issue to the subject of abortion, "presenting a range of views about the conditions under which abortion might be considered."[32]

The relative slowness with which white evangelicals joined the pro-life cause may surprise the modern reader. The Southern Baptist Convention of 1971 called upon Southern Baptists to advocate for policy change at the state level, not for the banning of all abortions, but the permitting of abortion in cases of rape, incest, and even fetal deformity and "the likelihood of damage to the emotional, mental, and physical health of the mother,"[33] which was the widest possible consideration given among the exceptions. As I will explore in chapter 6, "emotional health" was often subject to the widest possible interpretations by physicians and law enforcement. Moreover, the Southern Baptist Convention reaffirmed its 1971 position

---

29. FitzGerald, *Evangelicals,* 254–55. Italics mine.
30. Williams, *Defenders,* 67.
31. Williams, *Defenders,* 146.
32. FitzGerald, *Evangelicals,* 255.
33. FitzGerald, *Evangelicals,* 255.

every year until 1980. In fact, shortly after *Roe*, W. A. Criswell, president of the Southern Baptist Convention and pastor of the largest church in the denomination, First Baptist in Dallas, Texas, said something that would surprise many today: "I have always felt that it was only after a child was born and had a life separate from its mother that it became an individual person, and it has always, therefore, seemed to me that what is best for the mother and for the future should be allowed."[34] Outside of the Southern Baptist Convention, similar sentiments were widespread enough that in 1975, when Billy Graham gathered leaders from the National Association of Evangelicals, they condemned abortion-on-demand, that is, as a birth control method, but not abortion in every case.[35]

Within a few years, however, evangelicals repositioned the anti-abortion movement in the cause of social conservatism, anti-welfare capitalism, "states' rights," the "individual rights" of the fetus, and "religious freedom." Their narrative about abortion, and approach to abortion politics, lined up with and reinforced the commitment they had in the 1950s and 1960s: maintaining racially segregated, tax-exempt private schools and protesting *Brown v. Board of Education* (1954). Unlike the Catholic New Deal Democrats, who had seen abortion rates spike during the Great Depression, who argued that abortion was a feature of the lack of respect for all human life, the conservative Protestants allied themselves with the Republican Party and argued that abortion should be understood as the result of sexual promiscuity, of which poverty was more the result, and less the cause. Both Catholics and evangelicals explicitly denied the second-wave feminist argument that abortion simply reflected a woman's right to choose on the basis that it concerned her body alone. They rejected the sexual freedom movement of the 1960s and second-wave feminism.[36] Unlike the Catholic Democrats, though, who had paired anti-abortion policies with strong anti-poverty measures and a redistribution of power and wealth, the evangelicals criticized the liberal welfare state for financially supporting and supposedly encouraging unwed motherhood, single parenting, and therefore the further breakdown of the family.[37] The change in framing mattered a great deal, because a political and policy realignment was underway, intentionally, by Republican Party intellectuals and operatives. I will discuss this throughout future chapters.

---

34. Carter, "Bible."

35. FitzGerald, *Evangelicals*, 255, citing Cizik, "History"; also Harding, *Falwell*, 191.

36. Williams, *Defenders*, 107–21.

37. Roberts, *Killing*, 202–45 carefully rebuts this accusation. See also Franklin, *Ensuring Inequality*, for a very thorough treatment of how white supremacist legal and economic policies placed pressures on black families in various ways, from slavery through segregation.

Conservative evangelicals hardened their position that human personhood began at conception, which also seems to be more a *reaction* to science as a discipline (recall Georgia Congressman Paul Broun's dismissal of the field of embryology) than it was an honest response to Scripture, or even science itself. This created enormous tensions with the U.S. Constitution, and between the states, in regards to the legal philosophy and jurisprudence surrounding abortion. Conservative Christians, who had long felt marginalized by the culture—whether rightly or wrongly—sought authoritative certainty and accuracy akin to "science," to foreclose on ambiguity of all kinds, and to find moral causes around which they might still be relevant.

Scripture and Science Together on the Fetus

Reviewing just this slice of the history of Christian opinion on abortion produces two major impressions. First, we do not know as much about the fetus and abortion as we might think. Christians can and should care about the issue, but there were reasons why Christians in the past held differing opinions on it, and were aware of doing so. What is peculiar—and lamentable—about this current state of affairs is that the early Christian leaders, whose opinions on abortion became the benchmarks for the Eastern Orthodox, Roman Catholic, and Protestant churches for centuries, did not develop their views about the fetus and abortion from Scripture alone. They engaged with the medical and scientific knowledge of their day. The difference between the Orthodox and Roman Catholic positions on abortion reflects a consolidation of Christian opinion around different scientific views. This was *understandable*. Scripture informed their positions, but was not the only authoritative voice. Perhaps these Christian leaders did this to create bridges to information that was available to the general public in the Greco-Roman world.

Second, we must take great care to evaluate larger political movements into which people place abortion as an issue. I will continue to highlight many other social and political currents and subtexts, especially because Christians of different time periods aligned abortion policies alongside different views of women and men, responsibility, poverty, medicine and law, and other factors. Thus, to be clear, I believe Jews and Christians would be wise and correct to thoughtfully engage with the natural sciences, in as non-defensive and non-anxious a way as possible—for example, without reference to the "culture wars." We begin by examining the single most important biblical text on the unborn fetus, the text that demands that we accept a significant level of uncertainty about the moral weight of the fetus.

2

The Bible and Abortion: Exodus 21

Other Passages of Scripture Are Not Enough

THE PERSONHOOD INITIATIVE IS a broadly Christian movement trying to establish legal human personhood from the moment a sperm meets an egg. On their website, the Personhood Initiative says they hope to overturn *Roe v. Wade*, pass a personhood amendment, and define abortion as first-degree murder, not for the mother, but for the physician or other abortion provider who performs it.[1] Although in November 2011, Mississippi voters rejected an initiative to place an amendment on the state constitution to that effect, similar efforts are underway in other states.

As of this writing, on their website and booklet, the Personhood Initiative does not engage with Exodus 21:22–25, a passage that suggests that the death of a fetus is not equivalent to the death of a born child or an adult human person, based on the fact that there are different punishments specified for causing one or the other. Instead, in an effort to demonstrate that God treats a fetus as a fully human person from day one, the Personhood Initiative lists various passages from Scripture: Job 10:18; Jeremiah 20:17; and Judges 13:4–5. The organization does not list Psalm 139:13–16 and Jeremiah 1:5, but it could have, as those passages also speak of God calling his servants from the womb. Verses like this say:

> Why then did you bring me out of the womb?
> I wish I had died before any eye saw me. (Job 10:18)

> My frame was not hidden from You,

---

1. Personhood Initiative, www.personhoodinitiative.com, writes, "If the amendment that we are proposing is passed, then abortion would immediately be labeled as first degree murder, and anyone who performs an abortion would face either life imprisonment or the death penalty."

> When I was made in secret,
>
> And skillfully wrought in the depths of the earth
>
> Your eyes have seen my unformed substance. (Ps 139:15–16)

Passages like this clearly do indicate that while birth marks an important event, God's craft and care go back well before birth. But how much earlier?

New Testament scholar Richard B. Hays, in his book *The Moral Vision of the New Testament*, argues that using Scripture passages like this to determine the value of a just-fertilized egg is misleading and incorrect. It goes beyond what the passages were intending to answer. While also generally advocating against abortion, Hays points out that these passages, especially on account of their genre as poetic expressions, "cannot be pressed as a way of making claims about the status of the fetus as a 'person'; rather, they are confessions about God's divine foreknowledge and care."[2] Indeed, when Job complains, "Why then did you bring me out of the womb? I wish I had died before any eye saw me" (Job 10:18), Job is not making an ethical or scientific statement about *when* his life in the womb could have been regarded in terms of full human personhood. Still less is he saying that when his father's sperm and mother's egg met he possessed full human personhood, ontologically, morally, and legally, from that point. Even affirming that the poetic genre communicates truth about God's love for a yet unborn child, we are left with questions about the development of the life of the unborn fetus, both about its status as a fully human person at various points of development and our responsibility towards the unborn at different stages, especially when we examine the critical passage, Exodus 21:22–25.

For good measure, Hays addresses other biblical texts which are often enlisted to prove abortion is not simply immoral, but equivalent to murder.[3] He rightly points out, though, that those texts must assume what they claim to prove. Exodus 20:13 and Deuteronomy 5:17 prohibit murder, but these passages do not tell us definitively whether the fetus should be considered a fully human person, as Exodus 21 would *not* suggest. Galatians 5:20 refers to "sorcery" (*pharmakeia*) which might have included the practice of ingesting drugs to induce miscarriages, depending on some critical assumptions about cultural context. The term is far too generic to mean abortion in particular. Matthew 19:14 and Luke 18:15 recall Jesus affirming little children. The affirmations concern already born, not unborn, children, however. So to Exodus 21 we turn.

---

2. Hays, *Moral Vision*, 448.
3. Hays, *Moral Vision*, 446–48.

Exodus 21 and the Dilemma of Manuscripts

Without question, Exodus 21:22–25 has been the most important biblical text when trying to understand the value of an unborn fetus and ethics of abortion.[4] The text considers the case of two men fighting, where one strikes a pregnant woman. That much is clear. What follows is unclear. There is a curious but critical difference between the Hebrew Masoretic Text (MT) and Greek Septuagint (LXX) manuscripts.

Exodus 21:22–25, Hebrew Masoretic (NRSV)	Exodus 21:22–25, Greek Septuagint (Brenton's)
[22] When people who are fighting injure a pregnant woman so that there is a miscarriage, and yet no further harm follows, the one responsible shall be fined what the woman's husband demands, paying as much as the judges determine.	[22] And if two men strive and smite a woman with child, and her child be born imperfectly formed, he shall be forced to pay a penalty: as the woman's husband may lay upon him, he shall pay with a valuation.
[23] If any harm follows, then you shall give life for life, [24] eye for eye, tooth for tooth, hand for hand, foot for foot, [25] burn for burn, wound for wound, stripe for stripe.	[23] But if it be perfectly formed, he shall give life for life, [24] eye for eye, tooth for tooth, hand for hand, foot for foot, [25] burning for burning, wound for wound, stripe for stripe.

This is a subtle but very significant difference between manuscripts, and a rare instance where the manuscript differences make a rather big difference. The differences between these two manuscript families is important to mention because they introduce some uncertainty about how exactly to regard a fetus and involve the Jewish and Christian communities today in a centuries-long debate about which version is closest to the original.

---

4. It appears, for example, in Tertullian's and Augustine's comments on abortion, and in the Byzantine legal collection called the *Ecloga*. Troianos, "Embryo," 4, writes, "It is interesting to note that the so-called Appendix to the *Ecloga*—an aggregation of different unions of texts—includes the Mosaic Command, a collection of 70 fragments from the Pentateuch, that repeats the well known passage 21.22–23 from Exodus in chapter 27.29 strongly indicating that the problem of the 'figuration' or not of the embryo never ceased to be of practical significance." A reading of Jewish reflection on the topic of abortion produces the impression that Exodus 21:22–25 is the main biblical text explicitly considered. While Orthodox Jews are opposed to abortion except in case of the mother's life being threatened, Judaism is generally approving of abortion because of its more liberal approach to the biblical text. For a readable summary, see "What Do Orthodox Jews Think"; "Abortion and Judaism"; and "Issues in Jewish Ethics."

Traditionally, Jewish and Christian communities anchor their beliefs about God and God's commandments in texts. From the beginnings of Judaism, the Jewish community, and its leaders and scribes, worked from biblical manuscripts in the Hebrew language. They began translating those manuscripts into a common form of Greek in the third century BC because in the fourth century BC, Alexander the Great conquered much of the Eastern Mediterranean and Middle East, and established the use of a Greek dialect called *Koine* ("common") Greek throughout those regions. Alexander also built a string of cities stretching across this territory—all called Alexandria—which linked knowledge, trade, and influence to the westernmost of those cities: Alexandria, Egypt. In the third century BC, the Jewish community in Alexandria, Egypt, started translating the Hebrew Scriptures into Koine Greek because many Jews, especially those outside of Palestine but including some within, had lost touch with their native Hebrew. This Greek translation was called the Septuagint (for "seventy" and abbreviated by LXX) because of a pious origin story that seventy Jewish scholars worked independently to translate the Hebrew into Greek and arrived at the same version. Linguists accept the traditional date of the LXX Torah being translated in the third century BC from Alexandria, Egypt, based on the early form of Koine Greek utilized. The LXX version of Exodus, therefore, may come from the earliest possible Hebrew text. Other Greek translations developed, but the LXX was in popular use for centuries. If the *Letter to Aristeas* is to be believed on this particular point, the LXX was commissioned and approved by the Sanhedrin and high priest in Jerusalem, prior to any Jewish-Christian textual disputes, whereas the Hebrew Masoretic text had no such governing body. The LXX was widely used for centuries, by both Jews and Christians. It is vital for the study of the New Testament because the New Testament quotes from the LXX much more often than any other translation of the Old Testament.[5] Koine Greek is the language of the New Testament and most early Christian

---

5. For example, in addition to the "virgin" prophecy of LXX Isaiah 7:14, Luke 4:18 quotes from LXX Isaiah 61:1, which includes the phrase "and recovery of sight to the blind," whereas the MT does not. Acts 7:14 quotes from LXX Genesis 46:20–22 and Exodus 1:5 when Stephen refers to seventy-five people, whereas MT mentions only seventy people. Hebrews 1:6 contains the phrase, "And let all the angels of God worship him," from LXX Deuteronomy 32:43 and the Dead Sea Scrolls, which is not found in the MT. Hebrews 10:5 quotes from LXX Psalm 40:6, including the phrase, "A body You have prepared for me," whereas MT Psalm 40:6 does not. Paul quotes the LXX instead of the MT throughout his corpus, including LXX Isaiah 59:20 in Rom 11:26. We have evidence that the LXX was used very broadly by diaspora Jews, wherever Greek was spoken, because Hellenistic Jews, except for the educated rabbis, generally lost the ability to read and speak Hebrew, even in Palestine, and certainly in the diaspora. The LXX also played an enormous role in the spread of Christian faith, including the fact that the apostolic writers of the New Testament utilize it.

writing. The LXX continues to be the preferred manuscript for the Eastern Orthodox churches. Other manuscripts exist, including the Samaritan Pentateuch (dating perhaps to the late second century BC) and the Dead Sea Scrolls (dating variously from the third to first centuries BC), serve to corroborate the LXX at some times, and MT at others.

The Hebrew Masoretic manuscript takes its name from Jewish scribes, or *masoretes*, who flourished between the seventh to eleventh centuries AD in the regions of Palestine and Babylon. When Roman legions leveled Jerusalem in AD 70 in the Jewish-Roman War, and especially after Roman general Flavius Silva crushed the Jewish military encampment at Masada in AD 135, respected rabbis stepped into the leadership vacuum throughout the Jewish community, as the Jerusalem priestly class and the military wing of the Jews focused on an independent kingship became disheartened and disbanded. The military defeats also destroyed a great many biblical manuscripts and gave new impetus to texts being meticulously preserved and copied. Strains continued to develop between Christians and Jews, which is not surprising given that strains are evident in New Testament literature between Jesus and the Jewish leaders of his day. As rabbinical teachers formalized their responses to Christian claims about Jesus, they came to be dissatisfied with the LXX. Eventually, in the tenth century and under Islamic rule, Jewish scribes and scholars made an impressive effort to standardize the text of the twenty-four sacred books, adding vowel markings to the consonant-only text of the original Hebrew, along with notes in Aramaic where they found small variations among the manuscripts they possessed. The work and reputation of these scholars ensured the respect of the Hebrew Masoretic Text (abbreviated MT), and it became the authoritative text for rabbinic Judaism. The MT is also the standard manuscript for some Catholic Bibles and all Protestant Bibles.

The MT, in translations like the New Revised Standard Version, distinguishes between injury to the fetus, at whatever stage of development it is miscarried, and injury to the woman. Actually there is yet another interpretive question that I will discuss below.[6] In the NRSV, loss of a fetus may or may not be classified as a homicide; we cannot be sure. For a murder, Jewish law established the "life for life" principle in Exodus 21:23–25, which echoes the language of Genesis 9:5–6, where God permitted capital punishment in response to murder, to offset the violence that had set in among human beings in the primal history after the fall, as Cain demonstrated in Genesis 4. A forced miscarriage could have fallen into that category, but it does not. Nor

---

6. A minority of translators and interpreters view the passage as discussing an early delivery; see below.

does the forced miscarriage seem to fall into the category of an unintentional manslaughter, since the remedy for that was for an accidental offender to flee to a city of refuge (Exod 21:13; Num 35:11–24; Deut 19:1–13) to escape vigilante retribution. Criminal negligence resulting in someone's death could be handled with a steep fine (Exod 21:28–31), so forced miscarriage could fall into that same general category. Whatever the case, though, in the MT, the fetus, *at whatever stage of development,* apparently, is not regarded as a full human person, based on how the assailant is held accountable, or what was permitted to happen to the assailant.

Surely, we might ask of the MT, there is some point at which the fetus is so near to term that it could and should count as a full human person? If someone struck a woman who is eight and a half months pregnant, and the fetus in her womb were injured or miscarried, why would that not count as the homicide of a full human person? For example, according to U.S. federal law, specifically the Unborn Victims of Violence Act of 2004, if a motorist strikes a pregnant woman and both the mother and the fetus in her womb die, then the motorist is guilty of two homicides, not one, even if that woman was on her way to a hospital or clinic to abort the fetus. As of this writing, thirty-eight States count the fetus as a separate legal person for purposes of crimes committed against the pregnant mother.[7] So this is a very basic question to ask of the Exodus case law. Perhaps the MT envisions the offender paying a fine on a sliding scale based on stage of pregnancy. How obvious was the woman's pregnancy? Is that a relevant factor? Also, what is the motive of the assailant? Was the assailant trying to injure the wife of the man who was opposing him, as if there were a feud between two men, or two households? Or does the law assume that the assailant accidentally struck the pregnant woman? Was the woman wielding a weapon and taking an offensive role in the fight, as in Deuteronomy 25:11–12, when a woman seeks to harm a man's genitals? What if the assailant was acting in self-defense? Does that matter? Many of these questions go unanswered.

The LXX seems to anticipate a few questions—but only a few—like this related to the developmental stage of the fetus. The LXX makes a further distinction about the miscarriage. It asks whether the fetus was "imperfectly formed" (v. 22) or "perfectly formed" (v. 23) in order to determine the penalty. This might reflect an interest the LXX translators, or the original Hebrew text, had in distinguishing between a woman who was more obviously pregnant than a woman who was not yet showing. A man who struck the latter might understandably have less responsibility than if he struck the

---

7. Sanders, "When Does Life Begin?"

former. Or, as later commentators understood this verse, the developmental stage of the fetus itself made a fundamental difference.

The LXX, then, is ethically *more discerning and demanding* than the MT because the LXX introduces the developmental stage where the fetus is treated as a full human person as shown by the level of accountability for taking it. The LXX is also more textually clear. The LXX, moreover, takes away the phrase "as the judges decide" (Exod 21:22), which could have been an adjustment to the varying conditions of diaspora Judaism, where synagogue officials might not have called themselves "judges" (a "judge" is the Hebrew *hassopet*; Greek *kritou* in Deut 17:12; whereas the "synagogue official" is called *archon* in Matt 9:18; Luke 8:41).

Of course, Exodus 21 does not speak of abortion, but forced miscarriage. Did the assailant know the woman was pregnant? That consideration is not discussed. Did the assailant intentionally strike the pregnant woman so as to cause a miscarriage? Does Jewish law necessarily protect a fetus from a voluntary abortion by its own mother and/or father? We will consider how this text figures into Jewish tradition's views about abortion and human personhood. Given the curious silence of the biblical text about such factors, we must consider contextual clues, subsequent Jewish and Christian interaction with this text, and gauge the appropriate amount of uncertainty we must have in dealing with this issue.

Further Ambiguity in Exodus 21

Complicating the matter even further, a few translations of the MT treat Exodus 21:22 as addressing premature delivery but not miscarriage: Amplified Bible, Christian Standard Bible, Darby, English Standard Version, Geneva Version. The Amplified Bible, for example, translates Exodus 21:22:

> If men fight with each other and injure a pregnant woman so that she gives birth prematurely [and the baby lives], yet there is no further injury, the one who hurt her must be punished with a fine [paid] to the woman's husband, as much as the judges decide.

The material in brackets is added by the translators. The English Standard Version, although a bit vague, gives the same impression:

> When men strive together and hit a pregnant woman, so that her children come out, but there is no harm, the one who hit her shall surely be fined, as the woman's husband shall impose on him, and he shall pay as the judges determine.

Is this passage now about premature but safe delivery? This was the view of John Calvin and a minority of English interpreters.[8] If so, then the fine imposed on the offender is for causing a premature delivery and risking the physical health of the mother and fetus.

Some pro-life advocates argue for this interpretation in order to *also* make more room for the possibility that a forced miscarriage—at whatever stage of fetal development—would count in the "life for life" category, granting the fetus fully human personhood in Jewish law. In a 1992 issue of *Ministry Magazine*, a Seventh Day Adventist publication, ethicist Ron du Preez advocates for this position.[9] In the article, du Preez argues that the English word "further" modifying the word "harm" in English translations of v. 22 is unwarranted. If so, then the phrase "so that her child/children come out" refers to a premature delivery, and the word "harm" could refer to either the mother or the child. Furthermore, the *lex talionis* consequences in v. 23 would pertain to either the mother or the child: "But if there is injury, then . . . life for life, eye for eye." If the passage is read that way, then the fetus would be accorded full personhood.

Naturally, du Preez's presentation can be questioned. His own translations of certain Hebrew words are at times forced.[10] He does not consider that the Hebrew word *nagaph* ("smite"), which is used to denote the strike that one man deals upon the pregnant woman, is used everywhere else in the Torah to denote a mortal strike *exclusively* (Exod 8:2; 12:23, 27; 21:35; 32:35; Lev 26:17; Num 14:42; Deut 1:42; 28:7, 25), giving strong indication that his was a death-dealing blow, but to the fetus and not the mother, which would make the English word "further" precisely appropriate. Du Preez does not attempt to explain how the ancient Jewish rabbinical consensus about this text lasted for so long based on other sensibilities about the Hebrew language, and other moral factors like immoral conception or whether a fetus should die with its mother in a capital punishment, as the premature delivery view was put forward only by English translators interpreting the MT starting in the sixteenth century. Nor does du Preez engage

---

8. Calvin, *Commentaries*, 41–42. See du Preez, "Fetus," n. 14.

9. du Preez, "Fetus."

10. For instance, du Preez insists that the word *shakol*, used in Exodus 23:26, definitely indicates "miscarriage" and therefore provides a strong contrast with the word *yatsa* in Exodus 21:22, which he argues cannot mean that. While *shakol* is translated "miscarriage" in two cases (Gen 31:38; Hos 9:14), it is translated "abort" in one (Job 21:10), and in fourteen cases *shakol* carries the meaning of "bereavement" without being so specific (e.g. Gen 27:45; 42:36; 43:14; Lev 26:22; etc.). That fact diminishes du Preez's case that *yatsa* in Exodus 21:22 necessarily provides a *contrasting* meaning, as in "birth" in an ordinary sense requiring a living baby. The term *yatsa* is not so restrained and could in fact encompass a miscarriage in its meaning.

at all with the LXX manuscript, which does regard the central issue as a forced miscarriage, not a premature delivery. Nor does he engage the wider biblical context of Exodus 21 and beyond (see below). Nor does he engage with early Christian commentators. His article is limited on its own terms, and is far from producing certainty overall.

Exodus 21 in Context

Can the context of this passage help us? The larger narrative context is always important, and in this case, although it does not answer the key question before us, it adds some perspective. Exodus 21:2—23:33 is the first set of laws God gave Israel after he delivered them from Egypt, and provided the Ten Commandments. Exodus 24:1–8 is a narrative "seal" of those particular commandments, where Israel agreed to this covenant. Israel later broke this covenant (Exod 32), which required further mediation from Moses (Exod 33–34) and the institutionalization of his mediator role to stabilize the covenant (Exod 35—Lev 27). As such, there is a relationship between the commands God gave in Exodus 21–23 and all the narrative material that came before. In the immediate sense, God wanted to eliminate "Pharaonic slave practices" from Israel, to help a traumatized people not traumatize each other or foreigners in their midst. Moreover, in the larger context of salvation history, God was bringing Israel into a new garden land to be a renewed version of Adam and Eve, reminding Israel of the original garden and his vision for human bodies and relationships. Throughout the biblical narrative God retells the same basic storyline—or recapitulates what he has done before. Even the water of the Red Sea (Exod 14) was a reminder of the waters of the primordial creation (Gen 1); on the other side of water is a garden land.

Hence, the very first subjects presented after the Ten Commandments are servitude and freedom, bodily injuries and compensation. The clearest textual evidence for linking these laws to their narrative context occurs in Exod 21:16. God commands Israel to not kidnap people into slavery, on pain of death (Exod 21:16). This command serves at least two purposes. First, it is a commentary on the eighth commandment, "do not steal" (Exod 20:15), since kidnapping a person is the most egregious form of stealing. Second, it is a retrospective condemnation on Pharaoh's theft of Israel's labor through forcible enslavement.

God commanded Israel to not keep people in a certain form of servitude for more than six years (Exod 21:2–6). That principle fits a sabbath pattern involving the number seven. God wanted indentured servants ("slave" is now a dangerous mistranslation of the Hebrew *ebed*) to rest and be freed on the seventh year, which also seems to be a retrospective condemnation of how Laban tricked the vulnerable Jacob to serve two seven-year terms (Gen 29:20; 30). God was rebuilding his vision of the creation order—with the Sabbath on the original seventh "day" (Gen 2:1–3)—back into Israel's way of life. This echo of creation fits a pattern of recapitulation in the biblical narrative.

The other commandments in Exodus 21:2–36 and the remainder of this section of case law (Exod 22:1—23:33) can be understood in these ways. God commanded Israel to not impose harsh or unlimited beatings (Exod 21:18-21), as Pharaoh inflicted on them (Exod 1:8-14). He commanded Israel to not injure vulnerable infants (Exod 21:22-27) as Pharaoh once did to their infants (Exod 1:15-22). He even commanded Israelites to end cycles of retaliatory violence (Exod 21:12-14) which Moses failed to do back in Egypt (Exod 2:11-15). Perceiving the commands against these short-term (Egypt) and long-term (creation) frameworks has an impact on how we read Exodus 21:22-25.

No matter which manuscript tradition we take—Hebrew Masoretic or the Greek Septuagint—there appears to be a narrative intention behind this entire section and its placement: generally, to prevent bodily harm and bodily enslavement. Positioning damage done to a fetus against the damage done by Pharaoh to Israelite baby boys is especially illuminating. In fact, the biblical authors regularly dress up Israelites who break God's commandments in the literary garb of "Pharaoh" motifs. The thought that one Israelite might enslave another through debt triggers the reminder that "I am the LORD your God who brought you out of Egypt" (e.g., Lev 25:55). Much later, King Solomon's building projects and severe tax policy invite the narrator of Kings to dress him up as a type of Pharaoh: "forced labor" (1 Kgs 9:15); "storage cities" (9:19); "slave labor" (9:21); and even an explicit alliance with Pharaoh via marriage to "Pharaoh's daughter" (9:24). King Solomon, later in life, acted like *Pharaoh*. Any Israelite who enslaves others would be acting like *Pharaoh*. Unless there are moral circumstances to be considered, like when the life of the mother is threatened, or perhaps immoral conception, anyone who takes the life of a vulnerable fetus is, to some degree and on some level, acting like *Pharaoh*. Therefore, it is difficult to imagine that the miscarriage example in Exodus 21 could be interpreted in such a way so as to make abortion just one casual birth control method among others.

The literary structure of Exodus 21:2–36 helps us weigh the options before us. It seems to be in the form of a chiasm. In a chiasm, the first point matches the last point, the second point matches the second to last point, and so on, until you get to the center point. The center point is the main point. In the flow of conversation, or story, the center point is often a turning point where something important happens or is revealed. In English, we use small chiasms like this:

> A. Chris: "Pat, are you going to the party?"
> B. Pat: "Are you going?"
> B'. Chris: "Yes, I'm going."
> A'. Pat: "Then yes, I'm definitely going!"

In the short conversation above, the first point, "Are you going?" is answered by the last point, "Yes, I'm going." Pat is going to the party. The second point and second to last point ask and answer that for Chris. Pat's answer depended on Chris's answer. It is the "inside" story of the "outside" story of Pat's decision to go to the party. Chiastic structures happen very often in ancient literature, including the Bible. They are important because they help us understand how a passage is organized and the author's intention in organizing the passage. Here is Exodus 21:2–36 in chiastic outline:

A. Restoration Without Payment: Indenture; Betrothal (21:2–11)
  B. Sacredness of Bodies and Relations; Offenders Punished (21:12–17)
    C. Injuries from a Physical Fight; Service Toward Full Healing (21:18–19)
      D. The Full Humanity of the Servant; Murder vs. Homicide (21:20–21)
    C'. Injuries from a Physical Fight; Full Compensation for Miscarriage (21:22–25)
  B'. Sacredness of Bodies and Relations; Servants Freed (21:26–27)
A'. Restoration With Payment: Indirect Injuries; Compensation (21:28–36)

As mentioned before, the narrative context seems to influence the selection of examples here. In Egypt, the Israelites were vulnerable to injuries and violations of bodies and relations. While time and space do not permit me to address every question that arises about this section,[11] I do wish to make some important points about the miscarriage case addressed in C'.

    11. Chief among them: Exodus 21:20–21 involves yet another manuscript question. In the Masoretic Hebrew and the Greek Septuagint manuscripts of v. 21, a man who beats his servant and accidentally commits homicide (as opposed to premeditated murder) should not be punished: "No vengeance shall be taken" (NASB). That poses a moral irregularity and difficulty. Should he not face consequences for a homicide? However, the Samaritan Pentateuch variant contains the phrase, "He shall not die," instead. Meaning, for a homicide with unclear intent, a punishment short of death is called for, since "he shall die" for the homicide with clearer brutal intent in v. 20 is the comparison point. See Garratt, "On the Samaritan Text."

The connection between C and C' shows the unlikelihood of the premature delivery interpretation of MT Exodus 21:22. Although I am certainly not in favor of hitting a pregnant woman, or any woman, I find it difficult to imagine that a man who struck a pregnant woman without injuring her or her baby *at all* should pay a fine, as she was likely helping her husband in the struggle, and possibly trying to injure the other man, as per Deuteronomy 25:11–12. The problems and their consequences strongly suggest bodily *damage*. In point C, two men fight and one temporarily injures and incapacitates the other, requiring the former to give to the latter restitution through service. In point C', two men fight and a pregnant woman gets involved and suffers a bodily injury to her fetus, requiring one side to give to the other restitution through payment.

Fines indicated serious or lasting bodily harm in other cases, and another comparison of consequences helps here. In point C, the law of bodily injury of Exodus 21:18–19, injuring another person requires serving that person "until he is completely healed." In point B', if a master inflicted permanent bodily harm on a servant, the servant could instantly go free. Comparatively speaking, if no one was harmed, even in a limited sense, it seems unlikely that a fine would be imposed. Thus, I side with the English translators—and the vast majority of interpreters, Jewish and Christian—who see in Exodus 21:22–25 the situation of forced miscarriage, not premature delivery. Other translations that treat the passage as addressing a miscarriage are: Common English Bible, Contemporary English Version, Good News Translation, The Message, Revised Standard Version. Translations that use ambiguous English language are: King James Version, New American Standard Bible, New International Version, New Living Translation.

Christians cannot simply lift passages out of Jewish law and apply them, but examining wider patterns is important. In particular, the consequences meted out by Jewish law might help us consider whether some form of restitution payment could be a legal punishment for abortion, at least in some cases. Making abortion a first-degree murder, punishable by death, as some conservatives would like to do, is also questioned by Scripture itself in the MT manuscript.

Compensation is always preferred by Jewish tradition, certainly in cases of bodily injury and sometimes even homicide, and that compensation level helps underscore the moral weight of the situation. Since the payment for a forced miscarriage (in the MT as interpreted by the majority) is less than the consequence for the homicide of an already born child or adult, this case law reinforces the sense that the unborn fetus is not considered equivalent to a born child or adult. Or, if we consider the LXX, an early degree of fetal development (in the LXX) calls for the same. Unfortunately, the reasons for the difference are unexplained by the text itself.

Jewish rabbinical commentators interpret the *lex talionis* "eye for an eye" principle in Exodus 21:23–25 as not strictly retributive, as if it always required death or the same level of injury. At times, it required an offender to help heal the harm he had done. It is an outer limit of proportionality for cases of bodily harm, meant to represent proportional financial compensation (Talmud Bava Kamma 83b–84a) or, in some cases, lashes (Makot 1:1). Rabbinical authorities actually make a type of joke out of the wording involved in "an eye for an eye." They ask, "What if the offender is already blind? One cannot blind an already blind man!" So they believe that the "life for life, eye for an eye" is meant as proportional compensation first and foremost. If you blind someone's eye, *you become* his "second eye." A critical lesson emerges here: just because this phrase in Jewish law appears in the Babylonian Code of Hammurabi does not mean that it has the same *meaning* there as here. Context matters. Otherwise, we might have found the principle of "miscarriage for miscarriage" lurking somewhere in the biblical text—a troubling prospect.

This restorative justice reading—of undoing harm and restoring health if at all possible—is reinforced by the following facts. First, in Exodus 21:18–19 (point C), parallel to this example of bodily harm in 21:22–25 (point C'), the offender must care for the injured victim until he is "completely healed." The former point helps interpret the latter. Second, in Exodus 21:22 (in point C') and 30 (in point A'), financial compensation is named *again*, this time for homicide by criminal negligence. The owner of a goring ox who knew about the danger of the ox to humans, whose ox gored someone to death, was guilty of negligence and "life for life," in principle. However, the family's demand of a "ransom" appears to be expected. If the ox's victim was *also* an indentured servant, the ox's owner had to pay something to the servant's master for labor lost (21:32), *in addition* to paying something named by the servant's family and to them (21:28–31).

Third, moving to other portions of Scripture more broadly, in Leviticus 19:17–18, in what is often called the heart of Jewish law, God instructs Israelites to "not hate" or "take vengeance" upon one's neighbor for a wrongdoing, but instead to "reprove" and "love" one's neighbor. These commands are mutually interpreting.[12] The only way to reconcile the "do not take vengeance" command in Leviticus 19:17–18 with the principle of "life for life, eye for an eye" in Exodus 21:23–25 (and Lev 24:17–22 and Deut 19:15–21)

---

12. Snyder-Belousek, *Atonement*, 408.

is to interpret the latter as establishing a range of compensations for loss, so the offender can help restore the harm he has done.

Fourth, considering the Torah as a narrative, God anticipated Israel's exile from the garden land and loss of political sovereignty (Deut 27–28; Exod 20:4–6). That exile would reenact Adam and Eve's exile from the garden of Eden (Gen 3:20–24). God knew Israel would not be able to enact capital punishment while being ruled by another nation. So the principle of restoration and compensation was important to establish from the start. Fifth, a later incident affirms compensation as an apparent ideal. When King David pronounced a verdict that a certain man deserved death (even though he was unwittingly condemning himself), he said that the sentence would not be capital punishment, but restitution fourfold (2 Sam 12:5–6). Even if David was thinking about theft and speaking hyperbolically, his judgment is still of interest. Taking the health, and sometimes the life, of someone else, then, was seen as a theft, where thieves had to pay back between two to five times the value of what they stole. Not coincidentally, theft and compensation are the subjects of *the very next passage* (Exod 22:1–14). Therefore, when the covenant itself was not threatened, Jewish law was about restoring and undoing harm (victim-oriented and restorative), not primarily about "equivalent injury" (offender-oriented and retributive) in nature. Once again, the fact that the loss of an unformed fetus (LXX), or a fetus in general (MT), is *not* compensated at the same level as a born child or adult means something.

What a Difference a Manuscript Makes

What, then, do we make of the difference between MT and LXX on the possibility that the fetus's death be treated as the death of an ordinary human person? Could the LXX be a "synthesis" of Jewish oral law and the MT, or Jewish tradition as developed from the MT, or an application of the MT? It is fair to wonder if the LXX translators were influenced by Aristotle, or attempting to engage the basic understanding posed by Greek science. Aristotle made observations of miscarried fetuses and related the question of ensoulment to the physical development of the fetus.[13] The proper "form" in Aristotle's view was a precondition for ensoulment when Christian concerns were combined with it. Aristotle's student Ptolemy had become Alexandria's ruler after it was founded by Alexander the Great. In very little time, Alexandria surpassed Athens as the intellectual and cultural center of the Greek-speaking world. So there can be little doubt that educated

---

13. Aristotle, *History of Animals* 7.3.

Alexandrians—including the Hellenistic Jews there—knew the writings of the older Athenian philosophers and playwrights. And the LXX reflects a fairly robust engagement with Hellenism.[14]

Protestant scholar Richard B. Hays makes short shrift of this question when he dismisses the LXX on the basis "that Protestant theological tradition has historically affirmed the canonical priority of the Hebrew text over the Septuagint."[15] It is true that on these particular verses, the Samaritan Pentateuch, which dates to approximately 122 BC, agrees with the Hebrew Masoretic.[16] So does the Dead Sea Scroll fragment of Exodus known as 4Q22, which dates to 100–25 BC.[17] But larger textual and historical considerations have to be mentioned. LXX Exodus might still come from the earliest possible Hebrew text, and it was long approved for widespread synagogue use by the Jewish authorities who sat in Jerusalem, while the city stood. The LXX was widely used for centuries, by both Jews and Christians, and had a heavy presence in the thoughts of Jesus and the apostles in the New Testament.

Therefore, Hays's abrupt dismissal of the LXX is not satisfactory. It is logically self-defeating, as it raises the notorious and amusing question of whether Protestants—who cry "sola scriptura" over "tradition"—can invoke "tradition" to resolve an issue of competing biblical manuscripts, arguably the most fundamental of all issues. It is exegetically questionable, because of the clear appreciation Jesus and the apostles had for the LXX, even if we do not assume their endorsement of the entire translation. It is historically presumptuous, because the Hebrew Masoretic text has not been categorically vindicated over the LXX on every issue, even with the discovery of the Dead Sea Scrolls; rather, the opposite is true on many finer textual points.[18]

---

14. Gavrilyuk, *Suffering*, 21–63, points out that the LXX reflects a tendency to diminish the rich anthropomorphic and anthropopathic language for God given in the original Hebrew, perhaps out of a concern to avoid the impression that the God of Israel is like Zeus, and to at least engage (some might say "accommodate") the sensibilities of Hellenistic philosophical speculation about divinity.

15. Hays, *Moral Vision*, 447.

16. Samaritan Pentateuch Book of Exodus, https://www.stepbible.org/?q=version=SPE|reference=Exo.21.

17. 4Q22 PaleoExodus 21:22, 24, http://dssenglishbible.com/scroll4Q22.htm.

18. E.g., MT 1 Samuel 14:41 reads, "Therefore Saul said unto the LORD God of Israel, 'Give Thummim.' And Saul and Jonathan were taken: but the people escaped." This makes very little sense, and seems to be the error of a scribe who skipped a line. LXX 1 Samuel 14:41 reads, "Therefore Saul said, 'O LORD God of Israel, why have you not answered your servant this day? If this guilt is in me or in Jonathan my son, O LORD, God of Israel, give Urim. But if this guilt is in your people Israel, give Thummim.' And Jonathan and Saul were taken, but the people escaped." The word "pierced" in LXX Psalm 22:16 has been replaced by "lion" in the MT, which makes little sense. LXX Psalm

And it is ecclesiologically narrow, for Protestants cannot simply distance themselves from the Catholic and Orthodox traditions, who hold the LXX in higher regard. Certainly, both historic Jewish and Christian communities have been influenced by *both* the LXX translation with its focus on the developmental stage of the fetus *and* the Masoretic translation with its focus on the mother. Simply out of respect,[19] if not because of genuine uncertainty, we must consider both manuscript families.

As we have seen in this chapter, Scripture alone does not speak "with one voice" on the issue of the fetus. While the range of appropriate interpretations of Exodus 21 is not so diffuse as to be meaningless, this uncertainty means Bible-believing Christians know less about the fetus and abortion than they think. To understand Jewish and Christian ethical positions on a pregnant mother taking the life of her own fetus, or a father wishing his unborn fetus to be aborted, we also have to consider other biblical texts and other moral and scientific considerations. Are there other biblical passages and principles to consider? How did the early Christians understand the issue? How did they factor in other social problems, like poverty?

145:13 is omitted from the MT. The Dead Sea Scroll known as 4Q44 Deuteronomy containing Deut 32:9–10, 37–43 appears to agree with the LXX and not the MT, although 4Q44 Deut 32:43 is still missing a phrase.

19. The LXX forms the basis for the Old Latin, Slavonic, Syriac, Old Armenian, Old Georgian, and Coptic versions of the Old Testament.

3

Early Jewish and Christian Thought on Abortion and Exodus 21

Greek and Roman Contexts

JEWS AND CHRISTIANS SHARPLY disagreed with the Greco-Roman civilizations about abortion. For centuries, Jews and Christians contended with cultural and military powers that were far larger than them, not least on issues of fetuses, abortion, infanticide, and children. Into the Greco-Roman worlds, Jews and Christian deployed their sacred texts and community practices, cherishing their own children and those of others.

On the whole, pagan Greek and Roman law, philosophy, and culture held that infants had absolutely no inherent rights per se. Plato, in *The Republic*, records a conversation between Socrates and Glaucon in which they approve of both infanticide and abortion: infanticide in cases of "inferior parents" or children "born defective," and abortion in cases of women who become pregnant after the age of forty.[1] Similarly, Aristotle stated:

> Let there be a law that no deformed child shall live. But as to an excess in the number of children, if the established customs of the state forbid this (for in our state population has a limit), no child is to be exposed. But when couples have children in excess, let abortion be procured before sense and life have begun; what may or may not be lawfully done in these cases depends on the question of life and sensation.[2]

In *History of Animals* 7.3, Aristotle relays his observations of miscarried fetuses and relates the question of ensoulment to the physical development of the fetus. For various reasons related to his observations, he says that this

---

1. Plato, *Republic*, book 5, 460b–c and 460e–461c.
2. Aristotle, *Politics*, 7.16.

"form" is acquired by male fetuses at around forty days, and by female fetuses at around ninety.[3] The proper "form" was a precondition for ensoulment. This was one of the prevailing views of Greek science. Another view was that of the Stoics, who held that ensoulment and human personhood occurred when the fetus was born and drew its first breath of air. Prior to birth, believed the Stoics, the fetus was part of the mother's body, like fruit was part of a tree. Another view was that of Hippocrates, author of the famous oath adopted by physicians "to do no harm." Hippocrates had medical knowledge of how to induce an abortion, but he and Pythagoras viewed abortions at any stage as wrong. They were in the minority in their day.

In the days of the pagan Roman Republic and Roman Empire, a new mother laid her newborn baby on the ground, and the father of the household had to pick it up in order for the household to embrace that child. Parents could legally discard such a child to the elements to die (*expositio*), prior to the eighth day for boys and the ninth day for girls. These practices indicate that social birth, not biological birth, was decisive. The ancient document known as Papyrus Oxyrrhynchus 744, dating to 1 BC, is probably typical of a father in the Roman Empire giving instruction to his wife about their newborn baby:

---

3. Aristotle, *History of Animals*, 7.3 writes, "In the case of male children, the first movement usually occurs on the right-hand side of the womb and about the fortieth day, but if the child is a female then on the left-hand side and about the ninetieth day. However, we must by no means assume this to be an accurate statement of fact, for there are many exceptions, in which the movement is manifested on the right-hand side though a female child is coming, and on the left-hand side though the infant is a male. And in short, these and all suchlike phenomena are usually subject to differences that may be summed up as differences of degree. About this period the embryo begins to resolve into distinct parts, it having previously consisted of a flesh-like substance without distinction of parts. What is called effluxion is a destruction of the embryo within the first week, while abortion occurs up to the fortieth day; and the greater number of such embryos as perish do so within the space of these forty days. In the case of a male embryo aborted at the fortieth day, if it is placed in cold water it holds together in a sort of membrane, but if it is placed in any other fluid it dissolves and disappears. If the membrane is pulled to bits the embryo is revealed, as big as one of the large kind of ants; and all the limbs are plain to see, including the penis, and the eyes also, which as in other animals are of great size. But the female embryo, if it suffer abortion during the first three months, is as a rule found to be undifferentiated. If however it reach the fourth month it comes to be subdivided and quickly attains further differentiation. In short, while within the womb, the female infant accomplishes the whole development of its parts more slowly than the male, and more frequently than the man-child takes ten months to come to perfection. But after birth, the females pass more quickly than the males through youth and maturity and age; and this is especially true of those that bear many children, as indeed I have already said."

> I am still in Alexandria [Egypt]. . . . I beg and plead with you to take care of our little child, and as soon as we receive wages, I will send them to you. In the meantime, if (good fortune to you!) you give birth, if it is a boy, let it live; if it is a girl, expose it.

Moreover, a husband could punish his wife for procuring an abortion on the grounds that she deprived him of an heir. An unmarried woman, however, faced no such restrictions. The Christian teaching about abortion stands in very stark contrast to all this.

Early Jewish Thought on Abortion and Exodus 21

Judaism as a whole understands the body as a gift from God to human beings—a gift, in fact, "on loan" to us. Multiple prohibitions on bodily acts, from eating to tattoos to suicide, illustrate the Jewish vision which rejects the idea that the individual has unfettered right to do whatever he or she pleases with the body. So what is the record of Jewish thought on Exodus 21?

The first-century Hellenistic Jewish commentator Philo of Alexandria (c. 25 BC–c. AD 50) is the earliest witness. Philo seems to use the LXX because he distinguishes between an "unshaped and undeveloped" fetus and a "shaped" one with "all the limbs." He comments:

> If a man comes to blows with a pregnant woman and strikes her on the belly and she miscarries, then, if the result of the miscarriage is unshapen and undeveloped, he must be fined both for the outrage and for obstructing the artist Nature in her creative work of bringing into life the fairest of living creatures, man. But, if the offspring is already shaped and all the limbs have their proper qualities and places in the system, he must die, for that which answers to this description is a human being, which he has destroyed in the laboratory of Nature who judges that the hour has not yet come for bringing it out into the light.[4]

Philo concentrates on the developmental stage of the fetus in the case of miscarriage. A fine is required for the "unshaped" fetus; death for the "shaped" one. While this means Philo accepts the LXX, we should not take his citation as a rejection of the MT. Philo's knowledge of Hebrew has been questioned.[5] It is possible that Philo was *only* familiar with the LXX on this point. On the other hand, the authors of the article "Issues in Jewish Ethics: Abortion" at the Jewish Virtual Library cite the Samaritan Targum

---

4. Philo, "On Special Laws," 3.108–9, cited by Hays, *Moral Vision*, 460 n. 3.
5. כהן-ישר and Kahn, "Did Philo Know Hebrew?"

(which traditionally dates to 20 BC, but could date to the third century AD) and "a substantial number of Karaite commentators" as agreeing with Philo.[6] Those authors most likely knew Hebrew and the MT, and chose the LXX on Exodus 21:22–25.

Flavius Josephus (AD 37–c. 100), the first-century Jewish historian, does not mention the developmental stage of the fetus. Because that consideration is absent, he appears to refer to the MT or a proto-MT:

> He that kicks a woman with child, so that the woman miscarry, let him pay a fine in money, as the judges shall determine, as having diminished the multitude by the destruction of what was in her womb; and let money also be given the woman's husband by him that kicked her; but if she die of the stroke, let him also be put to death, the law judging it equitable that life should go for life.[7]

Josephus does not say whether the man *intends* to make the woman miscarry, which is frustrating in its ambiguity or oversight. Clearly, he believed that the woman's life was worthy of the "life for life" principle. At the same time, elsewhere in a different work, Josephus comments on the case where a pregnant mother intentionally aborts her child:

> The Law has commanded to raise all the children and prohibited women from aborting or destroying seed; a woman who does so shall be judged a murderess of children for she has caused a soul to be lost and the family of man to be diminished.[8]

It is not clear, however, *where* Josephus believes the Jewish Law says this, which is another disappointment. It must be noted, too, that Josephus favored Roman goals and imperial order and sought to accommodate Jewish life to the Roman Empire.[9] Many first-century Jews would have considered Josephus a traitor to the cause of Judaism, for reasons that are too long to explain here. That is meaningful because *Roman* policy prevented a mother from robbing a father of offspring, but the father could order an abortion or simply let a newborn baby die (see below). Possibly, Josephus was accommodating a Roman prejudice. Otherwise, it is odd for a representative of Judaism to commend capital punishment to a woman who aborts but only a fine to a man who forces a miscarriage, without addressing his intent.

---

6. "Issues in Jewish Ethics."
7. Josephus, *Antiquities of the Jews*, 4.33.
8. Josephus, *Against Apion*, 2.202.
9. Wright, *New Testament*, 324–29, 373–84.

Almost certainly, the later Jewish midrashic tradition *does* show the pervasive influence of Aristotle's scientific views on diaspora Jews, and not just the LXX translation. According to the later rabbinic document Midrash Nidpas 3:7, the fetus was considered to be "fully formed" on the *forty-first day* after conception. Yevamot 69b describes the fetus *before forty days* as "mere water." A convergence to this level of detail is rather suspect. The time frame of forty days for "formation" is probably not a coincidental agreement but, rather, reflects dependence. It shows that a substantial portion of Jews in antiquity had respect for Aristotle and the LXX.

The opinion of Rabbi Ishmael ben Elisha (AD 90–135) is unusual. He is recorded, by Sanhedrin 57b, to have said that gentiles, but not Jews, incurred the death penalty for intentional abortions. Given that most Jews have held that Jews are bound by God to stricter laws than gentiles, Ishmael should probably be taken as making a rhetorical point communicating his horror at gentile practices. In any case, Orthodox Christian bioethicist H. Tristam Englehardt is mistaken for taking Rabbi Ishmael's opinion as characteristic of Judaism as a whole.[10] Other Talmudic authorities believed that abortion, while prohibited, did not constitute murder.[11] For some, abortion was not categorized as a transgression until the fetus was viable.[12]

Vastly complicating matters, however, almost all Jews today reject the LXX in favor of the Hebrew Masoretic Text. Of course, a Christian concern with this rejection is that it seems motivated by the widespread Christian usage of the LXX, and Christians have accused Jews of modifying the Old Testament text in certain places where messianic prophecies were involved, although this accusation itself has been challenged by more recent Christian scholarship as a misunderstanding.[13] Regardless of motivation, that Jewish decision to favor the Masoretic Text is reflected in the following statement by an Orthodox Jewish scholar:

> If she is not harmed in any other way, the Bible says, then the man who struck her has to pay her husband damages. From this one can deduce that feticide isn't murder, because the penalty for murder is death. Rather, removing a fetus is said to be like amputating a limb—which a woman is still not allowed to do for

---

10. Josephus, *Against Apion*, 2.202.

11. Tosefta Sanhedrin 59a; Chullin 33a.

12. *Mekhilta de-Rabbi Ishmael*, Exodus 21:22–25 (pp. 397–403); also see Talmud, Sanhedrin 84b and Niddah 44b.

13. Daniélou, *History*, 96–97.

mere economic or cosmetic reasons, since that would be self-mutilation, which is forbidden.[14]

This comment seems to constitute a basic denial that the LXX, with its interest in the fetus being "formed" versus "unformed" at some point, is a trustworthy authority on the situation. The Hebrew Masoretic Text contains no distinction about the developmental stages of the fetus, so treats all miscarriages equally. And any assailant of a pregnant woman who causes a miscarriage is subject to a fine, according to Jewish law. Implicit in this statement is that Exodus 21 refers to harm to the *mother*, either of a lesser nature with the loss of her fetus, or of a greater nature if she suffers even more bodily harm. More progressive Jews (Conservative, Reform, etc.) entertain a variety of positions which amount to imputing full human personhood somewhere after conception but before birth.[15] In any case, there is a robust intra-Jewish debate about when human personhood begins.

The Record of Christian Thought on Abortion and Exodus 21: First through Third Centuries

Christianity led to the perception and treatment of children as people for the first time in the Greco-Roman world. In his book *When Children Became People: The Birth of Childhood in Early Christianity*, O. M. Bakke narrates how Christians confronted the prevailing cultural and legal views about children.[16] As Christian faith spread from the communities of Palestinian and Diaspora Judaism to confront the Greco-Roman world, Christian literature from the first to third centuries uniformly condemns the practice of abortion and the exposure of infants and attests to Christians striving to honor children by rejecting abortion as an option. Yet, as I will examine in the next section, in the fourth and fifth centuries, there would be two, and perhaps three, different directions that Greek-, Latin-, and Syriac-speaking (roughly) would take, showing that there was a range of acceptable Christian approaches to regarding the fetus and abortion. Our task is to understand why this range developed and what it might mean for us today. Their engagement with Exodus 21 and the two different manuscripts are part of that difference, as was their approach to the dominant scientific views of their day.

The *Didache*, perhaps an example of Palestinian Jewish Christianity dating to AD 50–100, instructs Christian readers, male and female, "You

14. "What Do Orthodox Jews Think."
15. "Abortion and Judaism."
16. Bakke, *When Children*, 15–55.

shall not murder a child by abortion nor kill that which is begotten."[17] It also speaks against infanticide: "Those that kill children are destroyers of a creation of God."[18]

The *Epistle of Barnabus* (AD 70–130) says, "You shall not slay the child by procuring abortion; nor, again, shall you destroy it after it is born. You shall not withdraw your hand from your son, or from your daughter, but from their infancy you shall teach them the fear of the Lord."[19]

The *Apocalypse of Peter* (~ AD 130) warns, "And near this flame there is a great and very deep pit and into it there flow all kinds of things from everywhere: judgment, horrifying things and excretions. And the women (are) swallowed up (by this) up to their necks and are punished with great pain. These are they who have procured abortions and have ruined the work which he has created. . . . Tiny beasts that devour flesh . . . turn and torture them forever, with their husbands."[20] It is notable that this document ascribes guilt to both the mother *and* father.

Justin Martyr, in his *First Apology* (~ AD 150), says that Christians are taught not to expose (i.e., abandon) their infants: "But as for us, we have been taught that to expose newly-born children is the part of wicked men; and this we have been taught lest we should do any one an injury, and lest we should sin against God, first, because we see that almost all so exposed (not only the girls, but also the males) are brought up to prostitution. And as the ancients are said to have reared herds of oxen, or goats, or sheep, or grazing horses, so now we see you rear children only for this shameful use; and for this pollution a multitude of females and hermaphrodites and those who commit unmentionable iniquities, are found in every nation. And you receive the hire of these, and duty and taxes from them, whom you ought to exterminate from your realm. And any one who uses such persons, besides the godless and infamous and impure intercourse, may possibly be having intercourse with his own child, or relative, or brother. And there are some who prostitute even their own children and wives, and some are openly mutilated for the purpose of sodomy; and they refer these mysteries to the mother of the gods, and along with each of those whom you esteem gods there is painted a serpent, a great symbol and mystery."[21]

Athenagoras of Athens, in *A Plea for the Christians* (AD 177), written to the emperors Marcus Aurelius and Lucius Aurelius Commodus, notes,

17. *Didache* 2:2.
18. *Didache* 5:2.
19. *Epistle of Barnabus* 19:5.
20. *Apocalypse of Peter* 8.
21. Justin Martyr, *First Apology*, 27.

"Women who practice abortion are murderers and will render account to God for abortion."[22] Athenagoras does not mention the role of men.

Tertullian of Carthage, *Apology* (AD 197), says, "But with us, murder is forbidden once for all. We are not permitted to destroy even the fetus in the womb, as long as blood is still being drawn to form a human being. To prevent the birth of a child is a quicker way to murder. It makes no difference whether one destroys a soul already born or interferes with its coming to birth. It is a human being and one who is a man, for the whole fruit is already present in the seed."[23] Tertullian, *On the Soul* (AD 210-13), explains the Christian position as rooted in the Old Testament. "The law of Moses, indeed, punishes the man who causes an abortion."[24] Tertullian, curiously, sees a principle in Exodus 21 that the fetus is valuable, but his application of that principle (infanticide is the same as abortion) could only come from the LXX. To say, "It makes no difference" does not comport with the sense of the MT.

Clement of Alexandria, *Eclogae Propheticae* (~ AD 200), refers to God's care for vulnerable children, worked out in the church community: "Children who were exposed by parents are delivered to a protecting angel, by whom they are brought up and nourished. And they shall be, it says, as the faithful of a hundred years old here. . . . The *Apocalypse of Peter* says that children born abortively receive the better part. These are delivered to a care-taking angel."[25]

Hippolytus of Rome, *Refutation of All Heresies* (~ AD 228) writes, "Women who were reputed to be believers began to take drugs to render

22. Athenagoras of Athens, *Plea for the Christians*, 35.
23. Tertullian, *Apology*, 9.8.
24. Tertullian, *On the Soul*, 37; referring to Exodus 21:22-23; cf. 23-37 where Tertullian describes an abortion procedure: "Among surgeons' tools there is a certain instrument, which is formed with a nicely-adjusted flexible frame for opening the uterus first of all and keeping it open; it is further furnished with an annular blade, by means of which the limbs [of the child] within the womb are dissected with anxious but unfaltering care; its last appendage being a blunted or covered hook, wherewith the entire fetus is extracted by a violent delivery. There is also [another instrument in the shape of] a copper needle or spike, by which the actual death is managed in this furtive robbery of life: They give it, from its infanticide function, the name of *embruosphaktes*, [meaning] "the slayer of the infant," which of course was alive. . . . [The doctors who performed abortions] all knew well enough that a living being had been conceived, and [they] pitied this most luckless infant state, which had first to be put to death, to escape being tortured alive. . . . Now we allow that life begins with conception because we contend that the soul also begins from conception; life taking its commencement at the same moment and place that the soul does."
25. Clement of Alexandria, *Eclogae Propheticae*, 41, cited by Bakke, *When Children*, 118.

themselves sterile, and to bind themselves tightly so as to expel what was being conceived, since they would not, on account of relatives and excess wealth, want to have a child by a slave or by any insignificant person. See, then, into what great impiety that lawless one has proceeded, by teaching adultery and murder at the same time."[26]

Marcus Minucius Felix of Rome, *Octavius* (~ AD 230), writes, "And in fact, it is a practice of yours, I observe, to expose your own children to birds and wild beasts, or at times to smother and strangle them; a pitiful way to die; and there are women who swallow drugs to stifle in their own womb the beginnings of a man to be—committing infanticide before they give birth to their infant."[27]

The early literary evidence for Christians' posture(s) towards abortion is fairly compelling when taken as a whole. Everyone who mentions the practice criticizes it. However, it is important to point out that, with the exception of the *Didache*, these are not pastoral documents. The *Apocalypse of Peter* is probably comparable to modern-day Christian fiction. The *Didache*, on the face of it, is fairly abbreviated instruction from some Jewish Christians to some gentile Christians who were Greek-speaking and possibly Syriac, as early as the first century. The *Didache* enjoyed a good reputation; a few notable Christian leaders even treated it as Scripture.[28] Most, however, placed it into a category of important literature but less than Scripture. The rest of the literature comes from evangelists who were making pointed comparisons between Christian faith and other pagan beliefs and practices. Hippolytus might have led a rival faction of Christians in Rome, and therefore might have functioned as a bishop, or he might have been a teacher in another city and region.[29] But if we were to err on the side of caution, we cannot be sure what leadership position Hippolytus occupied. We must keep all this in mind when we compare the literature of the first to third centuries with the literature of the fourth century onward, when Christian bishops, with pastoral responsibilities, comment on abortion—how to think about it and address it.

Spyros Troianos, a modern scholar of Byzantine law and history, points out that the status of the fetus entered into Christian discussions on other

---

26. Hippolytus of Rome, *Refutation of All Heresies*, 9.7.

27. Minucius Felix, *Octavius*, 30–31.

28. Durant, *Caesar and Christ*, 746, notes that Clement of Alexandria treated it as part of the New Testament, as do the *Apostolic Constitutions* (Canon 85), John of Damascus (*Exposition of the Orthodox Faith*, 4.17) and the Ethiopian Orthodox Church. Other Christian teachers and leaders share material in common with the *Didache* without ascribing authority to the document per se.

29. Cross, "Hippolytus."

occasions, too. During the first three centuries, Christians also pondered the question of whether baptizing the adult mother in effect baptized the unborn fetus, too; they decided that it did not.[30] From that angle as well, the fetus in the womb was not reducible to a part of its mother's body.

The Record of Christian Thought on Abortion and Exodus 21: Fourth and Fifth Centuries

We now consider in some detail the momentous fourth and fifth centuries, which are important for several reasons. First, Christian leaders, in councils, coordinated their views about abortion with specific pastoral responses, like penance. Second, a difference of opinion about the status of the fetus emerged between three church regions. Basil of Caesarea, representing the Greek East and modern Orthodox churches, the authors of the *Apostolic Constitutions*, in the Syrian church, and Augustine of Hippo, who would come to represent the Latin West—Catholic and Protestant—for close to a millennium and a half went in different directions on the fetus and abortion, showing a range of legitimate Christian opinion. Third, the Roman Empire itself, and its laws and administration, started to embrace Christians and welcome Christian influence. This gives us some indication for how Christian concern for the unborn—and human life in general—was translated into concrete policies.

The Council of Elvira (~ AD 306) was an early local council of nineteen bishops, convened in Roman Hispania (southern Spain). They made two decisions about how they would treat abortion among their parishes. Canon 63 says that if a woman becomes pregnant by adultery while her husband is absent, then takes the child's life, she "shall not be given communion even at the end, since she has doubled her crime." Canon 68 says that if a female catechumen becomes pregnant after committing fornication and then causes the death of her child, "her baptism is to be postponed until the end of her life." By comparison, any act of fornication was declared to require five years of penance (canons 47 and 48). It must be added that Christian leaders were concerned not just to punish people, but to protect them, because there was biblical evidence in 1 Corinthians 11:28–32, and

---

30. Troianos, "The Embryo," 5, writes, "The problem was addressed at the local Synod of Neokaesareia (314–325 AD), where it was determined that the baptism of a pregnant woman, in whatever stage of gestation, did not include the embryo which, in principle, possessed ontological autonomy: 'The child-bearing woman must be enlightened [baptized] whenever she wills it. For in this respect the bearing woman has nothing in common with that which is born, because each of the two expresses its will through the affirmation of faith.' (can.6)."

perhaps in other places in the church's memory, that people who take the eucharist with an unworthy attitude might actually die.

The Council of Ancyra, in AD 314, in the capital of Galatia in modern Turkey, was a local meeting of about a dozen bishops from Asia Minor and possibly Syria also. They decide, in canon 21, "Women who prostitute themselves and who kill the children thus begotten, or who try to destroy them while in their wombs, are by ancient law [other translations read 'by former decree,' meaning the Council of Elvira] excommunicated to the end of their lives. We, however, have softened their punishment, and condemn them to the various appointed degrees of penance for ten years." This rule remained influential until well into the Middle Ages. It is noteworthy, however, that canon 22 was a decision about murderers, and it says, "Concerning wilful murderers let them remain prostrators; but at the end of life let them be indulged with full communion." This difference in prescribed pastoral response is of interest to us. From this difference we may fairly conclude that the Council of Ancyra saw abortion as a variation of murder, but also a distinct category within it.

The Fourth Century: Basil of Caesarea and the Orthodox Churches

Basil of Caesarea, in his *Epistle 188* (AD 374) to his protégé Amphilochius, bishop of Iconium, comments on the decisions of the Council of Ancyra. Basil explains, "A woman who deliberately destroys a fetus is answerable for murder." Basil uses the term *phonou*, which he also uses to denote manslaughter and homicide, so there is some ambiguity about how to render this word in this context.[31] Then, Basil addresses the Aristotelian distinction between being formed or unformed. I have found two translations of the next sentence: the former is prescriptive, the latter descriptive.

Nicene and Post-Nicene Fathers, edited by Philip Schaff and Henry Wace	*The Cambridge Edition of Early Christian Writings*, edited by Ellen Muehlberger
"And any fine distinction as to its being completely formed or unformed is not admissible amongst us."[32]	"Among us there has been no technical discussion of whether [the fetus] is or is not fully formed."[33]

31. Radde-Gallwitz, *Early Christian Writings*.
32. Basil of Caesarea, *Epistle 188*, 2, trans. Jackson.
33. Basil of Caesarea, "Epistle 188," 2, trans. Radde-Gallwitz.

Obviously the latter translation "softens" Basil's statement. This difference may be important when it comes to a historical inquiry as to Basil's own position. Whatever Basil intended, subsequent Orthodox tradition follows it prescriptively, as shown on the left hand side of the table, and as shown below.

Basil shows that he is aware of Christians coming to different conclusions about how to think about the fetus and abortion, and *he accepts that*. For who is the "us" of whom Basil speaks? "All Christians"? "Christians of Asia Minor"? The latter is much more likely. At the start of his letter, Basil states the importance of following local customs established by local Christian leaders and communities: "It is right to follow the custom obtaining in each region."[34] Basil is also conscious of "Asia" (meaning Asia Minor) being such a "region" when he says, "It has seemed to some of those of Asia that, for the sake of management of the majority" of schismatics returning to the church, the bishops decided this or that. Some interpret the Council of Ancyra of AD 314 to have been a meeting of bishops from both Asia Minor and Syria, which might be historically accurate, and this might be the administrative "region" which Basil has in mind. But this view does not explain why the authors of the *Apostolic Constitutions*, originating in Syria at around AD 380–400, discuss abortion while making the distinction between unformed and formed, unlike Basil. I discuss this below.

Basil continues,

> For in this case not only the child which is about to be born is vindicated, but also she herself who plotted against herself, since women usually die from such attempts. And there is added to this crime the destruction of the embryo, a second murder—at least that is the intent of those who dare these deeds. We should not, however, prolong their punishment until death, but should accept the term of ten years [of penance]; and we should not determine the treatment according to time but according to the manner of repentance.[35]

And when in the same letter he discusses the importance of intentional and unintentional homicides, he says,

> Women also who administer drugs to cause abortion, as well as those who take poisons to destroy unborn children, are murderesses.[36]

---

34. Basil of Caesarea, *Epistle 188*, 1 trans. Jackson.
35. Basil of Caesarea, *Epistle 188*, 2.
36. Basil of Caesarea, *Epistle 188*, 8.

Basil also says in *Epistle 217* that if a woman abandons

> her newborn child uncared-for on the road, if, although she was really able to save it, she disregarded it, either thinking in this way to conceal her sin or scheming in some entirely brutal and inhuman manner, let her be judged as for murder. [But] if she was unable to protect it and the child perished through destitution and the want of necessities of life, the mother is to be pardoned.[37]

We see in Basil the bishops being sensitive to poverty as an understandable and acceptable reason for a mother—and presumably a father when he was involved in the decision—to abandon her infant. In other words, they see the problem not just as a personal issue, but a social issue, in which one's social context affects how we understand personal choices. As I highlight in chapter 5, Basil and all the bishops from the fourth century onward radically challenge the wealthy to address the poverty of others, and several of them are quite explicit about the need to redistribute *land*. Basil believed that parenting involved very material resources, not to mention emotional, communal, and spiritual resources. To be without material resources, at minimum, *eliminated blameworthiness for abortion and infanticide.*

Taken together, Basil's positions are noteworthy for many reasons. First, in order to arrive at his positions, Basil rejects most Greek and Roman positions available to him: the Aristotelian position on the fetus being "unformed" versus "formed," and subsequent "quickening"; the Stoic position that the fetus became human per se at birth when it drew its first breath; and the Roman tradition of seeing the husband's permission as primary and determinative.[38] Basil opts for the Hippocratic position, which was more rare, and ostensibly practiced by trained physicians who took the Hippocratic Oath, among whom Basil was one. Second, for purposes of establishing the moral category, Basil categorizes abortion as both self-harm to the mother and other-harm to the child. He considers it a murder, but one that involves self-harm, which shows a complexity and sympathy to his views. Third, he accepts the Council of Ancyra's distinction for the purpose of establishing the length of penance (no eucharist) between abortion and murder in every other sense. However, fourth, he encourages bishops to use discretion about whether to shorten that period of ten years based on the sincerity of the mother's repentance, and, perhaps, the mother's social context, based on the evidence provided by *Epistle 217* that he was sympathetic to such

---

37. Basil of Caesarea, *Epistle 217*, 52.

38. Troianos, "Embryo," 5, writes, "The . . . view, that the embryo possessed ontological autonomy, was maintained by the adherents of Platonic philosophy." I presume Troianos includes Basil in the general orbit of a Christian Platonism.

factors as poverty. Finally, fifth, Basil does not actually explain from Scripture where he derives his view. This is unfortunate, because Basil might have helped us better understand the Hebrew and Greek manuscripts of Exodus 21:22–23 which discuss abortion.

Basil of Caesarea's willingness to reject the distinction between "unformed" and "formed" is unexpected.[39] Given his preference for the LXX translation of the Old Testament—not to mention the overwhelming Greek patristic preference for using it in the church's liturgy—one wonders how Basil justified disagreeing with it, and how the Eastern Orthodox churches came to regard him as their spokesperson on the issue.[40] Likely, Basil knew about MT Exodus 21 from his contact with the Jewish synagogue communities of Cappadocia and Asia Minor, which by all reports was sizable.[41] I find this possibility rather likely, but besides the point; MT Exodus 21 would not have led him in this direction.

We might consider the possibility that Basil's source was the Christian tradition he inherited. Did Basil understand his Christian predecessors to have consciously rejected the distinction between "unformed" and "formed," or "unquickened" and "quickened"? True, the *Didache*, the *Epistle of Barnabus*, and other early Christian literature did not make that distinction. And one can have such a high view of church tradition as to say that this position on abortion goes all the way back to a verbal dictum of Jesus himself. That is logically possible, and one cannot preclude it with absolute certainty. But we must also keep in mind that this early Christian literature, while historically valuable, also contains material that was ignored or rejected even within the same period in question.[42] Also, apologists like Justin Martyr of Rome, Athenagoras of Athens, Tertullian of Carthage, and Marcus Minucius Felix of Rome would not have found it relevant to make the distinction between "unformed" and "formed." They made their point simply by calling attention

---

39. Basil of Caesarea, *Epistle 188*, 2.

40. E.g., Hatzinikolaou, "Embryo," 10; Englehardt, *Foundations*, 275, cites Basil as an authority and representative of the whole Orthodox Church, which he makes clear on p. 328 in his discussion of n. 136.

41. Stephen, "Jews."

42. *Didache* 11–15 contains material on itinerant "apostles and prophets," which was not practiced when the church became more settled and stable in its leadership structures, by the late second century. The *Epistle of Barnabus* 10 is a bit too confident in allegorizing the unclean animals of Jewish law into archetypes for unclean human beings, and 11 is too supersessionist with regards to Israel in light of Romans 9–11. Pseudepigraphal literature was often met with deafening silence; only Clement of Alexandria quoted from the *Apocalypse of Peter*, for instance, and there only to make a very constrained, measured point. And so on.

to how poorly their pagan Roman peers treated children categorically. We would not expect them to address more subtle pastoral questions.

Basil's move might suggest that other biblical passages might have been equally, if not more, important. But which? A possible textual source for Basil's judgment, and the Eastern churches who follow him, is Luke 1:44. This is where Mary, pregnant with Jesus, went to visit Elizabeth, pregnant with John the Baptist. Elizabeth told Mary, "The child in my womb leaped for joy." In the respective wombs of their mothers, John the Baptist was acknowledging Jesus, the one he would serve as forerunner and herald. Indeed, Orthodox ethicists and theologians regularly cite this passage to prove that life begins at conception.[43] Hays objects, with strong words: "To extrapolate from this text—whose theological import is entirely christological—a general doctrine of the full personhood of the unborn is ridiculous and tendentious exegesis; indeed, it should not be dignified with the label 'exegesis.'"[44] To the extent that Hays, as a Protestant exegete, is responding to shallow Protestant usage of the text, this is a fair statement. But to the extent that he is open to engaging with Orthodox and Catholic theologians, Hays underestimates the intimate relationship between christology and theological anthropology, which is not provided by biblical exegesis alone. For those anchored in the Chalcedonian Creed of the Fourth Ecumenical Council of 451, the humanity of Jesus Christ is precisely a normative humanity. So to understand the humanity of Jesus, even in this prenatal stage, is to understand something of our own humanity.

We must simultaneously acknowledge, though, that Basil is silent about his process of reasoning. He does not indicate that he is persuaded by *christology* to go beyond MT Exodus 21, and even beyond LXX Exodus 21. Even if he did, his reasoning would not be impervious to questions.

Substantial evidence exists that Basil was motivated to respond to the scientific maxims and questions of his own day. Examining Basil in this light is relevant for examining Christian attempts to engage with scientific questions in the late nineteenth century onwards. Basil was a trained physician, philosopher, and Christian bishop-theologian who expounded on the Christian doctrine of *creation ex nihilo* in his famous nine sermons on the first six days of Genesis 1, called the *Hexaemeron*, which means "six days." Among his motivations was to compare the Christian understanding of creation against

---

43. Hatzinikolaou, "Embryo," 4, lists it first among the biblical passage he cites. Englehardt, *Foundations*, 328, notes that the Liturgy of St. Basil says, "O God, who knowest the age and the name of each, and knowest every man even from his mother's womb."

44. Hays, *Moral Vision*, 448.

the Greek pagan philosophers' explanations of the universe.[45] Christian faith was growing and expanding in his day, not contracting. In his *Address to Young Men on the Right Use of Greek Literature*, Basil said he was open to helpful knowledge being found outside of the church or Christian faith in a formal sense, so long as that knowledge did not conflict with what is true of God as found in Christ and in Scripture.[46] Emmanuel Clapsis points out that Basil "leaves freedom to his listeners to accept as plausible some rational explanations about the place of the earth in the universe and its immobility," while encouraging people not to wonder in amazement at nature but at God.[47] Basil even developed his own "theory of evolution"[48] which is worth appreciating. Nevertheless, Basil was also concerned to refute Origen's proposal of the eternal universe, which he understood to be an intrusion into Christian theology of a pantheistic flavor of Greek philosophy—philosophy which also expressed the science of that time.[49]

Over a century before Basil, the influential teacher Origen of Alexandria proposed that the souls of human beings existed *eternally* before being joined to human bodies as the souls fell away from God. Basil recognized that, among other things, Origen's view made the body more or less incidental to the human being and also made the body the product of the fall. Thus, Basil proposed that God created the human soul *shortly* before placing that soul in the human body. In a sermon, Basil says:

> Understand God as incorporeal, on the basis of the incorporeal soul which dwells in you. God is not circumscribed in a place just as the soul's intelligence has no residence in a place, *before*

---

45. Basil of Caesarea, *Hexaemeron*, 1.2–4, demonstrates his knowledge of the various theories promoted by Greek pagan philosophers, calling them insufficient and measuring them against Genesis and the Christian doctrine of *creation ex nihilo*. In 5:10; 8:1; and 9:2 Basil asserts that God gave the earth itself the power to produce life in its rich variety, even granting that some animals might still be spontaneously produced from the earth.

46. In the case of the creation, based on Basil's *Hexaemeron*, that would include the convictions that God was creator, the creation was not coeternal with God, God made creation originally good, and evil was the result of human beings misusing their faculty of will.

47. Clapsis, "St. Basil's Cosmology."

48. An anachronism, of course, but a meaningful one.

49. Basil of Caesarea, *Hexaemeron*, 1.3, says, "Do not then imagine, O man! That the visible world is without a beginning; and because the celestial bodies move in a circular course, and it is difficult for our senses to define the point where the circle begins, do not believe that bodies impelled by a circular movement are, from their nature, without a beginning." On Origen's views of the eternally existing creation, see Florovsky, "St. Athanasius."

the soul is joined to your body. Having gazed upon your soul, which is inaccessible to sight, believe in God as being invisible.[50]

In my experience, Orthodox Christians I have approached with this passage respond to it with surprise, as if Basil could not have said this. Yet the fact that this passage is translated and cited by an Orthodox clergyman (the author was then Metropolitan of Ainou) and theologian is weighty. Below, I consider the possibility that Gregory of Nyssa, the younger brother and close companion of Basil, tried to *correct* (in his view) his older brother's view on the subject. Regardless, it appears that at one time, Basil believed that God brought the soul into existence *before* joining it to the body. A unified embodied soul, and ensouled body, did not necessarily start at conception, in his view.

Basil can be both critiqued and appreciated for trying to synthesize sources of information available to him. Basil appears to be familiar with the Greek physician Galen on embryology, for instance, because he works with Galen's terms. Galen believed in three stages: conception, construction, and shaping.[51] Galen believed that during construction, the fetus's organs and parts of the body developed from the father's semen. Basil, faced with the Christian conviction that Jesus was conceived immaculately without a biological father's semen, proposes that Jesus' fetal body was "immediately perfect in the flesh," that is, without gradual construction.[52] Basil's assertion, though strange and almost certainly mistaken, demonstrates that his motivation was to develop, as far as possible, a unitary approach to knowledge, for science, theology, and ethics.

Curiously, Basil believes that the soul of an animal was an earthly substance related to their blood, which was another mistake but notable attempt at synthesis. He took Leviticus 17:11, "the life of the animal is in the blood," not just as a theological statement about animals within the scope of the Jewish sacrificial system, but as a scientific one about their embryonic life, though he denied that it applies to human beings in quite the same way.[53] Basil misappropriates and misapplies that particular bibli-

---

50. Basil of Caesarea, *Homilia in illud, Attende tibi ipsi* 7, PG 31:216A, cited by Arghioroussis, *In the Image*, 21.

51. Galen, "Construction," 177–201, cited by Rasmussen, "Vessel," 8–9.

52. Basil of Caesarea, *Homilia in sanctam Christi generationem*, 4, cited by Rasmussen, "Vessel," 8.

53. Basil of Caesarea, *Hexaemeron*, 8.2, says, "Why did the earth produce a living soul? So that you may make a difference between the soul of cattle and that of man. You will soon learn how the human soul was formed; hear now about the soul of creatures devoid of reason. Since, according to Scripture, 'the life of every creature is in the blood,' as the blood when thickened changes into flesh, and flesh when corrupted decomposes

cal text, and not just because modern science would later discover that human blood forms in the human embryo in the fifth week.[54] However, Basil's comment again demonstrates that he is quite interested in reconciling various branches of knowledge.[55]

Basil's understanding of Jesus' own conception is compatible with his view that the human soul was joined to the human body after the human body started its process of development. It is logically possible that there was a short time lapse between the angel's pronouncement and the formation of the fetal physical body of Jesus in the womb of Mary, and between that point and his human ensoulment. After all, the narrative of Genesis suggests (however playfully or allegorically) that God "formed" (a pottery term) the body of Adam from pre-human material—clay, dirt, and earth—and then, after some time, God breathed into him the breath of life. Then he became a living being (Gen 2:7; 1 Cor 15:45). The "fashioning" (an architectural term) of Eve from the "rib" or "side" of Adam (Gen 2:22) would seem to imply, again, that the physical body is prepared first, before the soul is invested there by God. It is possible, then, that even Jesus, as the "new Adam" (1 Cor 15:22, 45) undertook his humanity in a similar way as the old Adam. The sequence might have been: God formed a body of pre-human material in the womb of Mary before breathing in the human soul of Jesus. It might have taken seconds, or days. Thus, in the end, even Luke 1:44 and the consideration of Jesus' own conception are still indeterminate for purposes of this question. We simply do not know. And we are still left with the manuscript differences between the Greek Septuagint and Hebrew Masoretic on the developmental nature of the fetus.

Since Basil did not finish his *Hexaemeron* to include the creation of humanity, his brother Gregory of Nyssa took up the task of completing his brother's work after his death. Gregory said that the human body-soul union started at conception. Notably, Gregory denied that the story of God

---

into earth, so the soul of beasts is naturally an earthy substance. Let the earth bring forth a living soul. See the affinity of the soul with blood, of blood with flesh, of flesh with earth; and remounting in an inverse sense from the earth to the flesh, from the flesh to the blood, from the blood to the soul, you will find that the soul of beasts is earth." In 9.3, he says, "Thus when the soul of brutes appeared it was not concealed in the earth, but it was born by the command of God. Brutes have one and the same soul of which the common characteristic is absence of reason. But each animal is distinguished by peculiar qualities."

54. "Cardiovascular System."

55. Rasmussen, "Vessel" is an excellent paper on the subject. Basil, *Hexaemeron*, 1.10, shows his interest in cosmology (and the Ptolemaic theory of the geocentric universe) by arguing that the world must be at the center of the universe because it does not fall anywhere. Other examples abound.

creating Adam from clay is a paradigm God repeats to achieve delayed ensoulment:

> Nor again are we in our doctrine to begin by making up man like a clay figure, and to say that the soul came into being for the sake of this; for surely in that case the intellectual nature would be shown to be less precious than the clay figure. But as man is one, the being consisting of soul and body, we are to suppose that the beginning of his existence is one, common to both parts, so that he should not be found to be antecedent and posterior to himself, if the bodily element were first in point of time, and the other were a later addition; but we are to say that in the power of God's foreknowledge (according to the doctrine laid down a little earlier in our discourse), all the fullness of human nature had pre-existence (and to this the prophetic writing bears witness, which says that God knows all things before they be), and in the creation of individuals not to place the one element before the other, neither the soul before the body, nor the contrary, that man may not be at strife against himself, by being divided by the difference in point of time.[56]

It is not clear why, logically and biblically, the human being would be "at strife against himself" if the body and soul were unified at some point soon *after* conception and grew and developed together from that point. The Genesis narrative offers that in the cases of both Adam and Eve, their bodies were formed before their souls were introduced and united with their bodies, at least as far as the biblical narrative recounts the matter. Nor is it clear why Gregory believes that the soul would be inferior to the body if it were created by God after the body, since both the creation hymn of Genesis 1:1—2:3 and the Eden story (Gen 2:4-25), which begins the genealogy of Genesis 2:4—4:26, portray creation as getting better and better. Creation is developmental, and what comes later is greater and better than what came before. So Gregory of Nyssa's assertion unfortunately finds no supporting basis, and in any case there is some doubt as to whether his brother Basil would have agreed with these underlying assumptions.

While Basil might have been more or less content to be uncertain, Gregory made the effort to be precise in his views.[57] For purposes of this

---

56. Gregory of Nyssa, *Making of Man*, 29.1.

57. Although I am not entirely sure he was terminologically consistent. In his sensitive and admirable pastoral work *On Infants' Early Deaths*, Gregory compares the newborn to the fetus in the womb, saying, "A human being enters on the scene of life, draws in the air, beginning the process of living with a cry of pain, pays the tribute of a tear to Nature, just tastes life's sorrows, before any of its sweets have been his, before his

study, I am content to let Gregory of Nyssa speak for his brother Basil, thus making Gregory represent Basil's mature view, assuming Basil's thinking on the subject changed.

Regarding abortion and the fetus, the likely reasons behind Basil's statements are his training as a Greek Hippocratic physician and his cautious sympathy for the theology of Origen of Alexandria.[58] Regardless, though, of how we reconstruct Basil's personal biography, his position on abortion and its reception are still surprising. As regards abortion ethics for Christians in the church, we are still left with the fact that neither Basil nor Gregory left behind in writing *why* they set aside the "unformed" versus "formed" fetal distinction between the two manuscript options on Exodus 21, or *how* they deduced the moral significance of human life in the womb.

Perhaps Basil (and/or Gregory) was trying to bring out what he believed to be the *latent significance* of Exodus 21:22–25 regardless of manuscript uncertainties, since the text can be understood as addressing the case of unintentional forced miscarriage. What if we had to consider the case of intentional abortion? Basil was probably taking up a position from his physician's training and Hippocratic oath, which he believed had a satisfying level of internal consistency, even if the proposal itself was not the *only* way to achieve internal consistency. In any event, it must be admitted that he, too, went beyond the biblical text—both the Hebrew Masoretic Text *and* the Septuagint. In view of the ecclesial, textual, and practical ramifications of taking the more challenging ethical stance, what is remarkable is that Basil provides no justification at all. From a strictly exegetical standpoint, while Exodus 21 is the most relevant biblical passage on the subject, Basil appears to have *ignored* the Scripture that was available to him.

Basil's position on abortion was adopted by the Orthodox churches. In 691–92, 215 bishops from the Eastern Roman Empire convened the Council of Troullos. This larger council—also called the Quinisext Council—was

---

feelings have gained any strength; still loose in all his joints, tender, pulpy, unset; in a word, *before he is even human* (if the gift of reason is man's peculiarity, and he has never had it in him), such an one, with no advantage over the embryo in the womb except that he has seen the air, so short-lived, dies and goes to pieces again; being either exposed or suffocated, or else of his own accord ceasing to live from weakness. What are we to think about him? How are we to feel about such deaths?" (emphasis mine). By describing the newborn as "before he is even human," Gregory is probably making a rhetorical point about *flourishing* as a human, by developing his mind, and for the purpose of this study, I'm willing to grant him that.

58. Meredith, *Cappadocians*, 21–22, narrates how Basil and his friend Gregory of Nazianzus collaborated to sift through Origen's writings and collect the most meaningful. This was known as *The Philocalia* of Origen. Basil would have had a personal motivation to do this because his grandparents had come to Christian faith through the ministry of Gregory Thaumaturgus, who had been a student of Origen.

located in the imperial palace of the capital, Constantinople. The Orthodox Church regards this council as an addendum to the Fifth and Sixth Ecumenical Councils, although the Roman Catholic Church never accepted the council as authoritative or "ecumenical." This council affirmed Canons 2 and 8 of Basil (from his *Epistle 188*) and Canon 21 of Ancyra.

The Fourth Century: The *Apostolic Constitutions* and the Syriac Church

Meanwhile, other Christians expressed in writing a different view about abortion, and different ways of getting there as far as the biblical manuscripts were concerned. The fourth-century church in Syria—which spoke both Greek and Syriac-Aramaic—according to Spyros Troianos gives evidence of being influenced by the LXX, as evidenced by the *Apostolic Constitutions*,[59] which began circulation among Syrian Christians between AD 380 and 400, contemporaneously with Basil of Caesarea at the height of his influence. Troianos refers to *Apostolic Constitutions 7.3*, which reads:

> You shall not slay your child by causing abortion, nor kill that which is begotten; for everything that is shaped [Troianos: "completely figured"], and has received a soul from God, if it be slain, shall be avenged, as being unjustly destroyed.[60]

Catholic scholar John T. Noonan agrees with Troianos: "The Apostolic Constitutions condemned the killing of a *formed* fetus."[61] The statement in the *Apostolic Constitutions* relates two conditions as being necessary and sufficient for defining a human person. The first involves the body ("is shaped"). The second involves the soul ("has received a soul from God"). As Troianos suggests, these two conditions reflect LXX Exodus 21.

Pastoral material like the *Didache* weighs heavily for the purpose of suggesting that, among the early Christians, abortion was forbidden from conception. But the *Apostolic Constitutions* does something remarkable. In Canon 85, it treats the *Didache* as Scripture. It styles itself as an expansion on the *Didache*, originates from the same region, and presents itself as wrapped in the same mantle of ancient Christian authority. Perhaps this

---

59. Troianos, "Embryo," 2, writes, "In the latter of these texts [i.e., the *Apostolic Constitutions*], the relevant passage is completed by a phrase, in which we find the term 'completely figured.' This augmentation shows the immediate dependence of this directive on the Old Testament excerpt as formed by the Seventy and by perceptions regarding the nature of the foetus expressed therein."

60. *Apostolic Constitutions* 7.3. Italics mine.

61. Noonan, *Contraception*, 88. Italics mine.

was an appeal to Syriac Christians who were aware of the *Didache* on some level—either in a general, popular level, or in its elite circles who knew something of Christian history from three centuries previous. Whatever the case, the *Apostolic Constitutions* does something even more remarkable. It either *modifies* or *clarifies* its predecessor on this very ethical question of abortion by using LXX Exodus 21:22–23. The authors of the *Apostolic Constitutions* do this at the very same time that Basil of Caesarea wrote on the same subject.

The implications arranged behind this literary presentation are astonishing. The *Apostolic Constitutions* presents Jesus' authority as inhering in the *Didache* through its supposedly apostolic origin. It then further clarifies the *Didache* on the issue of abortion on the suggestion that ancient Christian practice had been concerned with the "form" and "soul" of the fetus from the start. The *Apostolic Constitutions* had to do this because a more "literal reading" of the *Didache* would more naturally convey an *absolute* ban on abortion, not a qualified one. The *Apostolic Constitutions* had to therefore present the *Didache* as if it had been a shorthand which needed expansion. But, as the authors of the new, later document assure their readers, the apostolic authors of the *Didache* would agree with this more expanded version, either because the church came before the "Scripture," or because there was some oral tradition that needed to accompany the written one, to provide the latter with the clarity it needs. In order to present the last four centuries of Christian history in such a way that presented Christian community practice on abortion as smooth, continuous, and unbroken, the *Apostolic Constitutions* had to imply that *Jesus himself had personally affirmed LXX Exodus 21:22–25 to his earliest followers*. Surprising as this presentation is, it is a historical option that we cannot logically rule out based on the limited data we have today. So declared at least one important portion of the Greek-Syriac speaking church for some unknown period of time.

The Fourth Century: Augustine of Hippo, Jerome, and the Roman Catholic Church

The Latin church, which would eventually understand itself as the Roman Catholic Church, took a different path to handling abortion. This difference reflects the thought and influence of Augustine of Hippo (AD 354–430), and the general admiration and use of the Greek Septuagint. Augustine was not an advocate of abortion; he calls parents who expose and abandon their newborn infants "heartless."[62] Nevertheless, Augustine accepted the

---

62. Augustine of Hippo, *Epistle 98*, 6, says, "Foundlings whom heartless parents

Aristotelian distinction between an "unquickened" and "quickened" fetus. In *Questions on Exodus*, he relies on LXX Exodus 21:22–23, which actually does focus attention on the fetus, and says that the fetus being "unformed" or "formed" matters. Augustine says:

> Well, the fact that the author did not want the unborn childbirth to belong to the homicide proves that he thought that it was not man that is carried in the mother's womb. Here the problem of the soul is usually posed, that is, if what is not formed cannot be said to be animated, and therefore, that it would not be a homicide, since it cannot be affirmed that a being that had not yet had soul.[63]

O. M. Bakke observes that Augustine "argues that the abortion of an unformed fetus is not murder, since one cannot say whether it already had a soul at that stage. Although the abortion even of an unformed fetus is morally reprehensible, the punishment for this act is limited to a fine."[64] Augustine's belief that the LXX was inspired in its translation from the Hebrew, and his endorsement of the earlier Aristotelian scientific view of the fetus being "unformed" or "formed" and then quickened, promoted by Aristotle, led him to a different position than Basil of Caesarea, who is held up as the representative spokesman for the Eastern Orthodox.

The witness of Jerome (c. AD 347–420) to this question of abortion is also valuable. In AD 382, Jerome was commissioned by his mentor Pope Damasus I of Rome to write the best Latin translation of the Bible possible. Jerome labored at this task until AD 405. Jerome started to translate the Old Testament directly from a Hebrew manuscript, not the Greek LXX. When he came to Exodus 21:22–23, Jerome transcribed:

> [22] *si rixati fuerint viri et percusserit quis mulierem praegnantem et abortivum quidem fecerit sed ipsa vixerit subiacebit damno quantum expetierit maritus mulieris et arbitri iudicarint*

> [22] If men quarrel, and one strike a woman with child and she miscarry indeed, but live herself: he shall be answerable for so much damage as the woman's husband shall require, and as arbiters shall award.

> [23] *sin autem mors eius fuerit subsecuta reddet animam pro anima*

---

have exposed in order that they may be cared for by any passer-by ... are presented for baptism by these persons" who picked up the children.

63. Augustine of Hippo, *Quaestiones in Heptateuchum*, 2.80, cites Exodus 21:22–23; Augustine of Hippo, *Epistle 121*, cites Jerome's agreement.

64. Bakke, *When Children*, 133.

23 But if her death ensue thereupon, he shall render life for life.

Although Augustine and most other Christians believed that the LXX was an inspired translation, Jerome came to believe that the divine inspiration rested in the Hebrew language. It is unclear whether he tethered his assertion to a particular Hebrew text, and it is unlikely that he did. Nevertheless, in his historical context, Jerome's position was unusual. Unfortunately, Jerome did not explain his every decision as a translator.

Jerome's translation became known as the Vulgate version of the Bible, and it became the Roman Catholic Church's official text until 1979. Jerome's decision to not follow the LXX on these verses is noteworthy. Jerome's opinion on this textual issue is significant to consider because he settled in Bethlehem and reportedly had access to a copy of Origen's *Hexapla*. Origen of Alexandria (c. AD 184–c. 253) was the greatest biblical-textual scholar of the early church, and his *Hexapla* was a massive undertaking to compare the available manuscripts of the Old Testament. Origen wrote in six columns, placing side by side (1) an unknown Hebrew consonantal text; (2) the Secunda, a transliteration of the Hebrew text into Greek characters, which might have been a preexisting older text, or a translational step undertaken by Origen himself; (3) the second-century Greek translation of Aquila (or, Onkelos) of Sinope dating to around AD 130—Aquila was said to have been a disciple of Rabbi Akiva; (4) the late second-century Greek translation of Symmachus, another Jewish interpreter who made wide use of elegant Greek idiomatic expressions; (5) the Septuagint translation with Origen's critical markings; and (6) the second-century translation of the Hellenistic Jewish scholar Theodotion, whose translation of the book of Daniel was so appreciated by the early Christians that they used it in place of the LXX. It is unknown whether the destruction of the temple in AD 70 also destroyed the "official" copy of the Hebrew Bible or whether the Hebrew texts in existence in the second century, which served as the basis for Aquila, Symmachus, and Theodotion, reflected the growing Jewish-Christian polemics about messianic passages.

Despite Jerome's choice to favor a non-LXX manuscript for Exodus 21, the story does not stop there. Jerome personally believed in delayed ensoulment as well. In Jerome's correspondence with Augustine of Hippo, which started in the mid-390s, Augustine mentions the translator's agreement.[65] This fact is curious. Two aspects of Jerome's personal biography are important as they relate to his probable reflection about the question of abortion, the textual question, and the different positions that Christians held on the matter when he began his translation work from 382–405. First, in 380–81,

---

65. Augustine of Hippo, *Epistle 121*; see quotation in Bakke, *When Children*, 133.

Jerome stayed for almost two years in Constantinople, where Basil of Caesarea's influence must have been felt, as Basil had just died in 379. Jerome developed a personal acquaintance with Basil of Caesarea's close friend Gregory of Nazianzus (c. 329-90), who was then serving in Constantinople as its bishop, and Basil's younger brother Gregory of Nyssa (c. 335-c. 395), who was serving as bishop of nearby Nyssa.[66] Second, in 382-85, Jerome was back in Rome. He was chiefly known as a Christian moralist and ethicist. He was especially critical of the Christians living a morally lax life in a cosmopolitan center like Rome. He also befriended a circle of women from aristocratic families who wanted to be taught about monastic life. He almost certainly would have reflected on abortion. Yet in spite of this, Jerome did not advance the position of Basil of Caesarea.

Belief in delayed ensoulment held by Augustine, Jerome, and the entire Roman Catholic Church until 1869 (when the official Catholic position changed to ensoulment at conception) demonstrates that Christians can hold to Scripture, using science to clarify certain moral conditions that Scripture itself left ambiguous. On the one hand, they maintained the Hebrew Masoretic Text with its less clear view of fetal development, generally. There was no *conflict* with Scripture, for one need not equate the fetus from conception with a full human person in order to have a moral foundation against intentional abortion. On the other hand, the Latin tradition incorporated the contribution of Aristotle's developmental view of the fetus, which had the strongest evidentiary grounding of its time. Compared to the Stoic tradition, at least Aristotle conducted careful and meaningful observation of miscarriages.

Placing ourselves in AD 400-410 and surveying the regional differences we can identify in the church, this is what we would observe:

- Christians in Syria, following the *Apostolic Constitutions*, accept LXX Exodus 21 and follow it;
- Christians in Asia Minor, following Basil, accept LXX Exodus 21 yet are more ethically demanding than the Scripture itself;
- Christians in Rome, following Jerome, accept MT Exodus 21 yet functionally follow LXX Exodus 21;

---

66. Jerome visited Constantinople in 380 and stayed until the end of 381. While there, he received the instruction of Gregory Nazianzen, calling him "a most eloquent man, and my instructor in the Scriptures" (Jerome, *De Viris Illustribus*, 117). Jerome frequently appeals to Gregory of Nazianzen's authority in his commentaries and letters (*Epistle 52*, 8, etc.). When Gregory of Nyssa personally visited Constantinople, he read *Against Eunomius* to Jerome and Gregory of Nazianzus (*De Viris Illustribus*, 128).

- Christians in Roman North Africa, following Augustine, accept LXX Exodus 21 yet will receive MT Exodus 21 from Jerome, and continue functionally following LXX Exodus 21.

Clearly, none of this means that Christians took the issue of abortion lightly. I wish to suggest, though, something about the tradition. In the first three centuries, the matter was not for society as a whole. There was some regional variation on how to respond to women and their male partners procuring abortions. But when emperors and other government officials started to become Christians, they began to shape civil law, with its multileveled arrays and challenges of enforcement and punishment, by Christian norms. These leaders started to change the character of the Roman Empire's laws from a pagan towards a Christian orientation.

The bishops, newly freed from the worries of imperial persecution, also took the opportunity to standardize their views and practices. Eventually Christian tradition settled on two. The Greek East settled on the approach of Basil, who as a physician himself seems to have been impressed with the minority Greek view of Hippocrates and Pythagoras on the *ethics of abortion*. Their approach to abortion presumably reflected a view or views on the fetus, but there was room to be somewhat imprecise or uncertain about human origins. Basil shows the signs of thoughtful borrowing from both scientific and theological considerations. Curiously, Basil may have been open to the view that the human soul and body did not originate in time at the same moment. Basil's younger brother Gregory supplied the view that ensoulment occurred at conception, but Basil's extant writings do not answer the precise question of the union of soul and body. Biological details of Basil's views about the human fetus, including Jesus' fetal development, have to be corrected by modern science. The Latin West, meanwhile, settled on the view of Augustine and Jerome, which interacted with the majority Greek view of Aristotle *on the fetus*. Aristotle had studied miscarriages and fetal development. Augustine and Jerome coordinated Aristotle's observations with LXX Exodus 21 and reasoned from that text that the distinction between different consequences for unformed and formed fetuses was rooted in ensoulment. The Syriac-speaking church, exemplified by the *Apostolic Constitutions*, seems to have followed suit for at least some time. Meanwhile, the Jewish tradition eventually developed a range of views and considerations with the majority holding that abortion was distasteful but acceptable given other moral considerations, because the fetus became fully human at birth, when it drew breath. This followed Exodus 21 in the MT, which Jewish scholars preferred because they became reserved about the LXX and Christians' use of it.

Moreover, and equally important to my argument, Christian leaders recognized that they had to consider social and economic conditions, like poverty. O. M. Bakke notes, for example, that Christian bishops and theologians adjusted their counsel on the subject of allowing poor parents to sell their children, rather than expose them. In effect, they chose what they believed was the lesser evil.[67] This demonstrates Christian leaders' need to both weigh different factors but also be more precise about their ethical pronouncements ever since Emperor Constantine became a Christian. The Christian teacher and writer Lactantius—who was a fierce critic of infanticide, who did not explicitly name abortion, curiously[68]—advised Emperor Constantine, which started a pattern of Christian teachers and bishops advising emperors and other governors. If Christian leaders became concerned to delineate further what exactly they meant, they were often right to do so, especially if they were distinguishing between church and society. Perhaps LXX Exodus 21, which had always been close at hand anyway, became more attractive to consider. If Christian leaders also felt compelled to respect the best knowledge about the human fetus from the physical sciences at the time, that too is certainly understandable.

Thus, until 1869, Roman Catholic canon law distinguished between a *foetus animatus* and a *foetus inanimatus*. Pope Gregory VI (1045–46) said, "He is not a murderer who brings about abortion before the soul is in the body."[69] The medieval theologian Anselm of Canterbury (1033/4–109) affirmed the "delayed ensoulment" view, saying, "No human intellect accepts the view that an infant has the rational soul from the moment of conception."[70] The influential Thomas Aquinas (1225–74) asserted that "movement" is one of the two necessary principles of life. While still viewing abortion as a type of sin less than homicide, Aquinas accepted Aristotle's theory of fetal development and ensoulment. In practical terms, Aquinas reinforced the

---

67. Bakke, *When Children*, 134–35. Page 128 introduces the subject thus: "Since an increasing number of Christian parents were poor and found it difficult to look after their children, the theologians were forced to take into account this situation and reflect anew on the question. This made it possible to take a more tolerant attitude toward poor people who exposed their children."

68. Lactantius, *Divine Institutes*, 6.20, writes, "For when God forbids us to kill, He not only prohibits us from open violence . . . but He warns us against the commission of those things which are esteemed lawful among men. . . . Therefore, with regard to this precept of God, there ought to be no exception at all; but that it is always unlawful to put to death a man, whom God willed to be a sacred animal. Therefore let no one imagine that even this is allowed, to strangle newly-born children, which is the greatest impiety; for God breathes into their souls for life, and not for death."

69. Flinn, "Abortion," 4.

70. Flinn, "Abortion," 4.

view that the infant became a human person when the mother felt the infant move. This was called "quickening" and was considered the point of ensoulment. Peter of Spain, a contemporary of Aquinas in the thirteenth century, wrote a book called *Treasury of the Poor*, which contained an exhaustive list of contraceptive herbs and medicines, including those believed to be effective as abortifacients recommended for terminating a pregnancy prior to ensoulment; Peter of Spain is believed to have become Pope John XXI in 1276. Pope Gregory XIII (1572–85) said it was not homicide to kill an embryo of less than forty days since it was not yet human. Pope Gregory XIV (1590–91) said Pope Sixtus's censures against abortion were to be treated as if he had never uttered them.[71] In 1621, the Vatican issued another pastoral directive permitting abortion up to forty days.

Although the Aristotelian tradition held that a boy in the womb was formed at forty days, and a girl at eighty or ninety days, at some point opinions settled on the forty-day threshold. English law also held to this distinction, which the Puritans brought to North America. This was the American common law understanding of fetal development at the time of the U.S. Constitution. I will discuss the implications of this in chapter 12.

Immoral Conception and Other Biblical Considerations

On the matter of the two manuscript traditions of Exodus 21:22–25, in the end, I see no logical way to choose between them. The remarkable conclusion one reaches when we consider all the evidence so far is this: *biblical textual criticism, biblical exegesis, and appeals to Jewish and Christian history cannot settle this manuscript question at the heart of the Jewish and Christian debates about abortion.*

It does not *seem* likely that ancient Jewish scholars and community leaders would move from a *more* ethically discerning and demanding text (LXX) to one that is *less* so (MT). This could weigh in favor of the MT being original, and the LXX being a context-specific translation or adaptation. It is possible, though, that the LXX translators were taking the opportunity to clarify a practical question, one that emerged within the Hellenistic Greek world, to be sure, but also one that would have emerged in everyday circumstances as well. It is possible the LXX translators were influenced by Aristotle, but this seems unprovable. How are we to establish beyond reasonable doubt causation over mere correlation, or intellectual dependence versus mere similarity? But both the MT and the LXX have their own internal integrity, and it does not seem absolutely possible to determine whether the LXX translators were working from an earlier, more "pristine" Hebrew text *on this*

---

71. De Rosa, *Vicars*, 374–75.

particular question. The LXX has proven to be more reliable than the MT in some ways, which I have enumerated in footnotes, but not all. For now, we must entertain the possibility that the LXX and the MT have equally valid claims to being the original text of Exodus 21:22-25.

Having said that, Jewish tradition incorporates Exodus 21:22-25 and the question of abortion into its understanding of other biblical texts and other life situations. This effort complicates the matter. Numbers 5:11-31 authorizes a test of a wife accused of adultery, and Deuteronomy 22:13-30 the death of an adulterous man and/or woman. In either case, the woman may have been pregnant from the liaison. Indeed, this may have been one of the concerns any husband had about the possibility that his wife had been unfaithful. In the case of Deuteronomy 22:13-19, a newlywed husband may have had concerns that his new wife had misrepresented herself; she might even be pregnant from another man. But in Deuteronomy, no consideration is given to delaying the woman's death. The Mishnah Arakhin 2 confirms that a pregnant woman who is sentenced to death should be put to death without regard for the fetus in her womb. This leads more recent Jewish scholars to discuss the following:

> The permissibility of abortion has also been discussed in relation to a pregnancy resulting from a prohibited (i.e., adulterous) union (see *Ḥavvat Ya'ir*). Jacob Emden permitted abortion to a married woman made pregnant through her adultery, since the offspring would be a mamzer [bastard], but not to an unmarried woman who becomes pregnant, since the taint of bastardy does not attach to her offspring (*She'elat Yavez*, loc. cit., S.V. Yuḥasin). In a later responsum it was decided that abortion was prohibited even in the former case (*Leḥem ha-Panim*, last Kunteres, no. 19), but this decision was reversed by Ouziel, in deciding that in the case of bastardous offspring abortion was permissible at the hands of the mother herself (*Mishpetei Uziel*, 3, no. 47).[72]

These are weighty representatives of Judaism. Jacob Emden (1697-1776) was a leading German rabbi and Talmud scholar who championed Orthodox Judaism. Ouziel refers to Rabbi Benzion Uziel (1880-1953), who was elected chief rabbi of Mandatory Palestine from 1939-48 and then chief rabbi of Israel from 1948-53. One can see that simply considering one or two other biblical texts increases the complexity of the issue. When might "immoral conception" take priority over "fetus," or vice versa? How might other biblical texts be either informed by, or shape the interpretation of, Exodus 21:22-25?

My purpose in raising this question is not to take a side in an intra-Jewish debate but to recognize that this debate exists and that it has important

72. "Issues in Jewish Ethics."

consequences. The State of Israel currently permits abortion subject to review by a termination committee made up of two physicians and a social worker, where one of those three committee members must be a woman. This law passed in 1977. Prior to that, abortion had been illegal. Abortions are legal for women under the legal age of marriage (eighteen years), or over the age of forty, for women who conceived outside of wedlock or under illegal circumstances (rape, statutory rape, incest), for risk of the mother's life, for risk of the mother's health, and detected birth defects. A 2014 law provided abortion services to women up to the age of thirty-three, paid for under the nationally funded health program. Significantly, a 2012 study found that half of all abortions occur in private clinics, without engaging the process of getting termination committee approval.[73] Women who procure abortions outside of the termination committee process do not face criminal penalties. The doctors who provide them are legally subject to a fine or up to five years of imprisonment. But there have been no known cases of doctors being prosecuted,[74] which raises the same question about the actual implementation of the law or not, in the State of Israel as in the United States. It is also significant that the State of Israel, through its national health program, subsidizes contraceptives, partially funds abortions for out of wedlock pregnancies, and fully funds abortions for teens nineteen years or younger, and for birth defects detected in the womb.[75] While Israel's laws might indeed change, the history of rabbinical opinion on this issue is weighty. Simply considering Numbers 5 and Deuteronomy 22 alongside Exodus 21 raises more, and fairly difficult, questions. Given the strong support white American evangelicals give to the State of Israel, the relative silence of those same evangelicals towards Israel's abortion policy is remarkable.

Moreover, by examining passages from the Torah, I am not suggesting that Christians can simply take these texts and apply them straightaway. I am, for now, sidestepping massive discussions about the exact relationship between Christians—including Jewish Christians—and the Jewish law. I will make clear that "theocracy" is not a valid option for Christians politically, as hostility to Jews is one direct result of that posture. I do think that there are various principles that Christians can live out and call for. But before explaining those positions, we must return to Christian interaction with science today over the questions of the fetus and abortion.

---

73. Jones, "Abortion in Israel."
74. "Israel: Reproduction and Abortion," sec. III.
75. "Israel: Reproduction and Abortion," sec. IV.B.

4

Science as a Friend in the Discernment of Fetal Life

Christians' Dependence on Science

MANY CHRISTIANS BELIEVE THAT their position on abortion comes straight from Scripture and its authority. In fact, it does not. In chapters 2 and 3, I examined Scripture and church history for several reasons. First, when confronted with the important difference between the Hebrew Masoretic Text (MT) and the Greek Septuagint Text (LXX) variations on Exodus 21:22–25, church leaders and scholars did not know which to prefer. Second, when they developed their actual positions for pastoral responses to people who had procured abortion, there was not uniformity about how to apply Exodus 21; nor was it the only text, or principle, they considered. Third, when they did make practical pastoral decisions about the fetus, they actually incorporated insights from the science of their day, and also social conditions. Basil of Caesarea, whose position on abortion practice became the policy for the Eastern Orthodox churches, appears to have relied not on Scripture alone, but on Hippocrates, and perhaps, to a lesser extent, Galen. Augustine of Hippo and Jerome in the Roman Catholic tradition relied on the LXX and Aristotle to develop a view about the fetus's development—that the moment of "quickening," when the mother felt the fetus move, was the moment of ensoulment and therefore personhood. For a season, the Syriac Church, if it can be represented by the *Apostolic Constitutions*, appears to have followed the LXX and probably Aristotle. This document and the Christian community it represents directly imply that Jesus himself had approved of LXX Exodus 21. Meanwhile, the Jewish community developed its view on abortion from the MT and included other ethical considerations from Scripture, such as the case of immoral conception.

Both manuscripts of Exodus 21:22–25 require that Christians ask for further clarity about the fetus using the natural sciences. MT Exodus 21:22 likely envisions the offender paying a fine relative to the stage of the woman's pregnancy, as I mentioned before. LXX Exodus 21:22 expresses that we should treat the fetus as a full human person at some stage where being "formed" is relevant. In other words, both manuscript families leave room for the people of God to offer their best attempt at responding to God, and partnering with God, on these questions. And, as a reminder, abortion policy is not the only relevant consideration related to the developmental stage of the fetus.

Based on what we now know scientifically about fetal life, one important marker is the formation of a nervous system at roughly twenty-three days of fetal life.[1] Coordinating beginning-of-life and end-of-life care is an important consideration here. When a human being's nervous system is present, healthy, and functioning, there is no real question about a human being's legal human personhood. We do have genuine questions, however, when a human being is on life support, comatose, with no activity in her/his brain and nervous system. Although "miracles" could happen, most family members, medical professionals, and ethicists (including Christian ethicists) would consider their moral responsibility towards the comatose person with an inactive brain and nervous system to cease. My point here is not to parse the finer details of the euthanasia debate, but simply to identify a minimum condition. If legal human personhood should be defined as consistently as possible with beginning-of-life care and end-of-life care in mind, then legal human personhood might be based on the presence of a functioning nervous system. As such, it is epistemically accessible to anyone. People who identify as not belonging to any major religious tradition can recognize this fact. That is, they can recognize it as a valid moral and legal argument. And as such, it can reflect one stable meeting place for public policy, although I do think fetuses will continue to fall into an ambiguous legal category. I also insert a caveat: Simply exploring this point does not mean I am supporting possibilities for enforcement typically put forward by the pro-life movement, for that also needs to be critically examined, which I do in chapters 5 and 6.

---

1. Catholic bioethicist Carol Tauer also finds this biological marker, on the earliest side "when the primitive streak [of the spinal column] appears," to be morally significant; see McCoy, "Catholic Moralist."

Implantation

How would this twenty-three-day developmental marker coordinate with other important biological and legal markers? Sperm can fertilize an egg from within minutes to five days after intercourse. A fertilized egg typically implants in the uterine wall five to six days after being fertilized. Until recently, based on scientific measures, it was believed that 50 percent of all fertilized eggs do not implant.[2] A Stanford University School of Medicine study has revised that upwards: 70 percent of fertilized eggs fail to proceed to the blastocyst stage.[3] If we coordinate human personhood with conception, we must conclude that 70 percent of all people die within a week of being conceived. That is an unsettling and staggering reality.

Complicating matters, commonly used substances affect pregnancy outcomes. A 2014 analysis done in Canada found the rate of miscarriage increases by 2.4 times if the woman takes Advil or other non-steroidal anti-inflammatory drugs (NSAIDs), especially around the time of conception.[4] That analysis has been debated,[5] but the National Health Service of the U.K affirms it as "large, well-conducted . . . replicated in other studies . . . likely to be reliable."[6] The biological mechanism is also "well-established": "non-steroidal anti-inflammatory drugs inhibit the production of prostaglandin, which is essential for successful embryonic implantation. Abnormal implantation increases the risk of miscarriage."[7] NSAIDs have also been associated with birth defects in animals.[8]

Caffeine is another drug that affects pregnancy outcomes. A 1988 study of healthy women trying to get pregnant showed that caffeinated drinks reduced the pregnancy rate by half, some of which may have been the result of caffeine increasing the rate of non-implantation.[9] In 2008, research showed that drinking more than 200 mg (one cup) of caffeinated coffee increased the risk of miscarriage by 1.4 to 2.2, depending on the amount.[10] The latest review of studies acknowledges that while the exact

---

2. "Conception: How It Works."
3. Conger, "Embryo Survival."
4. Nakhai-Pour et al., "Anti-Inflammatory Drugs." See also Nielsen et al., "Risk."
5. Daniel et al., "Fetal Exposure" found there was no correlation in a large population of Israeli women, but this study ruled out non-implantation, because the population was women who were detectably pregnant.
6. "Ibuprofen May." An early 2003 analysis was published by Li et al., "Exposure."
7. Li et al., "Use of Nonsteroidal Antiinflammatory Drugs."
8. Cook et al., "Analysis of the Nonsteroidal."
9. Wilcox et al., "Caffeinated Beverages."
10. Weng et al., "Maternal Caffeine Consumption." However, Signorello and

biological mechanism is obscure, "caffeine consumption during pregnancy is associated with adverse gestational outcomes."[11]

If we truly believed that full legal human personhood begins at conception, then non-implantation ought to place more ethical demands on us. Should employers be banned from giving out free coffee? Given our level of technology, should we do more to facilitate proper implantation? Should we do more to save the fertilized egg from non-implantation and a natural death? Should we invest more research funding into hormonal treatments that increase the likelihood of implantation, available to women hoping to become pregnant? If we can achieve rates of successful implantation through in vitro insemination that are higher than natural procreation, are we ethically bound to separate sex from procreation? Conversely, there is no clear way to ensure that pregnant women do not take Advil or have more than one cup of coffee per day. One particularly intrusive but effective approach would be mandating vasectomies for young men at adolescence and only reversing them when men are ready to become fathers. Of course, mandatory vasectomies is not likely to ever be feasible politically, but it would dramatically reduce the number of people lost to natural non-implantation, and to abortion.

The non-implantation rate is also awkward for the Christian on a theological level: Does God invest a human soul into every fertilized egg, only to lose half of them? Why does he not wait a little while longer? Analogies to human experience may be limited, but they are still powerful: In war, a general who sends soldiers into battle, a NASA chief who sends astronauts into space, or a public health official who sends medics against a disease, only to have 70 percent of them die at the outset, for no discernable reason, would be considered a disaster. While this conclusion is not an *absolutely* insurmountable problem for theodicy, as the high non-implantation rate may be "from the fall," neither is there a discernable reason why God could not wait to ensoul the zygote when it reaches the blastocyst phase. The twenty-three-day marker relieves us of the weight of the moral and theological questions related to non-implantation. Moreover, the rate of non-implantation gives us some baseline perspective with which to view the use of Emergency Contraceptive Pills (ECPs) and Intra-Uterine Devices (IUDs).

McLaughlin, "Caffeine and Miscarriage" debated the results because of possible memory recall bias by participants and insufficient controls on age and other consumption including alcohol and cigarettes. Note also Armstrong et al., "Maternal Caffeine Consumption," point out that Weng et.al. overstate their conclusion advising pregnant women to abstain from coffee because there was no miscarriage rate difference for women consuming less than 200 mg of caffeine.

11. Qian et al., "Impacts of Caffeine."

Twinning, Cell Potency, and Chimerism

The twenty-three-day marker also sidesteps the metaphysical issues related to twinning and chimerism. If monozygotic twinning occurs, it occurs within eight to ten days of fertilization, in three to five cases for every thousand pregnancies. How does a Christian considering ensoulment at fertilization explain twinning? When the body is divided, is the soul divided also? The soul has been defined by Christian theologians as uniquely personal and indivisible. This at least poses a question. How then can one entity become two? Is human twinning like an earthworm being cut in two, with each taking on its own "individuality"? Until recently, a Christian might answer from a pragmatic, functional standpoint and deploy the moral probability argument again: Maybe twinning is some variation of cloning.[12] Perhaps the pre-twinned embryo had two (or more) souls. Perhaps God invested the original conceptus with two souls, which then separate as the twin bodies form. Or, perhaps God invests the "second" embryo with a soul at the point of separation (but which is the "first" and which is the "second"?). Prior to cell potency research, Christians considering all this might have admitted that the metaphysics of their position were a bit puzzling and left room for mystery.

More recent research into cell potency, however, challenges that understanding. The fertilized human egg begins as a zygote. Within hours, the zygote cell divides into multiple totipotent cells, which are undifferentiated. The cells seem to be able to be separated in principle—thus, twinning. These cells divide for about four days while retaining their totipotency, then divide further into pluripotent cells, and then become more and more "committed" in their functions as they continue to divide over the course of about twenty-one days. By itself, this does not have any more metaphysical implications. However, totipotent cells can become embryonic or extraembryonic (placental). That poses a metaphysical question, because we would not normally consider the *placenta* to be part of the human personhood of the fetus. That is, Christians do not believe the placenta contains part of the human *soul* of the fetus. It is, of course, possible to say that the zygote "spins off" biological parts that are not absolutely essential to the human personhood of the fetus, in principle. For example, if a bizarre accident happened where one finger fell off the fetus, we would have no doubt about the status of the fetus as a whole. But that is not exactly the situation here. For about four days, the totipotent cell or cells do not give any physical evidence of differentiation. If a totipotent cell can eventually become a twin *or* a placenta,

---

12. "Twinning Challenge."

that raises a very puzzling metaphysical question. Can we declare what a totipotent cell is until it tells us what it has become?

Research into pluripotent cells raises further significant medical and metaphysical implications. Recent studies have found that electrical charges found in organic, living contexts affect what pluripotent cells eventually become.[13] For medical purposes, a team of Japanese scientists reported in 2017 that they reversed diabetes in mice by transplanting mice pancreases that were grown in rats but from pluripotent mouse cells.[14] It may one day be possible to transplant induced pluripotent stem cells of a human into an animal in order to develop human organs.[15] Whether we eventually accomplish that or not is beside the point here. Metaphysically, this means that a totipotent zygote cell, and even pluripotent cells, require a certain *context*—the womb of a human female—in order to develop into a full human being. Without that context, and in another, the pluripotent cells might develop into some *part* of a human being. But that is startling. Equally startling is the observation that a differentiated cell can be returned to an earlier state of pluripotency. The cell can then be placed in a different context and allowed to proceed along a different path of development. These facts would strongly suggest that the fertilized egg by itself is not yet a human person. It needs to be in a certain context—a relational context—in order to develop into one, along with more time. Having the DNA blueprint and raw materials for a complex building is not the same thing as having the building itself.

Human chimerism poses an even greater challenge. When chimerism occurs, two embryos fuse and result in one body and one consciousness with two sets of genomes.[16] Either two or more eggs are released from the ovum and fertilized and then combine, or an initial twinning process starts but the embryos recombine. Perhaps one embryo "dies," and the other embryo simply absorbs that DNA.[17] But of this we cannot be sure. In 1998, a study was done on a man with female sex organs, who was discovered to be a chimera from two different fertilized eggs that combined.[18] In 2002, Karen Keegan and her three sons were seeking to do a kidney transplant for Karen when they discovered that two of the sons were not genetically Karen's, but Karen's sibling's.[19] In 2002, Lydia Fairchild discovered she was

---

13. Yamada et al., "Electrical Stimulation," and Chen et al., "Electrical Stimulation."
14. Wade, "New Prospects."
15. Servick, "Embryo Experiments."
16. Sheets, "Chimerism Explained."
17. Rettner, "3 Human Chimeras."
18. Strain et al., "True Hermaphrodite Chimera."
19. Wolinsky, "Mythical Beast."

not the genetic mother of her children; her twin sister, whose DNA was in her body, was.[20] And so on.

How does chimerism result in one person in a spiritual and theological sense? This is a challenging question that Christians in the recent past have not adequately discussed and coordinated with their views on Scripture, fetal life, and abortion. Dr. Edwin C. Hui, an evangelical bioethicist and theologian who wrote an outstanding and detailed book on bioethics in 2002, confined his remarks about chimerism to one paragraph. Hui wrote that the recombination of embryos has only been observed to happen in laboratory conditions, including in vitro fertilization, which he took to justify his view that fertilization constitutes full personhood.[21] Hui's assertion can no longer stand with high confidence, however. Chimerism may be more common than we think because it only draws our attention when human beings present with different characteristics, or when some part of the body contains different DNA. In 1996, scientists in the Netherlands concluded that blood chimerism is remarkably common, and suggested that chimerism affects up to 30 percent of the population;[22] the study does not appear in Hui's bibliography. In 2005, autopsy studies done on seventy-five women (who had had no organ transplants) found that Y-chromosomes were present in these women's organs: thirteen kidneys, ten livers, and four hearts.[23] Scientists wonder whether intersex individuals—whom Augustine of Hippo apparently called *hermaphroditi* and *androgyni*[24]—are chimeric. As to *how* chimerism happens, whether one embryo "dies" and is absorbed by the other, we simply do not know. It would seem that "embryo death" is not always the case. After Hui published his book, the doctors who studied Karen Keegan and her sons concluded, "It wasn't that there actually was a twin that went fairly far along in development then was resorbed, but more likely that very early on the two fertilized eggs fused together."[25] If true, that would be a remarkable challenge for Christian bioethicists.

If a Christian believes that ensoulment and personhood occur at conception, chimerism presents a major puzzle. Those Christians must offer an explanation: What metaphysical step must God take to resolve the fact that there is evidence of a second body? Do chimeric individuals somehow have two souls? Were there ever two souls? Must Christians say

20. Murphy, "DNA at the Fringes."
21. Hui, *At the Beginning*, 70.
22. Van Dijk et al., "Blood Group Chimerism."
23. Koopmans et al., "Chimerism in Kidneys."
24. Augustine of Hippo, *City of God*, 663.
25. Wolinsky, "Mythical Beast."

that one embryo has "died"? Is that something we can say, a priori, before we understand it scientifically? Is that the only way to remove the problem of the second soul? While various proposals are logically possible, the acrobatic moves leave me uncomfortable. And, lest we forget, historically when Christians believed they must be committed to a scientific theory as "fact" before they actually observe it *scientifically*, things have not gone well for either the Christians or the scientists.

Hence, cell potency and the possibilities at the cellular level raise more questions about "being" and personhood than older arguments have acknowledged. Catholic writer Peter Kreeft, for instance, argues for personhood at fertilization by noting that we must distinguish between "being," which does not increase, and "functioning," which does. Hence, he says:

> The zygote has no brain, true, but it does have what will grow into a brain, just as an infant does not have speech but has what will grow into speech. Within the zygote is an already fully programmed individuality, from sex and aging to eye color and aversion to spinach. The personhood of the person is already there, like the tuliphood of the tulip bulb. One must actually be a human being, after all, to grow a human brain.[26]

The questions here are not purely physical, as Kreeft suggests, but a combination of the physical and the metaphysical. Yes, physical development of a zygote can produce a human brain, and eventually a human person. Or it can produce more than one such brain and one such person, along with other material, and the *path there matters*. Thus, *which* cells "contain" or result in the eventual human brain and human person? Can we say such a thing if all the cells are undifferentiated until some later point? One possible cell-level milestone for personhood might be the beginning of a period when cell recombination is no longer possible, which is yet unknown.

The fact that we have to ask these questions leads to more questions about how the soul interacts with the body. The metaphysical corollary is *which* cells contain the human *soul* and thus the human person, and *when*. As a Catholic, Kreeft strangely sidesteps the traditional Catholic question about ensoulment. Still another question is whether the ontological basis for "being" can be considered "individualistically," as secure attachment to a mother's uterus has been shown by pluripotency to be not just nourishment but minimally required to move from pluripotency to embryo. We cannot even say that the ontology of human personhood itself is recognizably achieved or achievable apart from a relational context until a certain point in fetal development. Since relationality is prior to, and determinative of,

26. Kreeft, "Human Personhood."

ontology, Kreeft is mistaken to suggest that the reverse is true. Yet another question is whether the physical development of the fetus needs to achieve a milestone like the nervous system streak or the twenty-three-day milestone of the brain and spinal cord. Related to those questions, and involving others, what biological milestone might be the wisest for any public policy related to the legal status of the fetus?

Indeed, Catholic bioethicist Carol Tauer, in her excellent 1984 article assessing the Catholic use of moral probabilism, revisits the biological data and agrees:

> The phenomenon of twinning and especially that of recombination offer strong positive evidence that the human soul is not yet present in the early embryo; for, in the traditional Catholic understanding, the soul is indivisible and indestructible, and souls cannot split, fuse, or disappear. The soul is the principle of selfhood, which, like it, is a unique and indivisible marker.[27]

Tauer's work also does not appear in Hui's bibliography, which is unfortunate. Tauer cites often overlooked Catholic opinions about conception, body-soul unity, and baptism, and finds:

> Both theological and magisterial opinion, up until the nineteenth century, were open to the view that the ensoulment of the early embryo is highly improbable, if not impossible.[28]

Tauer points out that moral probabilism might be applied meaningfully to animal life, especially where animals appear to come close to human rationality and self-consciousness, yet we do not apply moral probability to the question of animal suffering. Tauer therefore comes to her powerful conclusion:

> The reasoning of the Congregation in forbidding all abortions, including the destruction of zygotes, is linked to the stringency of the moral tradition regarding factual doubts in relation to human life. But the thesis that ensoulment is a matter of fact within this context *cannot be substantiated*.[29]

Perhaps God is involved in fetal life another way. Delayed ensoulment fits quite well with patterns of God's activity in Scripture, where God first frames, then fills; he builds the structure, then implants life. God created the physical universe and the planet as a temple, and then, only after the planet had

27. Tauer, "Tradition of Probabilism," 30.
28. Tauer, "Tradition of Probabilism," 31.
29. Tauer, "Tradition of Probabilism," 33.

become stable, placed his image—that is, His human image-bearers—within it (Gen 1:1—2:3). After the "creation hymn," in the complementary account of Genesis 2, God took preexisting physical material, shaped it, and only then breathed life into it, creating Adam (Gen 2:7). God took preexisting human material, fashioned it into a woman, and only then gave the woman life (Gen 2:21-22). For presumably, God did not make Eve consciously endure the physical development of her own body. Before God brought the Israelites as a nation into the garden land, he prepared for them cities, houses, cisterns, vineyards, and trees which they did not build or plant (Deut 6:10-11). God enlisted the help of the Israelites to build a tabernacle, then temple, then came in glory to dwell within it (Exod 40:34-38; 1 Kgs 8:10-11), reminding us of the pattern of preparing physical material first and bringing the life-bearing presence later. Jesus gave his Spirit to his disciples when he breathed on them, in a deliberate echo of God breathing into Adam, and an echo of God's shekinah glory entering the temple (John 20:22). There is no biblical data that requires us to believe that ensoulment begins at the precise moment of fertilization and ample biblical data to suggest it does not.

Contraception

This twenty-three-day marker would mean that the full range of Emergency Contraceptive Pills (ECPs) and Intra-Uterine Devices (IUDs) should be commercially available, not least because they are now standard medical treatment for women who have been raped. I will survey a few of the more widespread ECPs and IUDs in the United States to observe the public policy ramifications of these methods. My intention here is to be representative, not exhaustive, as I highlight the relevant ethical aspects.

The "Plan B" or "morning after" pill, which utilizes the progestin called levonorgestrel, does not cause an abortion, and should not be controversial. Levonorgestrel interferes with conception, either by delaying ovulation and/or interfering with sperm movement.[30] Although the U.S. FDA requires the packaging of levonorgestrel to say that the drug "may" interfere with implantation of the fertilized egg in the uterus, studies indicate that it does not. This conclusion has been reached by Catholic Italy (which almost certainly would not have permitted it otherwise), other European health authorities, the U.S. National Institutes of Health, and the Mayo Clinic, and it has been discussed by the U.S. Supreme Court.[31] At the dosage of the Plan B pill, levonorgestrel has an 89 percent effectiveness rate, which the packaging explains

---

30. Peck et al., "Levonorgestrel."
31. Belluck, "New Birth Control Label." See also Belluck, "Abortion Qualms."

by saying, "Seven out of every 8 women who would have gotten pregnant will not become pregnant."[32] At low doses, mifepristone (see below) has been used as a type of emergency contraception similar to levonorgestrel, with an 83 percent effectiveness rate if taken five days after intercourse.[33] Levonorgestrel, however, does increase the risk of an ectopic pregnancy in the future, which naturally occurs in about 1 to 2 percent of pregnancies.[34] This means that, in the future, the drug imposes a health risk onto the woman, a mortality risk onto a future fetus, and an economic risk to the health care system. Put differently, there is an *uncertain cost* which will be paid by three parties, potentially: the woman, *a future fetus (or more)*, and the health care system. I will discuss this subject in a later chapter.

The RU-486 pill, by comparison, causes the uterine wall to not receive the fertilized egg (conceptus). It is therefore nicknamed "The Abortion Pill" by anti-abortionists. It is a combination of two drugs in two doses: mifepristone and misoprostol. The first pill, the mifepristone, blocks the hormone progesterone needed to maintain the pregnancy in the uterus. The second pill, misoprostol, is taken twenty-four to seventy-two hours later, and causes the uterus to contract and expel the placenta and embryo. The combination is effective up to seven weeks of pregnancy. Studies have shown that the mifepristone dosage alone results in abortion within one to two weeks of being taken in 8–46 percent of pregnancies.[35] The usage of misoprostol increases that effectiveness to 90 percent of pregnancies. RU-486 is available by prescription, not over the counter, and its use requires three visits to a physician in case of any side effects. When a woman wants to become pregnant after using the RU-486 pill, she faces an increased risk of ectopic abortion that is nearly three times higher than usual (i.e., 3 percent), which is the same risk increase as surgical abortion.[36]

The copper IUD can prevent both conception and implantation. Its primary function is to increase the foreign body reaction in the uterus. The uterus recognizes a foreign body within it and produces extra white blood

---

32. "Plan B label information." The effectiveness rate is based on a statistical benchmark. On average, if 1,000 women have unprotected sex during the middle two weeks of their menstrual cycles, 80 women will become pregnant. The effectiveness rate of 83 percent reduces that number to 13.6. See Weismiller, "Emergency Contraception." However, Gemzell-Danielsson, "Mechanism of Action," found that levonorgestrel decreases the chance of pregnancy from 57–93 percent.

33. Piaggio et al., "Combined Estimates."

34. American Pregnancy Association, https://americanpregnancy.org/pregnancy-complications/ectopic-pregnancy/.

35. Grossman et al., "Continuing Pregnancy," and Paul et al., *Management*.

36. DeNoon, "Abortion Pill."

cells, prostaglandins, and other enzymes within the fluids of the uterus and fallopian tubes. Together with the copper ions contributed by the copper IUD, this biochemical reaction is very hostile to sperm, resulting in a very high effectiveness rate of 99.2 percent. It should be understood that the uterus normally treats sperm as foreign bodies; the IUD increases that particular response. The IUD would also likely prevent implantation of a fertilized egg, but in my view, since implantation already carries with it a 30/70 success/failure rate, and since it takes place within the twenty-three-day window, I would accept this risk. The IUD does not affect an already implanted fetus. An IUD must be prescribed by a health care provider, and only a doctor, nurse, or registered health care provider can insert one; it can be expensive (~$1,300) if not covered by insurance. However, copper IUDs do cause a higher risk of ectopic pregnancies if an unintended pregnancy occurs. IUDs with progestogen also cause an increased risk of ovarian cysts.[37]

Of course, women seeking to have an abortion after the twenty-three-day mark will still be able to consult their health care provider and acquire these methods to abort the fetus. However, we should look more broadly at the social and legal difficulties women face. The prevalence of rape, for instance, makes a compelling case for these birth control and abortion methods to be available to women through a confidential meeting with her health care provider. About one in six women will be the victim of a rape or attempted rape during her lifetime.[38] As mentioned above, one study of over four thousand women found that 5 percent of all rapes resulted in a pregnancy, even when a condom was used.[39] If a woman is raped, unfortunately the odds are high that the rapist is a family member or an acquaintance whom she will continue to see. Eight out of ten rapes are committed by someone known to the victim: 39 percent by an acquaintance; 33 percent by a current or former spouse, boyfriend, or girlfriend; 2.5 percent by a non-spouse relative; and 6 percent by more than one person.[40] In the case of juvenile victims of sexual abuse that were reported to law enforcement, 59 percent were acquaintances, 34 percent were family members, and only 7 percent were strangers to the victim.[41]

Therefore, bringing a rape accusation forward has formidable relational and legal obstacles. Depending on a woman's age, mental/emotional health, and social circumstances, a woman may not report a rape right away. Women

---

37. Bahamondes et al., "Enlarged Ovarian Follicles."
38. "18 Profound Statistics."
39. Holmes et al., "Rape-Related Pregnancy."
40. "National Crime Victimization Survey," cited by "Criminal Justice System."
41. "Sexual Assault of Young Children," cited by "Perpetrators of Sexual Violence."

who are victims of rape are often confused about their own agency because perpetrators often exploit issues of memory, shame, self-blame, and power. In some situations, the relational and financial costs of responding to rape through the criminal justice system are overwhelming. RAINN, the Rape, Abuse and Incest National Network, finds that only 310 out of every 1,000 sexual assault incidents are reported to the police, and only 5 out of every 1,000 rape perpetrators go to prison for their crime.[42] Indeed, the rape victim can legitimately ask what would happen even after a convicted rapist goes to prison—in the "best case scenario" if it is indeed that—and then comes out again. Understandably, a woman is much more likely to respond to a rape as a personal health issue rather than a criminal justice issue. From a policy standpoint, therefore, making the RU-486 pill and copper IUDs available through a confidential meeting with her health care provider makes sense because women can legitimately fear for their lives, otherwise.

Of course any policy is open to misuse or abuse, given the limitations of what we can do with law and technology. The question is which type of misuse and abuse are we willing to tolerate, and why. I am willing to accept the possibility that women will seek to procure an abortion, using the RU-486 or IUD, even after the time frame in which I hope they would not, if it means that a woman who is the victim of rape would not have to bear the child of her rapist.

Parental Selection

In this book, I do not examine severe fetal abnormality due to its complexity and this book's length already. I do think it is possible to comment on Down Syndrome, however. The twenty-three-day marker might be used as one important criterion to weigh as a factor against abortion for Down Syndrome. Down Syndrome is detectable in the fetus through chorionic villus sampling as early as nine weeks[43] or an amniocentesis as early as fifteen weeks. Between 67–90 percent of all babies who are detected with Down

---

42. "Criminal Justice System." RAINN's statistics come from (1) Department of Justice, Office of Justice Programs, Bureau of Justice Statistics, "National Crime Victimization Survey, 2010–2016" (2017); (2) Federal Bureau of Investigation, "National Incident-Based Reporting System, 2012–2016" (2017); (3) Federal Bureau of Investigation, "National Incident-Based Reporting System, 2012–2016" (2017); (4) Department of Justice, Office of Justice Programs, Bureau of Justice Statistics, "Felony Defendants in Large Urban Counties, 2009" (2013). RAINN points out, "This statistic combines information from several federal government reports. Because it combines data from studies with different methodologies, it is an approximation, not a scientific estimate."

43. "Pregnancy and Chorionic Villus."

Syndrome are aborted.[44] In the U.K., the figure is 90 percent,[45] while the absolute figures have "significantly increased" as the percentage stays the same.[46] In Iceland, it's 98 percent.[47]

In 2018, as the state legislature of Utah considered a bill banning abortion for Down Syndrome babies, a flurry of articles and opinion pieces talked about the pros and cons. *Washington Post* editor Ruth Marcus acknowledged and encouraged women to use abortion not just as a method for birth control, but as child selection.

> Technological advances in prenatal testing pose difficult moral choices about what, if any, genetic anomaly or defect justifies an abortion. Nearsightedness? Being short? There are creepy, eugenic aspects of the new technology that call for vigorous public debate. But in the end, the Constitution mandates—and a proper understanding of the rights of the individual against those of the state underscores—that these excruciating choices be left to individual women, not to government officials who believe they know best.[48]

Marcus called "for vigorous public debate," yet seemed to believe that *Roe v. Wade* (1973) and the Constitution had already decided in her favor. In fact, the Constitution was written when women did *not* legally have bodily autonomy in this particular way, during an era where eugenic racist attitudes were firmly ensconced and defended by a majority of white Americans, which is part of the challenge of working with the Constitution, as I will examine in chapter 12. Moreover, *Roe* by itself does *not* accord individual women with such an absolute right, since it set up a trimester system to "balance"—however awkwardly—the interests of the woman and the fetus. Finally, Marcus framed the matter as an issue of the individual (which individual?) against "the state," which is itself questionable.

Marcus expressed admiration for those parents who do welcome a Down Syndrome child into their midst, but for herself said that "limited capacity for independent living and financial security" made it impossible in her case. She did not provide details about her family's financial commitments, but moved from that point into the statistical fact that many other women make the same choice and there are legal battles happening in a few conservative states.

44. Natoli et al., "Prenatal Diagnosis."
45. Gee, "World without."
46. Bottone, "Down Syndrome."
47. "All Danish Babies."
48. Marcus, "I Would've Aborted."

On the one hand, having other children or elderly parents are very real commitments; support and social services for Down Syndrome children might be terribly lacking; and the woman might be staring down a long road of being a single parent (possibly through death of a spouse, or divorce, and not simply sex out of wedlock), working and raising a Down Syndrome child. If we as a society hope to lower the rate of abortion of Down Syndrome children, then we must surely do more at the societal level to dramatically lower the cost of childraising, and ordinary life, along with educating all people about the risks inherent in having a child. Thus, by raising this issue I am not unconditionally expressing agreement with the legislation banning doctors to abort children solely on the basis of detecting Down Syndrome; I believe socioeconomic conditions play an ethical factor, as I discuss in chapters 5 and 6.

On the other hand, Down Syndrome individuals themselves are not in physical or emotional pain because of their condition, making the parent's/parents' emotional and financial situation the main criterion for whether to keep or abort the child. So the fundamental issue here is control. If the financial cost is lessened and brought to within reason, then the primary cost would be emotional. Provided that a reasonable level of emotional support exists for parents of Down Syndrome children, I believe that that cost is reasonable to expect parents to bear. Yet the strong case can be made that Down Syndrome should not be a criterion for abortion. People with Down Syndrome rank high in levels of personal fulfillment, with 88 percent of siblings of people with Down Syndrome feeling that they were better brothers and sisters; parents of children with Down Syndrome have a lower rate of divorce than the general rate.[49] Moreover, the simple reality is that bringing *any* child into the world runs enormous risks far beyond any parent's ability to control. The apostle Paul said that all creation groans, including our mortal bodies, as we face the vulnerabilities we share to the world outside of Eden. Is it ethical for prospective parents to want and welcome a child only under certain conditions they can control? Is there not a cost to the child and to society when parents in this situation can treat a child as a commodity they can return to sender? And, as I explore in chapters 5 and 6, is there also not a cost when we as *neighbors* build a social system where we do not share with other potential parents in that uncertainty, but force them to go it alone? Especially if there are strong social supports for childraising (see chapters 5 and 6), the case for Down Syndrome abortions, which is a form of child selection, is further reduced.

---

49. Mancini, "People with Down Syndrome."

Fetal Rights? Against Who?

The fetus is treated very inconsistently by U.S. law today. For example, the fetus can inherit property. If a pregnant mother dies before or in childbirth, but the fetus survives and is born alive, courts have decided that the child can inherit property along with other living siblings, and the state will appoint guardians for the child if needed.[50]

The fetus's life legally overrides its mother's "religious freedom" interest in refusing blood transfusions if she is a Jehovah's Witness. In 1960, the New Jersey Supreme Court, in *Smith v. Brennan*, ruled that an expecting mother and father had the right to sue for damages done to a child still in the womb. In 1964, the same New Jersey court, in *Fitkin Memorial Hospital v. Anderson*, decreed that a pregnant woman who was a Jehovah's Witness did *not* have the right to refuse a blood transfusion when doctors believed that the procedure would preserve the life of the fetus she carried. The 1985 *In re Jamaica Hospital* case in New York's State Supreme Court decided the same. The New York court recognized the mother's right to an abortion at that stage in her pregnancy, but maintained that in the circumstance where the mother was in need of a blood transfusion for another emergency reason, the state's significant interest in protecting a midterm fetus's life outweighed her religious beliefs against blood transfusions.

The fetus can be the victim of personal injuries in assaults in thirty-eight states. For example, in November 2014, in California, Scott Peterson was convicted of the first-degree murder of his wife, Laci, and the second-degree murder of their unborn son, Connor.[51] In November 2017, in Texas, Devin Patrick Kelley committed a gun massacre at First Baptist Church in Sutherland, Texas, murdering twenty-six people, including Crystal Holcombe *and* her unborn child, who was at eight months of gestation and was counted as a person among the victims.[52] As mentioned earlier, the federal Unborn Victims of Violence Act of 2004 makes a motorist guilty of two homicides in motor vehicle accidents when both a pregnant mother and the fetus in her womb die, even if that woman was on her way to abort the fetus, ironically.

Under such laws, fetuses could have their interests defended against poisoning from lead in drinking water, biotoxin exposure, etc. as much as alcohol and other substances. In a helpful law journal article, Trindel highlights numerous examples of courts that have even upheld children's

---

50. Trindel, "Fetal Interests," 743–44.
51. "Scott Peterson Fast Facts."
52. Sanders, "When Does Life Begin?"

legal suits against a defendant "for prenatal injuries where the defendant's negligence occurred prior to the child's conception."[53] For example, in *Renslow v. Mennonite Hospital* (1977), a minor daughter who was also incompetent, represented by her mother, successfully sued a hospital for administering an improper blood transfusion to the mother eight years prior to her getting pregnant. The Rh incompatibility in the mother's blood caused brain, nervous system, and organ damage to her daughter.[54] A similar case occurred in *Bergstreser v. Mitchell* (8th Cir. 1978), concerning a child being adversely affected by the doctors who administered a caesarian section improperly to her mother for her *previous* child. In *Jorgensen v. Meade Johnson Laboratories, Inc.* (10th Cir. 1973), deformed twin infants, represented by their parents, successfully sued a birth control drug manufacturer for their condition, which included mental retardation, physical deformity, pain, and suffering.[55] The *Curlender v. Bio-Science Laboratories* (1980) case in California surprised many because a child successfully sued for a "wrongful life" cause. Her parents relied on the company's assurances that their genetic tests were reliable and that their child would not have genetic complications. She had come into existence and was in constant pain from Tay-Sachs disease. Whereas parents had been able to sue on the grounds of a wrongful birth cause, this was the first time in U.S. legal history where a child won a case on the grounds that she should not exist—that is, of a *wrongful life*. Observers in many fields registered their alarm at what *Curlender* meant for the legal jeopardy of science and medical professionals.[56] Taking that one step further, can a child sue the society into which it was born because it was born into poverty?

We should note, meanwhile, that in other areas of law, fetuses do not count as legal persons. The U.S. census does not count fetuses. A pregnant woman cannot drive in the carpool lane because she carries a fetus. In vitro fertilization clinics storing fertilized eggs do not count extra legal persons living at their address. Miscarriages do not count as legal deaths. No one shows an interest in monitoring non-implanted zygotes. Fetuses are not U.S. citizens until they are born, according to the Fourteenth Amendment, so technically they are *undocumented*. On what basis do undocumented persons have civil rights? Despite the fact that many legal rights are accorded to fetuses on account of their parents, or sometimes against their parents, no pro-life advocate, to my knowledge, has argued that being *conceived* on

53. Trindel, "Fetal Interests," 746.
54. *Renslow v. Mennonite Hospital* (367 N.E. 2d 1250, 1977).
55. *Jorgensen v. Meade Johnson Laboratories, Inc.* (483 F.2d 237, 10th Cir. 1973).
56. Marsh, "Prenatal Screening."

American soil, or being present on American soil at any time during gestation, might qualify one to be a U.S. citizen with all the rights accorded thereof. Can one person's lack of documentation (the mother) serve as the basis for deporting another person (the fetus) who was not personally guilty of the act of crossing the U.S. border illegally? Put bluntly, can the fetus of an undocumented Mexican woman use a proxy to sue the U.S. federal government for deporting both it and its mother? Can other people in the undocumented category, moreover, acquire rights akin to the rights of an undocumented fetus? Why or why not?

Wisdom and common sense suggest that mother and fetus must be treated as a dyad, whenever possible. As both conservatives and liberals (though more often conservatives) have accused American law of being schizophrenic, both parties might find some common ground over some of these issues. But on the other hand, bigger worldview questions may be at stake which prevent reaching more common ground without examining those worldview questions. There may not be easy resolutions to these conundrums because the mother-fetus relationship expresses a claim on one body by potentially two persons. As of today, fetuses continue to fall into an ambiguous category in the law, and I am not confident these ambiguities will ever be smoothed out.

One of the larger questions Christians have to answer is whether science can be our friend and partner in our efforts to understand how we can express our moral commitments. While Christians can understand the historical reasons for why Christians in the mid-1800s felt uneasy with science, and while certain technological developments might be very worthy of critique and condemnation, it seems painfully clear that Christians then and now have largely overreacted to scientific inquiry as a principle. In order to engage in the public sphere, science can be our friend and partner. If my reading of Exodus 21 and church history is correct, then at least with regards to fetal life, science *must* be our friend and partner. Christians must restrain our own fears that scientific inquiry will fundamentally undermine faith in Jesus Christ. It does not.

In the midst of these swirling issues, we must ask again: What is the firm intellectual and biblical basis by which to explain why one's church tradition takes the position that it does? It involves choosing one biblical manuscript over another, or rejecting both, which is a choice *one cannot fully justify*. It involves massaging away the Hebrew Masoretic Text's indication that human legal personhood be established at *birth*, a position for which no church today seems to argue, or the Greek Septuagint at *some point of fetal development*, which involves further interpretive decisions *which have no firm justification in the biblical text itself.* It involves the science of human fetal development, which in light of non-implantation, cell potency, twinning, and chimerism *does not strongly support the probability of ensoulment happening at conception.* It involves an assumption about ensoulment, which one can only take as a moral probability, and which is a puzzling way to reason because it presumes that Exodus 21 is irrelevant and *sidesteps the biblical text altogether.* It tends to ignore other biblical texts which could inform how Exodus 21 is applied, which involves more interpretive challenges *that are by no means easy.* It ignores the most relevant biblical pattern of God first building a *habitation* for life, then giving the *life.*

For Christians to call non-Christians to care for fetal life introduces still more questions and challenges. Only Christians would find arguments from the New Testament or church history persuasive, but neither resolve the issue anyway. The New Testament does not address abortion, but further complicates the challenge by raising thorny questions about how Christians use power, and what is the relation of the church, the states, and Israel. How do Christians and Jews and others now inhabit the same public space? Church history raises the same questions, and narrows the reasonable options but without totally settling them. If anything, the engagement of Christians in the fourth century with scientific and medical views suggests that Christians were willing to seek some potential areas of common ground with science and with non-Christians.

The administration of actual policies poses complex problems. For example: What options do we want women who are victims of rape or incest to have? If personhood begins at conception, what are the moral implications of doing nothing to lower the rate of non-implantation? Or miscarriages? Tobacco contains chemicals that are toxic for embryos: nicotine, carbon monoxide, and mutagens. One study found that for every ten cigarettes per day smoked by a pregnant woman, her risk of miscarriage increases by 20 percent.[57] One study shows that *paternal* tobacco use noticeably increases the rate of miscarriage because tobacco impacts sperm health; in 2009, Blanco-Muñoz et al. found that a father who smokes and a mother who does not are three times more likely to have a spontaneous abortion than a non-smoking couple.[58] Would limiting tobacco use to post-menopausal women and post-vasectomy men be a desirable policy proposal? From what scientific studies have shown, it seems like a combination of Advil, coffee, and cigarettes will have as high a probability of causing a spontaneous abortion as an IUD. Is that a concern?

---

57. Armstrong et al., "Cigarette, Alcohol, and Coffee."
58. Blanco-Muñoz et al., "Exposure to Tobacco."

All these considerations, if honestly acknowledged by Christians, can only produce *humility*. Clearly, we must care about this issue. We must consult both Scripture and science about fetal development and all the issues related to children, men and women, economic hardship, etc. Yet for all intents and purposes, many Christians have adopted a view about the fetus, and policies related to abortion, not from a thorough and careful examination of Scripture and church history and science, not to mention legal and administrative challenges, but from within their confessional, denominational allegiance to Orthodoxy, Roman Catholicism, or some branch of Protestantism—or, even worse, to a political party. And because these positions are often reactions to other social issues, as opposed to extended reflections where those motivations are also questioned, a position on abortion then becomes almost tantamount to an *identity*. As evidence, politically conservative Christians in the U.S. often deploy their argument against abortion not just with passion, but with *absolute certainty*, and at times, *single-minded and condescending arrogance*, as if this is the issue that trumps all others at every time and in every way.

Is it possible to take a more humble approach to abortion itself which respects the uncertainties we face? Is it possible to also take a wholistic approach to the factors that make abortion appealing as an alternative? And if we take more of a social welfare, and not merely a criminal justice, approach to lowering the abortion rate, are there matters about which we can feel more certain?

Part Two

Child-Raising and the Protection of Women

5

Men and Male Power in Scripture and Church History

Pregnant Women Lose Their Civil Rights

PERSONHOOD USA IS AN anti-abortion group advocating for giving a fertilized egg constitutional personhood status; they would like doctors and other health professionals to be mandatory reporters, with women's medical records open to them. In Wisconsin, where laws mandating that health professionals report to law enforcement have taken effect, Alicia Beltran was forced into residential drug treatment because she once confided to her doctor that she had abused drugs. After she had stopped using all substances, had become pregnant, and met with a new OB-GYN, she came home and was arrested by five police officers who handcuffed her and took her to an examination where she was pronounced fine. She was nonetheless taken to jail, held there, brought before a judge, where she met the lawyer assigned to defend her twelve-week-old fetus, and then ordered into a residential treatment center for ninety days. The program did not even offer the treatment that she was told she needed.[1]

Laws originally designed to protect pregnant women from abusive husbands and boyfriends are increasingly being used against pregnant women in the ostensible interest of their fetuses. In December 2010, a Chinese immigrant named Bei Bei Shuai attempted suicide by taking rat poison after her affair with a married man fell apart. She was thirty-three weeks pregnant, and her fetus survived ten days after her poisoning and two days after being delivered by caesarean section. She was convicted by an Indiana state court for the felony charge of feticide, jailed for 435 days, and released on bail. She later pled guilty to a misdemeanor charge of criminal recklessness, was sentenced to time already served, and then

1. Gross, "Personhood."

released.² In July 2013, in Indiana, Purvi Patel took abortion-inducing drugs and gave birth at home to a 1.5 pound boy who had died shortly before or after birth—the details are disputed. When she went to the hospital to be treated for her bleeding, she was arrested and in 2015 convicted of feticide and child neglect. She was sentenced to twenty years in prison, but her conviction was overturned by an Indiana court of appeals.³ These are merely two of the cases that gathered a lot of media coverage.

National Advocates for Pregnant Women (NAPW) found, between 1973 and 2005, 413 known criminal or civil cases where law enforcement intervened in the lives of pregnant women. In 112 of the cases they found, the health care or other helping professionals were the informants to law enforcement. Since 2005 to the publication of their report in January 2013, 250 more known cases had occurred. Their report found:

- "Arrests and incarceration of women because they ended a pregnancy or expressed an intention to end a pregnancy;
- "Arrests and incarceration of women who carried their pregnancies to term and gave birth to healthy babies;
- "Arrests and detentions of women who suffered unintentional pregnancy losses, both early and late in their pregnancies;
- "Arrests and detentions of women who could not guarantee a healthy birth outcome;
- "Forced medical interventions such as blood transfusions, vaginal exams, and cesarean surgery on pregnant women."⁴

The report found, unfortunately, that "medical misinformation and ignorance about science and evidence-based research, particularly regarding drug use and pregnant women, played a major role in fueling the arrests, detentions, and forced interventions of pregnant women." It also documented that the women who were subjected to "deprivations of physical liberty" were "overwhelmingly economically disadvantaged."

Furthermore, black women were significantly more likely to be "arrested, reported to state authorities by hospital staff, and subjected to felony charges." *State of Florida v. Johnson* (1989) was the first such criminal case in the U.S. Jennifer Clarise Johnson was a twenty-three-year-old black woman accused of administering crack cocaine to her children in

---

2. Pilkington, "Indiana Prosecuting."
3. "Judge Says Purvi Patel."
4. Paltrow and Flavin, "Arrests and Forced Interventions."

utero. Dorothy Roberts aptly points out that Johnson's race was not immaterial to the case, noting:

> The reason Black women are the primary targets of prosecutors is not because they are more guilty of fetal abuse. A study of twenty-four hospitals conducted by the South Carolina State Council on Maternal, Infant, and Child Health in 1991 found that high percentages of pregnant women were abusing marijuana, barbiturates, and opiates—drugs used primarily by white women.[5]

Johnson's case was later dismissed by a higher court, but the issues the case highlights are important. Many people have observed racial disparities in reporting, policing, and prosecuting crimes of various types. This is quickly becoming one more category in which racial bias—implicit or explicit—plays a factor. Even if we were able to eliminate the racial bias in these matters, which is admittedly unlikely, there is a much larger, complicated question about what kind of support and treatment the pregnant mother needs. Is there a way for policymakers to empower social workers and other care providers with the appropriate flexibility and meaningful tools to succeed?

This is a significant level of involvement by law enforcement into the medical profession and women's health care. Conservative movements like Personhood USA are mobilizing voters across the nation to place "personhood amendments" into state constitutions, with ramifications like the above for pregnant mothers, which needless to say, jeopardize their civil rights. As mentioned in a previous chapter, in 2011, Mississippi voters rejected a personhood amendment ballot question. Phil Bryant, the state's then Republican lieutenant governor, and governor, "campaigned hard for the measure."[6] Bryant was elected and served as governor from 2012–2020, which suggests something about future political winds. In 2013, North Dakota legislators successfully passed a personhood amendment to their state constitution; it was rejected by voters in November 2014.[7] In 2014, Tennessee became the first state to enact a criminal statute against pregnant women who use drugs.[8] In 2018, Alabama passed a personhood amendment called Amendment 2, the State Abortion Policy Amendment, to its state constitution, by a margin of 59 percent to 41.[9] If *Roe v. Wade* were overturned, it would immediately go into effect. In all this, there are few to no consequences for the father.

5. Roberts, *Killing*, 172.
6. Rovner, "'Personhood' Divides."
7. "Personhood Movement." Martin, "North Dakota."
8. "Personhood Movement."
9. Associated Press, "Advocacy Group."

Which leads me to the fact that there is a very important gender bias in the mere *perception* of the problem. In 77 percent of the cases found by NAPW, the father or male partner was not even mentioned in the report, despite the fact that a male partner was obviously involved in the conception of the fetus.[10] That gender bias is the topic of this chapter. The proposal below takes abortion just as seriously, but places much more responsibility on the father. But first we must back up and explore the *why*, before we consider the *how*.

Is a Good Man Hard to Find?

Every person, especially ethicists, educators, and Christian ministers, should linger long over the fact that women who procure abortions consistently report that "partner-related reasons" are high, if not highest, among their reasons for aborting the fetus. Indeed, in one particular study of 843 women, one week after their abortions, the women "felt more regret, sadness and anger about the pregnancy than about the abortion, and felt more relief and happiness about the abortion than about the pregnancy."[11]

These women, upon discovering that they were *pregnant*, reported feeling sadness (74 percent), regret (66 percent), guilt (62 percent), and anger (43 percent). Those negative emotions were not interpreted as mutually exclusive with relief and happiness, which registered 25 percent and 33 percent, respectively, but the women also reported feeling those positive emotions at much lower levels. Studies like these are typically used by pro-choice groups to highlight why abortion is preferable. I would like to use it to reflect on men and their character development in the United States.

These particular women reported that "partner-related reasons" ranked as the highest single factor for why they sought abortions. Who were those "partners"? Surely many relevant details about the male partners were lost by creating a category so large. One longs for qualitative and narrative texture which is admittedly hard to grasp in a study of this nature. The study's conclusion in reverse is also apropos. Abortion may or may not have been the "right" decision for these women, even under the circumstances. But all of these women perceived *the man in question* as responsible for putting them into a position where abortion became the more attractive option.

Educators, ministers, ethicists, and anyone involved in youth development or community development must take that seriously. It is perplexing, for example, that North Carolina stands in favor of the law that prevents a

---

10. Paltrow and Flavin, "Arrests and Forced Interventions."
11. Rovner, "'Personhood' Divides."

woman from withdrawing consent to sex after sex has begun,[12] even when the male partner removes his condom, which happens with unknown frequency, but one suspects often enough to be a major concern.[13] Kimberly Lawson, in her article for *Vice*, puts it bluntly: "Men Legally Allowed to Finish Sex Even If Woman Revokes Consent, NC Law States."[14] North Carolina is home to many conservative evangelical Christians—a full 35 percent of its population identifies as "evangelical,"[15] and fully half of North Carolina's religious adherents are Southern Baptist.[16] In conservative communities supposedly concerned about abortion, one would think that we would not find self-defeating, male-privileging laws and attitudes like the one in North Carolina. But we do find them. In effect, a woman who has concerns about the trustworthiness of his/her contraception, or her male partner per se, cannot stop the sex act. By contrast, in *People v. John Z* (2003), the California Supreme Court ruled that "a woman who initially consents to sexual intercourse does not thereby give up her right to end the encounter at whatever point she chooses. In other words, when a woman tells her partner to stop, and he forces her to continue, he is guilty of rape."[17] As with the principle of "limited liability" in corporate law, the United States enshrines cultural and legal practices that encourage men in particular to be irresponsible, even immature, *because the true costs of their actions are pushed onto someone else.*

I suspect that many conservative Christians feel challenged by this position because they have accommodated a male bias in sexual relations. In 1 Corinthians 7:39, Paul says that he wishes all married couples would "be as though they were not." If husbands and wives spent 100 percent of their time and energy trying to please each other emotionally and sexually, Paul would call them narcissistic. Paul wanted married Christians to tend to people's needs inside and outside the church beyond their marriage, which would involve being generous financially beyond the family, investing emotional energy building community and mentoring younger believers, applying Jesus' teaching to their professions, taking up geographical moves to serve Christ elsewhere, learning new languages and cultures, etc. The case can be made that Paul was encouraging Christians to have fewer children or none at all: the Emperor Augustus had issued a tax law encouraging citizens of the empire to have at minimum three children; married couples who did

12. Ortiz, "North Carolina."
13. Rosenblatt, "'Stealthing.'"
14. Lawson, "Men Legally Allowed."
15. Omondi, "Evangelical Protestant Population."
16. Stuart, "Overview of Religion in NC."
17. Colb, "Withdrawing Consent."

not do their duty were taxed at a higher rate; yet children as a motivation for marriage is not found in Paul's teaching. In fact, his larger point was not giving other people authority over one's own body, because Jesus claimed the believer's body as the leading partner in a joint venture concerning that body. Paul directed sexual desire to marriage (1 Cor 7:1–5) but, without overturning marriage per se, very much challenged it. He was explaining the "eunuch" statement of Jesus (Matt 19:12).

Yet I have heard from countless anecdotes that some pastors and youth ministers told single people (especially youth)—implicitly or explicitly—that if they abstain from sex before and outside marriage, then their reward will be lots of sex in marriage. In other words, they have incorporated a meritocratic mentality into their pastoral guidance, where the most enjoyable, meaningful reward is *sex*, and not *character formation, growing in our capacity for friendship by taming our own self-centeredness, and kingdom mission*. Sexual pleasure then becomes something that people feel entitled to, once they get married. While I do not wish to underestimate a woman's hope that sex with her future husband will be pleasurable, I am fairly confident that on the whole, men find this hope more appealing than women do.

Is it any surprise, then, that evangelicals have weak spiritual muscles to delay gratification for very long? One 2011 much discussed study found that a full 80 percent of unmarried evangelicals in the U.S. between the ages of 18 and 29 say they have had sex before marriage, just slightly lower than the 88 percent of the general population.[18] Of those 80 percent of evangelicals, 64 percent had done so within the past year, and 42 percent were in a sexual relationship at the time. The study also found that 65 percent of the women interviewed had had an abortion, which is perhaps 650,000 abortions. Of these women, 37 percent identified themselves as Protestant, 28 percent Catholic. Unless others can point me to more factors to consider, I would conclude that the law of North Carolina reflects the failure of the church to do authentic Christian discipleship. The majority of Christians in the state have probably taught delayed gratification, not personal transformation oriented to advancing the kingdom of God, and certainly not a fuller biblical picture of the relationships between men and women.

Scripture and the Power of Women Relative to Men

In Scripture, there are two situations where women are given *institutional* advantages over men. The first is in the realm of sex *within marriage*. In Israel in 1981, there was a Supreme Court case called *Cohen v. State of*

---

18. Kumar, "Are Most Single Christians"

Israel. Mr. Cohen had violently attacked his wife and forced her to have sex with him against her will. Subsequently, they were divorced. She accused him of rape retroactively. He appealed his conviction on the principle that a man cannot be legally guilty of raping his wife, which at the time was the principle upheld in both English and American law. Both English and American law, until the 1980s and 1990s, ruled that when a woman said "yes" at the altar, she said "yes" to sex anytime her husband wished it. Even in cases when a husband had contracted a sexually transmitted disease, or was estranged, a wife had no legal right to say no to sex.[19] Israeli Judge David Belchor noted the position of English law at the time, since English law influenced the State of Israel before 1948. Obviously repulsed by this, "Judge Belchor stated that he was 'delighted' not to have to follow English law on this issue because that would involve endorsing the marital rape exemption.... He said, 'The people of Israel can take pride *in the progressive and liberal approach of their blessed heritage and the position of Jewish law on this matter from time immemorial.*'"[20]

"Time immemorial"? Dr. Warren Goldstein, chief rabbi of South Africa, explained this position from its sources: the Bible; the Talmud; and the rabbinical commentaries. Not only are women made in the image of God equally with men (Gen 1:26–28), which is not always the case in other creation stories, but both "creation accounts" stress how God makes his creation get better and better. The Genesis 2 account uses more sophisticated language for the creation of Eve ("fashioned") than it does for Adam ("formed"), and the reunion marriage of Adam and Eve is the high point. Every subsequent marriage between man and woman, because of the "leaving and cleaving" of prioritizing the marriage over above family of origin, is portrayed as a "recapitulation" of the original reunion-marriage. The laws

---

19. Goldstein, *Defending*, 155–62, summarizes the history. In England in the 1980s and 1990s, three cases dealt with the crime of indecent assault within marriage. A wife was deemed to have consented to sexual intercourse with her husband at marriage, even if he had later contracted a venereal disease; additionally: *R v. Caswell* (1984): A married woman's consent to sexual intercourse covered all acts preliminary to that intercourse. *R v. H* (1990): The marital rape exemption applied even to an estranged couple. In the United States, despite some differences between the fifty states, until the late 1970s, all states held that a man was legally entitled to rape his wife. "A husband cannot be guilty of raping his wife unless he forces her to have sexual intercourse with a third person. Immunity shields the husband even though all the other elements of the offense are present—force, penetration, and lack of consent. He is immune from a rape charge in most states, however violent the force he uses and however long he and his wife have been living apart.... For instance, a wife whose husband comes home drunk every night and violently forces sex on her ... is not protected by the rape laws of forty-six states." Goldstein cites Pracher, "Marital Rape."

20. Goldstein, *Defending*, 168.

from Sinai even grant wives "conjugal rights" which it does not accord to husbands, and intentionally so (Exod 21:10). Jewish tradition perceives the "vulnerability principle" throughout the Torah, and finds that wives must be accorded protections from their husbands, even sexually. "A man is forbidden to compel his wife to have intercourse with him" (Talmud Eiruvin 100b). "This Talmudic ruling appears in all the major codifications of Jewish law."[21] "Certainly she is not subject to him incessantly when she does not wish it" (Responsa Maharit 1:5).[22] "According to Jewish law, sexual satisfaction is primarily the husband's duty and the wife's right. Married women need legal protection to ensure that their husbands treat them sensitively in the potentially volatile area of sexual relations. Men do not need to be protected; they need to be restrained and educated to think of their wives and not to view them as their sex objects."[23]

This Jewish position compares remarkably well against Hinduism and Islam. A Hindu text says, "Men may be lacking virtue, be sexual perverts, immoral and devoid of any good qualities, and yet women must constantly worship and serve their husbands" (Hindu Manusmriti 5.157).[24] An Islamic text says, "It is not permissible for her to rebel against him or to withhold herself from him, rather if she refuses him and persists in doing so, he may

21. Goldstein, *Defending*, 170, citing Rambam, Hilchot Ishut 15:17; Tur and Code of Jewish Law, Orach Chaim 240:3; Even HaEzer 25:2.

22. Goldstein, *Defending*, 168, notes that the agreement from later Jewish commentators is remarkable: "He may not rape her by having intercourse with her against her will, but rather, he must do it with her consent and in an atmosphere of open communication and joy" (Rambam [1135–1204 AD], *Hilchot Ishut* 15:17). "If she finds her husband repulsive, she is freed from her conjugal duties" (Rambam, Hilchot Ishut 14:8, quoted by Goldstein, *Defending*, 172). "Certainly she is not subject to him incessantly when she does not wish it" (Responsa Maharit 1:5). "Even those who would permit [unconventional sexual intercourse] do so only when the woman is willing, but if a husband forces it upon the woman he is called a sinner" (Responsa Yaskil Avdi 6:25). "The vulnerability principle is the most influential one when it comes to Jewish law's outlawing of rape in marriage" (Goldstein, *Defending*, 176). "A woman's conjugal duty is limited to having intercourse at certain regular intervals . . . determined with reference to, on the one hand, the wife's needs and, on the other hand, the husband's capacity (Goldstein, *Defending*, 186). "She is not required at all to ensure that her husband is sexually satisfied. He is responsible to guarantee to the best of his ability that his wife never feels unfulfilled sexual desire, which means that according to Jewish law a man must with great sensitivity constantly attune himself to his wife's sexual needs. . . . The reason is that fulfilling her desires constitutes a Biblical commandment, whereas fulfilling his does not" (Goldstein, *Defending*, 184–89).

23. Goldstein, *Defending*, 190.

24. See also: "Women have no divine right to perform any religious ritual, nor make vows or observe a fast. Her only duty is to obey and please her husband and she will for that reason alone be exalted in heaven" (Hindu Manusmriti 5.158)

hit her in a manner that does not cause injury" (Shaykh Al-Islaam Ibn Taymiyah, *Majmoo' al-Fataawa*, 32:279). And another says, "When a man calls his wife to fulfill his need, then let her come, even if she is at the oven" (Jami at-Tirmidhi 1160).[25]

One liberal scholar, Harold Bloom, even suspected that major portions of the Torah were authored by a woman because he could not imagine that male founders, teachers, and scribes of a religion would compile texts so favorable to women.[26] The Bible's concern for women has incredible apologetic value, as it suggests that ancient Israel did not simply copy their male-privileged neighbors in the Ancient Near East.

Jewish tradition thought hard about the situation in which women were the most vulnerable: *within marriage*. It gave wives moral and institutional advantages over husbands, and the downstream, social ramifications were unquestionably empowering to women. It deserves to be studied and appreciated. In the New Testament, Jesus said that the Jewish law empowered *wives to divorce their husbands* (Mark 10:12),[27] contrary to what most rabbis believed at the time, since Israel's exile under the gentile empires had encouraged Jewish opinion to move in the direction of the male-dominant Greeks and Romans. Jesus' remark is striking because he authoritatively interprets Moses' instruction about divorce (Deut 24:1), which was economically phrased using the male example; Jesus affirms that this was the inclusive male tense in Hebrew, linguistically. Moreover, Jesus called for his disciples to exercise a formidable level of internal self-discipline with regards to sexual desire (Matt 5:27-30), a spiritual discipline which he could only have expected them (men, especially) to practice within marriage as patience and consideration. Jesus' teaching complemented and radicalized the wider Jewish tradition of which he was a part. And, Jesus said that a man who divorced his wife incurred moral responsibility for her subsequent choice to remarry—he "makes her commit adultery" (Matt 5:31-32)—presumably because a divorced woman faced dire poverty in the circumstances of the first century, where Israel's family-land traditions had been disrupted by exile under the gentile empires. Even Paul's acknowledgement in 1 Corinthians

---

25. See also: "If a man calls his wife to his bed and she refuses, and he spends the night angry with her, the angels will curse her until morning" (Hadith al-Bukhaari, 2998, 4795; Hadith Sunan Abu Dawd 2159; and Qur'an 2:223). "No woman can fulfill her duty towards Allah until she fulfills her duty towards her husband. If he asks her (for intimacy) even if she is on her camel saddle, she should not refuse" (Hadith Sunan Ibn Majah 1853).

26. Bloom, *Book of J*.

27. Hence, Noonan, *Contraception*, 32, is mistaken when he says of the Jewish law, "Divorce may only be obtained by a husband (Deut 24:1-4)."

7:1–7, that sexual desires are a consideration within marriage and towards marriage, needs to be framed within the Jewish exegetical tradition which gives the woman's sexual interests preeminence, and a man's sexual interests something for him to more aggressively submit to Jesus.

Given that roughly 17 percent of abortions are sought by married women,[28] it follows that if conservative Christians believe that abortion is always a moral tragedy, then in the practicing of their faith, they should seek to reduce this further by prioritizing the sexual rights of the wife over the husband, and probably her sexual satisfaction, too. In the U.K. and the U.S., marital rape is now acknowledged legally, and criminalized, but that is a relatively recent phenomenon.

Clearly, though, Christians are capable of ignoring Scripture. In 2017, the Russian Orthodox Church supported Vladimir Putin's decriminalization of domestic violence in Russia. In the name of undoing the "destruction of the family," Patriarch Kirill supported Dimitri Smirnov, head of the Moscow Patriarchal Commission on Family Matters. "In a country where it is estimated that domestic violence kills a woman every forty minutes, he [Smirnov] said nothing about the damage to a marriage when a husband 'just' slaps his wife in the face. Indeed, he—and the Commission to Protect the Family—said nothing about spousal abuse at all."[29] Prior to the legal change, in 2013, Russian officials acknowledged that six hundred thousand women reported being physically or verbally abused at home, and fourteen thousand died because of intimate partner violence.[30] In April 2019, the independent *Moscow Times* said, according to "official sources," that the yearly average death toll was twelve thousand, remarkably.[31] Sadly, the Russian Orthodox Church has given cover to Putin's brutal policies: "The church's commission on family affairs even stated in 2015 that it considers the term 'domestic violence' to be a tool used by radical feminists. It similarly maintains that the West is behind efforts to make domestic violence a crime in Russia."[32]

In the U.S., President Donald Trump, in his 2018 budget, proposed a dramatic decrease in funding for programs designed to help women under the bipartisan Violence Against Women Act of 1994. VAWA funds programs related to transitional housing assistance, legal aid, women with disabilities, residents of tribal lands, and so on. "After the budget came out this week, the Trump administration rushed to reassure advocates. It advised them to ignore

28. "Women Who Have Abortions."
29. Kizenko, "Beat Her When You Are Alone."
30. Cauterucci, "Russia Decriminalized Domestic Violence."
31. "UN Committee Sides against Russia."
32. Denejkina, "In Russia, Feminist Memes."

the chart that shows funding for the programs holding steady in 2018, then plummeting from $460 million to eventually $30 million annually within a decade."[33] Congress refunded the program, however. It is also notable, though, that in 2013, Jeff Sessions, when he was a U.S. senator from Alabama, prior to becoming attorney general, voted against a bill to reauthorize funding for VAWA.[34] Also in 2013, Mick Mulvaney, Trump's budget director and then chief-of-staff, also voted against it when he was a U.S. congressman from South Carolina.[35] Jeff Sessions attends a United Methodist Church in Mobile, Alabama. Mick Mulvaney is Roman Catholic.

In 2018, President Trump and Attorney General William Barr changed the definition of "domestic violence" as related to the Office of Violence Against Women in the Department of Justice. Under Barack Obama, the definition included the financial, psychological, emotional, and verbal patterns of abuse that commonly eventuated in physical abuse.[36] Under Trump and Barr, though, only the physical harms that would constitute a misdemeanor or felony are considered "domestic violence." "A woman whose partner isolates her from her family and friends, monitors her every move, belittles and berates her, or denies her access to money to support herself and her children is not a victim of domestic violence in the eyes of Trump's Department of Justice. This makes no sense for an office charged with funding and implementing solutions to the problem of domestic violence rather than merely prosecuting individual abusers."[37] William Barr is Roman Catholic and a noted "culture warrior" and "religious liberty warrior" who believes secularism is responsible for crime,[38] even

33. Wise, "Massive Cuts." Cauterucci, "Trump's Planned Elimination."
34. "Roll Call Vote 113th Congress."
35. "S. 47 (113th): Violence Against Women Reauthorization."
36. "Domestic Violence."
37. Nanasi, "Trump Administration."
38. E.g. Dreher, "Bill Barr," exemplifies how conservative Christians use the term "religious liberty" to disguise "conservative Christian privilege." Dreher does not distinguish between parents being able to pass down the faith to their children (which is still very much legal and not threatened) and having your faith reinforced throughout the public sphere (e.g., in schools, on monuments, etc.) in the "Christendom model." Dreher does not understand how Christians can argue for *human rights without theocracy* in the tradition of Roger Williams and therefore embrace political pluralism on behalf of others. Boston, "Seeking God's Law," notes, "During an Oct. 6, 1992, speech in Washington, D.C., to the Catholic League for Religious and Civil Rights, a traditionalist Catholic group, Barr called for the imposition of a 'moral consensus' based on 'natural law'—a philosophical concept embraced by conservative Catholic theologians who insist that Catholic moral principles can be arrived at through secular reasoning. 'Because human nature is fallen, we will not automatically conform ourselves to God's law, but because we can know what is good . . . we are not doomed to be slaves in our

while he, in the Justice Department under Bush and Trump, has fought to make the executive above the law.[39]

Legally, the right for a woman—including a wife—to withdraw her consent to sex at any time needs to be firmly established, with the backdrop being *rape*. Giving women that institutional legal advantage over men in such a way not only should result in fewer unintended pregnancies and abortions, it makes sense by itself by various moral principles, including firmly biblical ones. It would also result in a culture change where men recognize that they are not entitled to sex and not entitled physically or visually to women's bodies. I also believe that public policy like this will encourage men generally to be much more self-reflective, and self-challenging, will require that Christians teach the orthodox position on sexuality from much more of the character-based and theological-ontological perspective true to the New Testament, and will actually force men in American culture to reckon with their own sexual self-centeredness to a greater extent that *many more will give their lives to Jesus*. The apostle Peter's admonition is relevant here: "For it is time for judgment to begin with the household of God; and if it begins with us first, what will be the outcome for those who do not obey the gospel of God?" (1 Pet 4:17).

The second case where Scripture gives institutional advantages to women over men is the case of a rape accusation in Deuteronomy 22:25–27. Normally, Jewish law required two or three witnesses to accuse a person (Deut 17:6); in case of rape, this principle is set aside. Procedurally, this variation gives significantly greater legal power to the woman over against the man. In theory, a Jewish woman who consensually had sex with a man could turn against him, become a false witness, and accuse him of rape. There are probably implicit procedural considerations for that possibility: the judicial council could have probably considered other witnesses who could attest that the man was elsewhere. Could the "ordeal" imposed by a suspicious husband against his wife (Num 5) be used to determine the truthfulness of a man accused of rape? Regardless, the risk that a woman would abuse this legal procedure is apparently *acceptable*, and that risk weighs *against men*. A woman who accused a man of rape was, in principle, *credible*. Her testimony had the force of two or three witnesses.

---

passions and wants,' Barr told the group. 'To the extent that a society's moral culture is based on God's law, it will guide men toward the best possible life.' Barr went on to attack 'modern secularists' for dismissing 'ultimate, practical, utilitarian rules for human conduct,' blaming a cultural decline on 'the long binge that began in the mid-1960s.'" See also Ford, "Bill Barr's First Epistle."

39. Maddow, "Barr Record of Deception." Stahl, "If Watergate Happened Today." Wehle, "Bill Barr's Constitution."

Perhaps that is because, in the covenantal context and sociology assumed by the Sinai covenant for biblical Israel, a woman had no real incentive to bear false witness in this circumstance.

If a man found that the risk of being accused of raping a woman was so great, then he might consider that he was already commanded to submit himself and his sexual desires to the God of Israel. He could subordinate those sexual desires to God's vision of marriage (e.g., Prov 5) where a husband does not dominate but rather serves his wife, as is the case in Judaism. He could be part of a moral community which helps him grow in his discernment about the character of any given woman. He could become absolutely transparent to others of good character about his intentions in friendship, dating, and courtship, and be as public as possible in his efforts to court a woman, with as many witnesses present as possible. Because of this simple procedural exception in the case of a rape accusation, women in the Sinai covenant were given institutional advantages, which would have resulted in social advantages over men in the realm of romance.

How Christians Historically Reshaped the Power of Women Relative to Men

Abortion is never just a personal act involving the pregnant mother. It takes place in a social context. Christians in Palestine, Egypt, Syria, Asia Minor, and Europe inherited the challenge from a pagan Greco-Roman context in which not only abortion but infanticide through abandonment was quite common. Abortion was considered wrong only if the mother did it without the father's knowledge, on the grounds that she was depriving him of an heir. Husbands had complete legal and social power over wives. Families preferred boys over girls. Prostitution and abduction into slavery, significantly, were relatively common. So Christians had to respond on multiple fronts to the assortment of issues they confronted, knowing all the while the obvious: a baby must be welcomed and raised by parents. This is also to say that abortion itself was embedded in a relational context and a social system, where typically the father and other agents involved in the abortion were routinely not held accountable for anything.

Therefore, Scripture and church history can be interpreted as the struggle for Christians to develop a complex and multi-pronged ethical response to issues including abortion, not just as a personal act, but as a part of larger social problems. The historically unfolding ethical response of church leaders to abortion might also be narrated in the following way: The church was growing incrementally in its ability to construct meaningful practices and policies that dealt with abortion as one of many social issues. When we consider the legal rights of women and wives, especially the interactions between men and women concerning sex and children, we are challenged to see how Christian faith might shape public policy and culture.

If we believe that women are more likely to treat their bodies with more respect and their relationships with men with more caution based on their level of education and sense of purpose in the world, then the following fact should catch our interest: sociologically, Christianity's most impactful contribution to uplifting women was *singleness*. Jesus (Matt 19:12) and Paul (1 Cor 7) encouraged a vision of singleness as a special type of Christian *vocation*. While singleness as a vocation may sound strange or surprising to modern ears, we must understand that people in classical times assumed that women were destined either for the household or the brothel. Men had a wider range of options, but their social roles also tended to be centered around the household (e.g., the Roman *paterfamilias*, where the father had absolute, life and death authority over his household), or have a return to the household in mind (e.g., Homer's *Odyssey* shows the journey home from war). For women, there simply was not a wide range of options, or even choice in the matter. Christian people, by contrast, were expected to develop a range of spiritual charisms ("gifts"). Married women and men also developed a sense of Christian vocation and giftedness, but those who were single had much more flexibility and availability. An early form of this sense of "spiritual vocation" seems to have existed in biblical Judaism: the Levites had a special role among the tribes; judges (including women like Deborah in Judges 4–5) traveled in geographical circuits, ruling on cases; individual prophets and schools of prophets emerged (including women like Huldah in 2 Kings 22 and Noadiah in Nehemiah 6); worship leaders and special servants of the sanctuary (including women like Jephthah's daughter in Judges 11 who preceded Samuel in 1 Samuel 1–2); and then scribes (e.g., Ezra), the Pharisaical movement, and itinerant rabbis.

This early Christian vision of women and singleness is also deeply relevant because conservative Christian movements around the world overlook it, ignore it, and/or seek to subvert it because they are pursuing "the breakdown of the family." Jesus gave women a robust sense of vocation and purpose no longer centered on the assumption that they would be wives and mothers. Widows had an honored role in the church; some seem to have been regarded as teachers and house church leaders (1 Tim 5:3–22). Some women were esteemed by the apostles as evangelists (e.g., John 4:39–42), prophetesses (e.g., Acts 21:9; 1 Cor 11:2–16), teachers (e.g., Priscilla in Rom 16:3; 1 Cor 16:19), and coworkers in Christian ministry (e.g., 1 Cor 1:11; Phil 4:2–3; Col 4:15). Junia was "among the apostles" (Rom 16:7), and Phoebe was a deacon who delivered and interpreted the longest letter of Paul (Rom 16:1–2). Initially, men and women modeled themselves after the itinerant "apostles and prophets" attested in the New Testament and the *Didache* and the evangelists and teachers who seemed to travel rather spontaneously (Acts 13:1–3). Around the entire Mediterranean region, the vibrant, long-lived popularity of the Acts of Paul and Thecla, a work of Christian fiction with probably a kernel of historical truth about a female disciple of Paul, who learned avidly, took a vow of chastity, and went about *preaching* the gospel to men *and baptizing*, attests to this fact.[40] Catherine of Alexandria, the fourth-century teenager who had a brief but brilliant career as a scholar, evangelist, orator, and then martyr, was the inspiration for Saint Catherine's Monastery at Mount Sinai. Meanwhile, as the early Christian movement developed, people organized themselves into groups with a common vocation. From the second century on, scholarly teachers established particular schools (e.g., Justin Martyr in Rome; Athenagoras, Pantaenus, and Clement in Alexandria; Origen in Caesarea; etc.); bands of Christians called *parabolani* (gamblers) risked their lives to serve plague-stricken cities; individual monastic Christians headed out to the outskirts of towns (e.g., Anthony of Egypt); and finally, Christian leaders organized monastery communities.[41] Christian women appear to have participated in all these modes of life.

The community monasteries are especially important because they gave women opportunities beyond the family. They originated in Egypt and Palestine, where the "Desert Mothers" studied and taught those who came to them.[42] John Cassian and Benedict of Nursia took this model to Roman Gaul and the West. In the fourth century, Basil of Caesarea developed a model of urban community monasticism and drew upon this community to staff his *Basileiad*, an incredible facility including a hospital. Basil's older sister Macrina the Younger—credited by their younger brother Gregory of Nyssa as his teacher, and an able Christian philosopher in her own right—cofounded (with her other brother Peter) two monasteries in Pontus: one for men and another for women. Melania the Elder devoted her massive wealth to founding monasteries, of which she became mother superior in one convent near the Mount of Olives. These are but a few examples. They coexisted with the established bishops in their cathedrals, sometimes uneasily. While monasteries developed Christian leaders, and many bishops came

40. Davis, *Cult of Saint Thecla*. Hylen, *A Modest Apostle*.

41. Brakke, *Athanasius and Asceticism*; *Demons*.

42. Cardman, "Desert Mothers," identifies Amma Syncletica of Alexandria, Theodora of Alexandria, Amma Sarah of the Desert, Melania the Elder, Melania the Younger, Olympias, Saint Paula and her daughter Eustochium, and several other women who were unnamed by Palladius in his *Lausiac History*.

from the ranks of monks (e.g., John Chrysostom), Augustine of Hippo worried about how much money the ordinary Christian citizenry were giving to these monasteries.[43] This mode of organization gave birth to the powerful Roman Catholic orders (e.g., Cluniacs, Franciscans, Dominicans, Jesuits, etc.), among which were the orders for women, or inclusive of women (e.g., Poor Clares, Benedictine Nuns, the Carmelites, etc.), and also the guilds, confraternities, and special societies. These were the major organizational forces that challenged the land-locked feudal manors. And the great orders eventually inspired a secular version, in England and the Netherlands: the state-chartered corporation. From there, we derive the modern corporation, a secularized version of an originally Judeo-Christian idea of holy vocation. From an institutional perspective, the secular versions now have great ethical challenges of their own. But this mode of organizing people around a sense of common purpose and vocation stands as a context in which people developed social "trust,"[44] a contributing foundation stone of the principle of peaceful freedom of political assembly in the First Amendment of the U.S. Constitution and the robust wealth of the West.[45]

As we look deeper into church history to see what we can learn about the Christian empowerment of women, I must confess up front: in my estimation, Christian leaders should have been much faster to allow the "eunuch" teaching of Jesus (Matt 19:12) and the "singleness" challenge of Paul (1 Cor 7) to make a much bigger impact from early times, *for women*. If Christian families and leaders expected God to call women into singleness and a Christian vocation as often as men were, which was an eminently reasonable assumption, then Christian ethical and political thought should have kept pace. Girls should have been educated as well as boys, with the expectation that Christian women would join their male brethren as practitioners of the trades as did the ideal woman of Proverbs 31, leaders of organizations with real administrative power like Deborah was in biblical Israel (Judg 4–5), and scholars of theology, philosophy, rhetoric, law, medicine, and the arts like Huldah, who advised King Josiah (2 Kgs 22:14–20). After all, the apostolic church in Philippi had its Lydia, a merchant in very expensive purple cloth (Acts 16:14), and the pagans had their Hypatia, a philosopher at Alexandria. If Christian widows could be heads of their own households (1 Tim 5:3–22), if female deacons were entrusted with the task of interpreting the writings of the apostles, if talented women could own

---

43. Augustine of Hippo, *On the Work of Monks*.

44. Fukuyama, *Trust*, 108, 286.

45. Rosenberg and Birdzell, *How the West Grew Rich*; Handlin, "Development of the Corporation."

land and manage convents, then the Christian community should have enacted legal change for women much earlier. The sixth-century reforms of Theodora and Justinian allowing women to own property in their own right, or divorce their husbands if they were unfaithful (see below), should have come much sooner. Legal and economic safeguards for the defense of women should have been enacted by Constantine. Women should have been given the right to vote in the Roman republic and hold positions of leadership in society at large. Since women and girls were especially vulnerable to being kidnapped, the abolition of the slave trade and of chattel slavery by King Clovis II and Queen Bathilde (even after Clovis II died) in the kingdom of the Franks in the 500s should have become the model for Christian rulers everywhere, even if space for debt-bondage and penal servitude were still permitted. And so on. In the U.S., women's suffrage reflects this basic Christian principle: women are not only theoretically equal to men, they may also be unmarried and called by Christ to his mission in some way that requires them to be quite independent. Therefore, in terms of a theology of Christian vocation, a woman's vote cannot be assumed to be represented by her husband or father; she must express it by herself. As Christian leaders thought on behalf of women in the institutions of the world they were trying to shape, *this trajectory*, seen in glimpses and fragments throughout church history, should have developed more quickly. Given the traditional Christian taboos on casual abortion, these social reforms would have had major ramifications to promote "a culture of life." Given the negative correlation between abortion rates and women's levels of education and social opportunity, it would have had an impact.

Nevertheless, despite the hiccups and obstacles, Christians did show impressive development in that direction. From church history, *prostitution* serves as a very helpful point of comparison to abortion, on the issue of comparative responsibility of men and women. Prostitution illustrates how Christian leaders, when possible, assigned responsibility to women and men for sins involving both. A substantial passage from Leah Lydia Otis is worth examining:

> Although the Church fathers fulminated against the commerce of the body with the same ferocity as against other sins of the flesh rampant in the Roman world, prostitution, being a social phenomenon rather than a personal sin (such as fornication), did not, strictly speaking, lie within the spiritual jurisdiction of the Church. Despite its condemnation of all premarital and extramarital sexual activity, the Church recognized prostitution to be an inevitable feature of worldly society, which it had no hope or ambition to reform. Saint Augustine even warned that the

abolition of prostitution, were it possible, would have disastrous consequences for society; the practice, he believed, was a necessary evil in an inevitably imperfect world. Canonical wrath was focused, rather, on those who profited from this commerce, for, while prostitution was regarded as a social phenomenon distinct from the sin of fornication, procuring was considered by the Church to be synonymous with the sinful act of encouraging debauch (since the latter is usually associated with a pecuniary motive, whereas fornication can be committed out of passion as well as out of desire for money). Procuring was therefore considered to be a matter of spiritual jurisdiction, and strong measures were taken against it at the Council of Elvira (c. 300), whose canons were included in most of the major canon-law collections of the Middle Ages.[46]

It may surprise the general reader to know that the church took this course of action, starting from the Council of Elvira, which is dated around AD 306. Decriminalizing the prostitute while prosecuting the (male) buyer and the (male) exploiter is precisely what many today call "progressive"—it is even nicknamed "the Nordic model."[47] It has been extremely successful. Seventeen centuries prior to Sweden, the church recognized that there could be many reasons for why a woman was a prostitute: she was desperately poor; she was kidnapped and forced to do it; she was being extorted and blackmailed; she was raised by a pimp or even parents who prostituted her; etc. It is always possible, theoretically, that a woman with sufficient knowledge became a prostitute voluntarily for financial reasons alone, without any coercion or sexual abuse in her background. But as a matter of public policy—or even pastoral policy—it was sufficient to assume that such a woman was emotionally wounded, mentally ill, or gravely self-deceived. There was only one reason for a man to purchase sex, however, and it was always sinful.

Prostitution is an imperfect analogy to abortion, of course. But thinking through prostitution does highlight relevant ethical and pragmatic categories: Women are often both moral agents and moral victims of men.

---

46. Otis, *Prostitution*, 12–13.

47. "Sweden's Prostitution Solution" says, "In just five years Sweden has dramatically reduced the number of its women in prostitution. In the capital city of Stockholm the number of women in street prostitution has been reduced by two thirds, and the number of johns has been reduced by 80%. There are other major Swedish cities where street prostitution has all but disappeared. Gone too, for the most part, are the renowned Swedish brothels and massage parlors which proliferated during the last three decades of the twentieth century when prostitution in Sweden was legal. . . . In 1999, after years of research and study, Sweden passed legislation that a) criminalizes the buying of sex, and b) decriminalizes the selling of sex."

Giving women (and young boys, too, who are victims of human trafficking) this sort of "institutional advantage" puts new power dynamics in place. Regarding abortion, the reason why a woman confronts an ethical decision to abort her child can be quite complex. She bears some personal responsibility, but others surrounding the woman—especially the man involved in fathering the child—typically have direct and indirect responsibilities as well. Even when a woman has ostensibly consented to having sex with a man, there is ground in Scripture itself to consider her to be a victim of male power, or false promises, or deception of some sort.

Women steadily benefited from the Christian impact on Greco-Roman law and culture. Emperor Constantine restricted a husband's right to divorce his wife, limiting his arbitrariness and addressing a particular vulnerability wives faced.[48] Although it is impossible to gather data relating slavery and abortion from late antiquity, it is well within reason to suggest that abortion rates must have went down if women were not regularly abducted into slavery, turned into sex slaves, and/or made to bear children for their abusers. In AD 313, only two years after professing a conversion to Christ, Constantine banned kidnapping and forced enslavement, making that crime punishable by death.[49] Christians were informed by Exodus 21:16, Deuteronomy 24:7, 1 Timothy 1:10, and 1 Corinthians 6:10 of the impressive biblical limitations on debt, and other considerations.[50] Three years after that, in AD 318, he banned the breaking up of enslaved families and declared infanticide to be a crime.[51] Constantine legalized the manumission of slaves before a Christian bishop, granting them immediate Roman citizenship, making it very easy procedurally to free slaves. In AD 319, he made the voluntary killing of a slave/servant a capital crime.

Constantine also gave financial assistance to impoverished parents during famines, on two occasions: AD 322 and 329. In 322, Constantine declared, "If any parent should report that he has offspring which on account of poverty he is not able to rear, there shall be no delay in issuing food and clothing, since the rearing of a newborn infant will not allow any delay." He was probably inspired by the Roman church, which had been running a food network for four thousand poor people. In 329,

---

48. Theodosius I, *Codex Theodosianus* 3.16.1.

49. Theodosius I, *Codex Theodosianus* 4.7.1; 9.40.2; Justinian I, *Codex Justinianus* 9.47.17; Sozomen, *Ecclesiastical History* 1.9

50. For fuller treatments of biblical passages on slavery/servitude of various sorts, and how Christians interacted with them, see my papers, Nagasawa, "Slavery in Christianity, Part 1" and also "Slavery in Christianity, Part 2," both available here: www.anastasiscenter.org/race-slavery-belief-systems.

51. Theodosius I, *Codex Theodosianus* 9.15.1.

Constantine declared, "Therefore if any such person should be found who is sustained by no substance of family fortune and who is supporting his children with suffering and difficulty, he shall be assisted through Our fisc before he becomes a prey to calamity."[52] These decisions must have made abortion and infanticide rates decrease.

The case of Pulcheria (AD 398/9–453) in the fourth century is very instructive for widening a sense of Christian vocation for women. Pulcheria inherited the throne as Empress Regent while fifteen years old as "augusta" (AD 414) until her younger brother Theodosius II came of age. Pulcheria took a vow of virginity, which was a Christian commitment that also conveniently warded off suitors, and led her family in prayer and devotion, winning praise by the Christian historian Sozomen.[53] Pulcheria remained influential, and formally reigned again as "augusta" in her early fifties (AD 450) until she wed Marcian and, remaining chaste, coreigned with him until 453. Pulcheria played roles during the great Third and Fourth Ecumenical Councils. This cultural and legal change concerning women touched the highest strata of law: the position of emperor. Whereas Plato and Aristotle believed that men should rule over women as over animals, and whereas the classical Roman father wielded the power of life and death over his wife and household (*patria potestas*), the Christianized Roman Empire changed that practice. Women later ruled as emperors when widowed until their oldest son came of age, or as older sisters until their younger brothers came of age. This is most likely due to the *Christian* practice of regarding a widow as head of her own house (1 Tim 5:3–22), including servants (1 Tim 6:1–2).

In the sixth century, Emperor Justinian (AD 482–565)—no doubt influenced by his wife, Empress Theodora (c. AD 500–548)—enacted sweeping changes to Roman law, which utterly changed the status and power of women. Theodora's prominence and approach to political power broke a "glass ceiling" for women. When Emperor Justinian held court, Empress Theodora sat right next to him, which was unprecedented. She was free to address anyone in the court. She was known to disagree with him publicly, and he did not get angry. Even more remarkably, Theodora was known to hold her own court in her imperial chambers, near the throne room where her husband sat. There,

---

52. Bakke, *When Children*, 135.

53. Sozomen, *Ecclesiastical History*, writes, "She devoted her virginity to God, and instructed her sisters to do likewise. To avoid cause of scandal and opportunities for intrigue, she permitted no man to enter her palace. In confirmation of her resolution she took God, the priests, and all the subjects of the Roman empire as witnesses. . . . They all pursue the same mode of life; they are sedulous in their attendance in the house of prayer, and evince great charity towards strangers and the poor . . . and pass their days and their nights together in singing the praises of God."

many people came to her not just to influence Emperor Justinian, but for actual justice and official imperial decisions.[54] "Because of her intelligence and unerring political sensibility, many believe that she, rather than Justinian, ruled Byzantium. Her name appears in nearly all the laws passed during that period, and she received foreign envoys and corresponded with foreign rulers, roles usually taken by the ruler."[55]

Even more astounding were the changes in law and policy regarding women enacted under this couple. Justinian and Theodora legislated that a wife had legal protections *from her husband*: to be coerced into marriage, to divorce, have child custody, and keep property.[56] Roman women could sometimes be pressured into marriage, perhaps when proposed to when her family was present. Theodora put forward a law that required the woman to give her consent twice: once at the proposal and then again before the marriage ceremony at some point.[57] This allowed her to change her mind. Theodora seems obviously responsible for removing the ban on intermarriage between social-economic classes. This meant women—even prostitutes, theater workers, etc.—had better marriage prospects. Since brothel-keepers tried to hold prostitutes to their "oaths" to never leave the brothel, Theodora made such oaths illegal, and mandated that the local Christian bishop had the authority to liberate a woman from prostitution if the provincial governor failed to uphold the law.[58] Theodora had the divorce law of mutual consent, which most often worked against women, removed from the divorce requirement. As a result of women legally owning property by themselves, they gained enormous economic and legal power. For instance, under Theodora and Justinian, rape became an offense punishable by death, regardless of the social standing of the offender, and the rapist's property was immediately transferred to the *rape victim*.[59] Far ranging in her concern, Theodora moved female prisoners from under the watch of male guards—who abused and probably raped them—and into a nunnery under the supervision of other women, which she herself ordered constructed. Needless to say, all these changes outraged certain cultural conservatives of the day who imagined that the empowerment of women would lead to "the breakdown of the family." Women were still legally prevented from being judges, bankers, and witnesses to contracts,

---

54. Evans, *Empress Theodora*; I am indebted to Burton, "Empress Theodora," for this survey of Theodora and references. See also Cesaretti, *Theodora*.

55. Lewis, "Biography of Empress Theodora," and references.

56. Justinian I, *Novellae* 5.2.

57. Justinian I, *Codex Justinianus*, book IX, title 13.

58. Justinian I, *Novellae* 51.

59. Justinian I, *Codex Justinianus*, book IX, title 13.

however.[60] Neither was slavery or concubinage completely abolished,[61] nor loopholes closed for male adulterers.[62] Christian leaders sometimes protested inconsistencies like these, but the imperial legislation did not change.[63] The assumption was still that daughters would grow up to become respectable Roman wives and mothers. Women who wished to remain single were drawn to the Christian monasteries.

Nevertheless, Theodora's policy legacy, with Justinian's, is impressive. Lest Justinian be interpreted unfavorably here because of the accomplishments of his wife, it must be mentioned that Justinian was an able theologian in his own right, which makes the passage of his pro-woman laws all the more significant from a Christian standpoint. His four part *Codex Justinianus*, the law code he organized and developed from all he inherited, is a mark of his genius and energy. Justinian's Code continued to anchor legal thought in the attempt of Byzantine Roman lawmakers to apply Christian principles of human dignity to the law, played a part in the Renaissance in the West to once again push back against the Frankish-Germanic tradition of law, served as the backbone of the Napoleonic Code, and continues to be influential in Eastern European jurisprudence. Justinian's Code became one of the most important and influential documents in the European tradition. That means the revolution in the legal standing of women, a key marker that pagan Rome had been transformed into Christian Rome, conforming it closer to Christian principles, carried out by imperfect people under the impress of Christian teaching, stands at the heart of what is commonly called "the West" and also "the Christian East." Judith Herrin's study of Byzantine women throughout the social classes, *Unrivalled Influence: Women and Empire in Byzantium*, is an outstanding collection of essays exploring women's empowerment and roles in the Byzantine millennium.[64]

The Christian Byzantine Roman Empire produced Irene (r. 797–802), Theodora (r. 842–55), Zoe "the Purple-born" (r. 1028–50), Theodora "the Purple-born" (r. 1042–56), and Maria of Antioch (r. 1180–82), who reigned not as figurehead empresses, but as regent *emperors* in their own right. The Franks, by contrast, established their own "Roman Empire" in the West, in part because Charlemagne did not accept Emperor Irene as a sovereign. Frankish law and custom did not allow for women to own land and be in such a position of authority. This Frankish position—which Pope Leo III

60. Harris, "Byzantium and the Rights of Women."
61. Nasaina, "Woman's Position."
62. Troianos, *Chapters*, 99; cited by Matzarioti-Kostara, "Theology of Gender."
63. Lascaratos and Poulakou-Rebelakou, "Child Sexual Abuse."
64. Herrin, *Unrivalled Influence*.

sadly *honored* when he crowned Charlemagne "Emperor of the Romans" in AD 800—reflects a failure of the church of Rome to adequately *disciple* the Franks on issues of power and gender. The Orthodox Church must be appreciated here by contrast.

It is sobering to recognize that the division between Eastern and Western Europe is related to the failure of Christian discipleship on issues of gender and power, and that other political divides happen today because of this same reason. No legal change is ever easy, because matters of law also involve matters of enforcement, which require public support and spiritual education. Perhaps it is instructive, though, to observe that the Christian transformation of culture and law often stops when it confronts the traditional forms of sexual and economic power that men had over women prior to Christian faith's engagement with that people group. It is disappointing that white American Protestants in the South largely accepted abortion when it was framed within concerns of white supremacy over black people in the 1800s, only to vigorously join the pro-life cause when second-wave feminism in the 1960s asserted that a woman should have the legal right to control her own body. Is this a coincidence? This is not to say that the argument from bodily autonomy is a morally sufficient basis for abortion, but it is to say that conservative evangelicalism shows hallmarks of male chauvinism, and also that male responsibility for women's abortions has been conspicuously under-examined in the public record.

Abortion in the Christianized Byzantine Roman Empire

The collaborative efforts between church bishops and political leaders in the Christianized Byzantine Empire to provide publicly funded health care and hospitals must have led to better health for women and mothers, fewer cases of impoverishment due to disease and death of a family member, and, therefore, reduced abortions. Of course we can only make sociological inferences here. The Byzantine Romans also had policies about how to handle abortion, some of which touched the physicians. Not only is the Eastern Roman Empire of great interest, then, from the standpoint of law, but also from the standpoint of *public health*.

The Christian origin of hospitals is relevant to this chapter and chapters 8 and 9 as part of the argument that Christians ought to enact public health policies. The early Christian monasteries often reserved rooms for sick visitors. The visionary and energetic Basil of Caesarea, impressed by this care, constructed a large facility called the *Basileiad*, in his native Cappadocia. It served as "the first formal soup kitchen, hospital, homeless shelter, hospice, poorhouse, orphanage, reform center for thieves, women's center for those leaving prostitution and many other ministries."[65] To this, he tied the urban monastic movement he sponsored, another innovation with which he is credited. Christians from the monastery helped staff the hospital. Over time, hospitals spread throughout the Eastern Roman Empire. Timothy S. Miller, in his book *The Birth of the Hospital in the Byzantine Empire*, sifts through an enormous amount of historical data to describe one of the most positive aspects of the millennium-long interaction between the Christian church and the Byzantine Roman state.[66] Healing the sick was thought of as an obligation of Christian charity. Disease prevention was thought of as a public good because in the New Testament, Jesus was a healer, and in the Old, God wanted Israel to suffer from "none of these diseases" (Exod 15:26). Byzantine Roman laws incentivized charity and the construction of hospitals. Imperial law even required doctors to work half their time in the hospitals, with reduced salaries during that time, leaving them their private practice the other half of the time, with their private salaries. This emphasis on public health is intriguing, and I will comment on recent developments in health policy in the U.S., as it impacts abortion, in later chapters.

The most thorough historical study of abortion in the Byzantine Roman Empire finds:

> The theoretical basis of the permanent and absolute condemnation of all kinds of abortions except those permitted for medical reasons [to prevent harm to the mother], is greatly influenced by the spirit of Christianity. . . . All legislation of Byzantium from the earliest times also condemned abortions. Consequently, foeticide was considered equal to murder and infanticide and the result was severe punishments for all persons who participated in an abortive technique reliant on drugs or other methods. The punishments could extend to exile, confiscation of property and death. The physicians followed the tradition of Ancient Greece, incorporated in the Hippocratic Oath, representative of the ideas of previous philosophers. According to this famous document, it is forbidden them to give a woman "an abortive suppository." The Orthodox faith reinforced this attitude, protective of every human life. On the other hand, the Church and the State accepted selective abortion based on medical data, such as prevention of dangerous conditions in pregnancy or anatomical difficulties involved. In conclusion, science, church and legislation had a

---

65. Jacobse, "St. Basil the Great"; Frangipani, "Cosmological Vision"; and Heyne, "Reconstructing."

66. Miller, *Birth of the Hospital*, and Ferngren, *Medicine and Health Care*.

common attitude to matters concerning abortion and this fact reveals an effort to apply a fair policy for the rights of the embryo and the protection of human life in Byzantine society.[67]

The summary statement makes several things clear. First, to shape their approach to abortion, the Byzantine Roman lawmakers drew upon both Christian theological and Greek medical-philosophical resources. From the Christian side came the general position of perceiving abortion as a form of infanticide, generally. Of particular prominence was the view attributed traditionally to Basil of Caesarea and Gregory of Nyssa. From the Greek side came the Hippocratic Oath, a cultural precedent which must have appeared more attractive because of the Christian influence. My only disagreement with Poulakou-Rebelakou et al. is that, based on the study of patristic texts in chapters 2 and 3, I believe the Greek-speaking Orthodox Christian position already incorporated an engagement with the Hippocratic Oath, whereas the authors seem to think there was only ever one Christian position on the subject.

Second, punishments for abortion were varied. Poulakou-Rebelakou et al. report that Justinian's *Digest*, one of the four books of his *Corpus Juris Civilis*, instructed banishment for women who procured abortions, divorce for a couple when the wife obtained an abortion without her husband's knowledge, and corporal punishments otherwise, especially for the unmarried. A later dynasty, the Isaurian, added the punishment of death for a widow who kills an embryo in order to favor her other children related to distributing an inheritance. A still later dynasty, the Macedonian, added a punishment for the physician or midwife based on their social class and the harms done. Yet another punishment was added in the fourteenth century for potion-makers who provided herbal remedies that acted as abortifacients.[68] In at least one significant and very interesting case, the father was also punished (see below).

Third, medical and scientific information about the dangers of pregnancy were incorporated, and abortions were performed to prevent a dangerous pregnancy which ostensibly threatened the life of the mother. The historical record shows that knowledge of how to induce abortions—while ancient—was well-preserved in the culture and the medical science of the time. The venerable Hippocrates, despite his stated opposition to abortion, knew of methods, and another ancient authority, Soranus, allowed it to save the mother's life.[69] Abortifacients were therefore well known; the historian

---

67. Poulakou-Rebelakou et al., "Abortions," 19.
68. Poulakou-Rebelakou et al., "Abortions," 21–22.
69. Poulakou-Rebelakou et al., "Abortions," 22–23.

Procopius (if he is to be believed on this point) writes that Theodora, during her early life in the theater and before her marriage to Emperor Justinian, used various drugs to induce abortions. Hard exertion or movements were also understood as inducing abortion. Both were known to be recommended by physicians and others at times. Bronze instruments for performing abortions have also been discovered—a survival of the practice from the older Roman Empire. However, we do not have written descriptions of surgical abortions from the Byzantine era.[70]

Two further observations are very significant in this article. The first concerns how the church canon law and Byzantine civil law began to diverge:

> Another remarkable point is that the Byzantine Church increases its clemency in sentencing the women who underwent an abortion, while the imperial legislation from the 8th c. increases its severity, adding whipping to exile.[71]

Unfortunately, Poulakou-Rebelakou et al. do not explore what I suspect to be the case: the reason why imperial legislation increased in severity about abortion policy was the army's need for men. Persia then Islam threatened the Byzantine Roman Empire from the east. The Franks and Venetians sacked Constantinople during the Fourth Crusade in 1204.

The second comment concerns increasing paternal responsibility for abortion in (at least) the civil law:

> A very interesting trial about an abortion case took place in Constantinople in the year 1370. A monk from the monastery of Theotokos Hodigitria, named Ioasaph and an anonymous nun from Saint-Andrew-in-Krisi convent were the defendants in this affair. It was a rather unusual trial involving the Patriarch Philotheus Kokkinos and the prosecution of the father of the embryo, because the law exclusively punished the mother. The physician Syropoulos who provided the abortifacient drug was condemned to exile. . . . The monk Ioasaph was punished with demotion and expulsion from his monastery.[72]

That Byzantine Roman civil law at this point in time punished the mother exclusively is impossible to defend. The earliest Christian literatures addressing abortion make clear that both mother and father were responsible, at least in the situations they were envisioning. The presumption at this point that fathers were innocent is far-fetched. This case in 1370 is

---

70. Poulakou-Rebelakou et al., "Abortions," 24.
71. Poulakou-Rebelakou et al., "Abortions," 22.
72. Poulakou-Rebelakou et al., "Abortions," 22.

the first clear example where the father of the aborted child was punished. The question of why church leaders and civic government officials did not make more of an effort to define the father's responsibility in cases of abortion might be variously attributed to male chauvinism, or to pragmatic legal uncertainties about paternity.

I would not wish to institutionalize a penalty on a physician per se, because it creates the perverse incentives to perform abortions in private, as I will highlight in chapter 6. Also, since physicians in the U.S. and most countries today have considerable latitude to define "risks to the mother's health," physicians might deny abortions to women of color or poor women, while granting them to wealthy women who pay out of pocket, which is what happened throughout U.S. history as the next chapter will discuss.

Finally, I am not sure that labeling the Byzantine church canon law on abortion a matter of increasing "clemency," as Poulakou-Rebelakou, et al. do, is the right, or the only, way to label this trajectory. We might also understand it as applying Christian principles in law and policy to grasp the complexity of abortion as a social, and not merely individual, problem. The Orthodox Church's canonical response to abortion per se yields a noteworthy pattern in itself. Christian bishops moved from withholding communion until death (Council of Elvira, early 300s) to withholding it for ten years (Council of Ancyra, 314) to varying it "according to repentance" (Basil, ~370, and the Quinisext Council, 691–92). Until Basil, church policies were pastoral responses unfolding within the church community. When Christians influenced government policies, the nexus of issues became much larger. As we have seen, the bishops factored in poverty and probably, on a case by case basis, helplessness. The case in Constantinople in 1370 gives us a clear example that Christian authorities, both church and governmental, were quite determined to hold responsible the baby's *father* whenever legally discernable and possible. That the decision came from the patriarch himself is quite impressive.

All this biblical and historical data gives us a broad foundation to revisit the relative positions of men and women in the issue of abortion.

6

Holding Men More Responsible Today

Paternity and Responsibility

It goes without saying that abortion rates will come down further—perhaps much further—when men are held more responsible for paternity. Contrary to the trajectory of Personhood USA and other similar organizations, Christians must hold fathers responsible. The science and technology we have today finally make this possible. The father's DNA can be extracted from both unborn and aborted fetuses, and, in theory, this can become part of abortion procedures. The father's DNA was obtained from an aborted fetus from Planned Parenthood by police via search warrant in Spokane, Washington, as they sought evidence for statutory rape committed against a teenage girl.[1] The father's DNA evidence from an aborted fetus was used to determine the guilt of Samuel Williams in the rape of a young woman in New Orleans.[2] Fathers' DNA from living, unborn fetuses are being used by women in the UK with more than one male sexual partner to help them identify paternity and decide whether or not to have abortions.[3]

One possibility, then, is to commission health care professionals to perform DNA testing on any candidate for abortion and/or surgically aborted fetus to determine its paternity. Perhaps those paternity records should be placed in a secure health care database, so that a woman concerned for her own physical, mental, and emotional wellness would be able to consult her doctor to inquire as to whether the man she is starting to date has fathered any children who were aborted, prompting at least a conversation with him about whether he believes abortion *is* simply a birth

---

1. Ertelt, "Police Obtain DNA."
2. Simermann, "DNA Evidence."
3. Fernandez, "Hundreds."

control method. We would need to modify existing health care privacy (HIPAA) laws to accommodate for this practice.

Lest this seem invasive, let us consider the fact that *women's* health records keep track of past "abortions"—not distinguishing between miscarriages or induced or medically necessary—because it is medically significant from a health perspective. Let us also consider the example from Wisconsin and the study cited at the beginning of chapter 5, where women's civil rights are violated once they become pregnant. Do we not think that a man's record of fathering aborted children might be medically significant to the health care system at large, or to a woman starting to date a man and consulting her doctor for information that would affect her overall well-being? This would be an example of giving women institutional advantages in an effort to hold men more accountable for abortions as a matter of social policy. Conservatives should welcome this idea because they welcome accountability. Many secular liberals should welcome this idea because abortion, in their view, is just another form of birth control. What reason do men have to be so private about it? If men feel shame, is that their own problem? If the general public believes that a man should be mature enough to disclose to a woman whether he will use a condom, then does he have a legitimate reason to hide this aspect of his personal history? Besides, that is much less intrusive and much more discreet than arresting pregnant women.

A further possibility is that the father of any aborted fetus be made to pay higher health insurance rates, taxed at a higher rate, or fined a financial penalty. Exodus 21:22–25 called for a financial payment, after all. Debates about male responsibility also occurred in the late 1800s and early 1900s among doctors, in medical journals. Historian Simone Caron points out that Dr. Denslow Lewis of Cook County Hospital in Chicago held men, not women, responsible for abortion. His reasoning was socioeconomic, then interpersonal:

> Women resorted to this procedure because capitalists exploited them with such meager wages that they had to seek supplemental food, clothing, and entertainment from male companions, leading to unintended pregnancy. Subsequent male desertion caused women to transform their "usual sentiment of affection and of joy" regarding motherhood into a "feeling of aversion." He criticized Christian hypocrisy for shunning these women rather than assisting them with "emotional support."[4]

Denslow accounts for women facing harder socioeconomic conditions at the hands of "capitalists," no doubt because of sexism in the labor market

---

4. Caron, *Who Chooses*, 41–42.

but also perhaps because of women's lesser physical strength. This socioeconomic vulnerability compounded the biological vulnerability of pregnancy women already faced. I explore the significance of poverty as a driver of abortion rates in the coming chapters.

A move of this sort to penalize men financially would be a resumption of English common law practices, which overlapped with colonial America. Joshua Zeitz, writing for *Politico*, notes:

> There was a surprising amount of abortion case law in colonial America and in 17th-century and 18th-century England. Criminal prosecutions usually targeted doctors or *male partners* who stood accused of aborting live or "quick" fetuses against the wishes of their female patients or lovers.[5]

If women were willing to testify against their male partners or their doctors, this implies agreement between the doctor and the male partner, and a conspiracy between them to coerce the woman to abort. One or the other would probably not be enough, and it would seem that the latter was the driving force—as in the case of a man wanting to hide an adulterous affair, for instance. These common law cases indicate that people were willing to view the woman as the victim of her male partner if she so attested. I believe she should be viewed that way even if she does not. A minimum fine might be the child support that he would ordinarily pay, under the law. Why? Because the system must not produce perverse incentives where the father might pressure the mother to abort the fetus if the cost was less. In order for the pregnant mother to make as non-coerced a choice as possible to have the child or not, she must be in a situation where the father of her child has no financial incentive one way or the other. He can stagger the payments over several years, payable to state agencies dealing with various related fields: medical care; mental health counseling services; foster child services; etc.

Naturally, the objection will be raised why the father needs to pay for anything of the sort. One reason is that many conservatives on abortion policy maintain that a man should pay child support to his child's mother. So in principle, conservatives should be willing to make the father pay something. Due consideration needs to be given to health care providers, though, and their willingness to be mandated reporters in this regard. Is it fair for the father to pay something to the government (or government insurer) if the mother has an abortion? Yes, because there are costs that are borne by both the mother and the larger community whenever an

---

5. Zeitz, "Why Conservatives."

abortion happens, even if it is successful. Those costs are uncertain and not always apparent in the moment, but they exist.

    Studies show that abortion is linked to various later health risks. Physically, for example, when a woman procures an induced abortion, her chances of getting an ectopic pregnancy at a later time increases, a risk which increases with each successive induced abortion.[6] Various researchers have also argued that increased risks for breast cancer accompany induced abortion, although the issue is debated. The costs, localized in the woman's body, therefore fall in the future: on the woman when she wants to be a mother; on a man who may want to be a father; on the woman and the health care professionals who would much rather avoid an ectopic pregnancy, even if there are some promising surgical techniques which could transplant an ectopic pregnancy to the uterus;[7] on the woman and the health care professionals who would rather deliver a healthy baby simply than perform ectopic treatments; and a health care system which would rather pay for a healthy baby to be born rather than surgically intervene and/or lose the fetus. There is also a cost to the fetus who might be aborted to save the mother's life in those cases, who would have had a greater chance at healthy development. Risks of an ectopic pregnancy are higher when women are using an IUD as contraception. In that light, it bears mentioning that one study found that in the U.S., among Medicaid recipients, women of color are more at risk of ectopic pregnancies (Native Hawaiian/Pacific Islander and black being highest) than white women,[8] for unexplained reasons, as the researchers only controlled for state and age, not the use of birth control, number of previous children, past abortions or miscarriages, adverse childhood experience, nutrition, stress, etc.

    Abortion procedures risk weakening the cervix. Women who have had induced abortions are therefore more at risk for cervical insufficiency,

---

    6. "Ectopic Pregnancy." Several studies confirm the link: Tharaux-Deneux et al., "Risk of Ectopic Pregnancy"; Parazzini et al., "Induced Abortions."

    7. Wallace, "Transplantations," describes his successful transplant of an ectopic pregnancy from the fallopian tube to the mother's uterus, in 1917. Shettles, "Tubal Embryo," describes the surgical procedure he conducted on a similar patient in 1990. Mavrelos et al., "Efficacy," conducted a study in London where they found that one-third of 333 pregnant women with ectopic pregnancies resolved and had live births without medical or surgical intervention. Fortenberry, "Ectopic Pregnancy," suggests that, according to several recent studies, using surgical transplantation to the uterus, 24 percent of all tubal pregnancies could result in a live birth, and between 5 to 60 percent of all abdominal pregnancies (another form of ectopic pregnancy).

    8. Stulberg et al., "Ectopic Pregnancy," finds that out of 19,135,106 women, the incidence risk ratio in comparison with white women was highest among Native Hawaiian/Pacific Islander (1.61), black (1.47), Asian (1.34), American Indian/Alaskan Native (1.34), and Hispanic (1.16).

meaning a premature birth with a later pregnancy, where the baby has low birth weight and requires hospital care. According to a 2010 study in *Human Reproduction*, black women already have a higher risk of cervical insufficiency than white women for unexplained reasons, and for any woman, each successive induced abortion increases the likelihood of a premature birth later.[9] In addition, the earlier the premature birth, the higher the risk to the child of having cerebral palsy.[10] Forsythe refers to over 140 published medical studies indicating the increased risk of cervical insufficiency.[11] Clearly, the greater the number of abortions, the greater the increased risk.

Some abortion procedures also risk scarring the uterus. For a later pregnancy, a scarred uterus might result in the placenta forming not at the top of the uterus, as it normally does in a healthy pregnancy, but in a place that blocks the cervical opening. This condition is called *placenta previa*, and if it continues to the onset of labor, it increases various risks: need for caesarian section; hemorrhaging which could be life-threatening to the mother; early onset of labor and birth; low infant birth weight; risk of death to the infant just before or after delivery. A study published in 2003 in *Obstetrical & Gynecological Survey* found that the risk of placenta previa increases by 30 percent with one induced abortion,[12] which is lower than previous studies that indicated the risk increased by 50 percent, with other studies indicating that the risk significantly increases with each successive abortion.[13]

What is the cost of widespread abortion? In 2007, Calhoun, Shadigian, and Rooney estimated that the cost to the health care system of complications due to preterm birth and low birth weight is $1.2 billion annually.[14] That increased cost is not just due to abortion after-effects alone, but abortion is probably a significant contributing factor. Without identifying or estimating underlying causes, which are many, the World Health Organization observed that the U.S. preterm delivery rate increased by 30 percent from 1981 to 2012.[15] Martin and Osterman find that the rate increased again from 2014 to 2016.[16] Currently, fathers participate in paying this cost very indirectly, if they are taxpayers. It would be of great interest to survey what percentage of men know any of the subsequent health risks

---

9. Anum et al., "Health Disparities."
10. Calhoun, et al., "Cost Consequences."
11. Forsythe, *Abuse*, 254–55.
12. Thorp et al., "Long-Term," 75.
13. Thorp et al., "Long-Term," 70–71.
14. Calhoun, et al., "Cost Consequences."
15. "Born Too Soon,"
16. Martin and Osterman, "Describing the Increase."

of abortion. I would be open to men categorically being charged a special federal tax according to the abortion rate in the country, to help foster a collective atmosphere of male education and personal *and* interpersonal responsibility. I acknowledge that proposals like this are bound to be politically unpopular at the moment, but I remain persuaded that they would be morally preferable. It is unacceptable on moral grounds why men have largely been able to escape the consequences of their own sexual choices bodily, legally, and economically.

Put in terms of the philosophy of classical liberalism which centers the issue of being free from injury and harm, women who believe they must seek abortions, and those who obtain abortions, are morally and physically injured themselves, by *men*, because the position into which they are put—choosing between her own livelihood and the fetus within her womb—is itself a position no woman should face, even if she thought she was prepared for it and willing to use abortion as a form of birth control. One Christian criticism of Lockean liberal political thought is that surely one can consent to one's own exploitation, whether out of pressure, ignorance, or a self-destructive tendency. One can appear to consent to one's own sexual exploitation, as Christians understood well with prostitution, and even economic exploitation, by agreeing to work for exploitative wages because the individual worker is less powerful than a capital-rich employer. A person can agree to take on compounding debts (a subject I will cover in chapter 8), which Christians also understood well prior to John Calvin as exploitation. For Christians, consent is necessary but not sufficient to define what is moral. In the case of a woman considering or obtaining an abortion, if she is using abortion as a form of birth control, then she has consented to her own exploitation. That does have some moral responsibility attached to it, surely, but perhaps focused at an earlier stage of her decision-making, or perhaps as an accomplice to a man. But the one who exploited her is the man who impregnated her. And on the analogy to the Christian diagnosis of prostitution, the woman probably has many reasons for doing this, and only skilled therapy or pastoral counsel could tease those reasons apart and help her respond appropriately, if some form of lifestyle change or repentance is needed. There may be some rare cases where a woman wants to have a man's child more out of a desire to possess the man and less out of love for the child, where some change in the man-woman relationship changes how the woman feels about her mother-child relationship. That poses its own ethical challenge. But even in those cases, the man in question can always be held responsible for placing that woman in the situation of considering an abortion.

Psychologically, women often pay an emotional cost for an abortion, although the phenomenon is complex. The interruption of the hormonal cycle occurs after both abortion and childbirth. While reliable studies show that for the general population of women there is not an increased risk of emotional and mental health distress *when compared* to carrying the baby to term,[17] those who tend to hold anti-abortion policies often maintain there are emotional and mental health costs borne by the woman in absolute terms. The American Pregnancy Association website states that emotional and psychological effects after abortion are more common than physical side effects, ranging from mild regret to depression.[18] The Health Research Funding website claims that teenage girls who have abortions are ten times more likely to attempt suicide than those who have never had an abortion, and that teenage girls are four times more likely to succeed at committing suicide when compared to older women who have had an abortion. HRF also says that 45 percent of women who have an abortion report having suicidal feelings immediately afterwards.[19] Indeed, the pro-choice Guttmacher Institute acknowledges that women who procure abortion might experience "negative emotions":

> Difficulty with the abortion decision and the degree to which the pregnancy had been planned were most important for women's postabortion emotional state. Experiencing negative emotions postabortion is different from believing that abortion was not the right decision.[20]

Studies like this are difficult because distinguishing between correlations and causes is challenging. Once again, for social conservatives who typically point to the emotional and mental costs borne by a woman procuring an abortion, *even to the woman herself in an attempt to dissuade her,* they

---

17. Biggs, "Explained: Abortion Research," cites sixteen studies conducted between 1989 (starting with Surgeon General C. Everett Koop, a Christian, who was under political pressure to declare that abortion increased risk of depression and suicide in women, but did not) and 2017. Also, Charles et al., "Abortion and Long-Term," systematically reviewed the medical literature on abortion and mental health, finding, "A clear trend emerges from this systematic review: the highest quality studies had findings that were mostly neutral, suggesting few, if any, differences between women who had abortions and their respective comparison groups in terms of mental health sequelae. Conversely, studies with the most flawed methodology found negative mental health sequelae of abortion." The recent Turnaway Study conducted by ANSIRH found after following almost one thousand women for five years across twenty-one states that there were no significant mental or emotional health costs.

18. "Emotional Side Effects."

19. "19 Shocking Statistics."

20. Rocca et al., "Women's Emotions."

should be absolutely willing to consider the emotional cost to the woman, in principle. Her need to access formal or informal channels of mental health care is one such cost.

Some studies compare procuring an abortion, on the one hand, and giving birth to an unexpected child, on the other. An approach like that bypasses the sensitive but usually overlooked question of whether the woman should have been pregnant at all, or whether, in some cases, a prior lack of emotional or mental stability may lead some women to become pregnant. Consider this case: "When a drug-addicted woman becomes pregnant, she has only one realistic avenue to escape criminal charges: abortion. Seeking drug treatment is usually not a viable alternative."[21] In these cases, there are further social costs that are difficult to quantify whenever any such woman gets pregnant and procures an abortion: costs to others to help her emotionally recover, for instance. Because conservatives have a tendency to first consider punitive methods to accomplish cultural goals, they should be comfortable with fining the man.

Are Physicians Always to Blame?

When then-presidential candidate Donald Trump said in early 2016 that women should be subject to "some form of punishment" for aborting a fetus, there were widespread denunciations of his remark from both conservative and liberal circles. Trump himself recanted, saying that he meant the abortion "doctor or any other person performing this illegal act" should be held responsible.[22] This incident highlighted two things. First, many wondered if a conservative had at last "said the quiet part out loud." After all, the social conservative position requires the woman to pay the much higher price of giving birth to the child and raising it, if she does not give the child up for adoption. This could be considered "some form of punishment." Some conservatives have not been so quiet: Bob Nonini, Idaho Republican state senator, said that women should be punished, a day after he said that the punishment should include the death penalty, though he later backed off.[23] An Idaho group called Abolish Abortion backed a 2018 ballot initiative to charge both the physician and the woman with first-degree murder.[24] An Ohio bill introduced in March 2018 sought to ban all abor-

21. Roberts, *Killing*, 181.
22. Flegenheimer and Haberman, "Donald Trump, Abortion Foe," and Kertscher, "In Context: Transcript."
23. Kruesi, "Punishing Women."
24. North, "Plenty of Conservatives."

tions without exception, and punish physician and woman with a homicide charge punishable with life in prison or the death penalty.[25] Quite possibly, pro-life advocates are offering these initiatives as direct challenges to *Roe v. Wade*, as opposed to sustainable law. Most pro-life advocates, however, are adamant that women be considered the second victim in an abortion, and should never be prosecuted.[26] It remains to be seen, politically, whether there is a tendency among intellectuals to be more disciplined about this point, and populists to be more punitive.

Second, the incident highlights the challenge conservatives face when they place abortion in a criminal justice category but do not hold the father fundamentally responsible. Whether out of political expedience or not, social conservatives assert that when an abortion is performed, there are two victims: the fetus and the woman. I agree with this. But a victim of *who*? The answer, according to social conservatives, is: *the abortion provider*. The infamous case of Kermit Gosnell can be considered an example where that is true on account of his clinic conditions and delegation to others. But that position is difficult, if not absurd, in the main. A woman seeking an abortion *wants* the service, and is usually quite determined and clear-headed about it. A doctor in that position might even feel caught in a catch-22 situation. If she can safely perform the abortion, and is morally willing to, then she could. But she may incur a moral injury by doing so. She might also incur a moral injury by *not* doing so, because she does not know whether the pregnant woman will seek an abortion under less safe conditions. In other words, the abortion provider can be considered a victim, as well.

To observe the moral discomfort and moral injury to gynecologists and other health care professionals, consider the experiences of pro-choice advocate Dr. Alan Guttmacher, pro-life advocate Dr. Anthony Levatino, and the various doctors surveyed in either the Physicians for Reproductive Health twenty-five-minute video, *Voices of Choice: Physicians Who Provided Abortions before Roe v. Wade*, or Carole E. Joffe's book *Doctors of Conscience: The Struggle to Provide Abortion before and after Roe v. Wade*.

Dr. Alan Guttmacher did his medical residency at Johns Hopkins in the mid-1920s and experienced the deaths of three women who had resorted to illegal abortions by "untrained nonprofessionals."[27] The first was a mother of four children; the second was a girl of fifteen; the third was a woman in middle age. When he sought to perform an abortion for a twelve-year-old girl who had been impregnated by her father, Guttmacher's mentor

25. Rosenberg, "Ohio GOP."
26. "One Untrue Thing."
27. Garrow, *Liberty*, 270.

responded negatively. Only the local district attorney could give them permission and exempt them as physicians from Maryland's criminal statute prohibiting all abortions except those to save the mother's life. As a result, Guttmacher delivered the girl's baby seven months later. In 1942, Guttmacher became chief of obstetrics at Baltimore's Sinai Hospital and became an outspoken advocate of repealing state anti-abortion laws, in favor of giving doctors more discretion. Since Guttmacher's name has been associated for decades with pro-choice advocacy, it might be surprising to find that he said this about physician responsibility in 1954:

> I do not feel that the obstetrician-gynecologist is simply the patient's agent who presents her request for interruption of pregnancy without himself evaluating it. I think he should pass this request on to the hospital authorities . . . only if he is convinced of the wisdom of the request. If he thinks the procedure unjustified, it behooves the physician consulted to discuss the matter in great detail with the patient and to attempt to persuade her to his viewpoint. If he fails to do this he has no further responsibility in the case.[28]

What interests us about Guttmacher's statement is how he understood the physician's role and responsibility. At least at that time, Guttmacher believed that physicians had a responsibility to dissuade a woman from aborting a pregnancy, at least under certain circumstances. Presumably this involved making sure the patient was fully informed of all the present and future health risks she would incur. The physician also operated in an organizational context and was responsible to inform others about the situation; Guttmacher was a member of his own hospital's therapeutic abortion committee. Being unable to dissuade the woman from aborting, the physician would then be free to perform the abortion but bore no moral responsibility for the act itself.

Guttmacher's statement gives more texture to how the phrase "a woman and her doctor" was used in different ways. According to *Roe v. Wade*, a woman seeking an abortion is merely acting via her right to privacy, and contracts with the physician, who bears no moral agency. It would seem that Guttmacher held to a view that the physician must first serve as educator, then counselor about the decision, before being the abortion provider. Various pro-life conservatives make a valid point, then, about *Roe* and *Doe* when they critique the woman's right to privacy being absolute in the first trimester. Framing the matter as a constitutional right means that the woman is the moral agent, a responsibility they say they do not wish to

28. Guttmacher, "Shrinking Non-Psychiatric Indications," 119.

assign to her. Guttmacher's process as a physician, however, clearly shows that he viewed the physician as having moral discomfort, agency, and possibly injury in the matter as well.

In 2015, Dr. Levatino testified before Congress about the development of his sense of moral injury and why he switched from being pro-choice to pro-life as a doctor and becoming a pro-life advocate. He describes performing a Dilation and Evacuation procedure, which is an abortion method usually done after fourteen weeks.

> Imagine if you can that you are a pro-choice obstetrician/gynecologist like I once was. Your patient today is 24 weeks pregnant. At twenty-four weeks from last menstrual period, her uterus is two finger-breadths above the umbilicus. If you could see her baby, which is quite easy on an ultrasound, she would be as long as your hand plus a half from the top of her head to the bottom of her rump not counting the legs. Your patient has been feeling her baby kick for the last month or more but now she is asleep on an operating room table and you are there to help her with her problem pregnancy.
>
> The first task is remove the laminaria that had earlier been placed in the cervix to dilate it sufficiently to allow the procedure you are about to perform. With that accomplished, direct your attention to the surgical instruments arranged on a small table to your right. The first instrument you reach for is a 14-French suction catheter. It is clear plastic and about nine inches long. It has a bore through the center approximately ¾ of an inch in diameter. Picture yourself introducing this catheter through the cervix and instructing the circulating nurse to turn on the suction machine which is connected through clear plastic tubing to the catheter. What you will see is a pale yellow fluid that looks a lot like urine coming through the catheter into a glass bottle on the suction machine. This is the amniotic fluid that surrounded the baby to protect her.
>
> With suction complete, look for your Sopher clamp. This instrument is about thirteen inches long and made of stainless steel. At the business end are located jaws about 2 ½ inches long and about ¾ on an inch wide with rows of sharp ridges or teeth. This instrument is for grasping and crushing tissue. When it gets hold of something, it does not let go. A second trimester D&E abortion is a blind procedure. The baby can be in any orientation or position inside the uterus. Picture yourself reaching in with the Sopher clamp and grasping anything you can. At

twenty-four weeks gestation, the uterus is thin and soft so be careful not to perforate or puncture the walls. Once you have grasped something inside, squeeze on the clamp to set the jaws and pull hard—really hard. You feel something let go and out pops a fully formed leg about six inches long. Reach in again and grasp whatever you can. Set the jaw and pull really hard once again and out pops an arm about the same length. Reach in again and again with that clamp and tear out the spine, intestines, heart and lungs.

The toughest part of a D&E abortion is extracting the baby's head. The head of a baby that age is about the size of a large plum and is now free floating inside the uterine cavity. You can be pretty sure you have hold of it if the Sopher clamp is spread about as far as your fingers will allow. You will know you have it right when you crush down on the clamp and see white gelatinous material coming through the cervix. That was the baby's brains. You can then extract the skull pieces. Many times a little face will come out and stare back at you. Congratulations! You have just successfully performed a second trimester Suction D&E abortion. You just affirmed her right to choose.[29]

While obviously not all doctors come to Dr. Levatino's position, his testimony is informative, not only on the factual level, but on the emotional and moral register, too. It should be noted that a miscarriage and a medication-induced abortion in the second trimester require clinically similar, if not identical, processes, so the skill itself is important from a medical perspective. Not all abortion procedures are the D&E, though, especially procedures performed earlier in the pregnancy. The National Academies of Science, Engineering, and Medicine report:

> Most abortions are performed early in pregnancy—50 percent by 7 weeks' gestation and 90 percent by 12 weeks' gestation—and length of gestation is the primary factor in deciding what abortion procedure is the most appropriate. Medication abortions are used up to 10 weeks' gestation; aspiration procedures may be used up to 14 to 16 weeks' gestation. When these are no longer feasible, dilation and evacuation (D&E) and induction methods are used.[30]

Obviously the later in the pregnancy, the more physically involved the method and the greater the physicians' concern for both the mother, the fetus, and

---

29. Levatino, "Planned Parenthood Exposed."
30. "Safety and Quality."

themselves. Studies debate whether the fetus can feel pain, especially before twenty-two weeks because pain signals cannot traverse the thalamus to the brain cortex because the connections have not formed,[31] or at twenty-six weeks because of other neuroanatomy being formed at that time.[32] That is surely a consideration for most physicians. If the preferred methods of abortion continue to change (in 2014, 31 percent of abortions were medical abortions, compared with 6 percent in 2001[33]) doctors' involvement and sense of participation might change, resulting in more doctors being willing to perform first trimester abortions. Studies suggest that doctors' willingness to offer abortion services might be increasing, but also that they may be reluctant to answer surveys. In 2011, a study found 14 percent of OB-GYNs offered abortion services;[34] a similar study in 2016–2017 suggested that about 24 percent do.[35] In theory, it is possible that the U.S., or parts of the country, could face a similar situation as Italy. Italy, by law, makes abortion legal up to ninety days. But 70 percent of gynecologists—and up to 83 percent in the more conservative regions in the south—do not perform abortions for religious or personal reasons.[36] Therefore, one should not assume that the moral cost to doctors performing abortions is negligible. While doctors may be willing to perform them,[37] no society as a whole can guarantee that they will be willing to, in steady or increasing numbers. My point here is not to make predictions per se, but only to highlight that doctors often do feel a sense of moral weightiness, even moral injury, in performing abortions of various kinds.

Yet physicians often feel a sense of moral weightiness or injury if they do not. Dr. Mildred S. Hanson is one of the physicians featured in the video documentary *Voices of Choice: Physicians Who Provided Abortions before Roe v. Wade*. She was head of a hospital committee on abortion and sterilization in the 1960s, overseeing hospital protocol. When explaining her decision to offer abortion services to women, she refers to an incident when she received a call from a frantic young woman. The young woman wanted to know about what the abortion process was like, but never gave her name or phone number. Later, Dr. Hanson learned that she had died by suicide, by jumping out of

31. Lee et al., "Fetal Pain," provides a helpful review of the relevant scientific literature to 2005, and Levitan, "Does a Fetus Feel Pain," surveys the literature to 2015.
32. Derbyshire, "Can Fetuses Feel Pain?" and Tighe, "Fetuses Can Feel Pain."
33. Healy, "OB-GYNs Remain Conflicted."
34. Gold, "Proportion of OB-GYNs."
35. Grossman et al., "Induced Abortion Provision."
36. Pianigiani, "On Paper."
37. Grossman et al., "Induced Abortion Provision," summarized by Healy, "OB-GYNs Remain Conflicted." In the U.K., "The Care of Women" notes, "Abortion accounts for a significant proportion of the workload of many gynaecologists."

a seventeenth-story window. Hanson says, "To this day, I still feel responsible for her death."[38] Categorically placing legal responsibility on physicians puts them into a conundrum. Not only are they placed into a situation where they are unable to help the patient before them, society loses the help of medical professionals as gatherers of stories and data as we try to address unintended pregnancy as a wider social problem.

This leaves only *one possible party* ultimately responsible for injuring the fetus, the mother, and the doctor: the man who impregnated the woman. Unless a man claims that a woman raped *him*—which is highly unusual, but does happen, and would present a different kind of legal challenge—his agency in the pregnancy needs to be the subject of much more accountability.

If it is argued that a man who wants to be a father is put into a defenseless position if the woman he impregnated wants an abortion, one can say that unfortunately, he trusted the wrong woman. He did not spend enough time getting to know the woman in question, restraining his own sexual desires until he did, and/or understanding the contraception available to them. That sounds like a heavy responsibility for a man to bear. Yet consider this: a system which gives institutional advantages to women only puts men into the very same position that women are in today. Women have to think about all those things, anyway. The institutional incentives would then be placed on men to approach women much more carefully, respectfully, wisely, with much more self-restraint, and with much more self-awareness on their part. Otherwise, our society may place women and physicians in a similar situation to the one they were in prior to 1973. To that subject we turn.

An Unknown: Can Health Professionals Function Well as Part of the Criminal Justice System?

Pro-life advocates often speak as if overturning *Roe v. Wade* would have a decisive impact on abortion rates, especially in comparison to other social policies. The assumption is that giving states legislative, budgetary, and judicial control over reproductive policies and medical professionals will lead to an overall reduction in abortions. This is a topic that pro-life and pro-choice advocates vigorously debate. Reading Mark Graber's 1996 evaluation of the practice of anti-abortion against constitutional principles of equal protection, Leslie Reagan's 1998 social history of abortion policy, indicating troubling patterns of law enforcement, and Clarke D. Forsythe's 2013 argument against *Roe v. Wade* leaves one with very different impressions about

38. Lee, "Doctors Who Performed." *Voices of Choice.*

the prospects of enforcement of anti-abortion statutes at the state or federal level. Forsythe, an attorney, argues that state law enforcement officials pursued anti-abortion policy in a more or less consistent manner. While he acknowledges "lapses" and "corruption like other areas of law enforcement," he cites numerous examples of abortionists being prosecuted.[39] Citing Reagan's work, Forsythe points out that even selective prosecution has the effect of deterrence.[40] All told, however, Forsythe devotes only about six pages to the challenge of enforcement. Unfortunately, he does not name Graber in his bibliography, who devotes an entire book to the topic. While the deterrence factor is surely real, the ethical issue here is not *whether* the law was ever enforced, but *how evenly and consistently* it was enforced and might be enforced should these laws be reinstated. Laws about capital punishment and drug use have regularly been used in the service of, if not motivated outright by, racial bias, and it is doubtful that deterrence is a sufficient moral or legal justification for discriminatory implementation that is completely foreseeable. Indeed, several of the examples raised by Forsythe reveal more troubling patterns. Therefore, Leslie Reagan's 1998 social history of abortion policy, indicating troubling patterns of law enforcement, and Mark Graber's 1996 evaluation of abortion policy against constitutional principles of equal protection, remain important.[41] Doctors' own accounts are vital as well. How were the anti-abortion policies in the United States actually administered in the decades just prior to *Roe v. Wade*?

Pro-life policy before *Roe* stopped abortions like the era of Prohibition stopped alcohol. Namely, it did not. For example, between 1923 and 1967, Dr. Robert Douglas Spencer performed an estimated one hundred thousand or more abortions in his spotless clinic in the midst of coal country in Ashland, Pennsylvania. He charged virtually nothing. Reports exist of him charging rates as low as $10, $25, and $50.[42] Explaining why he offered these women who came to him seeking abortions, he said, "I could see their point of view." How widespread were occurrences like this, and what patterns did they follow?

In the 1930s, says the *Oxford Companion to United States History*, licensed physicians performed about eight hundred thousand abortions per year, despite pro-life laws in every state.[43] During the 1940s, medical

39. Forsythe, *Abuse*, 192–97.
40. Forsythe, *Abuse*, 196–97.
41. Reagan, *When Abortion*, and Graber, *Rethinking Abortion*.
42. Brownmiller, "Dr. Spencer."
43. Boyer, *Oxford Companion*, 3. Reagan, *When Abortion*, 134–35, 305 n. 13. Garrow, *Liberty*, 272, calls this estimate "the best available demographic estimate."

advances—the use of penicillin, better use of anesthesia, and new surgical techniques for caesarian sections—reduced maternal risk factors but also made abortions easier. The increase in abortions for psychiatric reasons—referring to the emotional health of the mother—increased rapidly. If a woman told her doctor she was considering suicide because of an unintended pregnancy, that counted as a psychiatric reason, as the doctor could only take her word for it.[44] In 1954, Dr. Alan Guttmacher admitted that "the truly legal abortions, in which the procedure is absolutely essential to preserve the mother's life, are relatively few."[45]

Doctors in hospitals were almost never prosecuted for the abortions they performed. The law allowed for abortion performed for "therapeutic purposes," that is, to save the mother's life. In practice, hospitals were given wide leeway to define what conditions threatened the health of the mother. One physician admitted, "After starting a little bleeding I'd tell her to go home and call me back within twenty-four hours to let me know if the bleeding continued. If it did, which I expected that it would, I would then admit her as a threatened abortion and complete the process in a legitimate way."[46] Despite Catholic doctors spearheading the formation of hospital committees to provide oversight, physicians regularly admitted that the practice of performing abortions in hospitals was "inequitable, inconsistent, and largely illegal."[47] One survey of New York hospital practices in the 1950s concluded that in a five-year period, 90 percent of all so-called "therapeutic" abortions were actually illegal.[48] Reports abound of sympathetic doctors performing a "dilation and curettage": causing a small amount of uterine bleeding, telling the woman seeking an abortion to come back the next day, and providing an abortion on therapeutic grounds. This was a useful device for aborting the pregnancy for other, supposedly precautionary reasons. In one small hospital, reports show that 107 "diagnostic uterine curettages" were performed in one year; of those, 104 patients had been pregnant.[49] Concerning the

---

44. Williams, *Defenders*, 35, notes that Dr. Alan Guttmacher said in a 1961 private letter that in his practice, about 60 percent of abortions were psychiatric; in 1963, Buffalo hospitals reported that 88 percent of all abortions were for psychiatric reasons.

45. Guttmacher, "Shrinking Non-Psychiatric," 118.

46. Messer and May, *Back Rooms*, 179–80.

47. Hall, "Abortion in American Hospitals," 1933. Williams, *Defenders*, 35.

48. Graber, *Rethinking Abortion*, 49; see the long list of citations he provides.

49. Graber, *Rethinking Abortion*, 55, cites Bates and Zawadski, *Criminal Abortion*, 79–80, and Burtchaell, *Rachel Weeping*, 49. Graber adds in the footnote, "Several persons who wish to remain anonymous have informed me that large hospitals in New York City, Boston, and St. Louis also practiced this subterfuge."

1950s and 1960s, estimates range from 200,000 to 1.2 million per year.[50] I will comment on why there is reason to seriously doubt *both* the higher and lower estimates, below, but the more significant point here is the interaction between practitioners of law and medicine.

Surprisingly, then, just prior to *Roe v. Wade* in 1973, abortion law did not mean as much about the actual practice of abortion as one might think. Thirty states made abortion illegal in all cases without exception, sixteen states legalized abortion under ostensibly rare circumstances (rape, incest, threat to mother's life), three states legalized abortions but only for state residents, and New York allowed abortions generally. Meanwhile, "*Wealthy citizens usually had access to safe abortions even in jurisdictions with draconian restrictions on abortion on the books.*"[51] For example, prior to *Roe*, California law after 1967 stated that abortion was only legal when a mother's health would be gravely impaired. If law indicated practice, one would think that California would have a low abortion rate. Yet California officials were known to be so flexible with medical terminology, and so sympathetic to women seeking abortion, that they effectively "permitted abortion on demand."[52] By 1973, California's legal abortion rates were higher than those of states that had repealed all restrictions on abortion.

One reason for this startling gap between abortion law and abortion practice is the willingness of many actors to circumvent the law to protect abortionists they felt served them. Prior to *Roe*, while single women sought abortions too, the overwhelming majority of abortion requests were made by married women.[53] Especially when the women were white and middle- to upper-class, abortions were readily available. Pre-*Roe* policy created a vast gray market in abortion. In fact, the law enforcement agents themselves had a vested interest in not prosecuting cases, because they had either benefited themselves from abortion services or believed, with the community, that abortionists "performed a useful service":

> Anti-abortion advocates complained that "even the most outrageous abortionist" could not be convicted in a jury trial. One juror refused to convict a well-known abortionist because there was "nobody in Schuykill County that the doctor hasn't helped." Half the abortionists convicted in New York between 1925 and 1950 were sentenced only to probation. Dr. Milan

---

50. Calderone, *Abortion in the United States*, 80, cited by Graber, *Rethinking Abortion*, 42.
51. Graber, *Rethinking Abortion*, 19. Italics mine.
52. Graber, *Rethinking Abortion*, 19.
53. Graber, *Rethinking Abortion*, 42.

Vuitch, a prominent physician-abortionist, was arrested sixteen times for openly running an abortion clinic in Washington, D.C., but never went to jail.[54]

Since women did not consider themselves to be victims of a crime, law enforcement agents regularly found themselves lacking any witnesses and complainants. Recall the example of Dr. Robert Spencer in Ashland, Pennsylvania. As to why he was never prosecuted under criminal charges, Dr. Spencer's widow explains:

> No one was out to get him because he was such a good doctor. Besides, he was benefiting the local economy. People were coming here from all over the United States. They spent money in the hotels and restaurants. The local merchants, no matter what their attitudes about abortion, knew a good thing when they saw it, and they weren't about to kill the goose that laid the golden egg.[55]

In fact, one man ran as a candidate for district attorney, promising to prosecute Dr. Spencer and shut down his business. He was crushed in the next election.[56]

Those who assess law enforcement of anti-abortion laws concede that it was not merely erratic, but unquestionably *selective*. Garrow, on whom Forsythe substantially relies, admits that the police pursued "the most unskilled practitioners rather than the most successful."[57] The famous 1956 *Time* magazine story of an abortionist highlights how successful abortion physicians were rarely prosecuted. *Time* covered the story of a seventy-two-year-old doctor in Akron, Ohio, who was sentenced to four months in prison for performing abortions in his own clinic. He admitted to performing two to three hundred abortions per year since 1934, totaling about 5,500 abortions. He had never previously been arrested, probably because he had never caused a woman's fatality.

The case of Ruth Barnett is somewhat similar, but from another angle. In 1968, Barnett finally closed her abortion clinic, due to a combination of old age and a legal conviction, after performing an estimated forty thousand abortions over the course of about forty years. In 1929, Barnett opened her own abortion clinic in Portland, Oregon, after acquiring only a chiropractor's license, following apprenticeships to two doctors who also performed

---

54. Graber, *Rethinking Abortion*, 45.
55. Miller, *Worst of Times*, 123–25, 135.
56. Miller, *Worst of Times*, 127.
57. Garrow, *Liberty*, 274.

abortions; her business was very sought after, including in the Great Depression era.[58] Although she was implicated in an infection while visiting another practice in Las Vegas, while in Portland, she practiced without medical or legal incident until 1951, when Portland's mayor decided to crack down on crime in the city. Her clinic was raided and she was arrested. Barnett was arrested again in 1956. Then, under a new district attorney, she faced prosecution again in 1965, and was convicted in 1966 of manslaughter by abortion. She appealed, but her conviction was upheld by the Oregon Supreme Court in 1968, and she served a sentence as a seventy-three-year-old woman, "the oldest inmate to be sent to the state penitentiary."[59] Forsythe cites Barnett's prosecution as a positive example for his case, but the question posed by Schoen and others is whether Barnett's age, gender, and status as a chiropractor had anything to do with the timing of the prosecution she faced.[60]

Consider also the case of "Jane." From 1969 to 1973 in Chicago, a feminist group made up of 120 women performed between eleven thousand and thirteen thousand abortions in four years, despite Illinois's anti-abortion law. They went under the name "Jane," and were trained by abortion doctors and non-doctors to do dilation and curettage procedures on women who were up to fifteen weeks pregnant. Allusions occur in narratives told by other unlicensed abortion providers; one doctor knew of "feminist groups" who performed menstrual evacuations, a procedure relatively safe for the mother.[61] After *Roe* and legalization, "Jane" members in the Chicago area attested, "For the most part . . . there was a tacit understanding with police officers, who sent their wives, daughters and girlfriends to Jane for abortions."[62]

Carole E. Joffe opens her book *Doctors of Conscience: The Struggle to Provide Abortion before and after Roe v. Wade* with the story of Dr. Jane Hodgson. Hodgson was an obstetrician/gynecologist in St. Paul, Minnesota. She was a prominent and respected physician who had become head of the Minnesota Obstetrics/Gynecology Society in 1964. After treating many women who were bleeding or infected from incompetent abortionists, and also watching many of her male colleagues claim to be pro-life in public but ask her for referrals for their own wives or daughters to have a

58. Schoen, "Reconceiving Abortion," 355–56.
59. Schoen, "Reconceiving Abortion," 358.
60. Forsythe, *Abuse*, 407–8 n. 52.
61. Smothers, "What It Was Like," interviews Dr. Curtis Boyd, who recalls that in 1967, "Some feminist groups began to do menstrual extractions when abortion was still illegal."
62. Brotman, "Secret Abortion." Schoen, "Reconceiving Abortion," 359–61. Kaplan, *Story of Jane*.

safe abortion, Joffe became outspoken about legal reform. She became an advocate of women having the option to abort, and in 1971 performed an abortion on Nancy Widmeyer, a married mother of two who had contracted rubella from her children. In other states, rubella was an acceptable reason for a woman to seek an abortion because of the risk of fetal deformity. In Minnesota, it was not. After appealing the law in federal court in Minnesota and being denied, Hodgson performed the abortion in a deliberate attempt to challenge Minnesota's state law. She "became the *only* physician in United States history to be convicted of performing an abortion in a hospital."[63] The *only* hospital physician?

A similar phenomenon of non-policing and non-prosecution occurs in the State of Israel. Since 1977, abortion has been fully legal in Israel for a broad range of categories, subject to the pregnant woman coming before a termination committee, which by any interpretation is quite lenient.[64] Women who procure abortions outside of the termination committee process do not face criminal penalties. In theory, the doctors who provide them are legally subject to a fine or up to five years of imprisonment. No doctors have been prosecuted, however.[65] One government study estimates that about three-fifths of Israel's fifty thousand abortions per year occur outside of the committee process.[66]

In that light, consider a recent incident in American politics. U.S. Congressman Tim Murphy (R-PA) served for fifteen years, consistently advocating anti-abortion legislation. On October 21, 2017, Murphy abruptly resigned. Shannon Edwards, his thirty-two year old mistress (Murphy was then sixty-five), had just revealed that Murphy asked her to abort a child he thought they had conceived together. Edwards gave their text exchange to the *Pittsburgh Post-Gazette*, which read:

> Edwards: *"And you have zero issue posting your pro-life stance all over the place when you had no issue asking me to abort our unborn child just last week when we thought that was one of the options"*
>
> Murphy: *"I get what you say about my March for life messages. I've never written them. Staff does them. I read them and winced. I told staff don't write any more. I will."*[67]

63. Joffe, *Doctors*, 12. Italics mine.

64. "Israel: Reproduction and Abortion," sec. IV.A, points out, "Although Israeli law imposes strict limitations on abortions, in practice 98.5% of all requests for abortions to the committees were approved in 2009, and 98.7% in 2010."

65. "Israel: Reproduction and Abortion," sec. III.

66. Brackman and Lubitch, "Chief Rabbis: Fight."

67. Ward, "Rep. Tim Murphy."

Edwards's revelation and Murphy's resignation suggest much about the politics of abortion in the U.S.[68] They also indicate how a powerful and well-connected white man believed a white woman could obtain a safe abortion very easily and, apparently, very privately. A devastating article by Devorah Blachor called "Abortion Is Immoral, Except When It Comes to My Mistresses" deserves to be read by all.[69] Given these dynamics, it is hard to understand why Forsythe can begin his description of law enforcement of anti-abortion statutes by admitting it was "marked by lapses and marred by corruption" and finish by saying these laws were "regularly enforced."[70]

The number of abortions after *Roe* unquestionably went up. By how much, however, is highly contested. Pro-life advocates argue that the number of abortions prior to *Roe* was low to give the appearance that abortions vastly increased after 1973. Pro-choice advocates, on the other hand, suggest that the pre-*Roe* number was already high, to give the impression that *Roe* did not cause that much of an increase. Discussion of the high and low ends of these estimates is not only meaningful in itself, but also raises observations related to the larger relationship between law and medicine.

At the high end of the estimates for the years just before *Roe* is 1.2 million, which is commonly cited. Forsythe makes the important point that, prior to the late 1960s, there were only a small number of physicians performing a supposedly high volume of abortions. Dr. Mary Calderone, the medical director of Planned Parenthood, estimated in 1960 that 90 percent of all illegal abortions were done by licensed physicians, whereas Dr. Alan Guttmacher in 1967 estimated that percentage to be 80.[71] Those estimates, if accurate, certainly call into question how over a million abortions per year could be carried out by physicians alone. However, given the characterization

68. Ward, "Rep. Tim Murphy," says, "[Their] text exchange over abortion was prompted by a Jan. 24 Facebook post by Mr. Murphy: 'The United States is one of just seven countries worldwide that permits elective abortion more than halfway through pregnancy (beyond 20 weeks). It is a tragic shame that America is leading the world in discarding and disregarding the most vulnerable,' he wrote. Mr. Murphy noted in that post that he sponsored and voted for a bill prohibiting the use of federal funds to pay for abortions and said he had hope that 'we will once again be a nation committed to honoring life from the moment of conception and ensuring American taxpayer dollars are never spent to end a life before it even begins.' He is currently a co-sponsor with 181 other legislators of the Pain-Capable Unborn Child Protection Act, which would bar abortion after 20 weeks except in cases of rape, incest or where the pregnancy poses a threat to the life or physical health of the mother. Mr. Murphy voted for the bill Tuesday evening, according to Roll Call. It passed 237 to 189."

69. Blachor, "Abortion Is Immoral."

70. Forsythe, *Abuse*, 192, 194.

71. Calderone, "Illegal Abortion," 949, and Guttmacher, *Case*, 69, 71–72 discussed by Forsythe, *Abuse*, 201–2.

of the 1960s as the time of "free sex," it is difficult to believe that abortion rates did not go up dramatically. Calderone's and Guttmacher's may be underestimates, especially by the pregnant women themselves or by people who were not licensed physicians. If, in one year, a non-physician like Barnett the chiropractor could perform one thousand abortions, and groups like "Jane" could do two to four thousand, it is not hard to imagine that the national abortion rate would lean towards the higher side. One report extrapolated from North Carolina data alone in 1967 and concluded that, nation-wide, 829,000 illegal or self-induced abortions occurred in that year alone.[72]

One study gives a lower estimate of 210,000 illegal abortions per year. Graber highlights two major methodological problems used to arrive at that number. The data comes from Centers for Disease Control (CDC) data on abortion fatalities from 1940 to 1972, which CDC officials admit represents "a minimum estimate." The study also takes the number of women from New York City who died from illegal abortions to estimate the total number of abortions administered in NYC, then extrapolates that to the larger U.S. At that time, 94 percent of the women who died from illegal abortions in NYC were women of color. The study therefore underestimates the far greater access to abortion services—considered legal—that wealthy, white women had. Graber points out, "Nowhere do the authors explain why one would assume that black women in Harlem had access to anything remotely resembling the same quality abortion services as had white women who lived in such affluent suburbs as Scarsdale and Great Neck."[73]

Indeed, the available statistics for the experiences of black and Latino women, compared with those of middle- to upper-class white women, point to a troubling unevenness, which is an essential point here concerning the consistency of medical practice and law enforcement.[74] Women of color received nowhere near the same sympathy and access to safe abortion as white women, from the overwhelmingly white medical profession. For instance, one study of medical practices in Georgia concluded that, in 1970, single white women were twenty-five times more likely to be granted a "therapeutic abortion" than single black women.[75] Of course patterns like this pushed poor and minority women to procure unsafe abortions. Matters were not much better in the supposedly more tolerant North. A study by Gold et al. of abortions in New York City from 1951 to 1962 concluded that

72. Gold et al., "Lessons."
73. Graber, *Rethinking Abortion*, 23
74. Charles and Alexander, "Abortions for Poor," 150–51.
75. Rochat et al., "Epidemiological Analysis," 548. See also Rodman et al., *The Abortion Question*, 149–50, and Rosen, "Emotionally Sick," 73, for racially discriminatory distribution of abortions in Baltimore, Maryland.

108 white women died due to abortion, compared to 466 black and Puerto Rican women—over a 400 percent differential, despite white women making up a larger percentage of the population.[76] Polgar and Fried surveyed impoverished neighborhoods in New York City in 1965 and 1967, and based on respondents' answers, found that physicians were involved in only 2 percent of abortions.[77] Meanwhile, 93 percent of all therapeutic abortions were performed on white women, physician-approved.[78] It is difficult to imagine there being a biological or environmental reason for white women to be so disproportionately in need of therapeutic abortions. The sufficient explanation is white privilege operating in the medical field.

Women of color were much less likely than white women to be able to afford or acquire safe, physician-attended abortions. Hospitals routinely denied them legal therapeutic abortions. One's ability to find the right connections, speak the right terms, and navigate committees of doctors became a test of wealth. Rochat et al. observe that at a nationwide level, as anti-abortion enforcement increased in the mid-twentieth-century, albeit selectively, the mortality rate for black women due to abortion increased from two times that of white women in 1933 to *six times* that of white women in 1966.[79] Another study reported that illegal abortions accounted for *half* of all maternity-related deaths among black women in New York City in the 1960s, which is highly disproportionate.[80] By comparison, during the Great Depression, abortion was listed as the official cause of death for only 18 percent of women who died of maternal causes.[81] In the South, one would expect those disparities to be worse, and Packer indeed confirms it. In a single decade, in Georgia, the mortality rate for black women due to abortion went from four times that of white women in 1960 to *fourteen times* by 1969.[82] We must bear in mind that race might be the easiest characteristic to measure. Class is less obvious. Connectedness can only be inferred.

---

76. Gold et al., "Therapeutic Abortions," 964–66. Graber, *Rethinking Abortion*, 8, notes, "The persons responsible for administering abortion policy did, however, take steps that prevented competent abortionists from offering the same services to the general public. The resulting exclusive gray market . . . violates the philosophical and constitutional principle that persons must be governed only by general laws, rules of universal application made by their elected representatives."

77. Polgar and Fried, "Bad Old Days."

78. Gold et al., "Therapeutic Abortions," 966. Graber, *Rethinking Abortion*, 8.

79. Rochat et al., "Epidemiological Analysis," 543–44. Graber, *Rethinking Abortion*, 59.

80. Weisbord, *Genocide*, 116, discussed by Roberts, *Killing*, 102.

81. Gold, "Lessons."

82. Packer, *Limits*, 343. Graber, *Rethinking Abortion*, 59.

Equal Choice vs. Discriminatory Treatment

Given the state of actual anti-abortion policy as practiced on the ground, some constitutional scholars like Graber raise the question of *equal choice*. If medical policies are so selectively followed, and laws are so selectively enforced—especially in a patterned way that reflects other persistent social inequalities—is there a legal, even constitutional, problem? The Fourteenth Amendment guarantees to citizens the right to be treated equally under the law. One very early Supreme Court case demonstrates how equal treatment under the law is significant. In *Yick Wo v. Hopkins* (1886), Yick Wo was convicted of running a laundry business without a license. San Francisco denied licenses to all Chinese laundry operators. It granted licenses to all other laundry operators but one. Law enforcement had arrested more than a hundred Chinese people for operating laundries without licenses. The court overturned Wo's conviction, saying, "Though the law itself be fair on its face, and impartial in appearance, yet, if it is applied and administered by public authority with an evil eye and an unequal hand, so as practically to make unjust and illegal discriminations, between persons in similar circumstances... the denial of equal justice is still within the prohibition of the Constitution."[83] While this commitment has certainly been eroded by later Supreme Court decisions, especially *McClesky* (1987), the issue is relevant from the standpoint of constitutional meaning and Christian moral principles.

Christians should be deeply concerned about the "equal protection" clause of the Fourteenth Amendment and the consistency with which policies and laws are followed because of how deeply this concern resonates with biblical principles. In the Old Testament, God commanded procedural equality before the law, where Israel's judges were to uphold the principle that "there shall be one standard for you, for the stranger as well as the native" (Lev 19:22). This central idea came replete with command after command to refuse partiality, bribery, and the like (Exod 23:8; Deut 16:19, 27:25; Isa 1:23, 5:23, 33:15; Ezek 22:12; Amos 5:12; Mic 7:3; Ps 15:5; Prov 17:23; 2 Chron 19:6–9), which applies to both money and *services*, offerer and receiver. In Jesus' teaching, we find the Golden Rule: "Do unto others as you would have them do unto you" (Matt 7:12). Policies which allow for such discriminatory practices, administered "with an evil eye and unequal hand," which we can anticipate with reasonable certainty, are hard to morally justify. Arguing that deterrence nevertheless happens might not

---

83. Although the *McClesky v. Kemp* (1987) decision went contrary to this basic principle, the direction of the court is uncertain, and equal choice claims might still be upheld with *McClesky* remaining a judicial outlier, or even overturned. Discussed by Graber, *Rethinking Abortion*, 77–107, and Alexander, *New Jim Crow*, 109–14.

be sufficient moral counterweight. Such policies might be politically possible, but only because a majority of people who can still benefit from the corruption of medicine and law —again, along the lines of race, class, and connectedness—are willing to use statute laws as mere symbols. We will mention the Fourteenth Amendment again when we look at the movement towards state-level targeted restrictive abortion provider (TRAP) laws, and the Texas *Whole Woman's Health v. Hellerstadt* (2016) case.

One major problem therefore raised by the pre-*Roe* gray market in abortion is the vastly unequal treatment women face based on race, class, and connectedness. If there is reasonable belief that this will be the result, what are the moral and legal implications? Graber predicts:

> Recriminalizing abortion will not protect the unborn because pro-life laws on the books are nearly impossible to implement. Criminal measures succeed in practice only when the bulk of the community shares the sentiments embodied by the law. Because more Americans support abortion rights than in the past, localities that recriminalize abortion will experience even greater public pressure not to prosecute competent abortionists than we have seen historically. Fewer police officials will investigate or arrest competent abortionists, fewer jurors will convict them, and fewer judges will impose substantial sentences on them. Citizens and officials hostile to abortion rights will confront increasing numbers of pregnant women who can travel to jurisdictions where abortion is legal or can obtain such drugs as RU-486, a substance that promises relatively safe, self-induced abortions. Significantly, no major pro-life official has announced a plan for preventing the rebirth of the abortion underground.[84]

Graber's sober assessment of the sociology of law enforcement is critical to consider. I am left stunned by his assessment that recriminalizing abortion practice by physicians will not protect the unborn *at all*; I would expect laws on providers to have some small effect, but the confounding effect of a gray market in abortions, and women self-inducing abortion, is completely unnerving. Moreover, Graber's point in relation to privilege and underprivilege based on race, class, and connectedness is essential. We have decades of history in anti-abortion laws where a gray market in abortion emerged, resulting in a *segmented* market involving shades of legality and illegality. We also have years of history with Prohibition with which to compare, when public corruption became endemic because not enough people believed in

---

84. Graber, *Rethinking Abortion*, 73–74; see citations.

the law itself. If law enforcement officers are given wide latitude to police and prosecute crimes, then—similar to policing, prosecuting, and sentencing for drug use in the U.S.—we would expect to see very disparate results along the lines of race, class, and connectedness, which is what the National Advocates for Pregnant Women has already observed in this country. If there is implicit racial bias among health care professionals, which indeed has also been shown already, we would expect to see different levels of accuracy in mandatory reporting.

Troublingly, abortion rates prove to be stubborn despite the position of the law, even in other countries, and multiple reputable studies confirm it. From international data in 2003, researchers published in *The Lancet* that abortion rates in countries where abortion is legal are close to rates in countries where it is not, "suggesting that outlawing the procedure does little to deter women seeking it."[85] Another international study from 2016 published in *The Lancet* found that globally, 25 percent of all pregnancies now end in abortion, and again showing that anti-abortion law does little to reduce the abortion rate.[86] The 2016 study found that in Europe, Africa, Asia, and South America the majority of women who procure abortions are married. Poverty or financial hardship is a major, perhaps the driving, factor for abortion. Examining data to 2017, the Guttmacher Institute found that the presence of anti-abortion laws has a minimal effect on the abortion rate. In countries that make abortion illegal altogether, or only legal to save the mother's life, the abortion rate is 37 per 1,000 women. In countries that allow abortion without restrictions, the abortion rate is 34 per 1,000 women.[87] The preponderance of evidence pointing to the same thing is compelling. These studies strongly suggest that social policies are at least as important, if not more so, in reducing abortion than whether anti-abortion laws exist on the books. In economically developed countries, gestational limits, a mix of waiting and counseling periods required of women seeking abortions, and social policies designed to make childrearing affordable *do* seem to bring down abortion rates.[88]

85. Sedgh et al., "Induced Abortion," summarized by Rosenthal, "Legal or Not," who notes, "The wealth of information that comes out of the study provides some striking lessons, the researchers said. In Uganda, where abortion is illegal and sex education programs focus only on abstinence, the estimated abortion rate was 54 per 1,000 women in 2003, more than twice the rate in the United States, 21 per 1,000 in that year. The lowest rate, 12 per 1,000, was in Western Europe, with legal abortion and widely available contraception." See also Wise, "Abortion Rates."

86. Foster, "Unmet Need."

87. "Induced Abortion Worldwide."

88. Douthat, "What Reduces," also refers to Claeys, "Abortion Legislation," 14, who gives helpful commentary on how to understand abortion rates in various European

As further evidence, health economists Joyce, Tan, and Zhang found that, just prior to *Roe*, women who were financially able traveled great distances to get an abortion.[89] After New York legalized abortion in 1970, including for out-of-state women, many women traveled there. Even after abortion became legally available in six states and Washington, DC, in 1971, 84 percent of all known abortions occurring outside a woman's home state took place in New York. "There was a plane for women who wanted abortions that went from Detroit to Buffalo," said Joyce.[90] Among the twelve states that the study covered (New Jersey, Connecticut, Rhode Island, Massachusetts, New Hampshire, Vermont, Oregon, Michigan, Maine, Indiana and Illinois), with the assumption that New York was the likely destination, researchers found that each extra hundred miles of travel decreased the abortion rate by only 1 woman in 1,000, or made it only 12.2 percent less likely that a woman would procure an abortion. The researchers take note of race, class, and age, and due to limitations of the data, conclude cautiously that non-white, poor, and underage women found it harder to travel, but were uncertain of the magnitude of the impact. They conclude, "A reversal of *Roe* is unlikely to cause drastic increases in unintended childbearing, but it would likely have a significant impact on those with the least resources and wherewithal to adjust . . . we anticipate that the vast majority of women in states without legal abortion would access services in states where abortion remained accessible."[91]

Conversely, one impact of *Roe v. Wade* was that deaths of women from abortion procedures themselves virtually disappeared.[92] Data from other countries bears out this pattern. South Africa, for instance, legalized abortion in 1996, and showed a "90 percent decrease in mortality among women who had abortions."[93] The maternal death rate had already descended remarkably due to other medical advances in the abortion procedures themselves and the treatment for any complications, such as penicillin. So we cannot assign all the credit to *Roe* for doing that in the context of the U.S.[94] But we can assign to *Roe* credit for more equal treatment to women across the board. That was foreseeable, as New York had already learned; the year New York legalized abortion, women of color obtained

---

countries, as well as challenges with data collection.

89. Joyce et al., "Back to the Future?"
90. Thomson-DeVeaux. "When Abortion."
91. Joyce et al., "Back to the Future?" 26, 27.
92. Culp-Ressler, "Americans Have Forgotten."
93. Rosenthal, "Legal or Not."
94. Forsythe, *Abuse*, 203–7.

56 percent of all legal abortions, compared to 6 percent previously.[95] *Roe* also allowed state regulators, physicians, and researchers to work together, in the open, towards the goal of maximizing safety to the mother. The death rate from *legal* abortions fell from 18.6 per 100,000 procedures in 1970 to 0.5 per 100,000 procedures in 1980.[96]

Reflections

The opinion of medical professionals and their willingness to act according to set policies and enforce them among their peers has always driven abortion policy in the U.S. By 1967, an estimated 87 percent of American physicians favored the liberalization of abortion laws.[97] This almost certainly had an impact on the Supreme Court. Examining the uncertainties if *Roe* is overturned highlights the uncertainties of any given policy.

Can abortion be legal for the mother but illegal for the father? Can abortion practices and health privacy laws be modified in such a way to identify paternity? I acknowledge areas of deep concern and uncertainty about going down this road. I am not a physician, lawyer, law enforcement officer, or legislator, but as a citizen, after reading reflections by pro-choice and pro-life physicians in particular, and understanding some of the challenges of managing complex organizations, I am uncertain if *any* policies can be designed well and enforced. The effectiveness of any abortion policy depends first on health care providers being willing to consistently abide by certain policies, which seems to depend on whether physicians themselves believe that we as citizens are doing the best we possibly can to bring down the *overall* abortion rate, even if we cannot bring complete moral clarity to every single instance of abortion.

Law is not a subtle tool, and there are very serious challenges with trying to make legal distinctions involving intimate relationships between men and women, the private professional relationship between a woman and her physician, and the professional relationships between physicians and their colleagues. Would physicians actually feel comfortable identifying the paternity of an aborted fetus? If there were social or financial consequences for the father, would health care providers have the proper motivation and accountability to do that? Can the integrity of the data be assured? Both before and after *Roe*, women are vulnerable to being coerced

---

95. Graber, *Rethinking Abortion*, 67.
96. Graber, *Rethinking Abortion*, 68.
97. Mohr, *Abortion*, 248.

or pressured by others into seeking abortion,[98] which should be accounted for in any policy. What if a man pressures a woman he has impregnated to seek a "back room" abortion to avoid any exposure or financial penalty? Will she have the capacity to seek help from law enforcement? Will law enforcement take her seriously? Will she be able to overcome any racial bias in law enforcement or health care? What will be the mechanism for that? What if a married woman wants to get an abortion without implicating her husband, and their finances? Should a married couple be given the option of a financial penalty or a mandatory vasectomy for the husband? What if a pregnant woman has personal connections via family or friends or wealth to doctors willing to perform secret abortions?

All this adds to the complexity of what we do not know: we do not know how doctors, nurses, and health care administrators will respond to expectations that they function as an arm of law enforcement in this particular way, even if we effectively make abortion legal for the mother and illegal for the father. Will sexism and gender bias in favor of men undermine the policy? Or will the medical profession be largely persuaded by this approach and stabilize their beliefs about accountability?

I am more troubled by the level of certainty that the vast majority of today's pro-life conservatives feel about policy matters. As I have shown in chapters 2 and 3, the claim that many pro-life conservatives make about the fetus being a fully legal human person at the point of fertilization is not affirmed by Scripture itself. Not only does Scripture speak with more than one voice about the topic of when an unborn child should be so regarded, there are other important moral considerations. In this chapter, we have seen that we have strong indications that if we make abortion illegal for the physician, even if the mother is seen as the second victim, then women will search for illegal abortion options once again. Because physicians are the first to see and understand the costs of abortions done by unlicensed providers, including self-induced abortions, we can reasonably expect their opinions to fluctuate based on how much they are exposed to the

---

98. Dworkin, "Coerced Abortions," finds from three studies that "for women in violent relationships, somewhere between a third and half report having experienced some form of reproductive coercion. But even for women in relationships that are not violent, 15 percent report experiencing such controlling behaviors, according to a study of 1,300 women published in the journal *Contraception* in April." An oft-quoted statistic that up to 64 percent of women who procure abortions were coerced in some manner seems to be unreliable, as it originates from the Elliot Institute, whose founder David Reardon claims to have earned a PhD in biomedical ethics, but from an unaccredited institution with no classroom instruction, and which publishes very questionable material. Among human trafficking victims, see Lederer and Wetzel, "Health Consequences." See also Lederer, "Examining H.R. 5411."

costs in women's bodies. They will be caught in moral dilemmas of their own. Moreover, what is the plan to address the disturbing levels of privilege and discrimination in the segmented gray market created by any policy scorned by a substantial portion of the public?

From this vantage point of seeing how anti-abortion law led to unequal and discriminatory practices by medical and law enforcement professionals, and an acknowledgement of the uncertainties inherent in my own proposal as well as those in the proposals of the vast majority of anti-abortion advocates, I reiterate the necessity of approaching abortion from the perspective of broader social and economic policies designed to support childraising. In principle, anti-abortion statutes and child-friendly socioeconomic policies are not mutually exclusive. But in recent times, they have been politically arrayed against each other, perhaps because they reflect different beliefs about "rights" and "deservingness." We will therefore explore socioeconomic policies, and beliefs about those policies, as factors that drive the prevalence of abortion in the U.S. In many ways, it behooves us to consider reinvigorating the Catholic appreciation for the New Deal's social and economic vision, to make childraising more affordable and joyous.

7

God's Gift Economy and the Heretics' Reward Economy

Abortion and Economic Pressure

WHY DO WOMEN HAVE abortions? According to the Centers for Disease Control, married women accounted for 14.1 percent of all abortions in 2016.[1] That statistic suggests that the cost of raising children is a factor even in the conservative ideal of the two-parent family. Of the white women who procured abortions, 16.8 percent were married, meaning 83.2 percent of white women who procured abortions were unmarried. Of the black women who procured abortions, 7.9 percent were married; 92.1 percent of black women were unmarried. Of the "other race" women who procured abortions, 31.9 percent were married; 68.1 percent of other race women were unmarried. It stands to reason that when a woman is a single parent, because of the death, divorce, or desertion of a male partner, economic pressures will factor into her decision-making even more.

In one study conducted by the Guttmacher Institute in 2004, a survey was completed by 1,209 abortion patients at 11 large abortion-providing locations, with 38 women from 4 of those sites giving in-depth interviews. The researchers describe their results thus:

> The reasons most frequently cited were that having a child would interfere with a woman's education, work or ability to care for dependents (74 percent); that she could not afford a baby now (73 percent); and that she did not want to be a single mother or was having relationship problems (48 percent). Nearly four in 10 women said they had completed their childbearing, and almost one-third were not ready to have a child. Fewer than 1 percent said their parents' or partners' desire for them to have

1. Jatlaoui et al., "Abortion Surveillance."

an abortion was the most important reason. Younger women often reported that they were unprepared for the transition to motherhood, while older women regularly cited their responsibility to dependents.[2]

The study itself summarizes some previous research done on the topic, including a 1985 study of 500 women in Kansas, a 1987 study of 1,900 women at large abortion providers across the U.S., and various studies done in Scandinavia. One might raise valid questions about sampling bias. For example, perhaps women who feel pressured by parents or partners are less likely to fill out these surveys. The researchers themselves suggest some limitations of their study as well.[3] Yet studies like these provide us with concrete considerations for ethical reflection, as we approach the Scriptures and the perceptions of Christians about abortion, not simply as an individual, personal ethics issue within a church context, but as a social phenomenon. This means Christians must be thoughtful about how we influence laws that affect economics, especially the standing of women, whether we provide government-subsidized child care and public schooling, and how we encourage men and women to become emotionally mature in the societies in which they live. The issue of abortion therefore requires us to look at all our institutions, not simply the individual choice of a pregnant woman.

Poverty is one significant contributing factor to abortion. One oft-quoted study by Finer and Zolna found that, while the abortion rate for unintended pregnancies stayed the same between 2008 and 2011 (40 percent in 2008 and 42 percent in 2011), the number of abortions declined from 2008 to 2011 because the number of unintended pregnancies declined by 18 percent (from 54 per 1,000 in 2008 to 45 per 1,000 in 2011).[4] This news was roundly welcomed by all. Yet the same study found that women below the federal poverty level had rates of unintended pregnancy at two to three times the national average.

---

2. Finer et al., "Reasons."

3. Finer et al., "Reasons," 118, notes, "This study is subject to some limitations. Our sample is not strictly nationally representative. Also, only 58% of the abortion patients seen by the participating facilities completed the survey, and nonresponse on some variables—notably, income—was high. However, the social and demographic characteristics of respondents were similar to those of two nationally representative surveys, which provides some reassurance that the findings are representative of abortion patients in the United States."

4. Finer and Zolna, "Declines."

B Income as a Percentage of the Federal Poverty Level

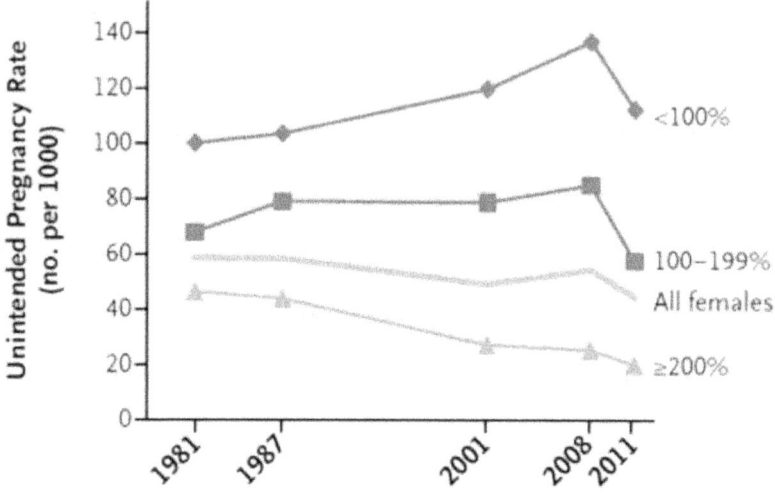

Women who were cohabiting also had rates of unintended pregnancy at two to three times the national average, but the study did not say whether those women were cohabiting because of economic reasons, at least in part. Women whose income was between 100 percent and 199 percent of the federal poverty level had a rate of unintended pregnancy at ~60 per 1,000, still higher than the national average of 45, but the rate had narrowed.

Other data can be integrated with this study to help explain why income and wealth greatly influence the rates of unintended pregnancies. Women worry for their physical safety, are paid ~80 cents for every dollar men are paid in the aggregate (for the same work, the gap is much narrower),[5] or 61.8 cents if they are black, or 54.5 cents if they are Hispanic,[6] are charged more than men for cars, car insurance, and mortgages, and pay higher prices for their clothes, dry-cleaning, haircuts, and even deodorant,[7] so they have physical and economic incentives to live with a boyfriend. Women are more than twice as likely than men to be unpaid caregivers to older adults in the home.[8] Workplace discrimination and family commitments contribute to a

---

5. Gould et al., "Gender Pay Gap"; Hegewisch and Tesfaselassie, "Gender Wage Gap." "State of the Gender Pay Gap."

6. Hegewisch and Tesfaselassie, "Gender Wage Gap"; Mora and Dávila, "Hispanic–White Wage Gap."

7. Hill, "6 Times."

8. Johnson and Weiner, "Profile."

large gap in poverty rates between women and men that begins at eighteen to twenty-four years of age, narrows with age but never closes, and then widens dramatically in old age.[9] After having a child, 23 percent of mothers are out of the workforce compared with 1 percent of fathers,[10] giving women less time to build their resumes and skills. It goes without saying that past childhood experience, parents' circumstances, lack of educational or job opportunities, debt, despair, discrimination against her as both worker and consumer, racial discrimination, and other financial pressures influence women to become sexually active and face an unintended pregnancy.

As Angela Davis observed, "When Black and Latina women resort to abortions in such large numbers, the stories they tell are not so much about the desire to be free of their pregnancy, but rather about the miserable social conditions which dissuade them from bringing new lives into the world."[11] Although it is true that poor and ethnic minority women's educational and economic prospects improve when abortion services are accessible (e.g., black women's high school and college completion rates increased by 1.3 and 9.6 percent, respectively, in states offering abortion services in the early 1970s[12]), Davis cautions us to read abortion statistics without assuming we know how the minds of the women procuring them. Does an abortion come with earlier or more access to jobs, higher wages, or better schools? Perhaps that is what an abortion means to white women of means. But black and Hispanic women of less means might not think of an abortion as a trade-off to other pursuits. They may believe they are sparing a child from sharing the miseries they cannot escape.

Unfortunately, Christians—especially white evangelicals—are more likely than the general public to blame economic hardship on people's own character. In one 2017 study done by *The Washington Post* and the Kaiser Family Foundation, among Americans who identified as atheist, agnostic, or without a religious affiliation, 65 percent said "difficult circumstances" were to blame for a person's poverty, compared to 31 percent who said "lack of effort" was chiefly to blame. By comparison, 46 percent of all Christians, and 53 percent of white evangelicals said that "lack of effort" was the chief cause.[13]

9. Gaines, "Straight Facts."
10. Gaines, "Straight Facts."
11. Davis, "Racism," discussed by Roberts, *Killing*, 302.

12. Angrist and Evans, "Schooling," 75–113. Cited by Institute for Women's Policy Research website.

13. Zauzmer, "Christians," and DeVega, "Christian Charity." Perhaps this contributes to why other communities are criminalizing homelessness: see Fessler, "U.S. Cities," who says in some cities, we are seeing "an increase in laws to criminalize homelessness, to make it illegal to camp, to panhandle, to, in fact, feed people—large groups

If those percentages hold constant nationwide, then the odds are 3.2 to 1 that white evangelicals, compared to the nonreligious, will say "lack of effort" causes poverty. Many white evangelicals and other conservatives criticize the welfare state because they believe it subsidizes an anti-family ethic, *promotes* abortion, while creating dependency on government "handouts."

Conservatives view economic hardship, therefore, as the appropriate *consequence* for immoral behavior, but other groups—not just today's so-called "liberals" but the older wave of Catholic pro-life activists as well—view economic hardship as a major *driver* of certain immoral behaviors, including abortion. Catholic doctors and clergy watched abortion rates climb during the Great Depression, for instance. At that time, poverty clearly contributed to abortion rates, which is why the Catholic New Deal Democrats fought for structural changes to the economy, anti-poverty policies, and stronger social safety nets. We saw a hint of the pressure of financial uncertainty more recently. Following the financial crisis of 2008–09, 44 percent of women reported wanting to reduce or delay their childbearing because of their financial uncertainties. Google searches of self-induced abortion jumped.[14] As manufacturing jobs went overseas, men became less likely to marry.[15] This question about economics is therefore central. If the U.S. is *not* a true meritocracy—if financial success and poverty are not simply the result of "effort," if income and wealth inequality is actually the *intended design* of public policy, and economic vulnerability is just as much a cause of abortions as the result—then conservatives must reexamine the relationship between government policies and individual responsibility and correct the difference between reality and their perception. Already, "meritocracy" is an untruth that is being applied unfairly, not least because socioeconomic policies also affect the *child* who has done nothing to "merit" anything one way or the other.

When we ask what a Christian ethical response to abortion *as a social phenomenon* might be, we must consider *all possible angles that have a bearing on abortion rates*. That is the difference between considering abortion as an issue for social ethics, as opposed to an issue simply for personal ethics. In this chapter, I constrain myself to addressing two angles that are borne out of specifically Protestant *heresies*. I do think the cost of child-raising is very deeply impacted by these heresies, even though most Christians do not recognize these factors as heresies per se, and have not thought very hard about how to repent from them.

---

of people—outside."

14. "Real Time Look." Stephens-Davidowitz, "Return."
15. Autor et al., "When Work Disappears."

Heresy #1: John Locke's Theory of Meritocracy

The first heresy concerns John Locke and his interpretation of Genesis 1, which impacts our view of work, land, and home. American Protestant evangelicals, and perhaps Americans in general, have a tradition of interpreting wealth as *reward*, and not as *gift*. Much of the credit for this goes to John Locke, Enlightenment philosopher, political economist, and dominant influence on the framers of the United States Constitution. Since European Protestants could not look to the Catholic popes' "Doctrine of Discovery"[16] as their justification for seizing Native American land, they turned to a novel interpretation of the biblical text. In his work *Second Treatise of Civil Government*, Locke draws out his notion of "property" and those entitled to property from his novel reading of Genesis 1.

> God gave the world to men in common; but since he gave it them for their benefit, and the greatest conveniencies [sic] of life they were capable to draw from it, it cannot be supposed he meant it should always remain common and uncultivated. He gave it to the use of the industrious and rational, (and labour was to be his title to [land];) not to the fancy or covetousness of the quarrelsome and contentious.[17]

Locke argued that according to Genesis 1, God gave land in common at first, but intended a shift of ownership to those who practice a certain kind of "labor." In Locke's mind, God's command to subdue and cultivate the land was synonymous with European-style settled agriculture and "improvement." For Locke, labor entitled people to property because, in his reading of Scripture, God did not want the land to remain "uncultivated" and "wild," but wanted the land to be used for "fruitful" production. Therefore, Locke asserted that land should be given to those who are "industrious" and "rational"—those capable of "working the land."

---

16. The "Doctrine of Discovery" refers to a body of papal declarations from 1452 into the early 1500s. They began with Pope Nicholas V, *Papal Bull Dum Diversas of June 18, 1452*, who said: "We . . . granted among other things free and ample faculty to the aforesaid King Alfonso—to invade, search out, capture, vanquish, and subdue *all Saracens and pagans* whatsoever, and other enemies of Christ wheresoever placed, and the kingdoms, dukedoms, principalities, dominions, possessions, *and all movable and immovable goods* whatsoever held and possessed by them *and to reduce their persons to perpetual slavery*, and to apply and appropriate to himself and his successors the kingdoms, dukedoms, counties, principalities, dominions, possessions, and goods, and to convert them to his and their use and profit." Translation sourced via http://www.doctrineofdiscovery.org/ (emphasis mine). See Charles and Rah, *Unsettling Truths*.

17. Locke, *Second Treatise*, ch. 5, sec. 41.

Not incidentally, Locke intentionally misrepresented Native Americans, even though he had better information in his own personal library.[18] He said they were not entitled to the land because they did not "labor in" or "improve" it.[19] Using the white European as the exemplar of labor and industry, Locke asserted that Native Americans waste the gift of rich lands. In his view, they refused to improve it by labor. In effect, John Locke became one of the first white people to accuse non-white people of "laziness"; his ideology of land acquisition required it.

Locke's influence on the United States is hard to overestimate.[20] The tradition which followed John Locke contributes to white American evangelicals, especially, having a meritocratic-retributive ethic in public life. I suspect Locke's framework is one reason why they often take the view that economic hardship is the appropriate consequence for those who choose to have sex and get pregnant. They tend to feel especially unsympathetic to sexually active single women. To them, economic hardship is the appropriate consequence for committing fornication and getting pregnant outside of marriage.

But is this view biblical? Prior to John Locke, moreover, Christians read Genesis 1 very differently. They learned from Genesis 1 that every human being was supposed to have a share of "dominion" in creation, and be nourished by creation, as well.

Basil of Caesarea (AD 329–79):

> That bread which you keep belongs to the hungry; that coat which you preserve in your wardrobe, to the naked; those shoes which are rotting in your possession, to the shoeless; that gold which you have hidden in the ground, to the needy. Wherefore,

---

18. Arneil, "'All the World,'" shows how Locke relied very selectively on travel journals and books in his library for information about Native Americans to portray them unfavorably.

19. Locke, *Second Treatise*, ch. 5, sec. 41 says, "There cannot be a clearer demonstration of any thing, than several nations of the Americans are of this, who are rich in land, and poor in all the comforts of life; whom nature having furnished as liberally as any other people, with the materials of plenty, i.e. a fruitful soil, apt to produce in abundance, what might serve for food, raiment, and delight; yet for want of improving it by *labour*, have not one hundredth part of the conveniencies we enjoy: and a king of a large and fruitful territory there, feeds, lodges, and is clad worse than a day-labourer in England" (italics mine).

20. Miura, *John Locke*, writes a devastating and integrated analysis of Locke, summarizing post-colonial scholarship on Locke, and proposes a non-conquest-oriented liberalism. For a shorter treatment, see Quiggin, "John Locke," who argues that Locke legitimized expropriation and enslavement, noting that the SCOTUS case *Keto v. City of New London, Connecticut* (2005) relied on faulty Lockean assumptions, which is indicative of how much American jurisprudence rests on Locke.

as often as you were able to help others, and refused, so often did you do them wrong. If that were true which you have affirmed, that you have obeyed the commandment of love from youth, and have given to everyone as much as to yourself, whence, I ask, have you all this wealth? For the care of the poor consumes wealth, when each one receives a little for one's needs, and all owners distribute their means simultaneously for the care of the needy. Hence, whoever loves the neighbor as oneself, will possess no more than one's neighbor.[21]

Gregory of Nyssa (c. AD 335–c. 395):

You condemn a person to slavery whose nature is free and independent, and in doing so you lay down a law in opposition to God, overturning the natural law established by Him. For you subject to the yoke of slavery one who was created precisely to be a master of the earth, and who was ordained to rule by the creator, as if you were deliberately attacking and fighting against the divine command.... What price did you put on reason? How [much money] did you pay as a fair price for the image of God? For how [much money] have you sold the nature specially formed by God? God said, "Let us make man in our image and likeness."[22]

Ambrose of Milan (AD 340–97):

Why do the injuries to nature delight you? For all has the world been created, which you few rich are trying to keep for yourselves.... When giving to the poor, you are not giving him what is yours; rather, you are paying him back what is his. Indeed, what is common to all, and has been given to all to make use of, you have usurped for yourselves alone. The earth belongs to all, and not only to the rich.... You are paying back, therefore, your debt; you are not giving gratuitously what you do not owe.[23]

Why do you drive out the fellow sharers of nature, and claim it all for yourselves? The earth was made for all, rich and poor, in common. Why do you rich claim it as your exclusive right? The soil was given to the rich and poor in common—wherefore, oh, ye rich, do you unjustly claim it for yourselves alone? Nature gave all things in common for the use of all; usurpation created

---

21. Basil of Caesarea, quoted by Avila, *Ownership*, 50. See also Basil the Great, *On Social Justice*, 69–70.
22. Gregory of Nyssa, *Fourth Homily*.
23. Ambrose of Milan, quoted by Avila, *Ownership*, 66.

> private rights. Property hath no rights. The earth is the Lord's, and we are his offspring. The pagans hold earth as property. They do blaspheme God.[24]

John Chrysostom of Constantinople (AD 340–407):

> Can you, ascending through many generations, show the acquisition [of your wealth to be] just? It cannot be. The root and origin of it must have been injustice. Why? God in the beginning did not make one man rich and another poor.... Are not the earth and the fullness thereof the Lord's? If, therefore, our possessions are the common gift of the Lord, they belong also to our fellows, for all the things of the Lord are common.[25]

Augustine of Hippo (AD 354–430):

> The superfluities of the rich are the necessaries of the poor. They who possess superfluities, possess the goods of others.[26]

> God commands sharing not as being from the property of them whom He commands, but as being from His own property.[27]

Gregory I of Rome (c. AD 540–604):

> In vain do they think themselves innocent who appropriate to their own use alone those goods which God gave in common; by not giving to others that which they themselves receive, they become homicides and murderers, inasmuch as in keeping for themselves those things which would alleviate the sufferings of the poor, we may say that every day they cause the death of as many persons as they might have fed and did not. When, therefore, we offer the means of living to the indigent, we do not give them anything of ours, but that which of right belongs to them. It is less a work of mercy which we perform than the payment of a debt.[28]

Thomas Aquinas (AD 1225–74), the most esteemed of Roman Catholic medieval theologians, continued this interpretation:

---

24. Ambrose of Milan, quoted by Sinclair, *Cry for Justice*, 397.

25. John Chrysostom, quoted by Avila, *Ownership*, 94–95. See also Van de Weyer, *On Living Simply*.

26. Augustine of Hippo, *Expositions*, on Ps 147:12, quoted by Sinclair, *Cry for Justice*, 398. See also Ward, "Porters," for an impressive, concise, and thorough summary of Augustine's teachings on wealth and ownership.

27. Augustine of Hippo, quoted in Avila, *Ownership*, 141.

28. Gregory the Great, quoted in Herron, *Caesar and Jesus*, 111–12.

> In cases of need, all things are common property. There is no sin in taking private property when need has made it common.[29]

The quotes above, most of which are ably discussed by Charles Avila, demonstrate the Orthodox and Catholic stance on Genesis 1, that God gifted the earth to all human beings in common, *before* they did any work or technological development, and *whether* they did any at all. Gregory of Nyssa's invocation of "natural law" is especially intriguing, since he anchors it in Genesis 1, using it as an *argument* against chattel slavery and *for* broad distributive economic justice. Ambrose's perception that "nature" is violated by poverty expresses the same idea. This stable tradition of interpretation confirms that John Locke's view of Genesis 1, and all Protestants who followed him, were following a specific Protestant error. John Locke effectively reversed the entirety of the Christian tradition before him. For most Christians, for most of church history, God gave land to humanity with "boundaries" (Gen 10; Deut 32:8; Amos 9:7; Acts 17:26–27). For Locke, humans could step over those boundaries by being more "productive" than the people who lived there before. Prior to Locke, for most Christians, the land was common, and need made all things common. For Locke, labor made *common* things *private*. Lockean thought contributes to the American culture of overwork, ecological devastation in the name of productivity, and suspicion that other hard-working immigrants will "replace" nativists.

God's Gift Economy and "Housing First" Vision

What patterns of land, work, gift, and merit do we see in Scripture? From creation, God called human beings to create "garden homes" for all the children who would come from us. He provided a "garden home" for Adam and Eve as a starter home. God even provided four rivers diverging from Eden (Gen 2:10–14) so human beings would have an easier time spreading the garden over the world. This is the most straightforward way to make sense of how God gave human beings a commission to multiply and fill the earth (Gen 1:26–28, 2:18–25) and also to cultivate and keep the garden (Gen 2:15). In other words, God had a "Housing First" policy, which had children in mind. Land, nutrition, clean water, safety, beauty, models for creativity—all of the basic forms of wealth—were not "rewards" given to human beings for their "hard work." They were gifts. The gifts we received from God, we were to "pay it forward" to others.

---

29. Thomas Aquinas, *Summa Theologica*, II-II, Q 66, Art 7.

Under the Sinai covenant, God brought the people of Israel back into a garden land, to give that garden land to their children, because their children were his children. God called Israel to be a renewal of Adam and Eve, in a sense, of what humanity should have been. While God let Israel develop and keep animals, clothes, crops, and currency, he established land as belonging to Israel's *future children*. God designed the Jubilee Year to re-gift the garden land to all his children, hitting an economic reset button regarding the land (Lev 25). Through the Jubilee arrangement, God prevented children and grandchildren from receiving all the advantage and disadvantage they could inherit. The Israelites were to set free any brethren in indentured service so they could go back to their own family land; this made them like God, because God delivered Israel out of Egypt and into the garden land (Lev 25:55). Along with Christian biblical scholars and ethicists like Christopher J. H. Wright, we can consider many aspects of this unusual practice.[30] For the Israelites, land was many things: the gift of God given through one's parents complementing God's wise commands (Prov 1:8); the basic form of wealth for people and animals; the source of agriculture and therefore nutrition and health; a school in which to learn wisdom; a first job where you contribute your labor; the source of the ability to be generous (Deut 24); the source of the ability to employ others who might need to learn something, work off a debt, recover from hardship, or were coming from a gentile background to faith in the God of Israel; a physical place in the community and therefore a major contributor to mental health; the potential source of unusual blessings from God (Deut 11); and perhaps most importantly, *the inheritance they gave their children*. By pushing the Jubilee Year reset button, in fact, God acted as though he were bringing every new generation of Israelites into the garden land anew, for the first time. God forbade an Israelite from stockpiling other people's land for his own children. God claimed all Israelites as his children, in his role as supreme gift-giver. In effect, God called all Israelite parents to recognize that *his* relationship to their children took precedence over *their* relationship to them. Before your children are *yours*, they are *his*.

There can be no "minimizing" the Jubilee principle on the supposed grounds that Israel did not practice it elsewhere in the biblical record. Leviticus 25 in particular, and God's garden vision in general, reverberates throughout the Scriptures. The plot of the book of Ruth revolves around the role of the kinsman-redeemer (Ruth 3:2–12; 4:1–6), which is only found in Leviticus 25:25–27. Ezekiel's vision of the new temple (Ezek 40–47) was based on the numbers associated with the Jubilee Year, found especially in

---

30. Wright, *Old Testament Ethics*.

Leviticus 25:10–15 because of its association with the idea of return from exile and displacement. Chronicles explained the seventy years of the Babylonian exile as the time needed for God to give the land its sabbaths (2 Chr 36:20–21), which only comes from Leviticus 25:1–7. Even if Israel did fail to practice the Jubilee Year in its fullness, which is unknown, the principle was integrated into the fabric of Israel's institutions and literature. Israel's prophets defended this vision (Isa 1–5, 58–59; Ezek 16, 22; Mic 4:1–5, 6:8; Amos 5; etc.), even against rapacious kings, like when King Ahab took land from Naboth, an average Israelite (1 Kgs 21). The psalmists sang of it, to nurture an ethical vision for the community in the people while they were in worship and giving thanks to God (Pss 1, 15, 37, 112, 119, etc.).

To the gentiles, God declared that Israel's laws would be "wisdom" (Deut 4:5–8). Strikingly, when Israel went into captivity among the gentile empires, the most tangible impact they had was influencing gentiles to care for the poor. In Egypt, Joseph cared for all of Egypt and the peoples roundabout, benefiting especially "the little ones" of both Israel (Gen 47:12) and Egypt (Gen 47:24). In Babylon, Daniel told Nebuchadnezzar to show "mercy to the poor" throughout the Babylonian Empire (Dan 4:27). Being the people of God among the gentile empires meant caring for the poor and vulnerable in some way that resembled God's vision within Israel. Job, in his cultural context, might have led a small clan and used some physical force: "I delivered the poor who cried for help, and the orphan who had no helper . . . I broke the jaws of the wicked and snatched the prey from his teeth" (Job 29:12, 17).

Embedded in God's vision for Israel, especially the Jubilee Year, is that children should not inherit the fundamental disadvantages that their parents and grandparents could bring down on them. While it is true that the Ten Commandments said that in some cases God will cause the consequences of the sins of the parents to extend across three or four generations (Exod 20:5–6), that was not an everlasting principle. It referred to Israel's exile, which took shape ultimately under Babylon, although there were less devastating precursors to it (e.g., Num 13–14). We can be quite certain of this because the "new covenant" promised on the other side of the exile said that children will no longer bear the consequences of their parents' sins (Ezek 18). Today, in an American society which is supposed to be "meritocratic," we can ask the question, "What have children done to merit all the advantages and disadvantages we put on them?" Since the answer is obviously "nothing," we should be very critical of inequality caused by intergenerational wealth transfers.

Jesus focused our attention on the day he will return and share God's garden planet with all God's children (Rom 8:18–25). He transformed Israel's "people on the land" experience to a "people around the table" experience with regards to wealth and community (Luke 6:21–49, 12:13–34, 14:7–35, 15:1–32, 16:19–31, 18:15—19:10), complete with regular storytelling around a meal (Luke 24:13–30; 1 Cor 11:17–24). To call and gather people into God's family, Jesus welcomed "children" (both biological and spiritual children), and challenged those people who were not willing to give to *other people's children*. The double story told by Matthew, Mark, and Luke of the children, followed by the rich ruler (Matt 19:13–30; Mark 10:13–31; Luke 18:15–30), demonstrates Jesus' mission to all and his challenge to us.

Jesus framed his commandments within the storyline that he was undoing the "hardness of heart" which had set in from the fall. In the story just before this (Matt 19:3–12), Jesus told the Pharisees that his teaching about marriage was a restatement of the original creation, from Genesis, before the fall (Gen 1:27 quoted in Matt 19:4; Gen 2:24 quoted in Matt 19:5). Jesus saw the divorce clause in the Sinaitic covenant (Deut 24:1–4 quoted in Matt 19:7) as a concession to Israel's "hardness of heart" (Matt 19:8), which set into humanity after the fall. "Hardness of heart" and its downstream effects of sin, adultery, and divorce (Matt 15:18–20) would not have affected human beings in the original creation. The Sinai covenant had to allow for "hardness of heart" with respect to marriage and divorce.

Jesus believed that "hardness of heart" held Israel back from even more economic generosity. Matthew alone uses the word "regeneration" (*palingenesia*) in his account of the rich young ruler (Matt 19:28; cf. Mark 10:13–31; Luke 18:15–30). The word "regeneration" refers to Jesus restoring human nature and human relationships back to the design God intended originally in the first "generation," the creation in Genesis.[31] Jesus tied the "regeneration" to his enthronement: the time when "the Son of Man will sit on his glorious throne" and the apostles will "sit upon twelve thrones, judging the twelve tribes of Israel" (Matt 19:28).[32] Jesus connected his enthronement and the "regeneration" to his resurrection when God gave him Adamic "authority over all things in heaven and earth" (Matt 28:16–20).[33] The Sinai covenant,

---

31. The word occurs only twice in the entire New Testament: once here in Matthew and once in Titus 3:5, where Paul speaks of "regeneration" by the baptismal "washing" which is a Christian practice reminding us of the waters of creation in Genesis 1.

32. The prophet Daniel envisioned that the Son of Man would rise enthroned above the other powers to vindicate Israel (Dan 7:13–14). Daniel's vision was built on the Genesis story of Adam in creation, in which Adam and all humanity were given authority by God. Therefore, the seating of the Son of Man "on his glorious throne" has Adamic authority as its primary concern. Jesus notably referred to Daniel several times just prior to his crucifixion (Matt 24:15, 27, 30, 39; 25:31; 26:64), showing that "the coming of the Son of Man" to the "throne" of authority was uppermost in his mind.

33. Whereas Luke is more explicit that Jesus' enthronement occurred at his

therefore, preserved in Israel only *part* of what God intended from the creation order for all human beings. But which parts?

Jesus went beyond the Jewish law on the what, when, how, where, and why of giving. Regarding "what" to do: Moses taught the Israelites to "generously lend" to fellow Israelites in need (Deut 15:8); Jesus commanded people to "give" to anyone in need without expectation of repayment (Matt 5:42, 6:12–15). On "when": Moses commanded the Israelites to forgive debt on certain cycles of time (Lev 25:40–41; Deut 15:1–17); Jesus made the "when" all the time, as apparently he believed that debt-forgiveness, generosity, and hospitality did not happen frequently enough! On "how": Moses told the Israelites to be generous while staying anchored on their ancestral land; Jesus told people to let go of the idea of a ethno-nationalist territory and go around the world, trusting God to provide, as the story of the rich ruler shows us (Matt 6:19–34, 19:27–29). Regarding "where": Moses taught Israel to stay in the land because God used the land as a tangible resource (Deut 11); Jesus told his followers to go into all the world (Matt 28:16–20) because God would use the whole world to resource his mission and his people (Matt 6:25–34). Finally, on "why": Moses taught the Israelites to set their brethren free because God delivered them out of bondage in Egypt and into the garden land (Lev 25:55); Jesus taught his disciples to remember his death and resurrection (Matt 26:26–29), by which he invites all people out of our bondage to sin and into the freedom of being true children of God. Jesus taught his disciples to relate to others and wealth to show the fall being undone, as if "hardness of heart" had never set into us.

The apostle Paul envisioned the far-flung church as one community journeying through a "wilderness period" together, relying on God's provision, waiting for a "new garden land" when Jesus returns (2 Cor 8–9). He concretely believed that the gentile Christians should share resources with the poverty-stricken Jewish Christians in Jerusalem and Judea. He reasoned, for one, that all Christians are informed by Jesus as exemplar—Jesus,

---

ascension (Acts 1:1–10), Matthew simply connects Jesus' authority to his resurrection, commissioning of the disciples, and to the downfall of the temple in Jerusalem in AD 70 as the sign of vindication that Jesus and his followers are now the new "temple-people" of God. Jesus and his disciples will henceforth be the explicit measure by which Israel is "judged," that is, truly constituted and defined. In other words, the "regeneration" in Matthew's and Paul's usage (Titus 3:5) is not in the far distant future when Jesus comes again. It is the age that dawned with Jesus' resurrection, which is unfolding all over the world through the mission of the disciples in the power of the Holy Spirit. The regeneration—the restoration of God's creation order, his true humanity, and his design for relationships—is happening right now. At his crucifixion, Jesus was crowned king of Israel, albeit in exile and ironically (Matt 27:27–37), in anticipation of God bestowing him "all authority" in his resurrection.

who "though He was rich, yet for your sake He became poor, so that you through His poverty might become rich" (2 Cor 8:9). Paul also reasoned that all Christians live in a period of God's timeline akin to biblical Israel's time in the wilderness, when God gave provision roughly equally to all his people, and all received a daily share of manna. Paul said:

> For this is not for the ease of others and for your affliction, but by way of equality—at this present time your abundance being a supply for their need, so that their abundance also may become a supply for your need, that there may be equality; as it is written, "He who gathered much did not have too much, and he who gathered little had no lack." (2 Cor 8:13–15, quoting Exod 16:18)

In other words, Paul reminds Christians that God is generous, too, and will richly provide for their needs (not all their wants or wishes) (2 Cor 8:10–15). Of course, this means working and sharing as opposed to stealing (Eph 4:28) or being outright lazy (2 Thess 3:10–13). It is absolutely true that the biblical writers look at one's job as one's way of earning a living and contributing to a community. But it is also absolutely true that they look at jobs as gifts, given to them, so people could participate in their community and feel their contributions were welcomed. The apostle's quotation from the manna story in Exodus seems quite strategic: God gave manna to Israel to provide their daily needs, for people to gather as well as eat, as we wait for God to bring us into his new garden land when Jesus returns (1 Cor 11:17–24).

As God invites everyone to become his adopted children in Christ (John 1:12, 3:16–21), why would Christians not work towards an economic vision where every human child is honored not just in the womb, but through their whole lives? Can we tilt our economic and social system so that a home and a job might be things people have to work to stay in, sure—but to start, what if a home and a job are gifts to every child by the community at large? Can Christians build a society so that each child might taste as a small gift what God gifts in full? How might Christians contribute to a gift economy, not just a reward economy?

Conservative Evangelical Ethics: Two Mistakes

When we look at the major voices shaping conservative evangelicals in America, we must appeal to them to correct some mistakes. Wayne Grudem's 2010 book *Politics according to the Bible* is a fairly good representation of an educated, conservative Christian approach to politics and power.

Grudem taught for twenty years at Trinity Evangelical Divinity School, where he was chairman of the department of biblical and systematic theology. He is a best-selling author in the subject of systematic theology in the Reformed tradition, a former president of the Evangelical Theological Society, the general editor of the English Standard Version translation of the Bible, and cofounder of the Council of Biblical Manhood and Womanhood. In *Politics*, Grudem seeks to be very comprehensive. In his chapter on economics, Grudem believes that God gave people the unlimited right to pass on economic inheritance to their children (Prov 19:14; Num 27:8–11) and that government should not interfere with that (Ezek 46:18). He says, "The Bible clearly takes the side of individual ownership of property. My conclusion is that the estate tax should be permanently repealed."[34] How did he arrive at this conclusion, so diametrically opposed to mine, and Christians' prior to John Locke?

Grudem quotes the Old Testament command against coveting (Exod 20:17) as assuming "private property." He takes this as a foundational point, despite the fact that God said of Israel's land, their fundamental economic resource, "The land, moreover, shall not be sold permanently, for the land is Mine; for you are but aliens and sojourners with Me" (Lev 25:23). The principle of "private property" did not extend to the land. Grudem's failure to recognize this fact—which is rooted in his functional agreement with John Locke—then impacts the rest of his scholarship. Grudem condemns public ownership of anything as a form of communism, on the grounds that it stands against the principle of private property. He fails, however, to note that the entire Levitical priesthood was a publicly funded group of not only religious leaders but scholars, educators, public health workers (Lev 13–15), welfare administrators (Deut 14:22–29), and peacekeepers through the cities of refuge, which were akin to publicly owned land (Num 35:11–24); Grudem also neglects to consider that God's commands to the Israelites to share with the poor and the foreigner in their communal festivals (Deut 14:28–29) and practices of agriculture (Deut 24:17–22) placed "human rights" over "property rights," as did God's limits on the power of disproportionate wealth (Deut 24:6–15) and lending capital (Deut 15:1–17). Grudem believes taxes should be as low as possible for all individuals, and lower than 20 percent for corporations, despite the fact that the material support for the Levites and the poor was quite substantial—probably greater than a third of all agricultural output. Grudem quotes 1 Samuel 8:10–18 (the warning of Samuel to Israel that a king will tax, take, and enslave) as evidence that big government power is always an evil, despite the fact that the Davidic kings were praised

---

34. Grudem, *Politics*, 309.

when they executed justice, especially in defending the poor (Ps 72:1–13; Prov 28:3, 15–16; 29:14) and promoted true worship. Not to mention the fact that judges, courts, elders, education, and public health roles all existed before the formal Davidic state did and were paid for by Israel according to ordinances given by God. Grudem is simply mistaken when he reads Leviticus 25 and concludes that "the estate tax should be permanently repealed." For people to have the unlimited ability to accumulate wealth—especially in real estate—and pass it on to their children is precisely the opposite of what Leviticus 25—and all of Scripture—says.

Jerry Falwell, founder of Liberty University and cofounder of the Moral Majority political advocacy group, serves as an earlier example of a conservative evangelical trying to read "free market capitalism" out of Scripture. In his 1980 book *Listen, America!* Falwell portrays the U.S. as a Christian nation in decline. He seeks to make personal Christian piety the foundation for economic, and even military, strength. My purpose here is not to evaluate all parts of Falwell's vision, but one part only: what Frances FitzGerald says about Falwell's use of Proverbs to link his version of religious-cultural conservatism to economic conservatism. "The free enterprise system is clearly outlined in the Book of Proverbs," said Falwell.[35] FitzGerald notes, "He opposed almost all forms of assistance to the poor, including food stamps, on the grounds that welfare programs sap the biblically mandated work ethic."[36]

Without dwelling on Falwell's approach, however, we can maintain that drawing a straight line from "hard work" in Proverbs to "free market capitalism" is not responsible. It is true that Proverbs supports the idea of "hard work" and "accountability" (e.g., Prov 10:4). Proverbs, after all, assumed the context of biblical Israel and its land practices. In the Sinai covenant, Israelites had to work their inheritance of family land, of course. But what system ensured that they had land? Like every other Old Testament passage about Israel's wealth, Proverbs takes the family-land vision as its starting point and foundation, and the Pentateuch must be understood *prior* to reading Proverbs. Proverbs 23:10–11, for example, recalls the laws of family and land:

> Do not move the ancient boundary,
> or go into the fields of the fatherless.
> For their Redeemer is strong;
> He will plead their case against you. (Prov 23:10–11)

---

35. Falwell, *Listen, America!* 12–13, 97–98, 104, 132 discussed by FitzGerald, *Evangelicals*, 305.

36. FitzGerald, *Evangelicals*, 305–6.

The "ancient boundary" refers to the family-based land boundaries which God decreed from Moses (e.g., Lev 25:10). These are the same boundary lines of which the Psalmist said, "The lines have fallen to me in pleasant places; my *inheritance* is beautiful to me" (Ps 16:6). The "fields of the fatherless" refers to the orphan's right (along with the alien's and widow's) to glean in anyone's field (Deut 24:19–22). But a field harvested once by the apparent "owner" becomes the orphan's field. This was not "charity" but legal justice. Indeed, although the tone of Proverbs is that of "advice wise and good," the subject matter is the very commands of God to Israel in the Sinai covenant on relational and economic matters (Prov 1:8). This is even more true when we find that Proverbs 28:7–9 affirms Jewish law's ban on interest rate lending, as I will explore below.

So "inheritance" in Proverbs includes God's "reset button" of Jubilee Year land redistribution to its original intended "ancient boundaries" and nothing beyond it. Proverbs certainly does not imply that parents should have the ability to pass down unlimited amounts of wealth and property to their children, especially when they gained it at someone else's expense, but even when they gained it "fairly." There were other forms of wealth, to be sure: animals, crops, clothing, artifacts, currency, etc. To the Israelites, however, land was not "private property" to be bought and sold on a "free market." Quite the contrary, God distributed a basic level of wealth *and work* through the land to each generation of Israelites, and each family. No one can make the case from Scripture that "pure meritocracy" or "free market capitalism" is the ideal economic system for Christians to support.

Heresy #2: John Calvin's Embrace of Interest Rate Lending

The second heresy concerns lending money with interest. "Payday lenders" are the most obvious example of how lending with interest can be harmful. "Payday lenders" charge exorbitant interest rates to people who are already financially desperate.

> While an interest rate may be presented by a lender as 15 percent, for instance, it actually is only for the two-week period until a person's next payday. The annual interest rate may be 400 percent or more, making it difficult for the borrower to repay the loan. It requires years for some people to pay off their debt. Predatory payday lending "grinds the faces of the poor into the ground," ERLC President Russell Moore said in a written statement announcing the coalition's formation. "As Christians, we are called by Jesus, by the prophets and by the apostles to care

for the poor, individually, and also about the way social and political and corporate structures contribute to the misery of the impoverished."[37]

We might be tempted to compartmentalize this problem as just affecting a few people facing hard times. Indebtedness, though, is a massive problem, not just individually, but in the economic system as a whole. It deeply affects how expensive child-raising is. We face mortgage debt, college debt, medical debt, car debt, and credit card debt. Why is this?

Lending money at interest (usury) was forbidden by the ancient Jews and the early Christians. The ancient Greeks and Romans frowned on it, too. Moses forbade it among the chosen people, three times (Exod 22:26–27; Lev 25:35–38; Deut 23:19). Moses instituted protections for a poor indebted person, such as keeping his collateral pledge at night, since it was usually his cloak which he needed to stay warm (Deut 24:10–24). Why? The basic problem with charging someone interest on a loan was what it implied about the relationship: why should loaning money, especially to the poor as an act of compassion, yield a profit? If a poor person has asked for a loan, usury is seen as extortion, a taking advantage of another person's misfortune. It was deemed inappropriate as measured against the type of relationship God envisioned for human beings, which involved compassion, generosity, and hospitality. Hence it violated God's relational vision and restorative principle of justice.

To God, indebtedness is a form of slavery, and while sometimes people do need to ask for a loan and pay it back, usury magnifies indebtedness, worsening it. By contrast, God wanted his people to be free to serve him. Israelites were permitted to loan money at interest to non-Israelites (Deut 15:3); apparently, there was a risk that the non-Israelite person might run off without paying it back. But otherwise, the Israelites were forbidden from charging interest. Israelites were not to be indebted to other people, or keep people indebted to them; they were to release indebted servants at the latest seven years from the point of indenture (Deut 15:1–17; cf. Exod 21:2), or on the Jubilee Year (Lev 25:39–41, 54–55).

King David condemned usury as being incompatible with godliness (Ps 15:5). King Solomon followed suit (Prov 28:7–9). Habakkuk and Ezekiel condemned interest rate lending as exploitative (Hab 2:6–7; Ezek 18:10–18, 22:12). Isaiah probably had it in mind when he cried out, "Loosen the bonds of wickedness . . . undo the bonds of the yoke . . . let the oppressed go free" (Isa 58:6). Nehemiah rebuked nobles in Israel for charging an interest rate

---

37. Strode, "Payday Loans," and Robbins, "Churches Step In."

on money loaned out to the poor; he called them to honor the standard Jewish law principle of abolishing usury (Neh 5:1–15).

Jesus deepened the posture. While Moses spoke of lending without interest, expecting to be repaid (Deut 15:8), Jesus spoke of giving without any such expectation (Matt 5:42). He taught his followers to pray, "Forgive us our debts, as we forgive those indebted to us" (Matt 6:14). And he told parables about forgiving outrageous amounts of money (Matt 18:21–35; Luke 7:36–50). This seems to align with Jesus' disclosure of God as being Father, Son, and Holy Spirit (Matt 3:13–17; 28:18–20). If we are to be like God and bear his image, we must reflect in our relationships the love within the Trinity (John 17:20–24). It is impossible to imagine the Son asking the Father, "May I share in your Spirit?" and the Father responding, "Only if you give me back more!" The very opposite is true: The Father generously gives us more than we ask or imagine (Luke 11:9–13; Eph 3:20; 1 Cor 2:9), including himself.

Even though many people see this biblical criticism of usury as outdated, the church prior to John Calvin was united in the opinion that lending money at interest was still a sin. Among other things, it exploited the poor, although that was not the only reason:

> On the iniquity of payment merely for the act of lending, theological opinion, whether liberal or conservative, was unanimous, and its modern interpreter, who sees in its indulgence to interesse the condonation of interest, would have created a scandal in any age before that of Calvin. To take usury is contrary to nature, for it is to live without labor; it is to sell time, which belongs to God, for the advantage of wicked men; it is to rob those who use the money lent, and to whom, since they make it profitable, the profits should belong; it is unjust in itself, for the benefit of the loan to the borrower cannot exceed the value of the principal sum lent him; it is in defiance of sound juristic principles, for when a loan of money is made, the property in the thing lent passes to the borrower, and why should the creditor demand payment from a man who is merely using what is now his own?[38]

The early Christians believed Jesus universalized the prohibition against Israelites lending to fellow Israelites at interest. The Council of Arles (AD 314, twelfth canon), First Council of Nicea (AD 325, seventeenth canon), Council of Laodicea (AD 372), First Council of Carthage (twelfth canon), and the Apostolic Canon (forty-fourth canon) and many others forbade clergy from

---

38. Tawney, *Religion*, 43, and Kerridge, *Usury*, 79–95.

trafficking in usury. John Chrysostom, bishop of Antioch from AD 389, and later archbishop of Constantinople, thundered against it.

The church called on political leaders to develop public policies in line with the Christian understanding that usury was exploitative. Thus, the Emperor Justinian (AD 482–565), the great organizer of Byzantine law, drove down legal interest rates to 4–8 percent for normal loans "depending on the status of the creditor" and 12.0–12.5 percent for maritime loans because of the greater risk.[39] Charlemagne (AD 747–814), however, made usury illegal for everyone. By the Synod of Pavia in AD 850, the united church in the eastern and western Roman Empire was decided and influential enough to declare that all lay people practicing usury would be excommunicated. The councils of the twelfth and thirteenth centuries forbade it to both clergy and laity and laid down the punishments for such behavior. Usurers were not to be given communion or Christian burial, their offerings were not to be accepted, and clergy who failed to punish them were to be suspended until they made satisfaction to their superior.[40] On paper, the Catholic teaching on social ethics continues to criticize interest-rate lending. Devout Muslims also avoid it because the Qur'an forbids them.

John Calvin and his theological heirs reversed centuries of Christian opinion about usury and embraced it.

> He advised his followers outside of Geneva to practice business in ways that enhanced social life in their respective locales, even prompting a German merchant with business overseas to exchange credit for a profit, the very tactic that Calvin had condemned in Geneva's tight credit market.[41]

In fairness, Calvin and his fellow Reformers tried to restrain usury, too, as did the Calvinist Puritans after them. But those caps proved to be based on thin sentiments which erected no real bulwark:

> Preachers subtly shifted the meaning of the sin of usury from any exchange of credit for a profit to mean-spirited lawsuits against impoverished debtors. . . . In sum, they began to legitimate the very exchange techniques once denounced as vile and inhumane: using credit as a commodity.[42]

39. Sydney and Sylla, *History of Interest Rates*, 55.
40. Tawney, *Religion*, 44 n. 60; 46 n. 65.
41. Valeri, "Calvin," 24; see also 37–38 n. 12.
42. Valeri, "Calvin," 27. Valeri also writes on 28, "Boston's Samuel Willard refrained from eschatological surmises and made the Calvinist-mercantilist connection more directly. He argued that the customary prohibitions against usury amounted to old Catholic superstitions long made anachronistic; that merchants who set their prices by

Their need for resources to fund the Reformation (for Calvin) or colonies (for the New England Puritans) led them to make alliances with merchants and bankers. In doing so, they reversed centuries of theological agreement about the problem of usury. Eventually, a predatory "buyer beware" logic took hold.

Reflection

If poverty was a factor that early Christian leaders viewed as excusing infanticide, and presumably abortion, it behooves us to look carefully at what drives poverty today. Surely there are many factors. But the fact that uniquely Protestant heresies are responsible for driving many into poverty should alarm us. Displacing people from their land on the basis of "productivity" or "merit," as if Genesis 1 meant that, was a mistake taught by John Locke. And subjecting people to potentially unlimited indebtedness was the outgrowth of John Calvin's teaching that the anti-usury laws of Scripture are no longer in effect. The former is the basis for race-based colonialism, land conquest, and genocide. The latter opened the doorway to the predatory financial capitalism of today's big banks. High abortion rates may be only one result of this combination of toxic ideas. Yet Christians are still called to care for all children, for they are all God's.

---

the market merely followed the laws of providence; and that the host of new techniques for making a profit in the market, from using lawyers and factors to trading bonds and securities, were godly practices."

8

How Christian Heresy Contributes to Economic Anxiety and Abortion

Inflated Child-Raising Costs as a Symptom of the American Racist-Reward Heresy

IN CHAPTER 7, I examined two heresies: John Locke's interpretation of land seizure and John Calvin's interpretation of the anti-usury laws. How, then, do these two heresies combine to raise the cost of child-raising and make abortion economically attractive? How might American Christians meaningfully repent with an eye to making child-raising more affordable, even for single mothers, to lower abortion rates? In this chapter, I will focus on housing in the U.S., not just because mortgage and rent are such large portions of household budgets, but because John Locke's heretical idea of "work for your land/home/belonging" and John Calvin's heretical embrace of interest-rate loans come together in the U.S. housing market quite clearly.

Americans might have a popular belief that housing is merely part of the free-market system of supply and demand, with minimal government intervention. In reality, American housing patterns have been a thoroughly government-funded and government-backed effort controlled by people committed to white supremacy. That vision itself was shaped by a third Christian heresy: white supremacy. White supremacy has its origins in Spanish Catholic fears that Jews were lying about conversion when pressured by the Spanish Inquisition,[1] in Catholic and Protestant colonialism when skin color became a virtual indicator of intelligence and criminality,[2] and in the notion that the biblical "curse of Ham" applied to

---

1. Carter, *Race*, explains how biblical Israel was a multi-ethnic faith, but Jewishness was interpreted according to the "blood theory of race" in Spain during the Spanish Inquisition and henceforth.

2. Jennings, *Christian Imagination*, discusses how Christian missionaries and

black people, so white Christians were justified in carrying out the never-ending retributive justice of God against them.³ Over the decades, white supremacist government policies backfired. While originally designed to keep whites and non-whites segregated so that white people could own homes, and have those homes appreciate in value, this distinctly American pattern (compared to other countries) now threatens to reduce most of the American population to a state of desperate indebtedness, where

---

theologians interpreting Americans and Africans developed the modern theories of "race" with which we now interact, as well as assumptions and stereotypes about intelligence and culture. For a brief summary of Jennings's work, see Yang and Nagasawa, "How 'Race' Emerged."

3. Goldenberg, *Curse of Ham*, 161–62 notes: "Ham was the ancestor of black Africans, that Ham was cursed by God, and that therefore Blacks have been eternally and divinely doomed to enslavement . . . A 1969 study of the educational materials (Sunday School lessons, primers, teachers' manuals, catechisms, etc.) of the American Lutheran Church found that the church had interpreted Gen 9:25–27 in a way that justified Black slavery and/or segregation, and it had done so both intentionally and inadvertently. 'There is no doubt left that the "curse of Ham" has been taught to our [i.e., American Lutheran] children as well as our adults, and application has been made of this curse to our black population. And this teaching is one which has been handed down from generation to generation.' The Lutherans were not alone. The Curse of Ham was commonly taught and believed in America up to recent times. As James Baldwin, the African American writer, said: 'I knew that, according to many Christians, I was a descendant of Ham, who had been cursed, and that I was therefore predestined to be a slave.'" "In a study of the mythic world of the antebellum South vis-à-vis Blacks, Thomas Peterson showed that the notion of Blacks as 'the children of Ham' was a well-entrenched belief: 'White southern Christians overwhelmingly thought that Ham was the aboriginal black man.' It was a notion well-entrenched in the North as well as the South. And it was a notion that went back, at least, to the year 1700, when the Puritan Samuel Sewall published one of the earliest anti-slavery tracts and argued against the idea that 'these Blackamores are the Posterity of Cham, and therefore are under the Curse of Slavery.'" Kendi, *Stamped*, 20–21, notes the presence of the "curse of Ham" theory in the notable Persian scholar Tabari (AD 838–923), but otherwise judges it to be a speculative idea in the medieval period. Slavery was too broad and diverse to give the "curse of Ham" real credence. However: "The shift to solely enslaving Black people, and justifying it using the curse of Ham, was in the offing. Once that shift occurred, the disempowered curse theory became empowered, and racist ideas truly came into being" (Kendi, 21). The "climate theory" of skin pigmentation "fell apart when [English traveler and writer George Best] saw on an Arctic voyage in 1577 that the Inuit people in northeastern Canada were darker than the people living in the hotter south" (Kendi, 31). He therefore advocated for the "hereditary" idea of the "curse of Ham" theory. This notion was rather thoroughly imbibed by the English Puritans like William Perkins (Kendi, 33), Richard Mather (Kendi, 33), Richard Baxter (Kendi, 48), Cotton Mather (Kendi, 59–64, 68–76). John Locke put forward the idea that "West African women had conceived babies with apes" (Kendi, 50). Some white Christians in Barbados even developed the idea that there was another human ancestor other than Adam from which their enslaved African people were descended (Kendi, 51).

children are seen as the biggest of all economic liabilities, and abortion, therefore, becomes economically attractive.

Since the early 1900s, white Americans designed zoning laws requiring new homes to be single-family houses, rather than the multi-family houses that enabled extended families to stay together, and made houses more affordable because of rental income.[4] Single family housing kept "those people" out through sheer unaffordability. At many cases, white people wrote "racial covenants" into the deeds of houses, which prevented a new buyer from selling to a black person or family; such covenants were enforced by the courts.[5] Housing prices in all-white or mostly white neighborhoods stayed high, but eventually contributed to today's housing crisis and car-fueled climate crisis.[6]

In 1911–14, the average down payment for (new and existing) single-family houses in twenty-two cities was almost 68 percent of the purchase price, and 46 percent of homes were acquired debt free.[7] Politicians committed to white supremacy and racial segregation expanded the role of mortgages to disguise the racism behind housing policy at the federal, state, and municipal levels. Franklin Delano Roosevelt created the Federal Housing Administration with the support of Southern democrats who were white supremacists. They required the FHA to have a whites-only stipulation.[8] The FHA was committed to racially segregated schools, warning that if children

---

4. Silver, "Racial Origins of Zoning." Anderson, "Maps" notes, "It was in 1924 that Portland voters approved the city's first zoning plan in a citywide vote, four years after having narrowly rejected the idea. It was a turbulent moment in Oregon politics. In 1922, the resurgent Ku Klux Klan had swept to electoral victory across the state, putting its members in the governor's mansion, the House speakership, and controlling the Multnomah County Commission. In 1923, the Klan-backed Alien Land Bill, banning Japanese nationals from owning property in Oregon, sailed through the Klansman-led state legislature with just one dissenting vote. A parallel national movement was afoot. A White House task force convened in 1921 was pushing U.S. cities to pass zoning codes. The task force's official documents never mentioned race, but its members were "outspoken segregationists" who (as documented by Richard Rothstein) wrote elsewhere that zoning could help segregate people by race."

5. Massey, *American Apartheid*. See Mapping Prejudice at https://www.mappingprejudice.org/ as an example of Minneapolis, Minnesota.

6. Wamsley, "Oregon Legislature," and Trickey, "How Minneapolis."

7. Collins and Margo, "Race and Home Ownership."

8. Rothstein, *Color of Law*, 64–65, notes that in 1934, the FHA "insured bank mortgages that covered 80 percent of purchase prices, had terms of twenty years, and were fully amortized. To be eligible for such insurance, the FHA insisted on doing its own appraisal of the property to make certain that the loan had a low risk of default. Because the FHA's appraisal standards included a whites-only requirement, racial segregation now became an official requirement of the federal mortgage insurance program."

are compelled to attend school where the majority or a considerable number of the pupils represents a far lower level of society or an incompatible racial element, the neighborhood under consideration will prove far less stable and desirable than if this condition did not exist.[9]

The FHA, through ratings and "red-lining," influenced how much houses in these neighborhoods appreciated, and how much mortgage financing was available to people who lived in certain neighborhoods.

After World War II, the Veterans Administration adopted the same standards as the FHA. So the federal government, through the mechanism of mortgage lending, subsidized white flight into new suburbs, especially for white GIs returning home from World War II. Black families received only 2 percent of those federally subsidized loans from 1945–59. By 1968, when Congress passed the Fair Housing Act and authorized the Department of Housing and Urban Development to try to undo some of the racial segregation built into the fabric of American home ownership, white families had a $120 billion head start, and Americans were more in debt.

Over time, this government strategy combining private indebtedness and racial segregation shifted enormous power from consumers to banks, which led to distortions in the housing market. Two additional legal changes in how we treat mortgage debt happened in the 1970s: (1) the Equal Credit Opportunity Act, which allowed banks to calculate mortgage eligibility based on two incomes rather than just one; and (2) the federal tax code was changed so people could deduct interest on mortgages, which not only distorts the housing market, but benefits the wealthy and penalizes the poor.[10] This incentivized people to take on more debt. Real estate developers simply built bigger, more expensive houses.[11]

9. Rothstein, *Color of Law*, 65–66.

10. "What are the Tax Elements" explains, "The deductions and exclusions available to homeowners are worth more to taxpayers in higher tax brackets than to those in lower brackets. For example, deducting $2,000 for property taxes paid saves a taxpayer in the 39.6 percent top tax bracket $792, but saves a taxpayer in the 15 percent bracket only $300. *Additionally, even though they only represent about 20 percent of all tax units, those with more than $100,000 in income receive over 85 percent of the mortgage interest deduction tax benefits. That difference results largely from three factors: compared with lower-income homeowners, those with higher incomes face higher marginal tax rates, typically pay more mortgage interest and property tax, and are more likely to itemize deductions on their tax returns*" (italics mine). See also Hanlon, "Mortgage Interest," who says, "Households with incomes between $40,000 and $75,000 receive, on average, $523 from the mortgage interest deduction. Households with incomes above $250,000 receive $5,459, or more than 10 times as much." See also Chait, "How Conservatives," and Thompson, "Shame."

11. Average home size data distilled from "Average Size of US Homes" and

1950: 983 square feet

1960: ~1,200

1970: ~1,400

1980: 1,825

1990: 2,165

2000: 2,509

2010: 2,692

2019: 2,806

Do the extra home office, guest room, and wine cellar contribute that much to happiness? Were Americans that unhappy with smaller homes in the 1950s to 1970s? I doubt it. People were (and are) not just trying to get into one nice house. They are looking to buy an entire experience: a place in a respectable community with a good school, and hopefully, growing home equity to pay for their kids' college tuition. This is, in part, a gamble. With residential segregation already built on a racist foundation, and public schools dependent on local property taxes, developers could charge vastly more for these houses and banks implicitly colluded with them. For some white people, even the desegregation of public community swimming pools was too much: they built private, backyard swimming pools and private club pools.[12] The price of housing skyrocketed:

"Characteristics of New Housing."

12. Wiltse, *Contested Waters*, and Appelbaum, "McKinney," who summarizes the trend thus: "Backyard pools and private clubs only proliferated after municipal pools were forcibly desegregated."

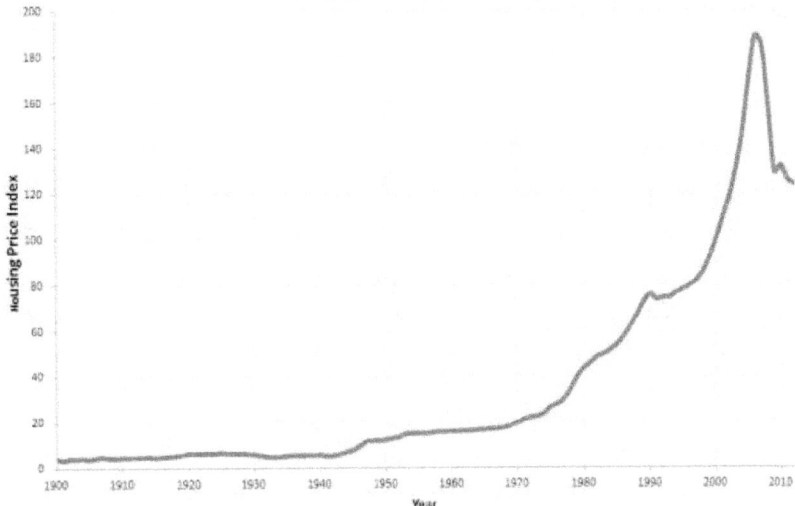

U.S. Housing Price Index Since 1900

Source: Observations (ObservationsAndNotes.blogspot.com)

The loose financing policies that once made it easy to own a home boomeranged to make it hard. Meanwhile, people in lower-income brackets suffered when Reagan abruptly changed course:

> Between 1980 and 1988, the Reagan administration decreased funding for the Department of Housing and Urban Development (HUD), the federal government body that oversees public housing, by 76%. Predictably, when the government began to starve public housing programs of necessary resources, public housing infrastructure deteriorated and quality of life for many residents declined.[13]

Banks also adjusted in cunning ways to anti-discrimination laws. The banks' policy of racially discriminatory exclusion became a policy of "predatory inclusion." Starting from the late 1970s, when foreclosures in black communities first began to rise, to the 2008–09 financial crisis, bank lenders issued predatory loans betting that black homebuyers would default on their

---

13. Gardner et al., "No Shelter," note, by contrast, "The Housing Act of 1949 [called] for the government to realize 'as soon as feasible . . . the goal of a decent home and a suitable living environment for every American family.' Federal legislation over the next several decades continued to support public housing and the government's role in maintaining it. By 1973, the US had more than 1.5 million units of subsidized housing, a threefold increase from 1961."

mortgages.[14] The financial crisis of 2008–09 disproportionately devastated black and brown homeownership and wealth.[15]

	White (median household)	Black (median household)
2005	$134,992	$12,124
2009	$113,149	$5,677

We are now seeing more American citizens squeezed by this economic philosophy which originated in the strategic use of debt in the service of white supremacy. The Federal Reserve Bank's quantitative easing policy from 2009 kept housing prices artificially inflated, rewarding boomer homeowners but penalizing asset-poor, already indebted millennials.[16]

Moreover, the U.S. housing market is, in principle, an international market at the expense of American citizens. From 2010 on, Chinese businessmen, investors from Canada, the U.K., Mexico, and India, and oil oligarchs from Russia and Saudi Arabia purchased real estate in the U.S. *with cash*—often with the very dollars that the U.S. Treasury used to repay its own debt to them, *with interest*. They further overheat the housing market, placing home ownership further out of reach for the average American while

14. Taylor, *Race for Profit*.

15. Bouie, "Crisis," observes, "In 2005, three years before the Great Recession, the median black household had a net worth of $12,124. Yes, this was far behind the median white household—which had a net worth of $134,992—but it was a huge improvement from previous decades, in which housing discrimination made wealth accumulation difficult (if not impossible) for the large majority of African-American families. By the official end of the recession in 2009, median household net worth for blacks had fallen to $5,677—a generation's worth of hard work and progress wiped out. (The number for whites, by comparison, was $113,149.) Overall, from 2007 to 2010, wealth for blacks declined by an average of 31 percent, home equity by an average of 28 percent, and retirement savings by an average of 35 percent. By contrast, whites lost 11 percent in wealth, lost 24 percent in home equity, and gained 9 percent in retirement savings. According to a 2013 report by researchers at Brandeis University, 'half the collective wealth of African-American families was stripped away during the Great Recession.'"

16. Shedlock, "Ben Bernanke" summarizes an article by McWilliams, "Quantitative Easing," writing, "Fed chairman Ben Bernanke's 'cash for trash' QE scheme drove up asset prices and bailed out the baby boomers. The cost of course, was pricing millennials out of the housing market. Unorthodox policy penalizes the asset poor. What assets do millennials have? Hardly any. Instead they are saddled with mountains of student debt which, thanks to president George W. Bush, could no longer be discharged in bankruptcy. The Bankruptcy Reform Act of 2005 would have better been called the Debt Slave Act of 2005. Then, when the Great Financial Crisis hit, the Fed came along bailed out the banks, bailed out the bondholders, bailed out Fannie Mae, and bailed out the asset holders in general, leaving millennials mired in debt unable to afford a house."

foreigners pay for houses in lump sums. Absolutely reliable data is hard to come by, as money sources can be disguised, but as of 2014, foreigners purchased 35 percent of all American real estate purchases, spending roughly $92.2 billion.[17] In 2017, even despite a strong dollar, foreigners bought real estate in the U.S. at record levels: $153 billion of real estate, an increase of 49 percent over the previous year.[18] John S. Allen, after observing the same push for home ownership in the U.K. under Margaret Thatcher, and the same problems resulting, argues that big banks exploit a human psychological desire for security and status.[19] In the U.S., bankers and capital investors learned to prey on black people. Now they simply prey on everyone, and invite their foreign counterparts to do the same.

Economic hardship is a matter of great concern to Christian ethics, and not just because economic hardship influences abortion rates and family stress levels. Generations later, wealth leveraged by homeownership is still the number one reason why white people have so much wealth and black people do not.[20] The number one factor in building wealth is not getting a college degree.[21] It is not raising children in a two-income married household.[22] It is not working more or spending less.[23] It is the leverage that white families have through home ownership, including through this

---

17. Rapoza, "These Are the Foreigners."

18. Olick, "Foreigners." For more information, see Levin, "Data Dig."

19. Allen, "Big Home Ownership Lie."

20. E.g., in Boston, "close to 80% of whites own a home, whereas only one-third of U.S. blacks . . . are homeowners," according to Munoz, et al., "Color of Wealth." Shin, "Racial Wealth Gap." Collins, "Wealthy Kids."

21. Traub et al., "Racial Wealth Gap," find that equalizing college graduation rates between whites and people of color would close the wealth gap by 1 percent for blacks and 3 percent for Latinos. Gaddis, "Discrimination," finds blacks who graduated from elite universities have the same chance in the job market as whites who graduated from less selective schools. In addition, black graduates are offered lower starting salaries and less prestigious starting jobs.

22. "Family Income" notes 15.2 million children living in poverty also live in married, two-parent families, and 16.7 million live with one parent. Traub et al., "Racial Wealth Gap," 7–8 find, "According to data from the Survey of Consumer Finances, the median white single parent has 2.2 times more wealth than the median black two-parent household and 1.9 times more wealth than the median Latino two-parent household." See also Badger, "Children with Married Parents," summarizing Howard and Reeves, "Marriage Effect."

23. Smith, "How to Reduce," features very good household data, though his proposal needs further consideration and is certainly not the only form of reparations being considered.

decades-long affirmative action government program for white people to create white suburbs.[24]

Meanwhile, white people in other parts of the country benefit from earlier waves of big government programs. The Homestead Acts of 1862 "were the most extensive, radical, redistributive government policy in American history," and the land transferred from Native Americans to whites, and excluding blacks, keeps paying dividends: in the year 2000, around 46 million people—about a quarter of the adult U.S. population—were descendants of Homestead recipients.[25] Blacks, on the other hand, were denied the forty acres and a mule originally promised them by Reconstruction, and commitment to the 1867 Southern Homestead Act was so dysfunctional, only approximately 4,000 to 5,500 black people out of 4 million newly freed blacks were given land grants, and only 6 percent of the land originally allocated was used.[26] Other big government interventions on behalf of white people can be mentioned: land grant colleges which allowed states to segregate facilities and funds;[27] discriminatory financing via the USDA to white farmers but not black which resulted in 98 percent of black farmers being dispossessed;[28] etc. All this attests to big government policies which tilted the scales towards white people.

As of 2013, a white high school dropout has more wealth than a black or Hispanic college graduate. An article titled "White High School Dropouts Are Wealthier Than Black or Latino College Graduates"[29] shows the following chart:

---

24. Traub et al., "Asset Value of Whiteness." Coy, "Big Reason."

25. Merritt, *Masterless Men*, 331.

26. Merritt, *Masterless Men*, 330. Williams, "Homestead Act," 10. Foner, *America's Unfinished Revolution*, 246, used the lower estimate of 4,000.

27. *Colleges of Agriculture*, 1.

28. Newkirk, "Great Land Robbery."

29. Bruenig, "White High School Dropouts," and Kurtzleben, "White High School Dropouts."

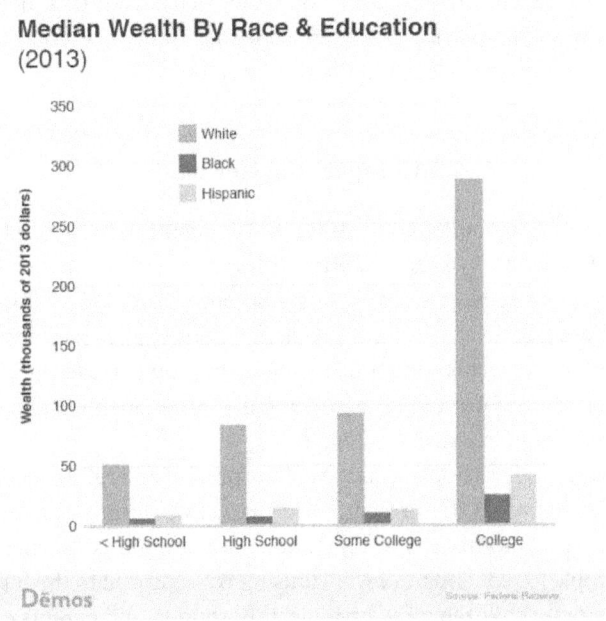

How can this be true in a society which claims to be a "meritocracy"? Confronting these facts makes us reevaluate our national mythology: the U.S. is not a "pure meritocracy," and never has been.[30] I am perfectly willing to grant that almost everyone worked hard. But their work did not earn them *equal results*. People experience life and results differently based on their zip code, if not the color of their skin outright. When children go to public schools, they greet the wealth disparities caused by residential racial segregation in the very place that is supposed to level the playing field for them, because public schools are funded largely by local property taxes.[31] People experience

---

30. McNamee, *Meritocracy Myth*, aptly says in the preface to the fourth edition, "We did not suggest that individual merit is a myth, or that it has nothing to do with who gets ahead and who falls behind. Instead, we made the case that the presumption that *the system as a whole* fundamentally operates on the basis of merit in determining who gets what and how much is a myth" (italics mine). McNamee helpfully examines non-merited benefits and disadvantages—economic, social, and cultural—that people *inherit*, and do not *earn*.

31. Spatig-Amerikaner, "Unequal Education." Illing, "Schools." "State Education Budgets." Some States have recognized that their public school systems have so much inequality that they violate the Fourteenth Amendment of the U.S. Constitution. See Harris, "Judge, Citing Inequality," who notes, "The current system 'has left rich school districts to flourish and poor school districts to flounder,' Judge Moukawsher said, betraying a promise in the State Constitution to give children a 'fair opportunity for an elementary and secondary school education.' . . . Bridgeport . . . has nearly eight times

police very differently by zip code—when they step outside their door,[32] when they receive a wellness visit,[33] or even while they sit on their couch eating ice cream[34]—in ways that are hardly "fair." And so on.

A Comparison: Germany

Germany's housing policy contrasts to housing policies in the United States. Eamonn Fingleton, a writer for *Forbes*, titles an article, "In World's Best-Run Economy, House Prices Keep Falling—Because That's What House Prices Are Supposed To Do." As of 2012, German house prices had decreased by 10 percent in real terms compared to 1982. That compares to the UK, where real prices rose by more than 230 percent in the same period.[35] How did Germany accomplish this? And why?

Germany views housing as part of the present and future labor market. Housing is linked to the present labor market because people need to be able to move to another city or region to take a new job, so Germany incentivizes people to rent and not own. Housing is also linked to the future labor market because children grow up in neighborhoods, and parents care about the quality of local schools. Therefore, Germany's policymakers oversee new development very carefully.

> A key to the story is that German municipal authorities consistently increase housing supply by releasing land for development on a regular basis. The ultimate driver is a central government policy of providing financial support to municipalities based on an up-to-date and accurate count of the number of residents in each area.[36]

This more carefully managed system results in housing developers working under different incentive structures than in the U.S.:

---

the population of nearby New Canaan, [where] property . . . is worth more than $1 billion more." New York faced a similar lawsuit in 2006, Kansas in 2016. Michigan has debated the problem.

32. Edwards et al., "Risk of Being Killed," finds that African Americans are 2.5 times more likely to be killed by police than white people. See Mock, "What New Research Says."
33. Tatum, "Fort Worth Police."
34. Martinez and Fernandez, "Trial Opens."
35. Fingleton, "In World's Best-Run Economy."
36. Fingleton, "In World's Best-Run Economy."

> In the German system moreover, house-builders rarely accumulate the huge large land banks that are such a dangerous distraction for U.S. house-builders like Pulte Homes, D. R. Horton, Lennar, and Toll Brothers. German house-builders just focus on building good-quality homes cheaply, secure in the knowledge that additional land will become available at reasonable cost when needed.[37]

The German approach to housing compares favorably with the American housing market, which is often imagined to be a "private market"—but wrongly so.

Does making child-raising more affordable reduce the rate of abortions? We might take a lesson from Germany here, too. As of 2010, Germany's abortion rate for women aged fifteen to forty-four years was 6.1 abortions per 1,000.[38] As of 2011, the U.S. abortion rate for women aged fifteen to forty-four years was just under 17 abortions per 1,000–almost three times higher. That should surely give us pause. On the one hand, it may be somewhat difficult to calculate exactly how much cost of living pressures—housing in particular—contribute to women getting abortions. On the other hand, it is fairly intuitive that there is a real relationship there.

Student Loan Debt and Medical Debt

No discussion of child-raising in America would be complete without at least mentioning the problem of overwhelming college student loan debt and, now, health care debt. In higher education, third party lenders—either the Department of Education or a private bank—are willing to make sizable loans to the student, so colleges and universities, in turn, *simply raise their tuition*. For every dollar the government gives in Pell Grants, colleges simply raise their tuition by 55–65 cents.[39] Universities expand their real estate footprint, build stunning gyms, make their dining services more expensive, etc. Student loan debt rose 157 percent from 2007 to 2018, and as of 2018, 44 million people owe money for their student loans, their average debt being $35,000.[40]

Even worse, for-profit colleges target (often with deceptive promises) lower-income families, Hispanic and black communities, those who might be first in their families to go to college, women, and single parents, including

---

37. Fingleton, "In World's Best-Run Economy."
38. "World Abortion Policies 2013."
39. Kristian, "Study: Federal Student Loans." Lucca et al., "Credit Supply."
40. Gold, "Who's at Fault."

those who are twenty-five years old and older—precisely the demographics that are most concerning in relation to unintended pregnancies and abortion. Even though the IRS says, "For-profit certificate programs do not pay off for the average student,"[41] the government has done little to shut them down, regulate them, or make alternatives more affordable. It is perhaps telling that Education Secretary Betsy DeVos, who stands in the Calvinist Dutch Reformed Church tradition, working for an administration that purports to be anti-abortion, delayed debt relief for nearly 180,000 students (disproportionately women, black, and Hispanic) who were lied to by for-profit Corinthian Colleges and ITT.[42] DeVos delayed so long she was sued by these students in June 2019, then finally reached a settlement in April 2020.[43]

The American people are now $1 trillion in medical debt.[44] Because people are willing to become indebted, drug companies charge higher prices for medicine, hospitals raise the price of care. Financiers looked at hospitals as possible cash-cows, and a furious merger and acquisitions wave began in the 1980s under Reagan's loosening of merger law that consolidated hospitals; as Matt Stoller notes, that is when "costs in American health care began exploding."[45] In economic terms, there is asymmetrical information and an element of gambling involved with both higher education and health care. People feel enormous pressure to buy a college education or top-quality health care, even though no one is certain how much these products *should* cost. People are risking their children's future and their own lives; they are therefore willing to pay a lot of money. Predatory corporations raise their prices when they find Americans, uncertain and anxious, willing to sink further into debt.

Reflection

I return to the study by Finer and Zolna mentioned at the early part of chapter 7.[46] For women below the federal poverty level to have rates of unintended pregnancy at two to three times the national average strongly suggests that for many women, financial hardship is not the *consequence* for having sex outside of marriage, or the *consequence* for not being proactive about birth control and getting one's tubes tied. Financial hardship is the *cause*, the *driver*,

---

41. Gold, "Who's at Fault." Harris, "Lifelong Cost." Berman, "Former For-Profit."
42. Douglas-Gabriel, "Courts Cleared."
43. Douglas-Gabriel, "DeVos Reaches Settlement."
44. Ashton et al., *End Medical Debt*, also discussed by Uyghur, "Medical Debt."
45. Stoller, *Goliath*, 380.
46. Finer and Zolna, "Declines."

the *motivating context* to see the support of one man, or even the affection of a child, as an oasis of personal connection in a world that is unremittingly cruel and anonymously harsh. The history I narrated above is directly relevant to abortion, again, because poverty and economic vulnerability encourage women—especially those who are poor, and/or black or Hispanic—to view living with a boyfriend as increasing their odds of survival. Rates of abortion are higher among black and Hispanic women than white women, but it is absolutely hypocritical to criticize black and brown communities for having higher abortion rates while supporting past policies or maintaining current ones that lopsidedly benefit white Americans. Meanwhile, white Americans constitute 42 percent of Americans in poverty,[47] and 30 percent of white children are born out of wedlock.[48] The structure of the economy impacts the cost of child-raising and, in turn, pressures low-income women to make survival-oriented choices, and influences even stable, two-parent families to view abortion as *financially attractive.*

Within American political discourse, therefore, Christians need to do some truth-telling. The economy is not simply the aggregation of individual choices. It has not been a laissez-faire affair. It followed various policies that had white supremacy in common. It was designed to be predatory, and now it consumes us. Christians must therefore call for more structural reform of the economy—especially in housing and banking—so we would not be prey. Repenting of the long-held heresies of the "myth of meritocracy" and the acceptability of interest-rate lending requires it.

Some say abortion is the modern-day expression of ancient child sacrifice. Not only do we take a consumeristic approach to sex, they say, we take a consumeristic approach to *everything*. One narrative blames this on the sexual freedom movement of the 1960s. Another narrative would blame the sexual freedom movement itself on earlier lies told about race and nation, money and power, and what happens when young people started to see through the lies. When young heroes who wanted change were assassinated (JFK, MLK Jr., RFK) and others were sent off to the Vietnam War, a war many did not believe in, and while a nuclear war loomed in the background at any moment, what else could people conclude? Why would they focus their sexual energy in more long-term directions? Our political and economic system wants people to consume, while cold corporations of immortal immorality seek *to consume us*. If our society simply views people as both consumers and the consumed, then many will consume, *even at the expense of their own children,* and *even their children themselves.* Perhaps

47. Kidd, "White Poverty."
48. DeParle and Tavernise, "For Women Under 30."

people were not just disappointed by standard lies, but *heresies*. The ancients told us that heresies invent gods who consume us.

To bring down abortion rates, not to mention to correct our complicity in heresy, Christians could adopt much more child-friendly, family-friendly, and planet-friendly policies. Dare we even take bold steps towards clean renewable energy? Towards renewing air, water, and land? Might we all feel excited to give our children and grandchildren a good inheritance in the garden planet?

Maybe we can make home ownership more broadly affordable to all. Maybe we can change zoning laws to allow for more multi-family "gentle density" housing. Pondering what we could regain by living in extended family units, even conservative commentator David Brooks said wistfully, "The Nuclear Family Was a Mistake."[49] Maybe we can prevent foreign capital investors from buying American real estate. If we are xenophobic, that would be a better use for that energy. Why not give restitution to black Americans for past housing discrimination by giving them access to zero percent interest loans directly from the Federal Reserve if they are purchasing a first home? Why not also extend that to all people who have incomes under twice the poverty level? Perhaps we could design a public bank supported by taxpayers (if banks are "too big to fail," we do that anyway) but returning all profits into our own community. Perhaps comprehensive reforms to the financial system and tax codes are still possible.

Perhaps it's not too late to support efforts by the Department of Housing and Urban Development to desegregate neighborhoods. Perhaps we could close the opportunity gap. And support "Housing First" programs wherever possible to alleviate homelessness? Perhaps we could give all our children green spaces and public parks, good schools and libraries.

Could we think of a job as a gift that we give to our children before we think of it as an impersonal process and corporate expense that is cheaper to ship overseas? Perhaps we could rebuild a "democracy of small businesses" as was envisioned by the American antitrust tradition and especially the New Deal, so that the "citizen as producer" might flourish. Might people actually feel more connected to each other through the contributions we make at work? Might employment and wages and satisfaction be higher?[50] Could we support equal pay for equal work in the marketplace, so that single mothers

---

49. Brooks, "Nuclear Family."

50. Stoller, *Goliath*, urges us to revive the American antitrust tradition which started with a Jeffersonian distrust of monopoly power—grounded in the experience of English state chartered corporations—and was reasserted in the Progressive Era and the New Deal Era. Stoller gives historical and political-economic arguments for why that would revive employment, wages, and local economy.

could provide for their children more fairly, laying a stronger foundation for them? Maybe Christians could support government-funded childcare as the Scandinavian countries, or the Netherlands, do. Might it be possible to tie executive pay to the wages of the lowest paid custodial worker in the firm by a fixed multiple, so children of blue-collar workers benefit? Might it be possible to reform corporate law so that the pre-distribution of wages flows more equally and real wages increase? Might it be time to consider reducing the workday again, from eight hours down to six, for instance?

The Catholic New Deal Democrats who championed the pro-life cause for decades believed in accountability but were not economically conservative. They were certainly not "communists," but they were economically *progressive*. They looked back to Christian inspirations before the Enlightenment, when the Western church believed that human political community was *natural* for us. Yes, of course we needed to grow in virtue in order to participate well and honorably in civic life—the *polis*, as Plato and Aristotle called it. But we were made from and for *relationship*, since we were created by a relational God who is Father, Son, and Holy Spirit.

The Protestant-individualist synthesis overthrew the Catholic-community synthesis by drawing Protestants in through the abortion issue. Various Enlightenment thinkers, who wanted to throw Christian faith completely out of the realm of justice and politics, said that humans were individuals, born free in the state of nature. The only sacred relations between people were contracts, made voluntarily. The individualism of the Western Enlightenment tradition said people did not owe much to each other, except to be left alone. This is what came to be known as "economic conservatism" with the "libertarian" camp at one end, arguing for minimal government. Since few to no libertarians envision a strong educational system empowering citizens in jurisprudence and litigation, however, it would seem that this vision leaves corporations to prey on people and the planet.

The true Christian moral conservative must be rooted in a vision of relational personhood, recognizing that we are intrinsically relational and bound together in community. This understanding comes from scientific, cultural, and historical realities but also trinitarian theology: God is a loving community of Father, Son, and Holy Spirit within God's self. If we are made in his image, we must expect that we are relational from the start, relational in our nature, and have growth in loving relationship as our intended moral goal. Therefore, the Christian moral conservative, anchored in trinitarian theology, must be economically progressive. We owe things to each other—for the sake of true liberty, our common life together, and for the sake of all our future children.

People who try to give gifts to their own children, while consuming everyone else's, build a society that simply consumes all children. I am persuaded that a fuller, deeper reading of Scripture and a fuller, deeper look at the challenge of abortion produces for us something we did not expect: a deeper love for all children. We will be even more surprised and challenged as we examine more facets of the issue.

9

How Christian Heresy Contributes to Health Care Policies and Abortion

Health Care Policies and Meritocracy

IN 1962, SHERRI FINKBINE sought an abortion of her fifth child. She and her husband had changed their mind about having this child because they had learned that the sedative that Sherri had taken early in her pregnancy to ease her morning sickness would likely result in birth defects. The Finkbine family lived in Arizona. Like most states, Arizona allowed abortion only in the case of a direct threat to the mother's life, but Finkbine told her doctor and hospital abortion committee that she would have a mental breakdown if she had a deformed child, and persuaded them to permit the abortion. Daniel K. Williams surmises that "Finkbine probably could have had the abortion quietly—as many women in similar situations did—if she had not informed a reporter of her intentions."[1] Finkbine was a star actress on *Romper Room*, a popular children's television program. The media attention divided the nation, including Catholics and Protestants. Catholics were largely against the abortion of a deformed fetus. Protestants and Jews were largely for it.[2]

The thalidomide controversy is but an extreme case study for why a publicly funded health plan is the most moral. The issue I focus on in this chapter is not the personal ethics of abortion, but the relation between fetal health, industrial development, and public health programs. Thalidomide was a sedative approved for use first in Germany because it was developed by a German company, Chemie Gruenenthal. Thalidomide was later found to deformities in limbs, internal organs, eyes, and ears. Many were born without

---

1. Williams, *Defenders*, 42.
2. Williams, *Defenders*, 41–43, notes that 50 percent of women and 54 percent of men said she did the right thing, as did 56 percent of Protestants and 33 percent of Catholics. It is poignant that various Catholic couples volunteered to adopt Finkbine's child.

an anus or genitals.³ Since 1958, across the world, thalidomide was probably responsible for countless miscarriages and infant deaths. In Germany alone, ten thousand babies survived with deformities. Unproven suspicions exist that thalidomide was originally developed by Nazi scientists, but a sensationalist interpretation of the drug is not necessary.

Chemicals developed under capitalist, socialist, and communist regimes alike have been found to cause birth defects and other health problems: brain damage, organ damage, deformed limbs, leukemia, spina bifida, Tay-Sachs, autism, asthma, etc. A 2009 article entitled "Environmental Factors in Birth Defects: What We Need to Know" points out that in the developed world, "in many regions birth defects are the largest single cause of infant deaths."⁴ A 2013 study of over eight hundred women who lived in an area known for high air pollution due to traffic—the San Joaquin Valley of California—found that women in the first two months of pregnancy who breathed high levels of carbon monoxide, due to vehicle exhaust, "were nearly twice as likely to have a baby with spina bifida or anencephaly as those with the lowest carbon monoxide exposure."⁵ A 2017 study done by the Cincinnati Children's Medical Center affirmed that pregnant women exposed to air pollution are at a higher risk of having children born with birth defects ranging from abnormal hearts to cleft lips and palates.⁶ A 2018 literature review of congenital heart defects in infants, which are the leading cause of spontaneous abortion and which cause 30 percent of infant deaths at birth, reveals that congenital heart defects are associated with exposure to smoking, vehicle exhaust, pesticides used on farms, byproducts of disinfectants used to clean public water supplies, toxic metals that can also be found in drinking water, landfill sites and incinerators, and phthalates which are found in plastics and common household products.⁷ The literature is overwhelming, staggering, and growing. Whether tobacco and other companies lie unscrupulously, or whether companies spew carbon monoxide, lead, and other toxins into the environment, or whether government regulators make profound mistakes, the issue is the same. All of these toxins land in the wombs of pregnant women.

In the U.S., a publicly funded health plan is the only moral and ethical way to comprehend the full cost of industrial development to people's health, especially fetal health and children's health. As such, it is the only long-term

3. Rennie, "Groundbreaking Drug."
4. Weinhold, "Environmental Factors."
5. Padula et al., "Association."
6. Ren et al. "Periconception Exposure"
7. Nicoll, "Environmental Contaminants."

way to make sure the public fully owns the full cost of industrial development and comprehends the pressures placed on families to abort a deformed child, hopefully to halt the underlying corporate causes more quickly. Any other proposal, in the U.S. context, is morally equivalent to letting capitalist shareholders profit from the poisoning of babies, and placing a moral burden on individual parents to consider an abortion, not just for their own sakes as parents, but for the child's sake. For example, it is morally unacceptable for pro-life advocates to tolerate oil, gas, and vehicle companies lobbying to relax environmental standards on vehicle emissions. In chapter 10, as we consider the Texas laws involving restrictive abortion provider laws that were put forward as promoting women's health, I will mention some very specific health challenges faced by Texan women due to industrial poisoning. That juxtaposition will illuminate the tensions of being morally conservative while trying to be economically conservative.

Generally speaking, American political conservatives apply the logic of "meritocracy" to health care. To put it bluntly, if you get sick, or pregnant, is it not mainly your own responsibility? If you smoke, isn't that your responsibility? The COVID-19 pandemic forced Americans to recognize that a disease can be so contagious that personal "merit" or "fault" cannot be assigned one way or the other, and therefore Americans were willing to pay for coronavirus testing and treatment through the Medicare program (i.e., funded by taxpayers). The same cannot be said of all diseases and conditions, though. How much truth is there to the notion that one's personal choices to diet and exercise are the main determinants of one's health? Is it true that someone who eats healthily and exercises should pay less in health insurance than someone who does not? Only if equally healthy food, clean air, and the like are available to all for the same price. Now that we know a person can be impacted, through no fault of their own, by inherit genetic disorders from their family, by the epigenetic transmission of trauma endured by their parents and grandparents,[8] in the womb by chemicals to which their mothers were exposed[9] or even a mother's diet and stress,[10] by environmental pollution like lead in water or car exhaust, by adverse childhood experiences (like violence, poverty, abuse, divorce, etc.),[11] and by

8. Molynn, *It Didn't Start with You*. See also Interlandi, "Toxins"; Wu, "Dads Pass"; Thomson, "Study of Holocaust Survivors."

9. Skarnulis, "Toxins." Raz et al., "Autism" is summarized by Rivas, "Air Pollution." Also Shelton et al., "Neurodevelopmental Disorders" is summarized by Olson, "Nearby Pesticides" and "Pregnant Mothers."

10. Doucleff, "Mom's Diet," discusses Dominguez-Salas et al., "Maternal Nutrition."

11. Felitti et al., "Relationship." Weder et al., "Child Abuse." Harris, "How Childhood Trauma." Bergland, "Social Disadvantage." Mitchell et al., "Social Disadvantage."

implicit racial bias by medical professionals,[12] we need to deeply revise our idea that health is purely individual and meritocratic.

I will develop my case in two stages. First, in this chapter, I will make the case that a universal health care policy is the only way to express an investment in all children and their well-being. This will help us not only support childbirth and childraising; it will help us as a society embrace the true costs of our economic actions as we place unborn children at risk and as some mothers and fathers among us face costs they did not expect because of our industrial development. Throughout this chapter, I ask my readers to keep in mind that the vulnerability of the fetus in the womb to chemicals and disease is not the only factor that is relevant to the argument for universal health care. Please keep in mind the obvious fact that children need their caregivers—certainly parents and often grandparents who might also be involved in caregiving—to be in good health. Otherwise, children may grow up in such a way that will make them vulnerable to becoming parents at a young age and repeating a cycle of vulnerability. The burden of this chapter is to show that applying "the myth of meritocracy" to health care has been hypocritical and counterproductive, and continues to be so.

Second, in chapter 10, I will make the case that contraception should be covered by that health care policy. Americans' view of women's sexual behavior and access to both contraception and abortion have also been shaped by the notion of "meritocracy." Social conservatives ask whether contraception is as effective as abstinence education at reducing unintended pregnancies. Even if contraception can be shown to be broadly effective, which studies do show, conservatives ask whether it promotes casual sex, which other social conservatives including Christians consider to be an expression of the breakdown of the family and an undesirable social outcome in itself, or an inevitable pathway to unintended pregnancy and the pressure to abort. Some traditional Catholics take a dim view of contraception as a whole because they maintain that married couples should only use natural family planning, a view I argue against in chapter 11. Other Christians and other conservatives, who are comfortable with contraception if it is one's own business and bought on the private market, question whether women "merit" free contraception, especially if it is publicly funded. Are taxpayer dollars encouraging sex outside of marriage? I will address those questions in chapters 10 and 11.

---

12. Chapman et al., "Physicians and Implicit Bias."

Health Insurance and the Notion of Meritocracy

Americans are accustomed to the notion that health insurance comes through a full time job. In some sense, Americans' belief that quality health care (via insurance) *should* come through an employer is rooted in the belief that the U.S. is a "meritocracy." This assumption, too, deserves comment. Shrewd U.S. policymakers in the WWII and Cold War eras built a hidden welfare system in health care. While other countries moved to a single-payer government health insurance plan, similar to Medicare but for all their citizens, the U.S. government strengthened its corporate sector and labor unions by shutting out the unemployed and underemployed.

By passing the Internal Revenue Code of 1954, Congress took the WWII-era tax loopholes and extended them to corporations so that they would provide health insurance to their employees through private health insurance companies. Tom Miller, a Fellow at the American Enterprise Institute and writer for *National Review*, notes that this employer-based approach to insurance "has been criticized for raising—and hiding—the overall costs of health insurance and health care."[13] Researchers at the National Bureau of Economic Research (NBER) point out that this system gives large firms an advantage over small businesses, gives high-income workers advantages over lower-income workers because insurance premiums are tax-exemptions, and may distort employment decisions and dampen entrepreneurship because people are tethered to their health insurance via their employer.[14]

This policy left out non-employed women who divorced their employed husbands, as well as other non-employed or part-time people. Nevertheless, Journalist Chris Ladd calls this "white socialism." While not all "white people" benefited from these policies, which is what Ladd's moniker would suggest, a large portion did get government assistance through the tax code, and still do:

> My family's generous health insurance costs about $20,000 a year, of which we pay only $4,000 in premiums. The rest is subsidized by taxpayers. You read that right. Like virtually everyone else on my block who isn't old enough for Medicare or employed by the government, my family is covered by private health insurance subsidized by taxpayers at a stupendous public cost. Well over 90% of white households earning over the white median income (about $75,000) carried health insurance

---

13. Miller, "Kill the Tax Exclusion."
14. Buchmueller and Monheit, "Employer-Sponsored Health Insurance."

even before the Affordable Care Act. White socialism is nice if you can get it.[15]

While companies deduct the cost of their employees' health insurance as a tax write off, employees do not report their employers' contribution to their health insurance as "income." Ladd writes:

> That results in roughly a $400 billion annual transfer of funds from state and federal treasuries to insurers to provide coverage for the Americans least in need of assistance. This is one of the defining features of white socialism, the most generous benefits go to those who are best suited to provide for themselves.[16]

Meanwhile, employment discrimination kept minorities out of good jobs *and* the health care system. Says Ladd:

> Until the decades after the Civil Rights Acts, very few women or minorities gained direct access to this system. Unsurprisingly, this was the era in which white attitudes about the social safety net and the Democratic Party began to pivot. Thanks to this silent racial legacy, socialism for white people retains its disproportionately white character, though that has weakened. Racial boundaries are now less explicit and more permeable, but still today white families are twice as likely as African-Americans to have access to private health insurance. Two thirds of white children are covered by private health insurance, while barely over one third of black children enjoy this benefit.[17]

If people believe that their "hard work" is the cause of all they enjoy—as if the U.S. is a "pure meritocracy"—then they become invested in turning the "hard work" argument against others, *and they will eventually turn it against themselves if they wish to preserve the myth.* This is a familiar political strategy going back as far as white Virginians' response to Bacon's Rebellion, an uprising of white indentured servants and black slaves. Virginia's powerful white elites responded by punishing the black people through passing the Virginia Slave Codes of 1705.[18] White landowners

---

15. Ladd, "Unspeakable Realities."
16. Ladd, "Unspeakable Realities."
17. Ladd, "Unspeakable Realities."
18. The Virginia Slave Codes of 1705 made slavery by race more pronounced, made it illegal for any black person to carry a gun, or strike a white person, or even employ a white person. Morgan, *American Slavery*, 270, notes, "But for those with eyes to see, there was an obvious lesson in the rebellion. Resentment of an alien race might be more powerful than resentment of an upper class. Virginians did not immediately grasp it. It would sink in as time went on."

invited poor white people into a realignment based on race, with token gestures of inclusion like the ability to own guns (the Slave Codes forbade black people from owning guns), so they would align themselves with the wealthy white landowning class for cultural and racial reasons, as opposed to black people for economic ones.

Throughout U.S. history, this political realignment has been effective. At key moments, on key issues, white people refuse public investment in schools, health care, etc. when black people would benefit by being included. For example, in 1944, Mississippi Congressman John Rankin gutted the G.I. Bill of 1944 of a provision that entitled all veterans to $20 per week of unemployment compensation for a year, because he believed the New Deal and veterans legislation should help as few black people as possible.[19] A broad example would be the lack of proper water and sewage systems—which depend on public funding and civic good will—which has led to "at least 12 million Americans" in the South and Midwest suffering from neglected tropical diseases.[20] That estimate was made in 2014 by Dr. Peter J. Hotez, dean of the National School of Tropical Medicine, who in 2017 led a team of scientists to Lowndes County, Alabama; they discovered that 34 percent of the residents have hookworm, a tropical parasite associated with extreme poverty in underdeveloped countries.[21] Alabama's water management systems are otherwise quite developed;[22] the state of Alabama simply opposes

---

19. Blakemore, "GI Bill's Promise," writes, "When lawmakers began drafting the GI Bill in 1944, some Southern Democrats feared that returning black veterans would use public sympathy for veterans to advocate against Jim Crow laws. To make sure the GI Bill largely benefited white people, the southern Democrats drew on tactics they had previously used to ensure that the New Deal helped as few black people as possible. During the drafting of the law, the chair of the House Veterans Committee, Mississippi Congressman John Rankin, played hardball and insisted that the program be administered by individual states instead of the federal government. He got his way. Rankin was known for his virulent racism: He defended segregation, opposed interracial marriage, and had even proposed legislation to confine, then deport, every person with Japanese heritage during World War II. When the bill came to a committee vote, he stonewalled in an attempt to gut another provision that entitled all veterans to $20 a week of unemployment compensation for a year. Rankin knew this would represent a significant gain for black Southerners, so he refused to cast a critical proxy vote in protest. The American Legion ended up tracking down the congressman who had left his proxy vote with Rankin and flying him to Washington to break the deadlock."

20. Hotez, "Neglected Parasitic Infections."

21. Pilkington, "Hookworm."

22. Hairston et al., "Water Resources in Alabama," point out, for instance, "Alabama ranks sixth and tenth, respectively, in water used for thermonuclear power generation and water withdrawn for industrial, commercial, or mining uses."

extending public infrastructure there.[23] Imagine being a child growing up next to a pool of water infested by hookworm.

The "myth of meritocracy" makes people curiously unable or unwilling to recognize when they and their children benefit from government activity. America's manufacturing economy was based on war, which means "big government."[24] During the four-decades-long Cold War, the federal government redistributed $12 trillion dollars into the economy.[25] Yet American political culture praises "entrepreneurs" and "job creators" as if government

---

23. "The Story of American Poverty" is a case study of how most Americans have benefited from massive public investment yet insist that American society is a "meritocracy of individual achievement," and why "small government conservatism" is often used as a smokescreen for "prejudice and systemic racial injustice." DeParle, "Why Do People," reviews Hochschild, *Strangers*, and writes, "Hochschild calls this the "Great Paradox"—opposition to federal help from people and places that need it—and sets off across Louisiana on an energetic, open-minded quest to understand it. A distinguished Berkeley sociologist, Hochschild is a woman of the left, but her mission is empathy, not polemics. She takes seriously the Tea Partiers' complaints that they have become the 'strangers' of the title—triply marginalized by flat or falling wages, rapid demographic change, and liberal culture that mocks their faith and patriotism. Her affection for her characters is palpable. But the resentments she finds are as toxic as the pollutants in the marsh and metastasizing throughout politics. What unites her subjects is the powerful feeling that others are 'cutting in line' and that the federal government is supporting people on the dole—'taking money from the workers and giving it to the idle.' Income is flowing up, but the anger points down. The people who feel this are white. The usurpers they picture are blacks and immigrants. Hochschild takes care not to call anyone racist but concludes that 'race is an essential part of this story.' When she asks a small-town mayor to describe his politics, his first two issues—or is it one in his mind?—are welfare and race: 'I don't like the government paying unwed mothers to have a lot of kids, and I don't go for affirmative action.'"

24. Goodwin, "Way We Won," discusses the rise of manufacturing being dependent on the U.S. military role globally. Zinn, *Postwar America*, 76–77, highlights how much money went to companies who were weapons manufacturers alone: "The United States in the 1960s was spending approximately $40 billion a year on weapon systems alone, two-thirds of the money going to twelve or fifteen industrial giants—corporations whose main reason for existence was to fulfil government contracts for death-dealing weapons. Senator Paul Douglas, who understood the situation well from his vantage point of chairman of the Joint Economic Committee, pointed out that 'six-sevenths of these contracts are not competitive but what are termed single supplier negotiable.' In the alleged interest of secrecy, the government picks a company and draws up a contract in more or less secret negotiations." Zinn, *Postwar America*, 77, also pointed out that despite the initial cost estimates, "it is customary for the ultimate costs to be double or treble the original estimates." A report by Senator William Proxmire found that in 1969, the top eleven companies of the top one hundred defense contractors "were awarded 47 per cent of the prime contracts received" by those one hundred. See also Lewis, "World War II Manufacturing," and Madrick, "Innovation," and PBS's "War Production."

25. "Cold War Mobilization" notes, "Over the course of four decades of U.S. resolve to 'contain' Communism abroad, Americans spent nearly $13 trillion on defense. Military readiness touched all aspects of American society and culture."

had nothing to do with it. If disempowered but socially conservative white citizens are encouraged to believe that the American system is a "pure meritocracy," they are assisted in their belief by media all too willing to portray government social services as "handouts," and beneficiaries as black and undeserving.[26] In 1980, lower-income white people were actually the biggest beneficiaries of food stamps and Medicaid when Ronald Reagan directed their resentment towards the "welfare queen"[27]—an implicitly black caricature exaggerated into nonexistence, but *she* was the one who abuses the system and requires its *reduction*. In 2009, "small government conservatives" were among those who held up signs saying "Keep your government hands off my Medicare."[28] An unusual number of Silicon Valley's population are vocal libertarians,[29] even though their very livelihoods were developed by, and still depend on, the Defense Department's military funding and the National Institutes of Health's grant money for scientific research.[30] Almost every component of Apple's iPhone, for instance, was designed by the military.[31] And eight out of the ten states that benefit the most from federal funds (*not* including military spending) are "conservative red states" that supposedly eschew government funding.[32]

Under the Obama administration, wealthy white elites tried to align poorer whites against public programs, especially the Affordable Care Act. From 2009, conservative media personalities like Rush Limbaugh, Bill O'Reilly, and Glenn Beck regularly accused Obama of secretly being for "reparations."[33] Instead of simply being for or against the economic stimu-

26. Gilens, *Why Americans Hate Welfare*, and Mettler, *Submerged State*.

27. Blake, "Return," and Gustafson, *Cheating Welfare*.

28. Krugman, "Health Care Realities." Rampell, "White Working Class," notes, "Americans (A) generally associate government spending with undeserving, nonworking, nonwhite people; and (B) are really bad at recognizing when they personally benefit from government programs."

29. Edwards, "Silicon Valley," highlights attitudes and policies criminalizing homelessness; the creation of a "meritocracy club"; ideas that Silicon Valley secede from California; and so on. Steve Case, venture capitalist and former CEO of AOL, argues that Silicon Valley has been "tone deaf" to middle America. See Castillo, "Silicon Valley."

30. Singer, "Federally Supported."

31. Malter, "Thank the Government," and Parramore, "What the Steve Jobs Movie."

32. Keirnan, "Most and Least."

33. Waldman, "Yes, Opposition," draws on valuable studies: "In a 2009 discussion about the stimulus bill, Rush Limbaugh told his listeners, 'Obama's entire economic program is reparations!' [. . .] Rush Limbaugh has the largest talk-radio audience in the United States, and he is admired and lauded by one Republican politician after another. But it isn't just him. Bill O'Reilly told his viewers, 'I think Mr. Obama allows historical grievances—things like slavery, bad treatment for Native Americans and U.S. exploitation of Third World countries—to shape his economic thinking . . . He

lus plan, health care expansion, labor rights, and progressive taxation, they cast a long shadow of suspicion on Obama personally, the bailout of the financial crisis, and the Affordable Care Act. This angry messaging was to the detriment of the entire population, not just poorer whites. Tea Party activists became publicly visible to protest "big government." Ironically, many of them benefited from the federal farm subsidy, and their protests had been cultivated and funded by the Koch brothers' corporate oil money and big tobacco companies since 2002.[34] They succeeded in electing representatives to Congress who sought to thwart Obama. One result: in 2015, those Tea Party Republicans refused to replenish the Strategic National Stockpile after the swine flu epidemic, which would come back to haunt the entire nation during the COVID-19 pandemic.[35]

Against Obama in 2012, Protestant Rick Santorum, Mormon Mitt Romney, and Roman Catholic Newt Gingrich deployed accusations of "non-meritocracy" which insinuated a plan to privilege black people. Santorum said, "I don't want to make black people's lives better by giving them somebody else's money." Later, he claimed he did not mean to say "black people," but simply "people." Mitt Romney repeatedly said that Obama wanted to turn America into an "entitlement society" and made the "47 percent" remark at a fundraiser he thought was private, which famously sank him. Newt Gingrich called Obama a "food-stamp president," said poor people should want paychecks, not handouts, and questioned the work ethic of poor children.[36]

Another Attempt at Governing Health Care by "the Myth of Meritocracy"

In 2016, many blue-collar voters rejected a party offering to fight for universal health insurance, and instead risked that Donald Trump would bring back

---

gives the bad things about America far too much weight, leading to his desire to redistribute wealth, thereby correcting historical grievance.' Almost any domestic policy choice, whether it involves taxes or budgets or health care, can be characterized as an act of racial vengeance exacted upon whites for the benefit of blacks. Glenn Beck has been another prominent advocate of the reparations theory. 'Everything that is getting pushed through Congress, including this health care bill,' he said in 2009, 'are transforming America. And they are all driven by President Obama's thinking on one idea: reparations.'"

34. Mayer, "Covert Operations." Nesbit, *Poison Tea*; "Secret Origins." Fallin et al., "'To Quarterback.'"

35. Torbati and Arnsdorf, "Tea Party Budget."

36. Blake, "Return." Gustafson, *Cheating Welfare*.

"jobs" while repealing the ACA and supposedly replacing it with "something better," which was unworkable on its face.[37] They hoped to get health care back through the dignity of "jobs"[38]—even coal mining jobs, for instance. The enthusiasm for coal mining jobs illustrated many points. U.S. manufacturing companies had for years offshored jobs to China and Mexico in search of cheaper labor, and blue-collar livelihoods were poignantly threatened. People had long been taught that their jobs—even fossil fuel jobs that, in the end, threatened to cause climate change and untold damage—were so much a part of their identity that suggesting a transition to clean energy jobs became a cultural issue involving personal pride. Unfortunately, the market assured coal's decline, and Trump himself threatened to hasten it because he also wanted to expand natural gas drilling, a cheaper competitor to coal. But the fantasy caught hold nevertheless. Most importantly, the 2016 campaign highlighted that many of these jobs had to be *provided* to these blue-collar voters, not by someone's "individual merit" and "hard work," but *through government policies* like trade negotiations, corporate tax policy, and spending on infrastructure and defense, the way it has always been since WWII. This is how the "myth of meritocracy" is preserved and how already disadvantaged children are made to suffer more.

Unfortunately, the Trump administration, with its own white supremacist elements, also failed to prepare for a massive public health disaster which was completely foreseen and forewarned by the outgoing Obama team, multiple scientists, public health experts, the Pentagon, other government officials, and even Bill Gates in a 2015 TED Talk.[39] Trump certainly cannot be held responsible for the virus itself, or for the actions of the Chinese government, but he can be for his preparedness and his response. After promoting the "birther" conspiracy falsely suggesting that Obama was born outside the U.S. and therefore "other," an effort the evangelical president

---

37. Trump wanted to overturn the "individual mandate," which required people to sign up for health insurance through the ACA website or face a financial penalty. Private health insurance companies needed the increased enrollment, especially from younger and healthier people, in order to financially cover older and less healthy citizens.

38. Ladd, "Unspeakable Realities."

39. On the Obama-Trump transition team simulation of a global pandemic, see Toosi et al., "Before Trump's Inauguration." On the Obama "Pandemic Playbook" manual, see Diamond and Toosi, "Trump Team Failed." On the Pentagon's warning to the White House, see Klippenstein, "Exclusive: The Military Knew." The original Pentagon report is now declassified and available online. On Bill Gates, see Sun, "Bill Gates." On the "Crimson Contagion" simulation, see "Crimson Contagion 2019" and Panetta, "Trump Administration Ran a Simulation." For a summary, see Sanger et al., "Before Virus Outbreak."

of Liberty University, Jerry Falwell, Jr., *praised*,[40] Trump was elected and set about undoing public health investments undertaken by Obama and Bush, perhaps motivated in part by his antipathy for Obama. This, despite very recent outbreaks of respiratory viruses—SARS (2002-03); the H5N1 "avian flu" (2003-04); the H1N1 "swine flu" (2009-10); MERS (2012); the H7N9 "bird flu" (2013)—and Ebola (2013-14). After Trump made a vulgar remark about African nations and Haiti on January 11, 2018,[41] on February 1, he dramatically shrank the scope of the infectious disease work done by the Centers for Disease Control and Prevention in 39 of 49 hot spot countries like China, Haiti, and African nations.[42] Shortly after another small MERS outbreak happened in Saudi Arabia, South Korea, and elsewhere in February 2018, Trump and newly appointed NSC head John Bolton either dismantled the Global Pandemic Team or otherwise reorganized it into ineffectiveness in May 2018.[43] In July 2019, Trump recalled Dr. Linda Quick from China. Dr. Quick was "a medical epidemiologist embedded in China's disease control agency." Trump did not replace her,[44] making the U.S. more dependent on the Chinese government for vital information, because it lost the eyes and ears of an American scientist in China. In January and February of 2020, while downplaying the coronavirus, Trump golfed eight times and held six campaign rallies.

During the pandemic, Trump and the Republican Party displayed a remarkable commitment to the tenets of economic conservatism and what could have been described as limited government[45] if Trump's administra-

40. Stripling, "Trump's Liberty U. Commencement."
41. Kiely, "What Did Trump Say."
42. Sun, "CDC to Cut by 80 Percent."

43. Grenoble, "Video of Trump." Sun, "Top White House Official." Yong, "Ebola Returns." Garrett, "Trump Has Sabotaged." For reference, see Jacobson and Knight, "Did Donald Trump Fire." Morrison, "No," claimed that Trump did not "dissolve" the team, but most people with work experience would raise eyebrows at the declaration that executives are downsizing a team, and removing its key experts, while claiming it would be just as effective and healthy as before. Mackay, "Trump Lies," evaluating the truthfulness of Morrison's article, pointed to statements by Dr. Fauci and other government officials who expressed alarm that the responsibility for pandemic response was downgraded and diluted. In any case, from a leadership standpoint, the question is moot. Whether Trump reorganized the relevant people out (Tom Bossert, Tim Ziemer, Dr. Linda Quick), hired people who ignored red-flag warning signs and documents (Alex Azar), or just didn't listen to them when he really needed to (Dr. Anthony Fauci, Alex Azar), Trump's failure was catastrophic.

44. Taylor, "Exclusive: U.S. Axed CDC Expert."

45. Chortimer, "Contrarian Coronavirus Theory," highlights an article about Richard Epstein, a legal scholar who is characterized as a key influence behind Trump's off-and-on denial that COVID-19 is a real crisis requiring government action. Two

tion did not also actively undermine state and local governments. Despite declaring war on the virus, Trump refused to use the Defense Production Act to compel American companies to make more medical masks, gowns, tests, ventilators, and other important medical equipment—executive authority that is standard in war and routine even in peacetimes to supply the military.[46] He instead allowed U.S. companies to sell badly needed equipment to other countries at premium prices.[47] When he did deploy the DPA (aside from once stopping a Brooklyn man from stockpiling and reselling equipment[48]), it was to empower the Federal Emergency Management Authority to routinely seize equipment from the states, despite the fact that he had told state governors to pursue what they needed and deflected their criticism or called them incompetent.[49] One anecdote encapsulates the dysfunction: Maryland's Republican Governor Larry Hogan was able to get an order of coronavirus test kits from South Korea, because his wife, Yumi, a Korean immigrant, had been able to initiate the order in Korean.[50] When the order arrived in Maryland in April, Governor Hogan called in the National Guard and state police to protect the supplies *from the federal government*.[51] Trump

---

points stand out: First, Epstein makes claims about the virus that are scientifically untrue, and makes important assumptions from these claims. He repeatedly said, "Viruses automatically weaken over time." He deduced that from his understanding of Darwin, where the living organism gets stronger against the virus. Unfortunately, this idea has no scientific support whatsoever. The very well documented experiences of AIDS, Ebola, and SARS contradict Epstein's idea that viruses weaken over time. The interviewer inserts statements from actual scientists and scholars he consulted, against the views of Epstein, who admits he is an amateur. Second, Epstein defends the political idea that government coercion is never necessary, even in a public health emergency. He believes that individuals act for their own self-preservation; therefore they will always do the right thing. Epstein did not comment on the spring breakers in Florida, the people who complained that St. Patrick's Day celebrations in New Orleans were cancelled, the "Coronavirus Party" in Kentucky, megachurches continuing to meet, etc.

46. Kanno-Youngs and Swanson, "Wartime Production," noted that even in the case of General Motors making ventilators, "With General Motors, it is unclear what the act accomplished. The company had already announced its intention to collaborate with the medical device firm Ventec Life Systems to produce ventilators. After the president threatened on Friday to invoke the Defense Production Act against G.M., the automaker announced that the venture would aim to produce up to 10,000 ventilators a month."

47. Fang, "Key Medical Supplies." On April 6, 2020, Trump was under enough political pressure to use the DPA to order 3M to stop exporting its respirator masks to Canadian and Latin American markets; see Brueninger, "Trump and 3M."

48. "Brooklyn Man Arrested."

49. Levey, "Hospitals Say." "FBI Discovers." Pickrell, "Maryland Called."

50. Nirappil et al., "With Focus."

51. Pickrell, "Maryland Called," points out, "President Moon Jae-in [of South Korea] phoned in via videoconference to say how proud Korea was of Yumi—believed to

also invoked the DPA to order conglomerate Tyson Foods to stay open and keep meat-packing laborers at high risk of getting the virus and bringing it home to their families.[52]

Meanwhile, at the Veterans' Administration, which manages the nation's largest hospital system, another variation of the tragedy of American health care unfolded. As lower-level staff cared for veterans' medical needs, they leaked news of shocking equipment shortages while higher level officials denied shortages in an effort to cover it up.[53] Trump's VA administered to 1,370 veteran patients hydroxychloroquine, a drug never approved by the FDA for this purpose, but enthusiastically promoted by Trump. The VA reported that 28 percent of veterans with COVID-19 who were given hydroxychloroquine plus standard care died, compared with 11 percent of veterans who were given only standard care.[54] Whether the administration of hydroxychloroquine reflected optimism or a willingness to reduce government expenses by risking veterans' premature deaths is uncertain.

The coronavirus highlighted and worsened health inequities related to race and poverty.[55] As of early June 2020, black people made up 23 percent of COVID-19 deaths, despite being only 13 percent of the population.[56] "These numbers indicate that they have a 2.3-fold excess risk of dying from COVID-19 compared to white Americans."[57] For any family that depends on grandparents to care for grandchildren, as lower-income families of all races more often do, COVID-19 was challenging, if not devastating. Politicians' adherence to economic conservatism, corporatism, and "the myth of meritocracy" only exacerbated these vulnerabilities and inequalities further.

Finally, Trump's administration was in the Supreme Court trying to overturn the ACA, jeopardizing the health care of more than 20 million people but protecting private insurance companies.[58] Trump eventually committed to covering people's COVID-19 related expenses under Medicaid, but

---

be the first Korean American first lady in U.S. history."

52. Colvin, "Trump Order."

53. Kesling, "Veterans Affairs Hospitals Facing"; "Veterans Affairs Hospitals Will Give."

54. Yen, "VA Says."

55. "COVID-19 in Racial and Ethnic Groups." As of early April, Johnson and Buford, "Early Data," report that in Milwaukee, "81% of its 27 deaths in a county whose population is 26% black." In Michigan, "where the state's population is 14% black, African Americans made up 35% of cases and 40% of deaths."

56. Luhby, "US Black-White Inequality."

57. Levine et al., "Racial Inequalities."

58. Eibner and Gidengil, "What If the Supreme Court."

declined to keep the ACA enrollment window open,[59] meaning that people who became unemployed would also lose their health insurance for all their other health-related needs. The whole nation is now paying for America's commitment to the "myth of meritocracy" and the white evangelical commitment to John Locke's heresy, as well as their suspicion of science.

Is Work a Requirement for Health, or Health a Requirement for Work?

Ray Mabus, a Democrat, former governor of Mississippi (1988–92) and Secretary of the Navy (2009–17) wrote an interesting opinion piece in the *Jackson Free Press* on April 23, 2020. Especially in light of the COVID-19 crisis, Mabus lamented the decision of Mississippi's political leaders to reject the Medicaid expansion under the ACA. Mabus recalled his own fight as governor to expand Medicaid in Mississippi, when the state became first in the nation to cover people to 180 percent of the federal poverty level. He praised the ACA as "an amazing deal for the states" because the federal government would pay for 90 percent of the cost of insuring its citizens. Mabus then said:

> Fourteen states including Mississippi opted not to expand Medicaid. These states had one thing in common: they were all governed by Republicans. This group also included some of the poorest states and states with the highest percentage of people lacking health insurance. There were no coherent reasons. It was pure, naked partisanship without regard to the suffering it would mean and a total absence of compassion.[60]

Some conservatives would surely disagree with Mabus, citing financial and moral concerns: Would taxpayers be able to afford more citizens incurring rising hospital costs due to the monopolistic consolidation of hospitals?—a fair concern, but one with more than one possible solution. Would taxpayers be paying for abortions, if the ACA's provision for IUDs as contraception might actually cause abortions in some cases? I will examine that concern below.

Mabus pointed to another cost, which was only accelerated during the COVID-19 pandemic. Hospitals in poor and especially rural areas financially suffered because they were not eligible to receive Medicaid reimbursements for their patients. Indeed, the Chartis Center for Rural Health

---

59. Luthi, "Trump Rejects Obamacare."
60. Mabus, "Moral Failure."

produced a report in February 2020 which found that 120 rural hospitals had closed since 2010. Additionally, they found that 453 out of the 1,844 rural hospitals in operation are vulnerable to closure. The states that lost the most rural hospitals since 2010 were Texas, Tennessee, Oklahoma, Georgia, Alabama, and Missouri—all states that refused to expand Medicaid through the ACA.[61] This has left 2.3 million people uninsured.[62]

Mabus then criticized conservatives' strategy of layering a "work requirement" on top of the Medicaid eligibility. He said this hearkened back to "the literacy tests for voting under Jim Crow," which is poignant in more ways than one. Mabus makes clear my point about why injecting the "myth of meritocracy" was harmful to people who became eligible under the ACA:

> Onerous "work requirements" were designed to deny people benefits under the demonstrably false and completely demeaning theory that the problem was that people who qualify for Medicaid were unwilling to work.[63]

Indeed, a person caring for elderly parents, going through rehab, or working two part-time jobs in the "gig economy" might be excluded by these "work requirements," depending on the state. The central complaint is that adding a "work requirement" moves Medicaid away from being a program that cares for lower-income people. Even more foundational is the question: is work for health, or is health for work?

Aside from all the other economic arguments about giving the federal government the legal authority to negotiate with drug companies (as Medicaid and the VA do), or making young people participate earlier because they almost certainly will when they are old and/or need the ER, or whether people would benefit economically by untethering their health insurance from their employer, etc., I agree there is a moral consideration. I seek to give more weight to that consideration.

Given that John Locke's "meritocracy" interpretation of Genesis 1 was heretical and designed to justify white supremacy, it is problematic for Christians to deploy "meritocracy," especially as a criterion for public health. People have many motivations to work, and other programs call forth those motivations. But health is not individualistic. There is no moral reason why Christians should help a for-profit health care industry stay afloat by excluding the most sick, poor, and vulnerable people from health care. This is a realm in which applying the "myth of meritocracy" as a litmus test on

---

61. "Rural Health Safety Net."
62. Scott, "1 in 4 Rural Hospitals."
63. Mabus, "Moral Failure."

people can only backfire because it neglects the biological reality of our genetic inheritance and human interaction in shared air and space. And as the COVID-19 pandemic shows us, it will backfire precisely at the time we need it the most. If the only way that that system can stay profitable is to exclude certain people from health care, then why should health insurance be a for-profit industry at all? And when the industry itself is for-profit, how can conservatives rid themselves of the suspicion that some actors in the system have incentives to profit from abortions, as the perennial suspicion of Planned Parenthood shows? Too, when we recognize the pressures that poverty itself places on rates of unintended pregnancy and abortion rates, what about the incentives for people to procure abortions because they cannot afford health care and other fairly important goods? Work should not be a requirement for health. Rather, health is a requirement for work.

If the ACA is an imperfect law—because it is fundamentally a for-profit, corporation-driven delivery system with a tax-payer funding solution—then the movement of policy cannot be to *increase* the economic pressures on people by striking it down. We can raise consumption taxes on tobacco and alcohol, and figure out other key lifestyle choices we want to disincentivize. For Christians in the U.S., however, the most moral direction of health care policy is to make health insurance a non-profit enterprise, because only when we remove the for-profit motivation can we instill a values-based, health-driven motivation, especially when other countries have shown that it is possible. This could be a completely publicly-funded, government-run health care system like the U.K.'s National Health Service, or a compromise solution of government and regulated private enterprise, like the Medicare For All proposal. We can redesign health care policy to better reflect the Christian conviction—which is shared by many others—that we share in the raising, care, and development of all (at least, citizens and legal immigrants) because God wants to adopt all into his family.

10

Contraception or Restrictive Abortion Laws?

The Myth of Meritocracy, Contraception, and Abortion

MAKING ABORTION POLICY SERVE the cause of social conservatism has counterproductive elements *even on its own terms*. Imposing the logic of "meritocracy" onto the realm of sexual conduct and childraising virtually requires that people suffer economically, not only when people are sexually immoral by conservative standards but also when things happen through no one's fault or certainly not the child's fault, like the death of a spouse, divorce, and developmental child handicaps. Collective actions might contribute to bringing down abortion rates, like imposing more limits on chemical companies which contribute to birth defects on the womb, but economic conservatism seems to want corporations to flourish while children and parents pay the cost. When we treat abortion as a social, public health challenge, and not merely as an individualized, criminal justice problem—or perhaps not at all that way—we will find more good options at our disposal.

As with housing, I would suggest that U.S. health policy and the health care industry—with its blanket of "meritocracy" hiding the actual white supremacy, corporatism, and militarism—has backfired, and that includes its impact on abortion. Lower-income women procure abortions at higher rates because of financial and relational pressures. Positioning the abortion debate within the cause of social and economic conservatism is another attempt to politically align people away from shared economic (and public health) interests, and into a religious and cultural alignment which winds up being white supremacist *de facto*, whether or not individual people intend it that way. By saying this, I am not suggesting that every person who votes this way is personally prejudiced, or insincere about their beliefs about abortion and fetal life. Nor am I necessarily suggesting that all people in this camp are purely cynical in their approach to politics. But I am saying that the "myth of meritocracy" draws people into political alliances that invariably make racial, economic, and gender tensions worse, and either *causes abortion rates to rise or shifts the circumstances of the abortions.*

Take for example conservative and liberal interpretations of the decline in abortion rates. In 1973, the abortion rate was 16.3 abortions per 1,000 women aged 15 to 44. According to data below collected by the Centers for Disease Control,[1] abortion rates have been declining more rapidly since 2009. What is notable about this decline in absolute numbers, rate, and ratio is that the overall population—particularly the number of women of childbearing age—has increased over this same time.

Table 8.1. Abortions Per Year, U.S.: 2002–16

Year	# of Abortions	Rate per 1,000 Women Aged 15–44	Ratio per 1,000 Live Births
2002	854,122		246
2003	848,163		246
2004	839,226		238
2005	820,151	15.7	236
2006	842,855	15.9	237
2007	827,609	15.6	229
2008	825,564	15.6	229
2009	789,217	14.9	224
2010	765,651	14.4	225
2011	730,322	13.7	217
2012	699,202	13.1	208
2013	664,435	12.4	198
2014	652,639	12.1	192
2015	638,169	11.8	188
2016	623,471	11.6	186

The challenges of data collection and the questions that are sometimes raised about these numbers are worth a brief mention. The CDC's data does not include California, Maryland, New Hampshire, and Washington, DC, because they choose not to report to the CDC. The Guttmacher Institute's

1. Jatlaoui et al., "Abortion Surveillance."

report is gathered by their own census of all known abortion providers. Neither includes data on abortions that might be procured outside of formal medical settings. Recognizing problems like these, a spokeswoman for Americans United for Life recently said, "There is no national abortion reporting law, making it impossible to know the true number of abortions."[2] The relevant question, though, is not whether we have *exhaustive* knowledge about abortions, but *sufficient* knowledge. As long as the CDC and the Guttmacher Institute have been consistent in their data gathering, then we have sufficient information, because we are observing meaningful trends that represent the whole picture.

Conservatives raise a more fundamental challenge with the data, however. Under the assumption that human personhood begins at conception, they oppose the use of IUDs, because there is a small chance that an IUD will do two things simultaneously: allow an egg to be fertilized, and then prevent the fertilized egg from implanting in the uterine wall. This, conservatives say, would constitute an abortion.[3] Since the use of IUDs appear to have been partly responsible for the reduction in abortion rates, the numbers above are misleading by definition. They do not count all the non-implantations caused by the IUD.

I addressed this difficulty in chapter 4. Simply put, I think it is metaphysically possible but unlikely that human personhood begins at conception. The high rate of non-implantation, along with the possibilities of twinning and chimerism, combined with cell potency, demand metaphysical adjustments to the theory of conception-personhood that strain credibility. The conception-personhood view seems more of a *reaction* to science—a leftover from the era where Christians felt threatened by science per se—than an authentic engagement with what we now understand about embryonic human life. I offered my own suggestion: use the twenty-three-day marker for human personhood based on the presence of a detectable, healthy nervous system; this would establish a knowable minimum to coordinate beginning of life and end of life care. I would therefore be comfortable with the IUDs. Even if one is not inclined to adopt my suggestion for consideration as related to policy, one must admit that the conception-personhood view is only a moral probability, and not even one that is easily reconciled with Exodus 21:22–25, the only biblical passage with enough detail to bear on this question. When we express this in reverse, as a moral *im*probability, or a moral unknown—since ensoulment and personhood might in fact happen at implantation or shortly afterwards—one would have to weigh that possibility

2. Agrawal, "Abortion Rate Declines."
3. Verlee, "Colorado Debates."

against the chances that an IUD fails at preventing fertilization but also succeeds in preventing an implantation, *over and above the natural 70 percent chance a woman's body will simply expel the fertilized egg on its own.*[4] Since the former cannot be expressed as a statistical probability, and the latter is very hard to measure but is likely quite small, one might approach this as a moral consideration which can be weighed against the apparent effectiveness IUDs have at lowering the measurable abortion rate.

Observers have suggested explanations for the decline in measurable abortions. Starting from the broadest possible lens, we must ask whether the decline in abortions is related to the fact that people are having sex less often. The decline in sex itself has been observed even in other industrialized countries which track this kind of data: not only high school aged young people[5] but Gen-Xers and Baby Boomers, and even married couples, surprisingly.[6] There are plausible reasons for the decline in sex. "Helicopter parenting" motivated by economic stress means that youth have less discretion. Young adults are living with their parents at higher rates because of stagnant wages and indebtedness. People's use of electronic social media either causes more personal anxiety and/or blunts sex drives. People's use of dating apps in a culture of casual hookups means that the less conventionally "good looking" people are left out of all the sex that "good looking" people are having. Some people are morally and/or emotionally turned off by the culture of casual hookups, and stand aloof from it. Women are less motivated to have sex because they have orgasms less frequently in this casual hookup culture. Men are less motivated to have sex because chemicals in the environment lead to lower testosterone levels. People are masturbating to pornography more often and having sex with a partner less often. We have culturally embraced asexuality as an orientation. People find other meaningful ways to connect with others and express, or distract, themselves. People are working longer hours and are more tired. People are depressed by climate change anxieties.[7]

Those who study abortion rates seem confident that the decline in sexual activity is not having any appreciable impact on the decline in abortion rates. My point is not to debate that. My purpose here is to help readers recognize the value judgments we make, or the emotions we feel, as we look at the factors above. Which factors are more or less desirable? Believable?

4. Conger, "Earlier, More Accurate Prediction."

5. The CDC's "National Youth Risk Behavior Survey" found that those who answered "ever had sexual intercourse" dropped from 54.1 percent in 1991 to 41.2 percent in 2015.

6. Julian, "Why Are Young People."

7. Copland, "The Many Reasons." Julian, "Why Are Young People." DePaulo, "7 Reasons Why."

If one believes that people should be having less sex, especially outside of marriage, is it worth climate change? More pornography use? Most observers will attribute moral meanings to these factors behind the slowdown in partnered sex, informed by a narrative about society (is society getting better or worse), which may have a religious frame. We place sexual activity, pregnancy, abortion, childbearing, and family into a larger story about meaning, love, virtue, health, and community.

The same is true when we consider the two factors contributing most directly to the decline in abortions: the Affordable Care Act enacted by Democratic lawmakers in 2010 which made contraception free via health care providers; and the tighter abortion policies enacted by Republican state lawmakers over this time period. Naturally, liberals tend to credit the former, and conservatives the latter.

These two areas of policy are *not* mutually exclusive. Citizens can certainly make contraception free even while they tighten abortion parameters. But these two paths are politicized and sometimes presented as if they *are* mutually exclusive. That is because, again, we place sexual behavior, morality, contraception, abortion, and health care policies into different narratives about society, which often have a religious frame. Moreover, people across the political spectrum have ideological debates about the role of government programs and their place and/or effectiveness, which they believe are informed by religious values. Even if a program may be effective, one might ask, what is the tradeoff? It takes a fair amount of emotional self-discipline to consider what steps to take going forward, especially when we lack information we wish we had.

National Data 2008–11

I briefly examine nationwide data on abortion from 2008–11, Colorado-specific data from 2009–14, Texas-specific data from 2011–15, and nationwide data from 2011–15. As I discuss the data, I will also highlight how some Christians have responded.

Prior to this period, women were becoming increasingly familiar with IUDs. From 2002–08, women started to use IUDs at an increasing rate, although "substantial geographic and age variations existed."[8] Nationally, use of IUDs increased by over six times, from 1.6 for every 1,000 women (of reproductive age) to 9.8. Use of the levonorgestrel-releasing intrauterine system (LNG-IUS) increased by over 19 times, from 0.4 for every 1,000 women to 7.7. Use of the copper IUD (T380A) increased by 2.5 times, from

---

8. Xu et al., "Revival of the Intrauterine Device."

0.6 for every 1,000 women to 1.5. The period 2002–08 did coincide with a decrease in abortion numbers of 28,558, from 854,122 to 825,564, but it is difficult to say whether this is statistically significant, because the abortion rate was already declining from 1990–2008 at an average of 2 percent per year.[9] This data set is helpful, however, as one possible explanation for why more women were more comfortable with IUDs later.

From 2008–11, prior to the implementation of the ACA, the annual number of abortions declined by 95,242, that is, by 13 percent. Fewer women had abortions in 2011 than in 2008 because fewer women became pregnant when they did not want to. Over this period, the proportion of pregnancies that were unintended declined from 51 percent to 45 percent, and the rate of unintended pregnancies dropped from 54 to 45 per 1,000 women, a decline of 18 percent. This constituted a drop of about 95,000 abortions.

How confident can we be that this decline is due to contraception availability and use? Researchers Rachel K. Jones and Jenna Jerman study this period, and I explain their comments here. They note that twenty-four states passed 106 abortion restrictions in the time frame 2008–11. Were these restrictions responsible for bringing down the abortion rates? For starters, 62 of the 106 abortion restrictions were enacted sometime in 2011, and "many were not implemented or enforced until late in the year." Those restrictions would not have a measurable effect until 2012. What of the other 54 restrictions? Some of the restrictions involved requiring that counseling materials include more information to be presented to women seeking abortions, which probably would not influence abortion incidence. Moreover, the decreases in abortion occurred in almost all states, not just those that passed the restrictions. This implies nationwide, not state-specific, trends. Jones and Jerman also note that, nationwide, the number of clinics—the target of restrictive policies—declined only by 1 percent. Since a full 95 percent of the abortions were performed in clinics, the remainder being in hospitals or physicians' offices, we must conclude that women had the same level of access to abortion services throughout 2008–11 as they did prior to 2008, meaning any decrease of access to abortion clinics cannot explain the decrease.[10]

At least in part, contraception does suffice as an explanation. In fact, the abortion decline appears to disproportionately come from more effective contraception use by lower-income women. From 2007–09, there was an increase of 130 percent in long-acting reversible contraception (LARC).[11]

9. Jones and Kooistra, "Abortion Incidence 2008."
10. Jones and Jerman, "Abortion Incidence 2014."
11. Finer et al., "Changes in Use."

The proportion of clients, though, using LARC at Title X–supported family planning clinics (Title X is a Nixon-era category of laws that serve lower-income individuals) increased from 7 percent in 2011 to 11 percent in 2014.[12] Women who are young *and* lower-income have the majority of unintended pregnancies, so they are disproportionately represented.[13] Any policy that lowers the unintended pregnancy rate for women aged eighteen to twenty-four will surely lower the abortion rate.

Colorado Data 2009–14

This conclusion is reinforced by the Colorado study. From 2009–13, the Colorado Family Planning Initiative offered thirty thousand LARCs (IUDs and hormone implants) for little to no cost to lower-income women at sixty-eight Title X clinics throughout the state. Ordinarily, these contraceptive methods would cost from $500 to over $1,000, a large expense for the average lower-income woman or family, especially if the expense is unforeseen and the need is urgent. Researchers noted that in 2009, the use of LARCs was fewer than 5 percent of the population of women of childbearing age; in 2011, it was 19 percent; in 2013, it was 26 percent.

The result? As of 2014, the abortion rate decreased by nearly 50 percent among women aged fifteen to nineteen and 18 percent among young women aged twenty to twenty-four. The unintended pregnancy rate declined by 40 percent among women aged fifteen to nineteen and 20 percent for women aged twenty to twenty-four. The birth rate declined by nearly 50 percent among women aged fifteen to nineteen and 20 percent among women twenty to twenty-four.[14] The program helped increase the average age of women giving birth to their first child. It reduced the number of births to unmarried women under the age of twenty-five without a high school diploma. The Colorado Department of Public Health and Environment estimated that it saved nearly $70 million in public assistance costs. Colorado would have to spend less on food programs for low-income mothers and children: enrollment in WIC supplemental nutrition declined 23 percent between 2008 and 2013.[15] Colorado Governor John Hickenlooper credited the program with three-quarters of the overall decline in Colorado's teen birthrate.[16]

---

12. Fowler et al., "Family Planning."
13. Finer and Zolna, "Declines in Unintended Pregnancy."
14. "Taking the Unintended."
15. Sullivan, "Colorado's Teen Birthrate."
16. Sullivan, "Colorado's Teen Birthrate."

At the state level, Colorado's abortion statistics, as reported to the CDC, are:

Table 8.2. Abortions Per Year, Colorado: 2007–15

Year	Residents Reporting Abortion	Occurrences of Abortion Reported
2007	10,556	11,363
2008	10,765	11,581
2009	10,735	11,598
2010	10,207	11,210
2011	9,284	10,474
2012	9,120	9,972
2013	9,175	10,199
2014	9,453	10,648
2015	8,975	10,114

The residents' abortion rate column is the relevant one, given the focus of the Colorado Family Planning Initiative. Between 2009–13, the abortion absolute number declined by 1,560—a 14.5 percent decline.

Republican state representative Don Coram, who sponsored a bill to expand the program in Colorado, said, "If you're anti-abortion and also a fiscal conservative, I think this is a win-win situation for you."[17] Most of Colorado's Republican state senators, however, objected to further expanding the initiative. They asserted that the initiative was redundant with other family planning services. They also said the possibility that IUDs would cause abortions, and not just act as contraception, made it unacceptable for public funding.[18] I will also discuss some conservatives' criticism of the Colorado initiative, and my evaluation of that critique, below. In the context of discussing the Affordable Care Act of 2010, below, I will return to the question raised by the Colorado Family Planning Initiative: what about lower-income women who are uninsured or underinsured? There are important questions raised by the Black Women's Reproductive Justice movement, for example, which must be examined.

---

17. Verlee, "Colorado Debates."
18. Verlee, "Colorado Debates."

Texas Data 2013–16

In 2013, Texas House Bill 2 banned abortions after twenty weeks of pregnancy, required abortion providers to have admitting privileges at a hospital nearby, required all abortions—not only surgeries but taking pills—to take place in "ambulatory surgical centers" on par with hospitals in cleanliness and one-way corridors and sizes of examination rooms, and discouraged doctors to prescribe drugs for medical abortion. Texas lawmakers asserted that these laws were helpful to protecting women's health. Of the state's forty-one clinics, only twenty-two remained open in November 2013,[19] and fifteen remained open as of November 2015.[20] Two clinics in the Rio Grande Valley which had together performed 2,634 abortions in 2011 closed in March 2014.[21] In 2014 alone, the number of abortions performed in Texas fell by 14 percent.

Conservatives are often critical of the media attention given to contraception and the ACA, citing such celebration as evidence of the media's liberal bias. Conservatives argue that abortion rates declined from 2011–15 because Republican state lawmakers passed restrictions on abortion providers, imposed mandatory counseling and a waiting period before an abortion, and put parental involvement and informed consent laws in place.[22] Between 2011 and 2015, thiry-one states passed a total of 288 such laws,[23] stating that they served the purpose of protecting women's health. Conservatives suggest the Texas laws of 2013 should be considered as preferable to contraception access through the ACA.

In 2013, one of the abortion clinics, Whole Woman's Health, sued the state and won an injunction staying parts of the law. In 2016, in a 5–3 decision in *Whole Woman's Health v. Hellerstedt*, the Supreme Court overturned two of the four parts of the Texas law. Had the Supreme Court sided with Texas and against Whole Woman's Health, a total of ten more clinics would have closed: four in Houston, two in El Paso and one each in Austin, Fort Worth, and San Antonio, as well as one in McAllen temporarily. This would have left Texas with nine or ten abortion facilities to serve 5.4 million women of reproductive age in the country's second-largest state by size and population.[24]

19. Fernandez and Goodnough, "Opinion Transforms."
20. "Research Brief: Texas Women's Experiences."
21. Carmon, "Texas Women."
22. New, "Obamacare."
23. Agrawal, "Abortion Rate Declines."
24. Grossman et al., "Change in Abortion Services."

In July 2016, the court declared that there was no clear connection between the Texas law and improving women's health. Abortion clinics need to be properly equipped and sanitary, obviously, but not to the level of a surgical room in a hospital. Supervised abortion procedures delivered by a health care professional are routine and do not result in immediate complications that require hospitalization. Justice Stephen Breyer observed:

> Abortions taking place in an abortion facility are safe—indeed, safer than numerous procedures that take place outside hospitals and to which Texas does not apply its surgical-center requirements. Nationwide, childbirth is 14 times more likely than abortion to result in death, but Texas law allows a midwife to oversee childbirth in the patient's own home. Colonoscopy, a procedure that typically takes place outside a hospital (or surgical center) setting, has a mortality rate 10 times higher than an abortion . . . the mortality rate for liposuction, another outpatient procedure, is 28 times higher than the mortality rate for abortion . . . Medical treatment after an incomplete miscarriage often involves a procedure identical to that involved in a nonmedical abortion, but it often takes place outside a hospital or surgical center.[25]

The Justices acknowledged that Philadelphia abortionist Kermit Gosnell's actions were scandalously wrong. "But," said Justice Breyer, "there is no reason to believe that an extra layer of regulation would have affected that behavior."[26]

There is a low risk of later complications with abortion. Women who do have complications resulting from either medical or surgical abortion experience them a few days after the abortion and would see their doctor at a hospital. The Texas law, in other words, governing the location of abortions per se did not contribute meaningfully to women's health outcomes. In fact, the justices noted that the lawyers representing the state of Texas could not identify a single woman whose health had been preserved or improved by the law:

> We add that, when directly asked at oral argument whether Texas knew of a single instance in which the new requirement would have helped even one woman obtain better treatment, Texas admitted that there was no evidence in the record of such a case.[27]

    25. *Whole Woman's Health et al. v. Hellerstedt* (136 S. Ct. 2292, 2315, 2016). See also Liptak, "Supreme Court."
    26. *Whole Woman's Health et al. v. Hellerstedt* (136 S. Ct. 2292, 2313, 2016).
    27. *Whole Woman's Health et al. v. Hellerstedt* (136 S. Ct. 2292, 2315, 2016).

The court declared that abortion physicians therefore did not need to have admitting privileges to a nearby hospital within thirty miles (as the Texas law mandated) in order to administer an abortion, especially to simply take two pills (a nonsurgical "medication abortion"), and that such a requirement imposed "a substantial obstacle" to a woman's right to procure an abortion, and an "undue burden" on her.[28] There was nothing unsafe about Texas abortion clinics at that time.

Nevertheless, due to the appointment of conservative judges Neil Gorsuch and Brett Kavanaugh to the Supreme Court, challenges to the 2016 decision are likely to recur.[29] At the time of this writing, the Louisiana case *June Medical Services v. Gee* is before the court. Meanwhile, other states have passed TRAP laws similar to those in Texas. Five states have one abortion provider: Missouri, Mississippi, North Dakota, South Dakota, and Wyoming.[30]

Did the Texas laws contribute to reduced abortions? They certainly did. *The Los Angeles Times* covered the Texas laws in a January 2017 article, in which researcher Dr. Daniel Grossman affirmed, "In Texas I don't think that the decline in abortion has been related to improvements in contraceptive use. I think it has more to do with barriers to accessing abortion."[31] Grossman is a professor of gynecology, obstetrics, and reproductive sciences at UC San Francisco's Bixby Center for Reproductive Health, director of the collaborative research group Advancing New Standards in Reproductive Health, and an investigator for the Texas Policy Evaluation Project (TxPEP).

The *L.A. Times* further reported that Dr. Grossman and colleagues "found that while the total number of abortions in Texas fell, the number performed during the second trimester rose." That number—a 27 percent increase from 2013–14 of second trimester abortions (from 4814 to 6117 procedures), characterized in other reports and before the Supreme Court as "small but significant,"[32] prompted Justice Anthony Kennedy to comment, "This law has really increased the number of surgical procedures as opposed to medical procedures, and this may not be medically wise."[33] Second trimester abortions, while safe, are associated with greater risks of

---

28. *Whole Woman's Health et al. v. Hellerstedt* (136 S. Ct. 2292, 2315, 2016).

29. "Reactions to Supreme Court."

30. Nash et al., "State Policy Trends 2019." See also Harrington and Gould, "Number of Abortion Clinics."

31. Agrawal, "Abortion Rate Declines."

32. Grossman, "Use of Public Health Evidence."

33. *Whole Woman's Health et al. v. Hellerstedt* (136 S. Ct. 2292, 2315, 2016).

complications, mostly hemorrhaging and/or infections.[34] There are fewer physicians who are willing to perform second trimester abortions, and it is more expensive.[35]

The TxPEP found that "medication abortions" (by taking the two RU-486 pills) declined by 70 percent in the first six months of the law going into effect. That is largely because the Texas law required women to go to an expensive "ambulatory surgical center" to simply ingest two pills for a "medication abortion."[36] Many of the lower-cost clinics which closed were located in communities on the U.S.-Mexico border—like El Paso in the west, and Brownsville and McAllen in the east—where doctors could not comply with the requirement that they retain admitting privileges at a nearby hospital.[37] The women in those communities are disproportionately lower-income and Latina, even overwhelmingly so.

Women's decisions whether to get an abortion were influenced by the distance they had to travel, which appears to be the "unofficial" but actual purpose of the law, which is what made the law unconstitutional. In urban areas where the distance to a clinic did not change for women, the abortion rate saw a small decline. However, in rural areas, where the distance did increase—sometimes dramatically—the abortion rate declined by nearly 50 percent.[38] Among women who lived an additional fifty to ninety-nine miles from the nearest clinic, the abortion rate declined by 36 percent; among women who lived one hundred miles away or more, the rate declined by half.[39] If we believe that the unintended pregnancy rate also halved, then we might end the discussion here. But if the unintended pregnancy rate stayed roughly the same, the question we must ask is what did those women do? Did women choose to carry their pregnancies to term, and keep their babies?

Some women administered abortions to themselves. While this is a difficult phenomenon to measure accurately, one economist estimated the number to be 5 per 1,000 women of childbearing age.[40] He found that women living in the ten states with the fewest abortion clinics had 54 percent fewer abortions than women living in the ten states with the most abortion clinics. That difference amounts to 11 abortions for every 1,000 women. Women in

34. Zane et al., "Abortion-Related Mortality."
35. Grossman, "Use of Public Health Evidence."
36. Carmon, "On Eve of SCOTUS."
37. Carmon, "On Eve of SCOTUS."
38. Wilkins, "Abortions Dropped."
39. Wilkins, "Abortions Dropped."
40. Stephens-Davidowitz, "Return."

the ten states with the fewest abortion clinics had 6 more live births for every 1,000 women. Assuming equal pregnancy rates, that left a gap of 5 abortions per 1,000 women. If that rate held true among Texas's population of women of childbearing age in 2012, which was between 5.5 and 6.0 million (assume the lower for this purpose), that would be 27,500 unreported abortions. If we assume that some of those abortions had been unreported even prior to the passage of HB2, and that the TRAP laws had a deterrence effect on unwanted pregnancies, then we might reduce the gap to 3, or 2, abortions per 1,000 women. By this method, we would estimate that Texas women had 16,500, or 11,000, unreported abortions, respectively.

Moreover, we have estimates based on very recent history in Texas. In 2012, the TxPEP took a state-wide survey of 779 representative women in Texas and asked them whether they knew if a "best friend" had ever attempted (successfully or not) a self-induced abortion. This is a common researchers' method to ask people about subjects they may be hesitant to reveal; it also gives an additional data point. The researchers then asked about the women themselves. It must be stressed that the timing of the survey was in 2012, and the questions were open-ended as to the timeframe of the abortions. This is about abortions at any point in time in the past. In response to the survey, 1.7 percent women said that they themselves had tried to end a pregnancy; 1.8 percent "were sure their best friend had done this"; an additional 2.3 percent said they suspected their best friend had done so.[41]

Extrapolated to the total number of women between the ages of eighteen and forty-nine living in Texas, which was 5,949,149 in 2012, the proportion suggests that between 100,000 and 240,000 women attempted a self-induced abortion, not in one year, but over their childbearing lifetime. The "lower figure counts only women who reported their own attempts; the higher one includes women who reported the actions of friends." Also, the lower figure is based on the 1.7 percent tally which is almost certainly underreported, because women tend to underreport their own abortions in surveys.[42]

The study also observed demographic patterns. "Latina women living in a county that borders Mexico" were significantly more likely to have attempted a self-induced abortion themselves, or known someone else who had. There was also an income and cost factor: "Women who reported that they had ever found it difficult to obtain reproductive health services like birth control or

---

41. Grossman et al., "Research Brief."
42. Grossman et al., "Research Brief."

Pap smears (for example, because of the cost of these services or because of difficulties arranging transport to a clinic)."[43]

Researchers also asked about the method of abortion. Misoprostol, also known by its brand name Cytotec, the second pill involved in the RU-486 treatment, was reported. It is known to be available in Mexican pharmacies and on the black market in the U.S. When used early in pregnancy, misoprostol is effective and safe. Other methods of attempted self-induced abortion reported include "herbs or homeopathic remedies, getting hit or punched in the abdomen, using alcohol or illicit drugs, or taking hormonal pills."[44] The frequency of each method used was unclear; women could have attempted more than one method.

Other women traveled remarkably long distances to obtain an abortion. Another TxPEP study of 398 Texan women found that those women whose closest abortion clinic closed traveled to the next one an average of 85 miles one way, whereas those women whose local clinic remained open traveled an average of 22 miles; the nationwide average is 30 miles. After the law's passage, 38 percent of the women had to travel an average of 70 miles one way, 25 percent lived more than 139 miles from their closest clinic, and another 10 percent of women lived more than 256 miles away.[45] Women in Corpus Christi traveled two hours each way to San Antonio.[46] Women in rural West Texas who would have gone to San Angelo may have had to travel three hours to the nearest city and clinic.[47] Some women who felt comfortable crossing the border to Mexico, and were able to do so, went to Mexican pharmacies to obtain pills.[48] Of course, these women had to consider expenses for travel, lost wages, child care, lodging, and food. Texas law requires a woman to have two appointments with an abortion provider separated by twenty-four hours, although this requirement is waived for women who travel over 100 miles.[49]

The TxPEP study found that nearly 40 percent of women whose closest clinic had closed were not able to obtain the medical abortion they wanted, and resorted to second-term surgical abortion, compared to 22 percent of

---

43. Grossman et al., "Research Brief."
44. Grossman et al., "Research Brief."
45. Gerdts et al., "Impact of Clinic Closures," discussed by Clark-Flory, "Supreme Court."
46. Stoeltje, "Abortion Clinic Closes."
47. Lopez, "For Supporters."
48. Eckholm, "Pill Available."
49. Lopez, "For Supporters."

women whose closest clinic stayed open.[50] Some women were *delayed* by the Texas law, which appears to have pushed more women into a more expensive category, with higher risk for complications.

There is quite good reason, then, to question the statistical conclusion that abortions in Texas decreased by 14 percent from 2013–14. The study by the TxPEP was conducted among women aged eighteen to forty-nine, spanning roughly thirty years of fertility. If we assume that 1/30th of the reported self-induced abortions occurred in each of the roughly thirty years represented by the women surveyed, we have an estimated range of 3,333 to 8,000 self-induced abortions per year. At least some of the women who self-administered an abortion visited an abortion clinic. So that data could, in theory, be partially comprehended already by the known CDC data for Texas, shown below:

Table 8.3. Abortions Per Year, Texas: 2002–16

Year	Residents Reporting Abortion	Occurrences of Abortion Reported
2002	76,539	79,929
2003	76,337	79,166
2004	72,978	74,801
2005	74,569	77,108
2006	79,266	81,883
2007	78,034	80,886
2008	78,464	81,366
2009	74,962	77,630
2010	75,151	77,463
2011	70,214	72,332
2012	66,349	68,201
2013	61,812	63,168
2014	54,401	54,148
2015	54,194	53,940
2016	53,567	53,481

---

50. Gerdts et al., "Impact of Clinic Closures," discussed by Clark-Flory, "Supreme Court."

It is very likely that in 2014, the number of attempted self-induced abortions was higher and that this range would need to be shifted upward, but by how much is uncertain. Recall that clinic closures under HB2 began in July 2013, and as of November 2019, while some clinics had returned, only twenty-two clinics were open in Texas due to the resources needed to restart.[51] Surely some women who attempted self-administered abortions *and were successful* at home do not appear in this data. If we assume that one-third of all women who attempted a self-induced abortion and were successful (via misoprostol, for instance[52]) did not go to an abortion clinic, then we have a range of about 1,111 to 2,667 to add to the 2014 numbers and later. The TxPEP researchers also point out that rates of attempted self-induced abortion are higher in Texas than the national average. Whereas less than 2 percent of women nationwide reported trying to cause an abortion prior to coming into a clinic, 7 percent of abortion clinic patients in Texas reported taking or doing something on their own to attempt an abortion beforehand.

I suggest the following comparison. If we add 1,111 to 2,667 more abortions to the reported numbers for 2014, 2015, and 2016, respectively, then we have low-adjusted and high-adjusted numbers, shown in columns 2 and 3. If we add the 11,000 abortions estimated by the statistical gap comparing clinics, we get the results in column 4.

Table 8.4. Abortions Per Year, Texas: 2012–2016 (Projections)

Year	Residents Reporting Abortion	+Self-Abort, Low TxPEP	+Self-Abort, High TxPEP	+Self-Abort, Gap by Clinics	Projected Without HB2
2012	66,349			66,349	66,349
2013	61,812			61,812	64,437
2014	54,401	55,512	57,068	65,401	62,580
2015	54,194	55,305	56,864	65,194	60,777
2016	53,567	54,678	56,234	64,567	59,026

There is also a factual narrative that must accompany the reported numbers in columns 2, 3, and 4: Women, and disproportionately poor and Hispanic women, chose to attempt self-induced abortions, using methods as safe

---

51. Lopez, "For Supporters," presumably drawing on data from the Guttmacher Institute

52. Jones and Jerman, "Abortion Incidence 2014," in their national study found that early medication abortions accounted for 31 percent of all nonhospital abortions in 2014, which was up from 24 percent in 2011.

as misoprostol, to methods as troubling as being hit in the abdomen and drinking alcohol. Other women, carrying their pregnancies to term, were surely pushed deeper into poverty.

Column 5 reflects the "do nothing" alternative for Texas. The abortion rate was decreasing in Texas from 2006–12 by an average of 2.9 percent per year. This decline was probably linked to a combination of increased contraception use, as in the rest of the country, and some mild abortion restrictions specific to Texas. If we extrapolate that data into 2013–16, and compare it to the official CDC numbers for Texas, we see a gradual decline.

The projected numbers in column 5 follow the most advantageous starting point for a decline: a peak in 2006. That is not unreasonable, however, as a point of reference for the "do nothing" alternative; nationwide, abortion numbers also hit a relative maximum in 2006. In point of fact, Texas did *less* than the "do nothing" alternative. Between 2000 and 2010, Texas cut its already underfunded lower-income Title X programs so that, in 2010, 46 percent of Texas's 1.7 million women who were in need of publicly funded contraceptive services and supplies were uninsured, causing a 30 percent rise in the number of women needing such services.[53] Then, in August 2012, Texas opted *out* of the Medicaid expansion under the ACA.

Had Texas enacted a modest contraception policy instead, it is likely that these projected numbers could have decreased even more substantially. Texas could have enacted policies that made contraception use even more accessible in particular areas, focusing on the Plan B pill, which affects fertilization and not implantation, and the LARCs (IUDs and hormones). Nationwide, as we recall from above, the abortion rate from 2008–11 decreased by 13 percent. If Texas decreased its abortion rate by 13 percent from 2013–16, the 2016 number would be 56,060.

If we consider these two policies to be mutually exclusive alternatives to each other, and if the goal for both was to reduce abortions, then the effectiveness gap between them might reasonably be said to be minimal, perhaps negligible.

If, however, Texas followed a more robust plan engaging young women, like Colorado 2009–13, they probably would have seen a substantially greater decrease. Recall that thirty thousand IUDs delivered in Colorado contributed to a 50 percent decrease in that state's abortion rate for fifteen- to nineteen-year-old women, and an 18 percent decrease for twenty- to twenty-four-year-olds. How might a similar effort in Texas have worked? Texas's CDC data reported by age group is:

---

53. Hasstedt, "State."

Table 8.5. Abortions Per Year by Age Group, Texas: 2011–16

Year	Age <15	Age 15–19	Age 20–24	Age 25–29	Age 30–34	Age 35–39	Age 40+
2011	176	7,548	23,363	19,139	12,141	6,866	3,059
2012	138	6,320	21,733	18,511	11,951	6,584	2,877
2013	194	6,939	20,268	16,763	10,700	6,038	2,226
2014	NA	NA	NA	NA	NA	NA	NA
2015	151	5,001	16,738	15,016	9,592	5,490	1,946
2016	107	4,903	16,152	15,085	9,758	5,601	1,875

Between 2012 and 2016, if Texas had taken the following actions, they might have seen the following results:

- If Texas had done education programs in connection with high schools, especially in border towns and major cities, the 2012 numbers for fifteen- to nineteen-year-olds might have been cut by 50 percent (per Colorado) from 6,320 to 3,160 in 2016. This would have surpassed the decline driven by the TRAP laws by almost 2,000.
- If Texas decided to follow a targeted but robust policy aimed at older women, even larger declines might be likely. One possibility might have been outreach to college-age women, young working women, and rural health clinics. If the 2012 numbers for twenty- to twenty-four-year-olds were reduced by 18 percent from 21,733 to 17,821, the number would have lagged the TRAP-related number by roughly 1,700. A 25 percent reduction would result in 16,300, roughly equivalent to the TRAP level.
- If Texas reached out to working women and urban and rural mothers of young children, the 2012 number for twenty-five- to twenty-nine-year-olds might have been reduced by 18 percent from 18,511 to 15,179 in 2016. That would have been comparable to the reduction under the TRAP laws. A 25 percent reduction would result in 13,883, nearly 1,300 less than the TRAP level.
- If the 2012 numbers for thirty- to thirty-four-year-olds were reduced by 18 percent from 11,951 to 9,799 in 2016, this would have been comparable to the TRAP decline. A 25 percent reduction would result in 8,963, about 800 less than the TRAP level.

This estimation calls into question the conservative assertion, in Texas and other states, that TRAP laws are more effective than, or equally effective as, increasing the availability of contraception. Do TRAP laws lower abortion rates *more* than the contraception alternative? From a statistical standpoint, that is not likely. There is sufficient evidence that restrictive laws do not have a deterring effect on unwanted pregnancies. States like Texas that implemented TRAP laws are very likely to have shifted abortion counts from visible and counted at the clinic to "invisible" and off the books—that is, significant numbers of women attempt self-induced abortions at home.

Moreover, in principle and in practice, a contraception plan has the ability to scale *up* its impact, and continue bringing abortion rates *down*, depending on how easy it is to engage women and supply them with contraception. The TRAP approach, by comparison, probably cannot. From a social policy standpoint, in order for TRAP laws to *increase* their impact, people would have to either abstain or get better and better at using the contraception they have; or the restrictions approach must become even more restrictive.

Are TRAP laws counter-productive? That is, do they actually increase abortion rates? An honest assessment has to compare TRAP laws to the "do nothing" alternative. By itself, implementing TRAP laws *does* lower abortion rates more than not implementing them. The question is whether that is the only goal and meaningful measurement. Problems enter in when we try to estimate other consequences, for example, the number of successfully self-administered abortions, which is likely to be quite substantial. We face another problem because social conservatives also prefer to implement "abstinence-only" sex education,[54] even though conservative states which implement that approach have the *highest* rates of teen pregnancy.[55] On that, see more below.

Other important concerns also enter in: How humane are these alternatives? How much do they cost to administer? How much do they cost when connected with other social welfare programs? What impact do these policies have on poverty rates? And so on.

Christian Ethics and Policy Principles Regarding TRAP Laws

From a Christian ethics standpoint, when comparing TRAP laws with contraception availability, there are several points to make. First, the issue of equal treatment under the law is an important one, even when

---

54. "20 Abstinence Only Statistics."
55. Stanger-Hall and Hall, "Abstinence-Only Education."

Christians find abortion law disagreeable. As the Supreme Court majority made clear, the Fourteenth Amendment is a formidable consideration, and one that has resonance with the biblical vision of how to treat people fairly. Christians should support it because of the connective tissue it has with the procedural equality tenet of Jewish law—"There shall be one standard for you, for the stranger as well as the native" (Lev 19:22)—and the Golden Rule tenet of Jesus' teaching—"Do unto others as you would have them do unto you" (Matt 7:12). Both Moses and Jesus are also concerned about substantive economic justice for the poor as a foundation for life and liberty (e.g., Lev 25:1–55; Deut 15:1–17, 24:10–22; Isa 58:1–14; Ezek 22:12; Luke 12:13–34, 14:12–25, 16:19–31, 18:15—19:10; Acts 2:41–45, 4:31–34; 2 Cor 8–9; 1 John 3:16–18; Jas 5:1–6).

Regardless of whether Texas lawmakers intended to impose on some women an undue burden to access abortion services, that was the *effect* of the law. Very early Supreme Court precedent demonstrates how equal treatment under the law is significant. Earlier in chapter 5, I discussed *Yick Wo v. Hopkins* (1886). That ruling is relevant here, and bears repeating: "Though the law itself be fair on its face, and impartial in appearance, yet, if it is applied and administered by public authority with an evil eye and an unequal hand, so as practically to make unjust and illegal discriminations, between persons in similar circumstances . . . the denial of equal justice is still within the prohibition of the Constitution."[56] The Fourteenth Amendment's "equal protection" clause is relevant, in addition to the "due process" clause.[57]

It is true that a state cannot guarantee a ready workforce of doctors who are willing to perform abortions, or other matters of accessibility via travel, affordability, and so on. Nor can the state order private physicians to move from urban to rural areas. But on the basis of the Fourteenth Amendment, the state should not erect more laws and economic barriers that further exacerbate those differences. Even if *Roe v. Wade* is overturned, state-specific statutes might still be relevant from a legal standpoint, if abortions are legal to twenty weeks in Texas. From a moral standpoint, if Christians want to pursue policies that will bring the abortion rate down, they are morally obliged to prefer policies that do not have an adverse discriminatory effect. Making contraception more accessible is the better option from that standpoint. I will comment on conservative Christian hesitation about that policy in chapter 11.

---

56. Although the *McClesky v. Kemp* (1987) decision went contrary to this basic principle, the direction of the court is uncertain, and equal choice claims might still be upheld with *McClesky* remaining a judicial outlier, or even overturned. Discussed by Graber, *Rethinking Abortion*, 77–107, and Alexander, *New Jim Crow*, 109–14.

57. Charles and Alexander, "Abortions." Graber, *Rethinking Abortion*.

Second, policies intended to reduce the rate of abortion should be honestly named as such. Christians are commanded not to lie (Exod 20:16). Lawmakers stated that their "official" objective was not to reduce abortion rates per se, probably because they would have to answer for why they did not want to expand contraception availability as well. Instead, Texas legislators put forward and defended these laws as contributing positively to women's health. Justice Alito wrote in his dissent that Texas legislators might have been motivated to protect Texas residents from the horrors of another Kermit Gosnell. Even if that was the intent of some, there is such a thing as going too far, as when governments use war to consolidate power. When we find, as the Supreme Court articulated, that these laws cannot be considered to serve the purpose of protecting women's health, why not be honest? From all appearances, the Texas laws were not put forward with sufficient integrity, perhaps on the part of the laws, and perhaps on the part of the lawmakers.

Another example related to information and integrity surfaced shortly before the final Supreme Court hearing. A Texas state employee confidentially spoke to NBC News, "accusing state officials overseeing the Department of Health Services of intentionally blocking the information and instructing staff members to mislead people who ask for it."[58] My purpose here is not to re-litigate this accusation, but to raise it as an example of a more general concern. If we are arguing from an outcomes-based orientation, then we cannot obstruct the gathering, analysis, or publication of all the relevant data.

Christians need to pressure both conservative and liberal policymakers (especially if that includes fellow Christians) to straightforwardly acknowledge the intended goals of our policies, knowing that they will not always do so. We believe that our policies have effects, because laws impact people's behavior, incentives, institutions, and organizations, and we would not invest the time and energy in policymaking and voting unless we believed they did. It is surprising to me that in 2016, the three SCOTUS justices who dissented—Alito, Roberts, and Thomas—said that there was no direct causal link proven between the Texas law and the closings of abortion clinics. They said this *as a joint reason* for their dissent, arguing that the closings might have been caused by Texas's decision to withdraw state funds, or doctors retiring, or a declining demand for abortion services. While I am not an expert on rules of evidence in the courtroom, I do not understand why the testimonies of doctors and clinic administrators themselves, who could not legally operate given the state's TRAP laws, were not sufficient. Asking for more

58. Carmon, "On Eve of SCOTUS."

evidence seems to be juristic handwaving to shield the closure of the clinics. The three justices reflected a surprising willingness to suddenly be ignorant about policy effectiveness. If conservatives are willing to credit the reduction of abortion rates to restrictive state laws, then they must be willing to explain how and why those laws have impact. Therefore, if conservatives are willing to *be uncertain* about a cause-effect relationship at such a direct, demonstrable level about the clinics, then they should be willing to be *largely ignorant* about cause-effect relationships at a higher, more abstract level. Perhaps the decline in abortion rates, then, is an unfathomable mystery—something that is happening independent of any laws. Would conservative lawmakers be willing to repeal TRAP laws because they suddenly find themselves in a cloud of unknowing about the effectiveness of law? I presume not, so any willful ignorance in this realm is self-defeating.

Third, Christians need to call policymakers to frankly acknowledge the unintended—or at least, unstated—consequences of our policies, as well. Anti-abortion laws seem to stop abortion like Prohibition stopped alcohol consumption. The "demand" for abortion as an economic product is fairly inelastic, as it is for alcohol. The Guttmacher Institute reports that globally, the abortion rate in countries that prohibit abortion altogether is roughly equal to that in countries that are relatively permissive: 37 per 1,000 women vs. 34 per 1,000 women.[59] The investigative studies done by the TxPEP in Texas bear out the same pattern and raise the same concerns. Outlawing abortion—or making abortion services extraordinarily hard to access—creates a vast gray market for abortions, further jeopardizing women's health, despite the stated objective. Surveys of both facilities and women suggest an unknown but significant rate of self-administered abortions. Researchers Jones and Jerman found that in 2014, 12 percent of nonhospital facilities (i.e., abortion clinics, non-specialized clinics, and physicians' offices) nationwide reported that they saw one or more woman who had attempted a self-induced abortion, but there were regional differences: 21 percent in the South, and 16 percent in the Midwest.[60] More than two-thirds of facilities were able to quantify this caseload, and three-quarters reported having treated ten or fewer of these patients in 2014. Yet another study done in 2014 suggests that this data will be hard to adequately understand close to real time: 34 percent of Americans who have ever been involved in an abortion—either as the mother or presumed father—told no one else.[61]

---

59. "Induced Abortion Worldwide."
60. Jones and Jerman, "Abortion Incidence 2014."
61. Cowan, "Secrets and Misperceptions."

Hence, Dr. Grossman and colleagues caution doctors in states with restrictive laws that they will certainly see a rise in women patients who self-administer abortions, and have complications. Complications include sepsis, hemorrhage, pelvic-organ injury, and toxic exposure. The combination of mifepristone and misoprostol is the safest method, even in the second trimester, although some women will probably use other, more dangerous methods, depending on their options or level of information.[62] These TRAP laws therefore increase the likelihood that women will see their doctors to perform surgical abortions during the second trimester, a procedure which is more expensive for the woman and for the health care system and psychically costly for the doctor as well.

Complicating matters, seven states make self-managed abortions (through RU-486) out to be a criminal offense, and twenty four others have laws that can be interpreted as doing so. Laws criminalizing self-managed abortion have the unintended or unstated effect of driving it into the shadows and driving women who need care further from care. It is notable that the American Medical Association and the American College of Obstetricians and Gynecologists "take strong positions against criminalization of self-managed abortion, because it deters patients with complications from seeking care."[63] Grossman recommends that doctors care about their patients' legal safety as well as their physical safety:

> No state mandates that health care providers report suspected or confirmed self-managed abortion, including for minors. Indeed, reporting may violate patients' privacy rights and result in penalties for those who report. Reporting is also problematic because caregivers are more likely to report women of color and low-income women than white or affluent women in similar circumstances.[64]

Since treating a miscarriage and a medication-induced abortion in the second trimester are clinically similar processes, a doctor can administer care without knowing whether the patient had experienced a spontaneous miscarriage or an induced abortion. This fact contributes to the slippage of anti-abortion policies when the rubber meets the road.

Fourth, in the case of Texas, Christians should point out that if state residents and lawmakers wish to protect women's health, there are many ways to do that beyond TRAP laws, including ways that impact maternal and prenatal health. Texas ranked forty-fourth out of the fifty states in the

---

62. Harris and Grossman, "Complications." See also "Doctors and Health Care."
63. Harris and Grossman, "Complications."
64. Harris and Grossman, "Complications."

Commonwealth Fund's evaluation of general health system performance by state.[65] Texas ranked dead last on the specific measure of health care access and affordability, forty-ninth on prevention and treatment, forty-eighth on low-income health equity, and thirty-second on race/ethnicity health equity. More than 6 million Texans have no health insurance of any kind, including 2.4 million women[66] and probably over 1 million children. In Texas and other states which connect moral conservatism to economic conservatism, not only anti-abortion laws but the individualistic, "meritocratic" approach to health policy drive women and families further into poverty, vulnerability, and poor health.

If economic conservatives dislike social entitlement policies and prefer policies stressing personal responsibility, then they might consider the significant damage Texas's big oil and gas companies do to people's health by poisoning their air, water, and land.[67] Industrial companies in Texas commit thousands of violations of the Clean Air Act, which have led to forty-two deaths and $241 million in *known* health-related costs *per year*, in Texas alone, absorbed by Texans against their will. Surely this has an impact on women's health. When a pregnant woman breathes in fine particulate air pollution—the kind given off by construction sites, unpaved roads, car and truck exhaust, power plants, and fires—the odds increase dramatically that her baby will have autism.[68] If she lives near a farm using certain pesticides, her child is 60 percent more likely to have autism.[69] Since we know that a woman's body expels certain toxins into her innocent fetus and breast milk, will this draw the ire of conservative activists? Also, what about elevated lead levels in Texas children?[70] Higher rates of leukemia and spina bifida in Texas children, probably because of exposure to benzene?[71] Increased asthma rates in children living within one mile of shale gas development sites, affecting 4.5 million Texans?[72] Increased asthma rates in children exposed while in the womb to certain plastics in women's nail polish, food packaging, and school supplies?[73]

65. Radley et al., "Aiming Higher."
66. Hasstedt, "State."
67. Pabst and Metzger, "Illegal Air Pollution."
68. Raz et al., "Autism Spectrum Disorder," summarized by Rivas, "Air Pollution."
69. Shelton et al., "Neurodevelopmental Disorders," summarized by Olson, "Nearby Pesticides" and Sagiv et al., "Prenatal Organophosphate."
70. Kurtin et al., "Demographic Risk Factors."
71. Whitworth et al., "Childhood Lymphohematopoietic Cancer." Lupo et al., "Maternal Exposure."
72. Willis et al., "Shale Gas."
73. Olson, "Pregnant Mothers."

In other ways, American law protects the fetus from harmful substances in utero. In chapter 5, we examined recent state-level laws, favored by conservatives, bearing directly on pregnant women, where their health care providers become mandatory reporters to law enforcement if they suspect that a pregnant woman is abusing substances. If the moral and legal basis for protecting the fetus from harmful substances has been established, why not prosecute industrial companies for chemically poisoning both pregnant mothers and their fetuses?

One root of this problem is corporate limited liability law, something evangelicals in Great Britain were firmly against when it was first considered there, on the grounds that not being fully liable for damages caused is a violation of Christian duty and grossly immoral.[74] Limited liability law allows fossil fuel companies to slough off "externalities" like chemical pollution from their accounting books, which is a considerable flaw in the argument of conservatives: why should actual people be fully responsible for what they do, while "corporate people"—if for a moment we accept the premise that corporations are people—are not?[75] Even Adam Smith—Mr. "Invisible Hand" himself—was *against* limited liability.[76] Why not repeal limited liability status, then? After all, citizens and lawmakers who stand up against abortion but allow chemicals into fetuses that cause brain damage, autism, asthma, spinal bifida, etc. undermine their own case. When a woman puts chemicals into her body to harm her fetus, they are outraged, but when other people put chemicals there against her will and usually her knowledge, they stand by and rationalize it. Is it really true that one can be a moral conservative and an economic conservative?

National Data 2011–16

My purpose in this section is not to defend the ACA per se, as I explained my ethical and economic rationales for preferring a single-payer public health insurance option in the previous chapter. My comments here are to primarily address two ethical concerns related to the implementation of using public, taxpayer money for women's reproductive health. Should public money

---

74. Hilton, *Age of Atonement*.

75. Mills and Schluter, *After Capitalism*, 127–43, advocate repealing corporate "limited liability" laws; Mills and Schluter are Christian economists and policy analysts at the Jubilee Centre, UK. See also Maizes, "Limited Liability"; Mattera, "Buck, Doesn't Stop"; Blankenburg et al., "Limited Liability."

76. Elliot, "Plc: The Prerogative."

fund an abortion? And should it fund contraception? The ACA has triggered debates about both questions, which are worth comment.

In the U.K., where almost all health care is public, taxpayer funded, and government-run, 97 percent of abortions have been covered by the National Health Service or another government department. Most abortions can be procured within twenty-four weeks. Acceptable vs. unacceptable reasons for abortion are not given on the NHS website. After twenty-four weeks, abortions can be performed if the mother's life is at stake or if the child would have severe deformities.[77]

In Canada, almost all abortions are paid for by taxpayers, though policy and availability can vary by province. Canada's policy states that "medical necessity" is what qualifies a woman to get an abortion, but no definition exists, and Canadian administrators are noticeably averse to defining it.[78] A 2011 poll showed that 54 percent believed that abortions for medical emergencies (rape, incest, threat to mother's life) should be taxpayer funded, and 64 percent did not support taxpayer funding for all abortions.[79]

In the U.S., a majority of the public generally disapproves of public funding for abortion, except for the following exceptions: rape, incest, and threat to the mother's life. The Hyde Amendment, an attachment to federal spending bills, prohibits federal funding to be allocated to abortion services through Medicaid or other Department of Health and Human Services (HHS) programs, except in cases where exceptions are granted. Since 1994, the exceptions include rape, incest, or "where a physical condition endangers a woman's life unless an abortion is performed." Between 1981 and 1993, rape and incest were not included. The Hyde Amendment is not permanent law, but a rider renewed by congressional approval to every budgetary bill. Policies like the Hyde Amendment have been attached elsewhere. For instance, though exceptions are granted, federal funding for abortion cannot be allocated to private insurance plans that cover federal employees, or accessed by women in federal prisons, the military,

---

77. "Abortion" (United Kingdom National Health Service).

78. "Funding: Tax-Funded Abortions" says, "In British Columbia, Alberta, Manitoba, Ontario, Quebec, and Newfoundland, abortion is paid for under the publicly funded system whether it is performed in a hospital or private clinic. In New Brunswick, hospital abortions are paid for by taxpayers but private clinic abortions are not. In Saskatchewan, the Northwest Territories, Nunavut, and Yukon hospital abortions are paid for by taxpayers but there are no private clinics. No abortions are performed in Prince Edward Island. The province does cover abortions performed elsewhere if they have been declared by a doctor to be medically necessary and have been pre-authorized and approved."

79. "Funding: Tax-Funded Abortions."

or Peace Corps.[80] It should be noted that many Democrats (the pro-life Democrats are in the minority) have called, unsuccessfully, to eliminate the Hyde Amendment. The Democratic Party's 2016 platform called for eliminating it. Conversely, Republicans have also tried, without success, to make the Hyde Amendment into permanent law. In 2019, HHS finalized a rule to require private insurers offering non-Hyde abortion services to collect at least $1 per month in premiums to cover abortion services and separate them from other premiums collected by the insurer.[81] Although some economic questions do exist, while the ACA is the law of the land, the Hyde Amendment is a workable moral solution, allowing pro-life citizens to opt in to private insurers which do not fund abortions, while allowing pro-choice citizens to opt in to insurers that do.

If the U.S. moves to a single-payer solution like Medicare For All, there would be a question about how to maintain this distinction. According to a poll, 75 percent of Americans are in favor of allowing abortions within the first three months (including 60 percent of Democrats and 78 percent of Independents), but with 54 percent of the American public opposed to taxpayer funding for abortions.[82] Given the staunch opposition of those opposed to taxpayer funded abortions, I assume the Hyde Amendment would become permanent law and stabilized to cover rape, incest, and the physical life of the mother. Public debate should be had about fetal deformities, tied to medical and social services. Those men and women who opt in to cover extra (non-Hyde) abortion services can pay some small additional amount on their federal taxes, in a progressive tax framework between $5 to $15 perhaps.[83]

Based on whether the public supports doing DNA testing to determine paternity, and changing the HIPAA laws, the public might consider increasing each biological father's tax contributions by small amounts based on the number of abortions associated with her or him. This reflects the health

80. Rovner, "Clash."
81. Norris, "ACA-Compliant Health."
82. Brown, "New Poll."
83. Based on data by Watson, "What Are the Different Types." An example: If there are 850,000 abortions per year, and 75 percent of them are non-Hyde, then 637,500 will need to be covered by the opt-in program. Assume 90 percent of those abortions are medical, not surgical, abortions at $500 each (within ten weeks of conception); 9 percent are D&E at $1,500 each; and 1 percent are evacuation abortions at roughly $3,000 each. Costs would be $319 million, $86 million, and $19 million, respectively, totaling $424 million. In 2017, 143.3 million people paid federal taxes. Depending how many people opt in to the non-Hyde abortion service, the effective tax could be $6 (if 70 million people) per year on average. A progressive tax would scale higher for higher-income women, lower for lower-income.

risks a woman takes on with each successive abortion; the cost to the health care system rises. If women and men use abortion services to cover non-Hyde services, they should probably be placed in this taxpayer category for at least some five to ten subsequent years of their tax-paying lives, even if they should later acquire religious reasons to prefer not to fund abortions. If paternity tests are done on aborted fetuses, men found to be fathers will be placed in the first category as well. Additional financial consequences for men might be considered, per the discussion in chapter 6.

Those women and men who opt out should pay the amount that covers Hyde category abortions, also in a progressive tax framework. The argument can be made that their contribution should be lower than the previous category, but I would argue not by much, to cover a larger respective portion of contraception education and materials. The rationale for this is a relational, not individualistic, view of citizenship: those who are highly committed to bringing abortion rates down by definition should be willing to pay for contraception and education related to it (relationalism), not just avoiding abortion themselves (individualism). After all, abortion is disproportionately lower-income, as poverty exposes women to hardships and pressures women into making relational choices that are not their first preference. Administratively, making contraceptives available to lower-income women is also more challenging.

The second question raised by government involvement in health care is whether or not public health insurance should cover contraception. In general, I argue for a "yes" to that question. As of this writing, women access contraception either through their health care providers without cost to themselves, or over the counter at their own expense. Since August 2012, due to the Affordable Care Act, private insurers now cover all FDA-approved contraception without charge to the women. The LARC devices (IUDs and hormone implants) are now free to women through their health care provider, whereas the copper IUD can cost up to $1,300 on the private market. However, some important caveats occur under this law.

Here is the practical argument (moral and biblical argument below) for a publicly funded health insurance program to cover contraceptive costs for every woman in country (at least citizens and all people here on a work visa). As of 2014, four of the top ten states with the largest declines in the abortion rates had no restrictive abortion laws (TRAP or otherwise) whatsoever.[84] The ostensible reason for the decline was contraception. Three studies show that between August 2012 (when the ACA took effect) and 2014, the use of long-acting reversible contraception increased from 2.4 percent of all

---

84. Jones and Jerman, "Abortion Incidence 2014."

contraceptive users to 14.3 percent.[85] The ACA has undoubtedly promoted women's use of more effective contraception, which has driven a decline in the abortion rate. Corroborating this, a 2012 study done in St. Louis, Missouri, called the Contraceptive CHOICE Project found that giving free birth control to 9,256 women between the ages of fourteen and forty-five, who were deemed to be at risk of unintended pregnancy, was effective. The researchers, from the Washington University School of Medicine, found that about 75 percent of the women chose IUDs or implants, once they were educated about them, together with short-term contraception (pills, rings, etc.). The program reduced abortion rates by 62–78 percent.[86]

Women who are contract workers, however, or are certain kinds of part-time workers, do not have employer-based health insurance. The part-time, contract graphic designer who enjoys the flexibility she has with her family does not have employer-based health insurance. Neither does the part-time barista at the coffee shop, the part-time hairdresser, ride-share driver, substitute teacher, nanny, or domestic cleaning lady, to name a few categories of women in the workforce. As a result, many women are not given equal access to contraception under the ACA. In Our Own Voice: Black Women's Reproductive Justice Agenda points out that 99 percent of all American women have used or are using contraception during childbearing age.[87] Yet black women are still 55 percent more likely to be uninsured than their white counterparts.[88] Hispanic women are probably even more likely. This is largely because of the type of employment they are able to find.

The ACA raised a major question that might need to be revisited on its own merits, if the U.S. decides to maintain the ACA as is. *Burnell v. Hobby Lobby* (2014) ruled that "closely held" for-profit companies, owned by people whose religious beliefs direct them against abortion, do not have to fund contraception which could cause abortions. The chain store Hobby Lobby was and is owned by the Green family, evangelical Christians; they employed twenty-one thousand people at the time of the case. The case involved Mardel Christian Education and Supply, owned by Mart Green, and Conestoga Wood Company, owned by the Mennonite Hahn family. David Green and his family believed that two emergency contraceptive pills (levonorgestrel, or Plan B; and ulipristal acetate, or Ella) and two IUDs (the copper IUD and the hormonal IUD) cause abortion. For that reason, they argued that the

85. Daniels et al., "Current Contraceptive Use"; "Use of Highly Effective Contraceptives"; Kavanaugh and Jerman, "Contraceptive Method," summarized by Snyder et al., "Impact."
86. Williams, "Access."
87. "Contraceptive Equity."
88. "The Facts" (In Our Own Voice).

ACA's requirement on employers to pay for their employees' contraceptive care should not apply to them. As employers, they did not want to contribute funds to the possibility of their employees committing abortion.

If the U.S. maintains the ACA as is, then I believe Christians themselves should work towards the reversal of the *Hobby Lobby* ruling. Prior to even considering the question of contraception and funding per se, there are corporate law and employment law questions. I explore corporate behaviors specific to Hobby Lobby in chapter 14, but for now, let me be more general. To what extent can we say that a for-profit corporation employing thousands of non-Christian people should be treated as a "religious organization," and in fact, a "person" or a "Christian person" that has religious rights? Is a Christian somehow less "Christian" if she starts a for-profit business with non-Christian business partners, pays for contraception, and honors Jewish and Muslim religious holidays? The answer to that is "no," highlighting the fact that Christians are not required by our faith to formally employ people in a for-profit business. When we do formally employ people, it is for ministry purposes in accordance with being a church or 501(c)3 non-profit organization. Hobby Lobby, Mardel, and Conestoga are not churches or religious non-profits, which have their own legal categorization. It is unclear why a for-profit corporation should be able to claim an exemption from a nation-wide employment law and employment tax, effectively, any more than it can claim exemption from corporate taxes because it might prefer to not support the U.S. military, or if Amish, to support technological development. In effect, the "freedom of religious conscience" principle is secondary here, because the Christian owners of the company are not engaging in a practice that is uniquely and solely Christian. Nor are they binding themselves to hire only Christians. Nor are they holding themselves to use ethically sourced labor, since their products are "Made in China," as I will explore in chapter 14. It is the designation "religious organization" itself that can be questioned. From the standpoint of Christian ethics and morality, should Christians who own stock in a publicly traded company have the right to influence non-adherence to employment law? I presume they should not. Are Christians in moral jeopardy when they, as employers, pay an employment tax for contraception, or as citizens, pay taxes so their government can pay for missiles, non-enforcement of racial equality, etc.? How diluted can the ownership of a company, or its employee pool, become to *disqualify* as a "religious organization"? Until American law answers those questions, the equation of a for-profit corporation as a "religious organization" should be dissolved.

If the U.S. adopts a public option for health insurance, then the questions above would be largely moot, but the questions below would still be relevant.

What about the forms of contraception that might operate as abortifacients? In chapter 4, I noted that the presence of a brain and nervous system in the fetus at twenty-three days marks the point of functional equivalency with end of life care and functional certainty about the status of the fetus. It is true that ulipristal acetate and the two IUDs have the possibility of interfering with implantation of the fertilized egg, but within the twenty-three-day period. Levonorgestrel should not be considered an abortifacient because it interferes with fertilization, not implantation. From a policy standpoint, I would feel comfortable with all of the above contraceptive methods.

Although the Supreme Court did not press this question, how much legal weight can we give evangelicals when they claim something that has not been historically true of the evangelical Christian tradition? Evangelical Christians, in particular, have *not* historically been advocates of the view that ensoulment/personhood begins at conception. In chapters 10 and 11, while examining the U.S. Constitution and reproductive politics, I explore the views of Protestant evangelicals in the U.S. to show that their views were not at all uniform in the 1700s and 1800s either. Prior to the 1960s, evangelicals were not particularly known for believing that human personhood begins at conception. In chapter 4, I highlighted the views of prominent evangelicals in the U.S. during the 1900s to show that it was not until the late 1960s and early 1970s that they made this claim. That was a Catholic position, and that only from 1869. If a Catholic hospital opened in 1871, how strongly should others take its assertion that it believed that personhood began at conception? Evangelicals wishing to maintain the view that ensoulment/personhood begins at fertilization must explain how a totipotent cell should be considered a human person when it could turn into either a twin or a placenta, how a pluripotent cell should be considered a human person when it could also turn into a human organ, and the other important scientific issues enumerated in chapter 4.

As I said above, two considerations need to be weighed against each other. On the one hand, it is very likely that if we adopt a nation-wide single-payer health insurance plan including contraception for women, the abortion rate would be reduced, especially among lower-income women, who are also disproportionately black and Hispanic. These statistical probabilities can be expressed.

On the other hand, there is a moral probability that personhood begins at conception and if so, then a statistical probability of abortion. The moral probability involves the possibility of ensoulment/personhood starting at fertilization, which cannot be expressed as a numerical possibility, but is a conceptual possibility. Given the significant doubts about that view raised by the biological realities of non-implantation rates, cell potency, twinning, and especially recombination (chimerism), could we take a functional perspective in policymaking? The statistical probability of abortion involves the probability of the contraception failing to prevent fertilization *and also* succeeding at preventing implantation, *over against* the 70 percent natural probability that a fertilized egg would fail to implant anyway. That is likely to be quite small, even assuming that personhood at conception is true.

The functional argument I make here is that, on this issue, the law should proceed with what can be adequately *known*. While future scientific research might be able to shed light on how close the fetus is to human personhood prior to twenty-three days, to this point what is *known* is that the twenty-third day of the fetus reflects a shared principle with end of life care: the presence of a healthy nervous system. Given that we are not taking steps against tobacco, painkillers, alcohol, caffeine, and environmental toxins as they relate to fetal and maternal health, we can also acknowledge the problems of uneven application and unknown causations of miscarriage. We are certainly allowing employers to provide unlimited coffee for their employees, even though caffeine and contraception both influence early fetal health, just by a matter of degree. All in all, it is very difficult to say whether the biological outcomes they influence occur solely because of the contraception, and it is also very difficult to say that the fertilized egg at conception is a human person.

11

Why Christians Fear Contraception

Contraception as an Orthodox and Catholic Concern: "Onanism"

WHY DO CONSERVATIVES DISAPPROVE of making contraception more available, even if it means bringing down the abortion rate? Part of the answer is that the Christian community formed reservations about contraception because some methods overlapped significantly with abortion. Contraception and abortion may have been hard to sharply distinguish before devices like birth control pills, condoms, tube-tying, and vasectomies came into widespread use. We embrace the help of science when we recognize that contraception and abortion are, or at least can be, two very distinct things that should be considered separately. That being said, early church leaders developed a theological stance against contraception per se, and whether their motivation was actually technical is debated. Catholic scholar John T. Noonan points out that human beings from ancient times knew of forms of contraception which did not risk abortion or harm to the mother, although many ingested contraceptive techniques had the same chemical ingredients as abortifacients and were often harmful—perhaps lethal—to the mother.[1] Now that the two categories are mostly very distinct things, some Christians remain suspicious. There are two sources of this attitude which I wish to engage: one comes from Orthodox and Catholic Christians; the other comes from Protestants.

Traditional Orthodox and Catholics maintain that the withdrawal method is the "sin of Onan," and is the reason why God struck Onan dead in Genesis 38.[2] Any form of contraception, therefore, is simply another ex-

---

1. Noonan, *Contraception*, 130, 136, 138, 157, etc.

2. For a Catholic articulation, see Broussard, "Onan," who says, "[The faulty] reasoning assumes that Onan's sin was merely a failure to uphold a transitory precept that was peculiar to the Mosaic law, but this not true. The penalty for not raising up

pression of this core attitude. While surveys show that in the U.S., a majority of Catholics and probably Orthodox simply ignore this part of the church's teaching,[3] the teaching itself should be examined in the interest of thoroughness. It is an important topic because a minority of Orthodox and Catholic Christians object to the use of contraception, including the withdrawal method. While this issue seems remote to Protestants and those outside of the Christian tradition altogether, out of respect for my Orthodox and Catholic brethren, I wish to engage the arguments put forward for it.

The interpretation that Onan died because he practiced the withdrawal method of contraception is problematic on biblical grounds. The Genesis narrative has a close relationship with the commandments given later throughout Exodus through Deuteronomy. Alan Dershowitz, for example, points out how decisions by characters in Genesis are interpreted or evaluated by the later commandments.[4] Most are explicitly critiqued or corrected, like Ham, who "uncovered his father's nakedness" (Gen 9:20–29; Lev 20:11), or Jacob, who played favorites among his sons (Gen 29–30; Deut 21:15–17). Noonan acknowledges, "That contraception as such is condemned seems unlikely. There is no commandment against contraception in any of the codes of law"[5]—whereas there *is* an explicit command against failing to raise up children for a brother (Deut 25:5–10).

Not only that, other biblical narratives explore this issue of interrupted lineage and inheritance, or take it as a central plot device (Num 36; Ruth 3:12—4:15). In Genesis 38, the question of a man raising up heirs for his brother through his widow, and partially for her, raises the issues of *his greed* and *her vulnerability*. If Onan's brother Er had no heirs, then there would be more inheritance for Onan: the future portion of Er's land inheritance would return to the family and Onan would get more of it. The particular case of

---

offspring for your deceased brother was public humiliation (Deut. 25:9), not death. The Lord took Onan's life because Onan engaged in contraceptive sex. The Lord's disapproval of this act was due to Onan violating the natural order of human sexuality. It was a sin against nature and thus a sin against God, since God's will is expressed in the order of nature. God ordered our sexual powers toward procreation and unitive love. And it is these ends that determine what is good for us in the sexual arena." For an Orthodox articulation, see Gleason, "Sacred Seed."

3. The original study was done in April 2011 by Guttmacher; "Guttmacher Statistic on Catholic Women," which found that 87 percent of sexually active Catholic women were using some form of birth control not approved by the Catholic Church formally. At the time of the survey, these women were aged fifteen to forty-four, so women older than forty-four were not included. At the time of being sexually active, they were Catholic and were not pregnant, post-partum, or trying to get pregnant. See also Nazworth, "Critics."

4. Dershowitz, *Genesis of Justice*.

5. Noonan, *Contraception*, 35.

Tamar also has to do with a Canaanite woman who converted, importantly. She wanted to be part of the faith and family of Israel and serves as a lesson of gentile inclusion via conversion, distributive justice, and participation in the story of God's development of "gardening partners," as she and her descendants would inherit the garden land, too.

Onan's death was more severe than the public humiliation prescribed under the Sinai covenant for the brother who refuses to carry out his duty (Deut 25:9). Therefore, advocates of "Onanism" argue, the failure could not be the brotherly duty per se, but the failure to consummate the conception.[6] The literary connection between Genesis 38 and Deuteronomy 25, however, does not require that the consequences be identical. In fact, the discontinuity between God's consequences in the two sections is precisely the point, because the biblical narrative stresses that something changed in the relationship between God and his people before and after the Sinai covenant.[7] In Genesis, God intervened fairly directly to protect his people, and dealt in consequences of life and death. During that period, he did not tell his people to deliver consequences on other people. He simply protected his people. God's consequence upon Noah's contemporaries, or Sodom and Gomorrah, etc., was death because it was mimetic and pedagogical: those who would threaten Israel with death were in reality killing themselves, because only through Israel would Jesus come to offer everyone new life, including those in the grave (1 Pet 3:18–20; 4:6). After the Sinai covenant, however, that dynamic changed. The Israelites became administrators and not just observers of God's activity. As such, the consequences changed, but that is not surprising. Once Israel came into the promised land, a typical Israelite widow had recourse to other Israelite family members for emotional and familial support. Again, by contrast, prior to the Sinai covenant, Tamar was a gentile woman who had just married into the nascent family prior to their nationhood, and she had no such recourse. Her exclusion from the family of Judah, then, was that much more dire. It was a form of spiritual death meted out to her by Onan. Onan was behaving like a gentile opposed to Israel; Tamar was behaving like a true Israelite. It was only fitting that God would protect her as he had protected his people before. For excluding Tamar, who wanted to be included in the family of faith, who wanted to be truly Israel, God's consequence upon Onan was death. Thus, to be precise, and to engage Catholic Thomist scholastic theologians, God did not take

---

6. E.g., Broussard, "Onan," see above.

7. Watson, *Paul*, 251–378; Sailhamer, *Pentateuch as Narrative*, 33–72, and *Meaning*, 221–459.

Onan's life because he violated the *order of nature*. God took Onan's life because he violated the *order of redemption*.

Furthermore, under the Sinai covenant, leaked emissions of semen were only a matter of ceremonial uncleanness for a very short time, not moral issues. Emissions of semen were concerns for a man by himself if he had a wet dream, or for both man and woman if semen leaked during or after sex (Lev 15:16–18), which is unavoidable; how else does one clean up afterwards? The placement of emissions in the context of Jewish ceremonial law in Leviticus 11–15 strongly suggests that the matter was for public health and for symbolism, but not for morality per se. Any skin discharge (Lev 15:1–15), and a woman's menstruation (Lev 15:19–33) had the same symbolic significance, because these experiences, too, symbolized life passing into death. Such matters had potential health ramifications as well, such as infections spreading through pus or blistering. The ordinance that such a person remain ceremonially unclean until sundown was their version of "social distancing"—a precautionary measure until health might be confirmed (Lev 13). If early Christians argued that Jesus fulfilled and set aside the ceremonial portion of the Jewish law (Heb 7–11), but took this section of Jewish ceremonial statutes as the inspiration to develop a *moral* argument against the withdrawal method of contraception, they were oddly inconsistent.

Additionally, the view that the sole purpose of marital sex is childbearing, as opposed to the union of the couple, has been thoroughly challenged on biblical and historical grounds. Says Noonan:

> The Song of Songs . . . concentrates almost exclusively on the personal relation between the lover and his beloved. "All mine is my true love, and I all his" (2:16). Human sexual love here has a value independent of fertility. In a more sober domestic vein the praise of a good wife in Proverbs is not of her fruitfulness, but of her prudence and the loving confidence her husband has in her (Prov 31:11), but it is clear that she is fruitful.[8]

This moves us to the heart of an important issue, very sensitive and long debated between Protestants and their Orthodox and Catholic brethren. Critics of the early church have argued that Christians were improperly influenced by Plato and the Platonic tradition's suspicion of the body and idealization of spiritual love giving birth to virtue.[9] While this critique has been

---

8. Noonan, *Contraception*, 32.

9. Noonan, *Contraception*, 86–87, credits Philo of Alexandria for being the first known Jewish or Christian writer who argued that married couples were "self-condemned" and simply lovers of pleasure if they did not have children; otherwise, they only had sex like animals. If Philo was the author of *De Vita Contemplativa*, then he

overstated, I accept part of it. It is certainly true that Christians from Justin Martyr onward saw Plato as a helpful precursor to the gospel, like Moses was to Christ, although Tatian the Assyrian (notably not a Greek) mocked the comparison by accusing Plato of poorly plagiarizing Moses. Relatedly, as a literary movement, the early Christians also had to engage other literary movements of their age, including the Hellenistic Alexandrians from the third century BC, who drew out allegorical interpretations from older, classical Greek literature, like Homer's *Iliad* and *Odyssey*, and took them in a Platonic direction.[10] Readers of the old poets faced difficulties because Homer and others seemed to promote vice and viciousness, at times. Since Homer could not be discarded, he was reinterpreted. Readers used the allegorical method to find new, "hidden" meanings that comported better with the Platonic virtues. Christians, starting with Clement and Origen in Alexandria, claimed that the apostle Paul read and applied the Old Testament in the same way (e.g., Gal 4:21–31; 1 Cor 10:1–13). It should be noted, though, that Christian allegorical interpretation often tried to speculate about a time prior to souls being embodied (e.g., Origen's view of Genesis 1) and what the heavens looked like (e.g., Origen and Gregory of Nyssa, following Philo, said Moses saw a heavenly tabernacle in Exodus 25:40), and sidestep the historicity of texts felt to be morally awkward or overly "Jewish" (e.g., Joshua's battles with the Canaanites). In that way, they tended to collapse the literary-historical distance between biblical Israel and the church. Paul, by contrast, was firmly committed to embodied history, reinforced already established biblical history, and respected the literary-historical distances between biblical Israel and the church.

This shift in interpretive direction touches on our subject. Monastic Christians committed to chastity were eager to allegorize the biblical book Song of Songs. They understandably preferred to not see in it the romantic courtship of a man and woman and their journey into wedded, embodied, erotic love with its relational challenges, but the spiritual love between God and his people. But without the former, can we understand the latter? Their mistake, in my opinion, was to misplace the "location" of the allegory: the

---

was impressed by the Therapeutae Jews in the diaspora and centered in Alexandria, who also renounced marriage and embraced chastity. From the third century onward, Christians were quite determined to interpret them as the first Christian monks. See Scouteris, "Therapeutae of Philo." Perhaps they could do this because there were no more actual Therapeutae Jews by this time. Hellenistic Christians were either influenced by Jews impressed by Plato or tried to outdo them in literary allegorizing. In any case, they departed from more traditional forms of Judaism.

10. For introduction, see MacDonald, "Alexandria and Allegory"; *Christianizing Homer*. Papanikolaou, "Allegorical Exegetical Method," gives an appreciative account and helpful background.

institution of human marriage is the allegory, but not the human couple in the Song of Songs in every detail. It is hard to allegorize the premarital courtship phase (Song 1:1—3:5) when the man chooses to *not* be sexually intimate (2:7; 3:5), compared to the wedding night when they are (4:12–16). And, it is likely that the husband is being portrayed as desirous of sex at an awkward, and possibly selfish, time of night (5:2), which he then stops to reconsider and confess before they are intimate again (8:4). The allegorical interpretation, which makes the husband out to be God, cannot permit that. Origen of Alexandria's and Gregory of Nyssa's commentaries allegorizing Song of Songs became quite popular, but the inconsistencies of their allegorical method, which I just noted, are evident.[11] Too, it is difficult to reconcile the biblical literature, when it says, "Let her breasts satisfy you at all times" (Prov 5:19) and revels in sexual, bodily humor and puns,[12] with the Greek patristic wish that a married husband and wife would have sex for procreative purposes only, with little to no lust.[13] Christian allegorism stepped over a limit, and this

11. Ambrose of Milan, *On Virgins*, 1:37–39, follows the pattern of allegorical reading that Origen and Gregory did, and quotes Song of Songs 4:7–11 to indicate that God is ardently drawn to human virtue, and in particular, the virtue of chastity. While this approach creates a poetically beautiful, compelling image of God's love for human virtue, it comes at a textual cost. Ambrose seems to avoid the admonitions to not be aroused. They simply do not serve his purpose, so he ignores them. Perrone, "'The Bride at the Crossroads,'" performs the complex task of reading and reconciling Origen's *Commentary and Homilies* on this book. Perrone, "'The Bride at the Crossroads,'" 92–94, recognizes that Origen, *Song* 1, interprets the Bride as initially addressing the Groom *in prayer*, therefore keeps the Groom "off stage," despite all the indications that Bride and Groom are physically proximate. Perrone, "'The Bride at the Crossroads,'" 100, remarks that another prominent scholar, Anders Nygren, believed that Origen had no literal sense for the Song.

12. Alter, *World*, 31–33 (Esther), 37–40 (Sarah and Abraham), 78 (Esther). Alter, *Art*, 185–203 (Song of Songs). Drazin, "What Did Ruth and Boaz."

13. Augustine of Hippo, *Marriage and Concupiscence*, 1.15.17, says that even if husbands are not actively trying to have children (which is ideal), they should be passively open to it with *every* sex act (which is acceptable, but barely): "I am supposing, then, although you are not lying [with your wife] for the sake of procreating offspring, you are not for the sake of lust obstructing their procreation by an evil prayer or an evil deed. Those who do this, although they are called husband and wife, are not; nor do they retain any reality of marriage, but with a respectable name cover a shame. Sometimes this lustful cruelty, or cruel lust, comes to this, that they even procure poisons of sterility [oral contraceptives]." Brown, *Augustine*, 500–501 puts it well: "[Augustine] was the contemporary of Jerome, who spoke of marriage as a tangled thornbush, good only to produce, in the form of children; of Gregory of Nyssa, whose gentle tone makes us forget the fact that he regarded sexuality with supreme lack of interest, as no more than an 'animal' appendance to humankind's original 'angelic' nature; and of Ambrose, who, when faced by married candidates to the episcopate, expected his readers to agree without question that *voluptas*, sensuality alone, had driven Adam from Paradise." Augustine insisted "that Adam's fall had resulted, instantly and visibly, in a loss of sexual

correlated with the church's growing distance from more traditional forms of Judaism. As Jewish synagogue communities themselves shed the influences of Platonism, the divide deepened.

Church leaders repositioned the Christian vocation of singleness into a framework where Christian marriage ideally excluded sexual desire. Pope Gregory the Great said, "Husbands and wives are to be admonished to remember that they are joined together for the sake of producing offspring; and, when, giving themselves to immoderate intercourse, they transfer the occasion of procreation to the service of pleasure, to consider that, though they go not outside wedlock yet in wedlock itself they exceed the just dues of wedlock."[14] To maintain a theoretical equality between singleness and marriage on the level of human motivation, though, church leaders had to reduce marriage to what made it functionally different from singleness: childbearing. In principle, that required the church to condemn all contraceptive methods, including withdrawal.

"Onanism" would seem to result in some pastoral problems and relational tensions, which are typically denied as exaggerations of the position. If "Onanism" is true, for example, then a post-menopausal woman might not be able to have sex with her husband in good conscience. Nor could the faith community fully celebrate the wedding of a sixty-year-old Christian man to a sixty-year-old Christian woman after each of them had been absolutely devoted to Christian ministry, separately and faithfully chaste. Or if both were widowed. The traditionalist might say that youth was the assumption and menopause was not, in both the Bible and early Christian writings, and that these concerns are overkill and overstated, but the sternness of the teachers from the fourth century onwards is absolutely daunting and uncompromising. A plain reading of the early church fathers on the issue of marital sex does not grant exceptions to old age. This, despite the fact that the founding matriarch, Sarah, asked God if she could have "pleasure" at the age of ninety (Gen 18:12). Was she *only* referring to *having* a child? Or was there a humorous double meaning? Was she also referring to *making* one?

Conservative Catholics sometimes assert that there is a cultural slippery slope down which we slide, if and when we separate procreation from

---

control" but, in a positive departure from the more stern Eastern Greek fathers, was "prepared to imagine what the intercourse of Adam and Eve in Paradise would have been like if they had not fallen. Such intercourse would have been an act of solemn delight, where two fully physical bodies followed the stirrings of their souls, 'all in a wondrous pitch of perfect peace.'" See especially the unparalleled work of Brown, *Body and Society*.

14. Gregory the Great, *Book of Pastoral Rule*, 27.

sex.[15] The slope begins with culturally approving contraception use. It ends with abortions. Then, men coerce women to get abortions, as what was once was an option becomes an obligation, and women and fetuses ultimately pay the price, because of male chauvinism. I agree that any instrumentalizing of a woman is a major problem—a moral failure in the biblical perspective. However, encouraging or forcing men to accept paternity and fatherhood does not necessarily unravel male chauvinism. In many cultural contexts, the two coexist perfectly well. In the U.S., if the rich man cannot pay for an abortion, he will simply pay for child support. In earlier times, a mafia man had a wife and a mistress, paid for the children of both, and attended Catholic Mass. Making women embody the consequences for men's sexual dalliances to "teach men a lesson" still slides into the problem of men instrumentalizing women.

In fact, another problem can be posed in response, partly in jest, and partly in seriousness. Given that a man can leak small amounts of semen and sperm prior to full ejaculation, does this now pose a technical problem? For the dogmatic scholastic, it might. "Onanism" means God requires that no seed be spilled. If one believes in "Onanism," then once vaginal sex begins, neither husband nor wife should stop it, even if they *both* wanted to, because *God wants them to finish*. Lest I be accused of being completely unserious, the absurdity of this scenario gestures to a more sinister problem: a variation on the disturbing North Carolina law entitling a man to finish sex once it starts (see chapter 5). "Onanism" in its full force requires a husband to instrumentalize his wife in the very act of sex, which is a different way of instrumentalizing a woman, and a potent one. Perhaps "Onanism" contributed to why marital rape was not recognized as a legal category, and a moral problem, in Christendom and post-Christendom, *until the late twentieth century*. Perhaps "Onanism" led to a culture which contributed to some of the very problems it purported to solve: a lack of interest in female orgasms and married women's mental health, unwanted pregnancies, and abortion. Moreover, one cannot help but wonder whether people under the teaching of "Onanism" suffered needless cycles of guilt and cognitive dissonance, on the one hand, or became dissociated and self-deceived, on the other. The Jewish tradition had a different response to male chauvinism from the start, which they discerned from the Scriptures. I believe Christians should follow suit.

Sadly, in my opinion, John Noonan's recommendation to Pope Paul IV to overturn the ban on birth control was turned down. As related to public policy when non-Christians are impacted, however, I maintain that contraception as a principle should be embraced outright. The details of

15. Dougherty and Gobry, "Time."

each pill or device may be worthy of discussion, I suppose, but I am speaking in general terms. If Orthodox and Catholic Christians cannot bring themselves to reconsider the tradition, they can simply allow contraception policy as the lesser of two evils.

Contraception as a Conservative Christian Concern: Political Narrative

Another part of the reason why conservative Christians are uncomfortable with contraception as public policy is *narrative*, and specifically *political narrative*. While some notable Roman Catholic figures come into view on this score, conservative evangelicals, who will have nothing to do with "Onanism," are motivated by *political narrative*. As some have wondered, when Emperor Theodosius made Christian faith the "official religion" of the Roman Empire in the late fourth century, and the "Christendom" model of church-state-society took hold, did Christian rhetoric and focus shift? I believe it did. Christians of every generation have to answer questions about how they will portray themselves against external foes—as "Christian Rome" had to confront the Persian Empire, then the Arab Islamic Empires—and how Christian parents will portray themselves to their children. Christians tend to use Christian rhetoric to fashion a political narrative, which will then enlist views of children, marriage, and sex into that political narrative.

Since colonial times, conservative American Christians have used laws involving marriage, sex, and children to sometimes express theocratic, but more often white supremacist, attitudes and identity markers. It is almost as if there were a "garden of Eden" state at some mythical point in American history where there were only heterosexual, lifelong, loving marriages—a point from which the only way was down. This, despite the actual history of 40 percent of Pilgrim children being born "early"; public masturbation in church courtyards and venereal disease epidemics in the Puritan colonies; etc.[16] Starting from laws passed in Virginia and Maryland, white men were legally able to rape black women with impunity, with nary a thought given to "the sanctity of life" that resulted. Simultaneously, conservative white Christians frowned on, and outlawed, white women having mixed-race children from the 1700s onwards, which resulted in abortions, infanticide, and the breaking up of parent-child relations, as I will highlight further in chapter

---

16. Holzwarth, "10 Weird Common Practices," writes a humorous, readable article. Solomon, "Sexual Practice and Fantasy," 24–35, gives a helpful, concise summary. See Emilio and Freedman, *Intimate Matters*; Smith, *Sex and Sexuality*; Block, *Rape and Sexual Power*.

11, because all this contributes to discussion about the U.S. Constitution. They treated consensual sexual sins as matters of criminal justice, outlawing mixed-race marriages from the 1700s until *Loving v. Virginia* (1967) struck down anti-miscegenation laws in all fifty states. They passed anti-sodomy laws from colonial times until *Lawrence v. Texas* (2003) ruled them unconstitutional in the remaining fourteen states which still had them; under those laws, sodomy was a felony, again despite the fact that Paul did not direct the Corinthian or Roman Christians toward such a use of law and public policy. They took up an anti-contraception position in the late 1800s because they feared science and modernism. In the early 2000s, rather than withdraw the word "marriage" from our legal language allowing for "civil unions" for all straight and gay couples to receive equal legal recognition, a move recommended by people across the political spectrum,[17] they fought a losing battle that culminated in the *Obergefell v. Hodges* (2015) decision, while discussing a constitutional amendment to define "marriage" as between a man and a woman. As a result, the public must call Newt Gingrich's relationship to Callista a "marriage" by law, even though he began that relationship as an affair, committing adultery with her while married to his second wife, which he began in the same way while married to his first wife. John the Baptist told King Herod the tetrarch that his relationship with Herodias was not a "marriage" by God's definition, because they began it while committing an affair, and Herodias's former husband, Herod's own brother, still lived (Matt 14:1–5; note Nathan's judgment on David for the same act, plus murder in 2 Sam 12:1–15). Just because Herod was male and Herodias was female did not make their union a proper "marriage" theologically. Moral context matters. "Marriage" is a sacramental or semi-sacramental term defined differently by different religious traditions, and yet Christian political conservatives wish the state to regulate a sacrament. A different legal principle would point out that differences about what is or is not a "marriage" should be permitted under the First Amendment's freedom of religious conscience clause, even in public spaces like public schools, and the only way to do that is to use the term "civil union" in formal law.[18]

17. Carter, "'Defending' Marriage." Tyrrell, "Another Peaceful Solution," now withdrawn from website. Paul, "Government." Boteach, "On Legalizing." Chartier, *Public Practice*. Richman, "Love, Marriage."

18. To address the issue of polygamy with Mormons and Muslims, I would be in favor of polygamous civil unions. As it is, conservative Mormons and Muslims in the U.S. benefit from welfare payments to single mothers. See "Who Foots Bill." In effect, welfare subsidizes polygamy. Dowling, "Welfare Encourages Polygamy," is an example of a conservative who uses this situation as an argument to abolish welfare. I take the opposite stance: abolish the theocratic definition of "marriage," adopt civil unions for all, take all the "single mothers" off of welfare, and make Mormon and Muslim husbands pay for

Politically conservative Protestants in the U.S. seem to believe, to various degrees, that the U.S. was a "Christian nation," and therefore should be again. In the 1930s, business leaders unhappy with FDR's New Deal regulations cultivated alliances with Protestant leaders and activists promoting a "Christian libertarianism" to fashion a political response that was anti-communist and anti-regulation.[19] Congregationalist minister James W. Fifield, Jr. founded an organization called Spiritual Mobilization that drew in laypeople and corporate leaders like J. Howard Pew, Jr., president of Sun Oil, eventually laying the groundwork for Billy Graham and setting a pattern of conservative Christians allying with fossil fuel.[20] They called for "freedom under God." The idea of the U.S. as a "Christian nation" tying moral conservatism and economic conservatism together emerged in this period. This coalition succeeded in backing and electing Dwight Eisenhower to the presidency. Eisenhower, a Protestant keen to tie together a general sense of Christian duty with post-WWII America's conception of itself, started the National Prayer Breakfasts, modeled after Methodist minister Abraham Vereide's "prayer breakfast movement." Eisenhower disappointed the libertarian, anti-state corporate backers, but supported Congress's move to add the phrase "under God" to the Pledge of Allegiance and printed "In God We Trust" on U.S. currency. This was but the latest version of the alliance that had existed since colonialism—an alliance between Christianity and capitalism, in a nation which thought of themselves as leading the world in the resistance to the Soviet Union. Hollywood cooperated in the effort by promoting movies like Cecil B. DeMille's *Ten Commandments* (1956), reflecting back to Americans the idea that they were inherently religious.

The raging theological controversies that constantly pitted Christian against Christian over such things as slavery, religion, and the rights of women were largely gone, so the time was opportune to rewrite that past. American conservatives made a fateful choice to hold up John Winthrop and the Puritans—with their "national covenant" notion—over Roger Williams and the citizens of Providence—with their human rights and principled "freedom of religious conscience" tradition—as the foundational vision for American life.[21] This idea is inspired by the portrait of biblical

---

their multiple civil unions.

19. Kruse, *One Nation*; "Christian America." Dochuk, *From Bible Belt*.

20. Phillips, *American Theocracy*. Nelson, *Shadow Network*.

21. Noll, *America's God*, 3–52, discusses this and shows historically that there was no way to have a "national covenant" because unbelieving children, excommunicated people, and newcomers made a "society" different from a "church." FitzGerald, *Evangelicals*, 361, points out George Marsden, Mark Noll, and Robert Hatch are evangelical historians who "felt compelled to write a response" directly in response to Francis

Israel under the Sinai covenant. That is, they believe that the nation is part of a "national covenant," where the nation in which they live either *is* a church, or a *type* of church, so their political vision is national and pseudo-theocratic, or theocratic outright. This idea had also been taken up by the Confederacy and the defeated South, in what is called "The Lost Cause" ideology, where Southerners placed Confederate flags in houses of worship because they believed the plantation system was originally God-ordained.[22] If God gave the white colonists a land as his covenant gift, like Israel inheriting the promised land and displacing the Canaanites, what better device with which to cover over their responsibility for illegally and immorally seizing land from Native Americans?[23] When Christians have an imaginary for a theocratic nation, they seem to use policies about marriage, sex, and children as primary markers for that nation.

Modern Christian conservatives do not seem to teach sexual ethics in the same way that Paul taught the Corinthians, and this is not simply stylistic, but *political*. In fact, Paul makes a comment in 1 Corinthians that should place consensual sexual sins far outside the realm of criminal justice in the minds of Christians. Paul believed that consensual sexual sin was a sin against one's own self: "the immoral man sins against his own body" (1 Cor 6:18). Note that I am not talking about non-consensual sins like rape, or involving people we deem unable to fully give consent, like minors, the mentally impaired, or sometimes those in the weaker position in a power dynamic. Consensual sexual sin falls into a category of Christian morality about which it is difficult to legislate. Law is effective at defining and punishing obvious harm that one person inflicts on another and the other person does not wish to be harmed. That comports with the admittedly limited statements in Scripture, where God commissions human beings to place limits on violence via limited violence (Gen 9:6). Paul comments on the state (Rom 13:1–7) with this apparent understanding, because he admonishes Christians to not retaliate with vengeance for the harm that others do them (Rom 12:17–21). Now, men might exercise power dynamics over women as I discussed in chapter 5 and 6, which make a woman's "consent" questionable in some cases, like in prostitution. Genuinely consensual sexual sin,

---

Schaeffer, *A Christian Manifesto*, and the notion of a "national covenant" and the idea that America was a Christian nation. Their response is found in Noll, et al., *Search*. FitzGerald, *Evangelicals*, 361, assesses the impact thus: "Their book did its work within the elite evangelical colleges, but not in popular right-wing circles." Bellah et al., *Good Society*, 241–43, cite Roger Williams as the earliest critic of the "national covenant." Williams pointedly said that America as a political nation "lay dead in sin."

22. Wilson, *Baptized in Blood*.
23. Bellah et al., *Good Society*, 241–43; Bellah, *Broken Covenant*, 1–60.

however, does not have that quality of non-consensual harm inflicted by one person on another. That is not to say that there are no consequences, or relational fallout, etc. from an inappropriate sexual relationship. There could be considerable pain involved. But on the interpersonal level, that would be a matter for therapists and ministers. It could involve divorce, a civil matter. On the broader, societal level, we might call certain types of sexual activity a "public health" matter which we would address outside of a criminal justice framework. But it is not a criminal matter.

What about the conservative concern about promoting contraception? As I mentioned above, some conservatives objected to the Colorado Family Planning Initiative, despite its apparent success. Bob Enyart, a Christian, and a spokesman for the conservative group Colorado Right to Life, warned that IUDs and hormone implants do not stop sexually transmitted diseases,[24] a perfectly valid and important point to make. While condoms reduce that particular threat, of course his point was that abstinence is the only sure way to avoid *both* STDs *and* unintended pregnancies, which is a point that I think is important as well. The unspoken message is that "abstinence-only" sex education is the best policy. Carrie Gordon Earll, senior director of public policy for the evangelical ministry Focus on the Family, went one step further: "What we have seen over many years is that access to contraception does not equal fewer unintended pregnancies and fewer abortions. Availability of contraception leads to increased sexual activity, which leads to unintended pregnancies and abortions."[25] Enyart additionally faulted Darwin's theory of evolution as encouraging promiscuity: "When you teach children that they're animals—that they have evolved from pigs and dogs and apes—then they act like animals." Enyart argued that offering contraception sends the message to teenagers that they can "have all the sex [they] want."[26]

Given the strong causal link Earll and Enyart predicted between contraception and sexual activity, and then sexual activity and pregnancy, I find it curious that they did not explain *why* the Colorado study was so effective towards goals conservatives seek—reducing unintended pregnancies and abortions—while leaving sexual activity unaddressed. Ostensibly, commenting on how different types of contraception have different levels of effectiveness would have been appropriate here, but they did not do that. Nor did they comment on whether lower-income girls and young women, especially in Colorado's lower-income Hispanic and white communities, face unusual economic, racial, and relational pressures which encourage

24. Maqbool, "Colorado Birth Control."
25. Draper, "Colorado Claims."
26. Maqbool, "Colorado Birth Control."

sexual activity outside of marriage and early in life. Could contraception and preventing young motherhood contribute to healthier relational choices? Economic advancement? Maturity later in life?

Clearly, moral and political conservatives want to help reduce sexual activity outside of marriage. Would they encourage youth to explore gay and lesbian sex, or get vasectomies, until they are ready for heterosexual marriage? No, partly because their best argument (in my opinion) argues that people must learn to stabilize their emotions, desire, and character for the sake of relationships—an older, pre-Enlightenment tradition where Jewish-Christian and Aristotelian virtue ethics converge. Most moral conservatives care whether teenagers think about becoming the type of people who could have a stable forty-year marriage, making it easier (and cheaper) for their own future children and grandchildren to care for them, and spend time with them. They see human personhood as embedded in relationships, especially relationships over time (which actually makes them *not* true economic conservatives, a rights-based worldview that flows from Enlightenment individualism). I am deeply sympathetic to this concern.

But if there existed a type of contraception that could *completely* eliminate unintended pregnancies and abortions, would conservatives welcome it? Or is it possible that some conservatives *want* the threat of an unintended pregnancy, along with the financial and emotional consequences of bringing a child into the world, to loom over people—especially adolescents—because they believe that that *is* the only incentive for people to not have sex outside of marriage? Or to see the church as morally relevant?

If sexual activity outside of marriage increased, but unintended pregnancy and abortion went to zero, how would conservatives weigh those different outcomes? Put differently, and also practically, how would Bob Enyart preach abstinence in nursing homes, where rates of promiscuity and sexually transmitted diseases are quite shocking, but with no risk of pregnancy? For background: from 2014–17, AthenaHealth found that the elderly suffered from STDs by an increased rate of 23 percent.[27] AthenaHealth's study also found that "seniors have the lowest condom use of any population." What do conservatives do in response to these facts? Do they call for single-sex facilities? Of course not. Non-Christian conservatives might very well hand out condoms in nursing homes, with a wink and a nod. Can Christians?

Conservatives make a *moral* association between sexual activity and pregnancy within a certain narrative. As is only human, often their real goal is to *affirm a narrative*. People feel challenged if and when certain associations

---

27. Pereto, "Patients over 60?" Howley, "What to Know."

they have long taken for granted can be questioned or even broken, because their larger narrative might be called into question.

Christian political conservatives in particular need to reflect on that issue, because Christians' attitudes towards sex are inescapably tied up with *political narratives*—politics because they involve the raising and rearing of children, the communities we form as we do, and the narratives we tell ourselves and our children about sex, other people's sexual choices, and our own views about sex. For instance, in response to the Colorado study, Bob Enyart cited Christian creational theology from Genesis to make his point: "We are made in God's image, and God's likeness, and for 13-, 14-, 15-year-old girls to be having sex is destructive for them."[28] I agree wholeheartedly that these young women are made in God's image, and that God's vision for sex is based on marriage. Understandably, when they are of childbearing age and might get pregnant, the stakes are higher for them. But from a Christian perspective, their age is actually morally secondary.

What is our "origin story" and what does that tell us about how our relationships should be? To the Corinthians, the apostle Paul, like Enyart, quotes the Genesis creation account. In the midst of a robust section about sex (1 Cor 5:1—7:39), Paul quotes Genesis 2:24: "The two shall become one flesh" (1 Cor 6:16). It is very important to notice that our "origin story" as far as sex and marriage are concerned *is not a national, political one*. It is about all humanity. As Paul understood it, and unlike Enyart's application, this "one flesh" union was true on two levels at once. On one level, two human beings could enact the "one flesh" union. Hence, Paul warned the Corinthians not to have sex with prostitutes, because sex forms a "one body" union between the client and the prostitute (6:16), and that would be "immoral" (6:18). He clearly takes the Genesis account as God's vision establishing what is moral and what is not. Simultaneously, on another level, the human believer forms a "one flesh" union with Christ by the Spirit. Thus, Paul had a deeper understanding of the human body and what it was designed for than his Jewish contemporaries: On a deeper level, "the body is for the Lord" (6:13), our "bodies are members of Christ" (6:15), and one's "body is a temple of the Holy Spirit who is in you" (6:19), "therefore, glorify [reveal, reflect] God in your body" (6:20). For we do not simply become "one body" but "one spirit with him" (6:17).

Paul radically *deepens* what Genesis 2:24 means by adding a distinctively Christ-centered *significance* to it. Paul says that God's creation vision is transfigured because in Christ God has become one with a human body, and even filled it with resurrection power and life (6:14) after slaying its

---

28. Maqbool, "Colorado Birth Control."

mortality (15:12-58). Paul's Christ-centered vision of the individual body being joined to Christ by the Spirit drives his sense of polity and politics. Paul's goal was to encourage and ensure, as far as he could, the distinctiveness of Christian believers' union with Christ, including how they conducted their ethical reasoning (6:12-20), even if the Christians needed to sadly excommunicate someone who was no longer faithful (5:1-13). Whether or not this led to "cultural improvements" in Corinth's sexual practices seemed not to enter his mind. For Paul, the Genesis creation account could not even be meaningfully discussed apart from Christ, or separated from Christ's mission to people all over the world. For him, the creation vision is inseparably transfigured and united to the "new creation" vision of Jesus, who is the "last Adam" (15:22, 45). Because Jesus calls all humanity as the "last Adam," the Christian belongs to a human community—a new *polis*—far beyond the political reach and demands of any one nation.

To put a fine point on it, Paul evangelized Corinth and established Christian sexual norms among the Corinthians without controlling public policy or controlling Corinthian law. Paul did not claim that Corinth would or should become a "Christian nation." He did not suggest that God would "covenantally bless" (economically? militarily?) the city of Corinth per se if the Corinthian Christians did this or that. He gave no indication that Christians had responsibility for the "culture" of Corinth. These facts already reframe the comparison I wish to make between Christian political conservatives in the U.S. and the vision of the church's ministry provided by the New Testament.

Critically, Paul does *not* broaden out Christian sexual morality to a level where non-Christians could share it *while remaining non-Christians*. The Jewish community of Paul's day, for example, could also feel an allegiance to the creation story of Genesis 1 and 2 regarding human marriage. True, Paul's sexual ethics rest on a creational vision of marriage from Genesis. But they rest even further upon a "theology of the body" where Jesus is the leading authority over the Christian's body: "Do you not know that your body is a temple of the Holy Spirit who is in you, whom you have from God, and that you are not your own? For you have been bought with a price: therefore glorify God in your body" (1 Cor 6:19-20). Because Jesus is Lord over each believer's body, individually, Paul gives cautions *against* giving other people *any* degree of authority over one's body. He says "no" to gentiles being physically circumcised (7:17-20), critiques slavery (7:21-23), and calls Christian married couples to "be as though they had" no spouse, even going so far as to encourage singleness if Christians can manage it, for the sake of ministry (7:7-9, 25-40), while still honoring and blessing Christian marriage (7:1-6, 36-39). While this raises fascinating questions about how to view "household codes" in Ephesians and Colossians, in Paul's view in 1 Corinthians, an allegiance to Christ qualifies and limits social hierarchies *and even Christian marriage relationships.*[29] Paul does not help non-Christian Jewish people

---

29. Conservative evangelicals tend to interpret Ephesians, Colossians, and 1 Peter without regard for 1 Corinthians, which is one way they arrive at a gender hierarchy. But when Paul uses the "head-body" language in Ephesians 5 for marriage, must we not first consider what he said about "head-body" language in 1 Corinthians, where he discusses shared leadership in preaching and teaching? Paul in 1 Corinthians extensively discusses the meaning of "headship," "head-body" relations, how to understand Adam and Eve's original relationship in creation, the nature of godly authority, and a woman's ability to preach in the congregation, as well as the vexing issue of "slavery" and what it means—far more so than do Ephesians, Colossians, and 1 Peter. Notably, Paul affirms the categorical right and importance of women praying and prophesying in the congregation (11:2–16), including a wife bearing an authoritative word from God to the congregation while her husband sat in the audience, or a daughter to her father, or an ex-prostitute to men of standing.

Some conservative scholars assert that Paul expected the immanent return of Jesus in 1 Corinthians, but became more interested in "stability" in Ephesians and Colossians. But nothing about his ethical framework in 1 Corinthians can be set aside. What if we understand 1 Corinthians before we read Ephesians? There are solid reasons for doing this. First, in AD 55, Paul wrote 1 Corinthians from Ephesus (1 Cor 16:8–9). It is reasonable to assume that the Ephesian believers in all likelihood retained a copy of 1 Corinthians, or at least an awareness of what Paul taught in it. Second, Paul had been in Corinth for eighteen months (Acts 18), and then went to Ephesus for three years (Acts 19–20), from which he wrote back to the Corinthians. It is fairly reasonable to think that the Ephesian believers were vulnerable to the same errors that the Corinthian believers were. So it is reasonable to think that Paul taught the Ephesians in person what he taught the Corinthians in writing. The fact that he stayed twice the amount of time in Ephesus as he did in Corinth gave him ample time to do so. Asia Minor was quickly surpassing Jerusalem as the missional and intellectual center of the broad Christian community, due in part to the personal investments poured there by Peter, Paul, and John. Paul wrote Ephesians (arguably) and Colossians from his imprisonment in Rome in AD 60–62, a full five to seven years after writing 1 Corinthians. And third, Paul refers to congregational worship practices that are common to every church, by the design of the apostles (1 Cor 11:2, 16). Those practices involve men and women praying for and prophesying to the congregation, in a mode of authority which Paul refers to as a "headship." Paul says that this is standard Christian practice, including of course in Asia Minor.

In Ephesians 5–6, Paul *limits* the scope of the husband's "headship" from household to wife, in addition to redefining the "head-body" relationship altogether (Eph 1:22–23; 4:15–16). In pagan Roman culture, the Roman father ruled his entire household: wife, children, and servants. If he had wanted to be culturally agreeable, Paul might have deployed the word "head" for the father over everyone else in his household in a pagan sense. But Paul does not do that at all. He does not accept the Roman legal concept of *patria potestas*, the absolute authority of the father. Rather, Paul positions Christ differently in each of the three relationships in Ephesians 5:22—6:9. The head-body analogy is notably absent from the parent-child relationship (Eph 6:1–4), because there comes a time for children to honor their parents but obey the Lord, and see themselves as too fundamentally distinct from their parents. Parents also need to parent with that

share his theological vision, or live it out while remaining non-Christians. He does not simply throw a layer of generic moral obligation over biological facts about where babies come from. He does not appeal to a "natural law" knowable by non-Christians, so prized by traditional Catholics in their attempt to appeal to non-Christians as such in a common society, to adjust Christian faith in the "Christendom model."[30]

---

endgame in mind. The head-body analogy is also absent from the master-slave relationship (Eph 6:5–9). For a master to unilaterally "do the same" things that Paul had instructed servants to do to masters, and additionally to "give up threatening" (6:9) means that Paul is dismantling the dynamic of power because Christ is above both parties. So Christ is *within* marriage. Christ is the *end goal* of parenting. And Christ is *above* all other relationships. Thus, the husband-wife relationship is set apart from other types of relationships because of the way Paul is using the "head-body" image. And within the mutuality of submission, the husband is to pay special attention to the way he speaks to his wife and about her, not distancing her from himself in criticism (Eph 5:22–33), which is the particular and precise dimension of Jesus' relationship with his body that Paul applies to the husband. This meaning is fully compatible with Paul's goal in 1 Corinthians 6–7 not to position Jesus over an existing social hierarchy, but to insert Jesus into every relationship to qualify it, asserting Jesus' lordship over each person's body, putting Jesus before any other relationships and breaking in principle every social hierarchy to radically limit any other authority over the believer.

30. See O'Donovan, *Resurrection*, xi–xv, to understand his critique of John Finnis, a popular Catholic thinker and proponent of an updated version of "natural law." The Lutheran-Reformed theologian Karl Barth and Reformed theologian T. F. Torrance challenge the notion of natural law based on the centrality of God's revelation in Christ. The secular philosopher David Hume also used the "is-ought" distinction to argue that while we might know what is, we do not know what ought to be. We might even "know" goodness and value in something, but not know how it compares with something else with goodness and value, like various principles of justice: meritocratic-retributive; restorative; substantive-distributive; libertarian. Having full, communicable knowledge of Jesus' moral teaching, or even God's creation order, and an epistemological foundation for it, is not the same as having the preliminary knowledge prior to that: a combination of a knowledge of one's self as broken, needing healing, with an intuitive, often vague awareness of God's interest in you. Paul clearly did believe each human being had a "conscience" (Rom 2:12–16) which brought them some knowledge of God and a moral awareness of themselves. But as Catholic tradition developed, it assumed that the conscience, which Paul coordinated with the Sinai covenant, more or less accessed the actual moral commandments God gave to Israel (or, interestingly, Christian developments of the Jewish law), rather than the underlying purpose of those commandments: to help Israel know the corruption of sin within each person's human nature, as Paul himself learned (Rom 7:14–25). The Sinaitic commandments and the Sinai covenant framework called for the Israelites to present their human nature back to God in a purified state, which Moses called "circumcision of the heart" (Deut 10:16, 30:6). The Sinai covenant thereby directed them to the healing of human nature in the Messiah, Jesus (Rom 8:3, 6:6, 2:28–29). Hence, Paul argues that humans can be aware of being in moral decline (Rom 1:21–32), even measured against *one's own* principles of judging *others* (Rom 2:1–4). Therefore, the notion that human beings can use independent principles of rationality to arrive at the moral vision of Jesus has been adequately

Remarkably, while assuming gender difference and honoring marriage, Paul articulates a Christian understanding of sex *without referring to children*. Whereas Genesis 1 explicitly names the fruitfulness of children, making it attractive to politically conservative Christians like Bob Enyart, Genesis 2 does not. This seems strategic on Paul's part, and not just because he might wish to honor weddings between two fifty-year-old people as much as two twenty-five-year-olds. Since the real power and beauty for his vision of human sexuality comes from the uniting of divinity and humanity in Jesus Christ, where the potential for having children is important but secondary, Paul's vision has the same power and attraction regardless of how old they are. This has surprising implications. Paul need not be committed to the "young earth" theory of Genesis 1, or to rejecting the notion that God used some form of "theistic evolution"—when Genesis 2 portrays God using the preexisting human material of Adam to fashion Eve, what intrinsic problem is there? Most importantly, this means Paul would not teach Christian youth about sex by playing up their *fears about reproduction*.

If Paul were a youth educator in today's world, he probably would *not* endorse the notion that young people should remain ignorant of sexual matters while learning only "abstinence-only education." Indeed, it is hard to see how he could: A reading of the *Old Testament* itself—which the apostle would surely encourage (1 Tim 4:13; 2 Tim 3:16)—invites readers to ask countless questions about sex. Was there rape and/or incest and/or homosexuality in Noah's family, and what exactly made Noah upset (Gen 9:20–29)? Can an old, married man have sex with a younger, relatively powerless woman whom he has hired, have a child with her (Gen 16), and then discard them both (Gen 21)? How do people older than grandpa and grandma have a baby (Gen 17–18)? Could anal sex count as love, or does it only communicate rape and power (Gen 19:5)? Should daughters rape their drunken father and have his children (Gen 19:30–38)? Why would a man have sex with his sister-in-law but ejaculate outside her, and how reliable is the withdrawal method of birth control, anyway (Gen 38:8–9)? Why would a woman who pretends to be a prostitute, deceives her father-in-law into sex, and has his children be more righteous than him (Gen 38:24–26)? Did people actually have sexual relationships with family members and animals (Lev 18, 20)? Why would a woman's breasts satisfy a man (Prov 5:19)? What makes adultery wrong, exactly (Prov 5:20)? Is oral sex in the Bible (Song 5:11, 16)? If I have sex with someone else and then destroy everything around me to hide it, or use my positional power to coerce a vulnerable, married woman, would God still bless me (2 Sam 11–12)? These questions relate to

---

disproven from both Christian and non-Christian angles.

very commonly read passages. The Bible does not try to hide factual information about all manner of sexual relationships and sexual acts, because the Bible uses *facts* to discuss *values*, including *facts* about human failings to discuss the *values* of God's wisdom and redemption. That is the very *nature* of the Bible. It frames the body, sex, marriage, children, and relationships in the larger context of God's desire to restore garden-of-Eden-like qualities on the earth (Joseph became God's partner in gardening in Egypt; Moses led Israel into a new "garden land"; etc.) and enlist more partners to do it. In relation to God's larger purpose, everything else has *value*: faith, character, and the meaning of healthy relationship.

Yet Christian conservatives seem uncomfortable with young people having basic factual information, because they confuse facts with values, or equate the giving of facts with the promotion of values, inherently. For example, even though Texas has high rates of teen pregnancy and sexually transmitted diseases, Texas governor Rick Perry insisted that the Texas education system teach abstinence-only-until-marriage as its sex education curriculum.[31] Of course abstinence should be included, and a fine case made for it. And of course, whether the *instructor* shows respect to students, choices, and various frameworks of values—even without personally being a spokesperson for one—is an important question. But that is a professional matter and should be handled that way. Fundamentally, facts and values are not the same. More to the point, *withholding facts* is not a biblical *value*. If it were, Christians might as well fault *the Bible itself* for introducing youth to the withdrawal method of contraception.

Regarding contraception, it seems plausible to make contraception available, especially in lower-income communities, and to younger women. Of course the availability of contraceptives can be abused. However, as I discussed in chapter 4 with regards to contraception, there may be cases of rape (by a family member, for instance) which a young woman would prefer to not report to a parent. The quality of relationships in a nuclear family and extended family might be considerably unhealthy so as to place a young woman at a tremendous legal disadvantage, otherwise. There are ample relational and legal reasons why a woman would want to handle rape as a public health matter, and not a criminal justice matter.

Of course I am aware that the children of Christian parents will be legally able to access contraception, too. But was that not true in Paul's Corinth? Focus on the Family's Carrie Gordon Earll was troubled that Colorado gave contraceptives to minors without requiring them to be

---

31. Smith, "An Hour with Rick Perry," unfortunately removed the video and the interview was not transcribed. See also Perlberg, "Texas GOP."

accompanied by an adult. In response to the Colorado initiative, she said, "It totally undermines parental rights."[32] Parental *concern* I understand. Christian parents must have ways of speaking to their children about sex in age-appropriate ways, in light of biblical values: humanity is made in God's image in a good creation, human nature is fallen, and our desires and relationships are laced with both tremendous goodness and deadly selfishness. From what authority, though, does Earll derive her "parental right"? Neither Old nor New Testament addresses the age at which a child should be considered an adult. Broadly speaking, the Jewish community celebrates bar- and bat-mitzvahs when children reach the age of thirteen, a tradition which might have been formalized in the Middle Ages. In American law, the Supreme Court declared in *Carey v. Population Services International* (1977) that people younger than eighteen can access contraceptives without their parents. As of 2020, Washington, DC, and twenty-seven states (including Colorado) allow all individuals to receive contraception, nineteen states place some limitations on people younger than eighteen, and four states have no explicit policy.[33] It is unclear to me, then, what the moral and legal basis for Earll's complaint was, or would be today.

Is there a connection between the Christian politically conservative posture that they must "preserve civilization" and their vision for sex, the body, and community becoming curiously depleted of anything specifically Christ-centered—that is, truly Christian? Sadly, many even seem willing to obscure or distort basic factual information about science, history, law, and educational outcomes.[34] A different narrative makes a big difference. Christians in the U.S. can be morally conservative, biblically evangelical, and theologically orthodox, yet take different policy positions than political conservatives have because they inhabit a different political narrative.

If conservatives modify or discard the idea that the United States should be a theocratic "Christian nation," perhaps in favor of the vision of a politically pluralistic nation with Christian influence, will they be better able to consider something like contraception policy? Have they been shaped by misguided Christian teaching and political myth-making to believe that more is at stake than it is? To what extent do Christian conservatives fear that the hormones of youth and the intellectual attacks of secularism will overwhelm the beauty of the biblical vision? Do they fear that a culture of wisdom cannot actually contend with a secular culture of casual sex? Do they believe that the best strategy to deal with non-Christian

32. Draper, "Colorado Claims."
33. "An Overview of Consent."
34. Culp-Ressler, "GOP Platform."

influence is to be relationally separate and to withhold facts from youth? Or are there deeper problems stemming from Western Christian theology? Does Augustine's attempt to hold together God's goodness with double predestination force Christians to accept irrationalities in their own faith, leaving them intellectually weakened towards others? Does his theology of total depravity, at least as deployed by Luther and Calvin, leave Christians with deep suspicion, distrust, and misgivings about ordinary emotions? Does an image of God as punitive and retributive leave Christians more responsive to emotions of fear, anger, and anxiety about survival? Do Christian conservatives believe our common, human desires for goodness, beauty, justice, etc. are weak? On the ground, are they less able to cultivate those desires in others? To what extent do Christian political conservatives want a strong sex-pregnancy link in place via *public policy* because they have forgotten how to nurture a truly Christian vision of the body, other than delaying sexual gratification for marriage? In effect, do these Christians rely on biology and government to do their discipleship for them? Do they rely on marriage to offset the breakdown of community under capitalism? Do they rely on capitalism to penalize the breakdown of marriage? Is "Christian political conservatism" actually Christian?

Part Three

Abortion in the Context of the United States Constitution

12

Roe v. Wade and the U.S. Constitution in Context

The Constitution and Abortion: An Introduction

IN THIS CHAPTER, I discuss the legal history behind *Roe v. Wade* in order to narrate, in part, the spiritual history of the United States.

Other countries handle abortion policy by amending their constitutions. For example, of the thirty-six European countries that allow abortion on request, the vast majority impose time limits of around twelve weeks.[1] They change their constitutions fairly regularly. But therein lies the rub: the "Founding Fathers" of the U.S. made the Constitution hard—quite hard, in fact—to change.[2] They did this because they distrusted widespread democracy and desired *to protect slavery*. Recall that in the original Constitution, only landowning white men were allowed to vote, and U.S. Senators were not elected by the popular vote but *selected* by state senators. On the issue of abortion, this feature of the Constitution has forced American political activists, politicians, and strategists, along with Christians, into positions and alliances that are questionable and arguably counterproductive to the very goals they hope to accomplish.

Just after *Roe*, the pro-life movement proposed various constitutional amendments, mostly aimed at a "Human Life Amendment."[3] The sheer

---

1. Llana, "In Europe." Brunet, "Abortion Laws."

2. Posner, "U.S. Constitution," writes, "Most liberal democracies—including the nice, stable ones in Western Europe—amend their constitutions with great frequency. Germany amends its Basic Law almost once per year, and France a bit more than once every two years. Indeed, most states in the U.S. amend their constitutions every couple of years. Many have completely replaced their original founding documents. The procedures for amendment in states and most liberal democracies are much easier than they are for the U.S Constitution. For example, in Germany, an amendment requires a two-thirds majority in each House, and that's it. In all these cases, no one complains about the lack of constitutional stability."

3. Williams, *Defenders*, 8.

political difficulty of doing this frustrated the pro-life camp so much that they carried the platform from the Democratic Party to the Republican Party, adopting an economic and political conservatism by doing so. Many became single-issue voters, hoping to elect a pro-life president who would appoint pro-life justices to the Supreme Court, to not only overturn *Roe v. Wade* but to find "legal human personhood at conception" somewhere in the Constitution's use of the word "life," legally and historically speaking.

Unfortunately, though, "legal human personhood at conception" was not the "original meaning" of the Constitution. Although "originalism" is typically associated with conservatives, whose approach to the law more heavily weights the original meaning of words and their contexts, compared to the "living Constitution" view associated with liberals, no amount of "originalism" can find such an idea. This is suggested by the fact that *Planned Parenthood v. Casey* (1992) affirmed a woman's right to have an early abortion from *Roe*, abolished the trimester system by updating the standards for states because scientific developments moved the milestone of fetal viability earlier, and established the principle of the "undue burden" test for those standards. It is notable that eight of the nine Supreme Court justices in *Planned Parenthood v. Casey* were appointed by Republican presidents.

Throughout U.S. history, Protestant views about the fetus and abortion were complicated and compromised by American chattel slavery, racial animus, nativism, and another political current related to the regulation of medicine. *Abortion was used as a political tool towards those other ends; state laws reflect this long-standing dynamic.* Therefore, while aspects of *Roe* can certainly be debated, the anti-abortion strategy of getting judicial appointees to the Supreme Court to reinterpret the Constitution is not an intellectually honest or valid approach to the issue. The strategy is even counterproductive as a political one to bring down abortion rates or promote the welfare of women and children. Those liberals who wish to find "bodily autonomy" for women in the Constitution have long known that they cannot find it there; those conservatives who decry liberals as "legislating from the bench" or "exercising judicial activism," however, are vulnerable to the very same charge. This chapter explains why that is.

This chapter explains why a major problem for abortion policy is the nature of the U.S. Constitution itself, and the structure of American law and governance. Those who were committed to anti-slavery, racial equality, and women's suffrage had to recognize that long ago. I think it is important that evangelicals who want some restrictions on abortion (myself included), but who imagine that the Constitution is the answer (unlike me), have to acknowledge that *the Constitution is itself part of the problem.* That would involve a reckoning on the part of conservatives, however—a reckoning that would challenge a deeply held political narrative about the nation and the role of evangelicals within it. This chapter does involve legal history, but again, the primary objective here is to narrate a *spiritual history*. The next chapter explores the responses that pro-life advocates have taken to events after *Roe v. Wade*, and what the ramifications have been on American political, and even spiritual, life.

Factor #1: Abortion at the Time of the Constitution

From a constitutional perspective, some abortion was legal and even religiously acceptable in the minds of the Puritans, the American "Founding Fathers," and the authors of the U.S. Constitution.[4] This goes all the way back to the influence on Western Christianity of the Greek Septuagint (LXX) translation of Exodus 21:22–25, which made a critical distinction between a fetus being "formed" or "unformed," as I explored in chapter 2. This invited biblical interpreters to coordinate those terms with observable, practical considerations.

One of the most respected scientific minds in the classical world offered an answer: Aristotle. As I explained in chapter 3, based on his studies of miscarriages, Aristotle asserted that the fetus had to acquire the proper "form" and shape before it was ensouled. Augustine of Hippo, in the early fifth century, accepted Aristotle's view. While still holding that abortion was immoral, Augustine did not equate it with murder:

> One who procures abortion before the soul is infused into the body is not a murderer. An embryo which is not yet formed cannot be murdered, nor can it properly be considered a human being in the womb. This depends on the soul, for when something is unformed and has no soul, it cannot be murdered.[5]

The medieval theologian Anselm of Canterbury affirmed this view: "No human intellect accepts the view that an infant has the rational soul from the moment of conception."[6] The Catholic doctor of the faith, Thomas Aquinas, asserted that "movement" is one of the two necessary principles of life. Aquinas reinforced the Aristotelian theory that fetal movement was evidence of ensoulment, or "quickening." While still viewing abortion as a type of sin less than homicide, the abortion of a fetus prior to movement was not a murder. Until 1869, Roman Catholic canon law distinguished between a *foetus*

---

4. Dine, "Scarlett Letters." Pollitt, "Abortion."
5. Augustine of Hippo, *Quaestiones in Heptateuchum*, 2.80.
6. Flinn, "Abortion," 4.

animatus and a *foetus inanimatus*. English law also held to this distinction, which the Puritans brought to North America.

Therefore, the Catholic and Protestant West held that human personhood began at "quickening," the first time the mother felt the baby kick in the womb, typically between sixteen and twenty-two weeks of pregnancy. While the "quickening" view seems antiquated from our modern standpoint, we have to appreciate that there was no other reliable method to test for a pregnancy. There was simply no sure way to conclude why a woman skipped a menstrual cycle. When a woman's menstrual flow was obstructed, she had reason to worry for her own health, as harm was known to result. Today, we understand those harms to potentially involve cysts or scar tissue buildup in the uterus, and hormonal disturbances related to the pituitary gland and hypothalamus. Medically, the treatment of an obstruction of a menstrual period was the same as an abortion.

Until the time of the writing of the Constitution and its ratification, and well into the 1800s, abortion was not only relatively common, but also indelibly linked to slavery and white Protestant supremacy. Although we do not have medical records from the time, it is very likely that white men regularly imposed abortion on women of color, if they were embarrassed about fathering a biracial child or, more likely, found it economically disadvantageous at the time. It is also very likely that white men pressured white women to have abortions if white women had sexual relations with black or Native American men. This history—largely, the history of Christian interpretation of fetal life and abortion—makes legal matters complex in its own right. But the traces of such attitudes are found in American law, before and after the Constitution. They are part of what makes abortion policy in the U.S. so difficult to navigate and stabilize. As the history of chattel slavery and the construction of race complicate everything in U.S. political life, so also with abortion and reproductive policies.

Factor #2: Abortion and Slavery in the Colonies

In December of 1662, white colonial Virginians passed the third of their many slave laws. This particular law declared that the legal status of a child—free or slave—was determined by the legal status of the mother.[7]

---

7. Virginia Slave Act of December 1662: "Whereas some doubts have arisen whether children got by any Englishman upon a Negro woman should be slave or free, be it therefore enacted and declared by this present Grand Assembly, that all children born in this country shall be held bond or free only according to the condition of the mother; and that if any Christian shall commit fornication with a Negro man or woman, he or she so offending shall pay double the fines imposed by the former act."

"Blackness" was already defined as having any amount of African ancestry. In Maryland in 1664, white legislators decreed when "English women . . . intermarry with Negro slaves," that "it was a "disgrace to our Nation." With laws like this taking place throughout the colonies, "white enslavers could now reap financial rewards from relations 'upon a negro woman.' But they wanted to prevent the limited number of White women from engaging in similar interracial relations (as their biracial babies would become free)."[8] Virginia and Maryland therefore placed severe fines and penalties on white women engaging in relationship with non-white men. In 1662, for example, Virginia altered its law prohibiting fornication to punish more severely fornication if the parties were of different races. Then in 1682, Virginia passed another slave law which said that "whatsoever English, or other white man or woman, being free, [who] shall intermarry with a negro or mulatto man or woman, bond or free, shall, by judgment of the county court, be committed to prison, and there remain, during the space of six months, without bail or mainprize; and shall forfeit and pay ten pounds current money of Virginia, to the use of the parish, as aforesaid."[9] Dorothy Roberts points out, "Because a child took on the status of the mother, mulattoes born to white mothers were free. But these children were treated more harshly than free Black children; those with white mothers were generally required to become indentured servants until they reached thirty years of age. Unlike the racially mixed children of Black women, they represented a corruption of the *white* race."[10] White men were meanwhile free, legally, "to engage in sexual relations with all women."[11]

The social history behind these laws is important to understanding American abortion law and practice. Observers and historians of the period of American slavery now call our attention to the occurrences of white women sexually abusing black men, which must have meant abortion was a practice that was relatively well-known and practiced. For example, the African American writer Harriet Jacobs, in her mid-nineteenth-century autobiography as a slave woman in North Carolina who escaped to freedom in New York, noted that sex between white women and black men was not terribly unusual. More recently, Thomas A. Foster provides numerous examples in early American literature spanning the time of the Constitution.[12] In effect,

8. Kendi, *Stamped*, 41.

9. Virginia Slave Law of 1682, Article XIX. The Virginia Slave Law of 1705 criminalized a Christian minister performing any marriage ceremony between a white person and a non-white person.

10. Roberts, *Killing*, 268.

11. Kendi, *Stamped*, 41.

12. Foster, "Sexual Abuse," 135–40.

this historical research challenges the stereotype of the sexually aggressive black man and the sexually passive but greatly desired white woman. It also strongly suggests that the sexual contact between white women and black men prohibited by colonial Virginia and Maryland were in fact real concerns expressed by the white men controlling those legislatures. Jessica Millward notes that black people in Maryland did try to legally petition for their freedom, based on the claim that they were descended from a free woman; Millward also notes the resistance these actions provoked among white people.[13] Given that American laws also specified that both the racial identity and the legal status of the mother determined the race and legal status of her offspring, and given that white American society had a vested interest in keeping the number of free black people to a small number, and also given that black children resulting from such liaisons were more often given to slave families and held in slavery, abortion must have been relatively widely accessible to white women. White women, and the white men in their families, must have resorted to abortion to hide evidence of a sexual history which embarrassed and threatened them.[14]

In addition, white slaveholders had at least some economic interest in *preventing* enslaved black women from having children, suggesting that abortifacient potions were available and used. Historians have held that white slaveholding men had an economic incentive to father children with enslaved women, arrange for forced coupling, and even permit slave families. However, more recent scholars have raised questions about how often this happened.[15] Children diverted the energies of enslaved women for significant periods of time. As victims of trafficking, women were consistently bought and sold for lower prices than men, which suggests that white slaveholders purchased women primarily for economic motivations and not their potential childbearing. White slaveholders regularly speculated that black women knew and drank herbal remedies to induce abortion.

---

13. Millward, "Wombs of Liberation," discusses cases when black people attempted to petition for their freedom based on the claim that they were descended from a free woman.

14. Foster, "Sexual Abuse," 140, notes that white women, compared to black women, "had greater access to contraceptive information and technologies."

15. Burnard, "Toiling."

Factor #3: State Laws on Abortion as Anti-Quack, Anti-Immigrant, and Anti-Black

This colonial data informs our understanding of abortion in the original understanding of the Constitution and the development of abortion law in early national history. During the early 1800s, white Americans parted ways with the British Parliament, which moved in a more restrictive direction on abortion. In 1803, the British Parliament passed Lord Ellenborough's Act of 1803 which made abortion before quickening a criminal act.[16] The early United States drew apart from English law, which is notable and significant to any analysis of the Constitution. The 1812 Massachusetts Supreme Court case *Commonwealth v. Bangs* demonstrated a commitment to the "quickening" doctrine. Isaiah Bangs was accused of beating his lover, Lucy Holman, and forcing her to drink an abortifacient potion. Lucy Holman either could not or would not attest to the fact that the fetus had quickened. Therefore, the court decided that they must dismiss the charge of abortion. Historian James C. Mohr says, "In Massachusetts, the court was asserting, an abortion early in pregnancy would remain beyond the scope of the law and not a crime."[17]

From the early 1800s, doctors on both sides of the Atlantic were increasing their knowledge of fetal life, questioning the "quickening" marker, and called for tightening abortion law. No doubt some doctors stood on genuinely moral concerns, as formally trained doctors took seriously the Hippocratic Oath and saw human life as a continuum from conception. But other motivations were also present. In the U.S., between 1800 and 1840, doctors called for tighter abortion laws because it was one of many issues where they faced economic competition from "quacks," the unsafe practitioners who presented themselves as healers, but without license or training.[18] Some "medicines" contained alcohol or opium. The larger issue was the American public's acceptance of an unregulated profession. Physicians made abortion one of the pivotal issues on which to lobby for legislative change. As a result of this physicians' campaign, states started to pass abortion laws: Connecticut in 1821; Missouri in 1825; Illinois in 1827; New York in 1828. By 1840, ten more states had joined that group. Most regulations made abortion a crime after "quickening," not before, although New York did consider pre-quickening abortion a misdemeanor compared with second-degree manslaughter for a post-quickening abortion, and

---

16. Mohr, *Abortion*, 23–24.
17. Mohr, *Abortion*, 5.
18. Mohr, *Abortion*, 3–45.

held responsible the one who did the procedure, not the woman seeking it. "The immunity of women suggests that laws were intended to regulate incompetent practitioners, not proscribe abortion."[19]

Mohr examines the Connecticut 1821 law in detail. He observes that its language concerned "poison" and took "quickening" as a baseline.

> Every person who shall, wilfully [sic] and maliciously administer to, or cause to be administer to, or taken by, any person or persons, any deadly poison, or other noxious and destructive substance with an intention him, her, or them, thereby to murder, or thereby to cause or procure the miscarriage of any woman, then being quick with child, and shall be thereof duly convicted, shall suffer imprisonment, in newgate prison, during his natural life, or for such other term as the court having cognizance of the offence shall determine.[20]

This was the first time any American legislature had addressed abortion in statute form. The fact that it was concerned with attempted murder by poisoning shows the interest among professional physicians to curtail the activities of the irregular, unlicensed dealers in herbal remedies. Historian Simone M. Caron writes, "The immunity of women suggests that laws were intended to regulate incompetent practitioners, not proscribe abortion."[21] Notably, the Connecticut law accepted the quickening doctrine. Mohr observes, "Prior to quickening there continued to be no crime. Phrased differently, the revisers of 1821 chose to preserve for Connecticut women their long-standing common law right to attempt to rid themselves of a suspected pregnancy they did not want before the pregnancy confirmed itself, even though they risked poisoning themselves in the process."[22] This understanding is significant because the other states which developed abortion restrictions in the period of 1821–41 would take this law's essential features. Mohr identifies this as "the first stage in the evolution of American abortion policy."[23]

The second stage began with a great upsurge in abortions among white Protestant women. American public schools began to teach more scientific knowledge about the human body. Licensed physicians of this period believed that this education in physiology was a large contributing factor in

19. Caron, *Who Chooses*, 24.

20. Connecticut "Crimes and Punishments" law of 1821, section 14; discussed by Mohr, *Abortion*, 21.

21. Caron, *Who Chooses*, 24.

22. Mohr, *Abortion*, 22.

23. Mohr, *Abortion*, 21.

"the sharp increase in abortion rates that began in the 1840s."[24] Some physicians, seeing women have health problems they thought were resulting from herbal abortion remedies, began to openly oppose such instruction, in an effort to reduce abortion. Some women became confident enough to use instruments at home, such as the vaginal syringes made by Parke, Davis, and Company in Detroit and the Davol Manufacturing Company in Providence. Or they went to clinics which offered surgical techniques, like the ones operated by the notorious Mrs. W. H. Maxwell in New York City or Catherine Costello in Jersey City.

Physicians founded the American Medical Association in 1847 in an effort to regulate the profession, and leaders like Dr. Horatio Robinson Storer launched a physician-led anti-abortion campaign aimed at changing not only state-level legislation, but also public opinion.[25] One homeopathic physician who led a rival organization to the AMA, Dr. Edwin M. Hale, in 1860 estimated the prevalence of abortion based on his own practice in Chicago: "There is not one married female in ten who has not had an abortion, or at least attempted one!" Husbands, as could be expected, gave their approval if not active partnership: not one husband sued his wife for aborting their child.[26] Numerous other physicians' records indicate the high rates of abortion. This is remarkable since 1860 is the year evangelical historian Mark A. Noll says was one the highest rates of church participation in U.S. history: one-third to two-fifths of Americans were formal members in churches, and the number of people participating regularly in church life claimed 66–80 percent of all Americans.[27] On the eve of the Civil War, Protestants were inundated with biblical literature for and against slavery; although they may have been hermeneutically naïve, they were reasonably biblically literate, and yet *they did not see abortion as a moral issue.*

Anti-immigrant and anti-Catholic sentiments gathered up anti-abortion attitudes along the way. Between 1840 and 1860, the white, Protestant elite males who filled the ranks of licensed doctors were also alarmed about the mass immigration of Irish Catholics to the U.S., who provoked fears of a "hostile take-over" because of their much higher birthrates. Politically, the Know-Nothing party expressed the nativist hostility towards these immigrants. Meanwhile, another round of anti-abortion sentiment swept white Protestant circles because Protestant women had been procuring abortions, even to express their Christian piety, interestingly. "With smaller families,

---

24. Mohr, *Abortion*, 69.
25. Mohr, *Abortion*, 147–70.
26. Mohr, *Abortion*, 113–18.
27. Noll, *Civil War*, 11.

white middle- and upper-class mothers could intensify their maternal 'duties' to raise pious children."[28] After studying pamphlets, letters, and literature from this time period, Caron observes, "Physicians' fears of Protestant reproductive rates falling behind those of Catholics undoubtedly fueled the campaign, which included a vested interest in the continued Protestant domination of society."[29] Dr. Storer looked westward from his home in Boston and restated his belief in Manifest Destiny in firmly white, Anglo-Saxon Protestant terms: "Shall these regions be filled by our own children or by those of aliens? This is a question our women must answer; upon their loins depends the future destiny of the nation."[30] Storer wrote a book intended for the popular audience titled *Why Not? A Book for Every Woman*. As Leslie Reagan notes, "Hostility to immigrants, Catholics, and people of color fueled this campaign to criminalize abortion. White male patriotism demanded that maternity be enforced among white Protestant women."[31] Storer did this as he advocated for women to be wives and mothers, and simultaneously championed keeping medicine an all-male profession.

The earliest Protestant minister to join the physicians' cause was a friend of Storer, Congregationalist John Todd of Massachusetts in 1867. Todd shared white Protestant supremacist sentiments with the leading physicians, which he too tied into the abortion debate. Writing an article entitled "Fashionable Murder" in the journal *Congregationalist and Boston Recorder*, Todd said, "God has given this continent to the strongest race on earth, and to the freest and best educated part of that race, and I do not believe he is going to let it drop out of hands that can handle the globe, and put it into hands that are hands without educated brains."[32] More Protestant ministers and laypeople joined, becoming writers and activists in their denominations and states.

The anti-abortion movement, like prohibition sentiments, gathered steam most quickly in the states with the largest immigrant populations. In 1843, anti-Catholic and anti-immigrant attitudes coalesced in New York in the newly formed American Republican Party, in response to Irish and German immigration.[33] In 1845–46, New York removed the mother's legal immunity to hold her liable for second degree manslaughter with either three to twelve months in prison or a fine of $1,000 or both. In 1869,

28. Caron, *Who Chooses*, 18–28.
29. Caron, *Who Chooses*, 25.
30. Reagan, *When Abortion*, 11. Mohr, *Abortion*, 166–68.
31. Reagan, "When Abortion" (1997).
32. Todd quoted in Takaki, *Iron Cages*, 216; also cited by Caron, *Who Chooses*, 26.
33. Leonard, "Rise and Fall."

New York removed the "quickening" doctrine from its laws.[34] Massachusetts passed an anti-abortion law in 1845 and outlawed written materials promoting abortion in 1847, while Boston's budget for relief for the poor tripled from 1845-53, culminating in 1854 when Know-Nothings took 397 of 400 seats in the Massachusetts legislature. In 1849-50, California outlawed abortion at any stage of pregnancy in the midst of the Gold Rush and growing white opposition to Chicanos, Mexican immigrants, and Chinese immigrants; in 1854, a Know-Nothing chapter was organized in San Francisco, which included a California Supreme Court judge who ruled that Chinese people could not testify against white people in court;[35] in 1870, California eliminated the mother's immunity. Historians Mohr and Caron review the legal history, state by state.[36]

By contrast, most Southern states, while making some small legal changes, maintained the "quickening" doctrine and focused on the physician's role, not the mother's. One should bear in mind that "quickening" is a hard evidentiary hurdle for a court to establish, because it essentially relies on the woman to testify against her doctor, which was unlikely. In 1840, Alabama maintained that abortion was only illegal after quickening. In 1866, under the influence of the North and Reconstruction, Alabama altered the penalty for abortion from three to six months to three to twelve months—probably an allowance to judges' discretion that seems suited for the post-Civil War situation, where white judges handed down shorter or longer sentences based on race. In 1848, Mississippi made abortion of a quickened child a first-degree manslaughter charge, with attempted abortion second-degree manslaughter. It said nothing about a fetus prior to quickening, and this abortion law remained Mississippi law well into the twentieth century. In 1876, Georgia made abortion of a quickened child punishable by death, whereas abortion of an unquickened fetus was considered, strangely, assault with intent to murder. In 1881, North Carolina made abortion of a quickened child a felony charge punishable by one to ten years in prison, whereas abortion of an unquickened fetus was a misdemeanor charge punishable by one to five years.[37] In 1883, South Carolina's legislative process saw a battle between the "regular" physicians who sought not only anti-abortion policies but also a stronger state board of health, against the "lingering champions of

---

34. Mohr, *Abortion*, 124, notes, however, that the law incriminating the mother was never pursued at any time in the nineteenth century. Also, in practice, the quickening doctrine was present in NY legislation "into the 1880s."

35. LeMay, *Transforming America*.

36. Mohr, *Abortion*, 200-225. Caron, *Who Chooses*, 26-28.

37. Caron, *Who Chooses*, 28.

laissez faire medicine," who also opposed the abortion bill.[38] Kentucky made no abortion law whatsoever until 1910. Caron says the "nativist fears of immigrants destroying Protestant hegemony" were "an anxiety not as relevant to Southern states as to Northern states."[39]

Racial and religious reasons must be considered explanatory factors for holding on to the "quickening" doctrine in particular. Keri Leigh Merritt notes that prior to the Civil War, poor white Southerners, landless and slaveless, had surprisingly close relations with enslaved black people. Because sexual relationships between poor white women and black men happened frequently, "infanticide was far from an uncommon occurrence."[40] Surveying legal records, Merritt says, "There are literally scores of these interracial infanticide cases throughout every county of the Deep South."[41] One can reasonably assume that abortion was also frequent and a standard part of poor white culture. After the Civil War, however, racial hostilities *increased*. Children of interracial unions were no longer acceptable by white society. If Jim Crow–era anecdotes are any indication,[42] white men still raped black women with relative impunity. The children of those unions, who could no longer be turned into slave labor, were now socially undesirable by white people and brought economic advantage to no one. It is probable that sexual relations between black men and lower-income white women continued to a lesser degree, and white men likely pressured white women in their families to abort mixed-race children. If both black and white women had recourse to abortion prior to "quickening," it served the white supremacist, patriarchal order. Religiously, the King James Version of the Bible used the Hebrew Masoretic text of Exodus 21:22–25, which suggested that a fetus was not even a full human person anyway. Although the "quickening" doctrine went beyond what the KJV indicated, still it was common law, and white male Protestant Southerners benefited from its utility.

Whatever the various motivations, this legal history matters because it shows that the states did not uniformly move towards overturning "quickening" despite growing awareness from the medical and scientific community about the fetus. Forsythe, who raises good questions about the motivations,

---

38. Mohr, *Abortion*, 228.

39. Caron, *Who Chooses*, 28. Louisiana and South Carolina were unusual in that they adopted more stringent measures. In 1856, Louisiana prohibited all drugs inducing abortion, and in 1870, prohibited all methods. In 1883, South Carolina banned all abortions. See Caron, *Who Chooses*, 27.

40. Merritt, *Masterless Men*, 128.

41. Merritt, *Masterless Men*, 130.

42. Hines, "Rape and the Inner Lives." McGuire, *At the Dark End*.

legitimacy, and wisdom of *Roe v. Wade*, presents a more or less uncomplicated movement by the states. He says:

> In the nineteenth century, the American states updated the English common law by passing specific statutes to eliminate the quickening distinction, prompted by developments in medical science that produced a new understanding of fetal development. The AMA strongly endorsed these legal changes in the 1860s. By the 1860s, many states had prohibited abortion after conception except to save the life of the mother, which was called "therapeutic abortion."
>
> When medical science challenged the quickening rule in the 1800s by showing that conception was the beginning of the life of a human being, states quickly moved to repeal the quickening rule and replace it with an abortion prohibition from conception.[43]

Forsythe seems to have this impression because he did not engage with Caron's 2008 work. Caron improves on Mohr's 1978 study by more extensively examining the Southern states, as well as situating abortion politics within white Protestant attitudes towards other issues related to reproduction and the perception of *other people's children*. Insofar as Forsythe portrays the development of American abortion laws state by state as simply a response to updated medical information, he is incorrect. That development shows the interference of other political motivations related to elite physicians trying to discredit the practice of unregulated medicine, anti-immigrant and anti-Catholic sentiment in the North, and anti-blackness in the South. Social history is admittedly not the same as legal history, but in this case, it does actually make American legal history more complicated, and the discrediting of *Roe* more difficult. Protestants, in churches and state houses, clearly understood and cleverly manipulated the wiggle room afforded to them by the circumstances of their common law inheritance on abortion.

From 1900–1930, the Protestant establishment largely lost interest in abortion policy and turned to contraception policy and notions of eugenics and racial purity. The medical profession could rest assured in its legal licensing and regulation, having banished the "quacks" and laissez-faire medicine from the American public, and quietly returned to conducting the business of abortion.[44] Around 1895, some doctors estimated that *two*

43. Forsythe, *Abuse*, 84, 108.
44. Mohr, *Abortion*, 226–45 points out that physicians practiced this way, but some state laws also continued to make a distinction using the quickening marker. In 1881,

million abortions occurred annually, prompting some physicians to call for another public campaign against it.[45] According to medical records, more single and fewer married women sought it, coinciding with the increase in contraceptive options.[46] In the South, Jim Crow contained the black community, but the flight of Southern blacks to cities in the North and West provoked alarmed reactions there. Meanwhile, ordinary Protestants in other parts of the country turned to battle immigration head-on. The Irish, German, Italian, Polish, and Mexican Catholics had much higher birthrates than the white Protestants. White Protestants passed laws against cross-racial marriages with blacks and, in some western states, Asians. Immigration surged after World War I, especially from the southeastern European nations; white Protestants considered them "inferior" and "darker."[47] The Ku Klux Klan resurged, and Congress passed restrictive immigration laws in 1921 and 1924.

White Protestant fears of racial suicide were more overt, and appeals to eugenics more explicit, but no further changes could be made to abortion policy by that time, except to move to the more extreme Catholic position against abortion, which no one was willing to do. Theodore Roosevelt exemplifies leading figures who became increasingly outspoken about their fears of "race suicide." He appealed to Yankee women to have more children and use less contraception as a matter of "duty," accusing them of being "cold and selfish" otherwise, even "criminal against the race,"[48] but that was all anyone could do. Protestants turned their energy to promoting contraception and population control policies, such as sterilization, among black and immigrant communities, the poor, rapists and certain criminal classes, and "the morons." They therefore turned against the anti-contraception Comstock Laws, and against the Catholics on the issue.

Protestants generally accepted eugenics, whereas Catholics did not. Connecticut led the way to expand marriage bans against epileptics, "imbeciles," and the "feeble-minded" in 1895, and by 1913, twenty-four states had followed suit, along with Washington, DC, and Puerto Rico.[49] As the first vasectomy had been performed in 1897 in Chicago, in 1907, Indiana became the first state to sterilize state-institutionalized "imbeciles,"

New York used quickening to distinguish between misdemeanor and felony charges (227–28).

45. Caron, *Who Chooses*, 41, citing Petchesky, *Abortion*, 53. Reagan, *When Abortion*, 23, citing Gordon, *Woman's Body*, 493 n. 23.

46. Mohr, *Abortion*, 242–43.

47. Caron, *Who Chooses*, 62.

48. Caron, *Who Chooses*, 46.

49. Caron, *Who Chooses*, 53.

convicts, and rapists; by 1913, sixteen states had passed similar laws, although courts challenged the laws. *Buck v. Bell* (1927) declared that sterilization of such men and women was constitutional. Twenty-three states had such sterilization laws by the late 1920s.

It is very instructive to observe Catholic and Protestant attitudes about abortion and other issues in reproduction. Western Christians, seeing the colonialism-Christendom model collapse but interpreting it as only Christendom collapsing, tied abortion to other goals they wished to accomplish. During this time, the Roman Catholic Church stiffened its resistance to abortion. As I noted earlier in chapter 4, Catholic anxieties about the use of the scientific method to criticize the Bible and Christian faith drove Vatican I's decision in 1869 to declare that human personhood began at conception and in 1870 the doctrine of papal infallibility. The former ensured its moral claim and relevance within the scientific framework that had just displaced Aristotle; the latter asserted that the church had an epistemological foundation that could compete with science. By 1895, the Catholic Church declared that abortion of a non-viable fetus was unjustified even to save the mother's life, and in 1902 forbade the removal of an ectopic embryo per se, making a non-viable fetus worth *more* than its mother. Church authorities made an "exception" for the removal of the entire fallopian tube which contained the ectopic embryo, on the grounds that it directly saved the mother's life but only indirectly caused the death of the embryo. Protestants and Jews recoiled from these conclusions, finding the moral calculus impossible to replicate or needlessly circuitous. Clearly, the main Roman Catholic concern, even adversary at times, was science, including medical science.

The declarations of the Catholic bishops compare to the instability among U.S. Protestants, who positioned abortion against immigration and race. American Protestants kept one eye on the Catholic immigrants in an adversarial sense, and enlisted abortion as a focal issue or a tool, modifying their position within the range of possible positions permitted by Scripture, as it suited their more urgent political needs: in the North and West, against Catholic immigrants with large families; in the South, against blacks to control their population. These patterns reflected, and contributed to, the basic instability of American policy on abortion.

Christian views on the fetus, if they were derived from Scripture and science, might have a searching and tentative quality, with intelligence, humility, and some flexibility, appropriate to what we can and cannot know for certain. Christian views on abortion law and policy, if Christians consulted the broadest possible range of Scripture, science, and social science, might reflect economic options to bring down abortion rates while not instrumentalizing women or stigmatizing others. But in the U.S., Christians seem to take positions about the fetus and abortion from larger political and cultural anxieties. Christians develop a view on the fetus that may technically be *possible* from within the range of Christian epistemology and ethics. But they do so by portraying it as if it were the *only* possible option. With considerable dedication, they harden in their position on the fetus, and not that issue alone, but the other political-cultural commitments to which they fuse it. Christians would repeat the pattern in the latter half of the twentieth century.

The Role of Early American Law in *Roe v. Wade*

The heightened tensions between Protestants and Catholics in the U.S. because of immigration largely prevented any collaboration on abortion policies. Such collaboration would have to wait over a century. I will discuss that phase in the next chapter.

With this legal and social history in mind, we can reflect on the Supreme Court justices' positions in *Roe v. Wade* (1973). The justices behind *Roe* cited this historical material as significant to the meaning and intention of the Constitution.[50] Not cited in *Roe* is the cataclysmic trauma of the Civil War and the attempt at fixing certain aspects of the U.S. Constitution through the Reconstruction Amendments; we will continue to see below why *the legal history of slavery* is important to understanding principles of American law, including abortion law.

Norma McCorvey was a single mother of two, pregnant with her third child, in Dallas County, Texas, when she sought an abortion in 1970. The state law of Texas forbade her from getting one because her life was not physically in danger—the only exception for which an abortion was legal. She sued Henry Wade, the district attorney of Dallas County, in an effort to overturn the Texas law as unconstitutional. McCorvey was given the pseudonym "Jane Roe" to protect her privacy. In January 1973, the Supreme Court decided 7–2 in her favor that the Due Process Clause of the Fourteenth Amendment gave her a "right to privacy" originally possessed by all citizens which made abortion legal. The court held that this right was not absolute, however, and balanced the interest of the state in protecting a mother's life and the fetus's life by setting up a trimester system. The mother's right to an abortion held for the first trimester. The state's right to protect a mother's life and health pertained to the second trimester, and the court ruled that individual states could impose requirements or limits on abortion related to protecting the mother's health. The state's right to protect the fetus's life related to the third

---

50. *Roe v. Wade* (410 U.S. 113, 1973); https://supreme.justia.com/cases/federal/us/410/113.

trimester, and the court ruled that states could forbid abortions entirely except in cases of the mother's life or health.

Doe v. Bolton (1973) was a companion case to *Roe*. "Mary Doe" sued the attorney general of Georgia because the state prohibited her from getting an abortion at nine weeks, though she later dropped her own case. The Supreme Court decided to rule on the case anyway, treating it as a kind of representative or anticipatory litigation. In this case, the court stated that a woman may have an abortion after the fetus was viable for reason of her "health." The court gave physicians maximum leeway to define "health" as pertaining to all types of health: "The medical judgment may be exercised in the light of all factors—physical, emotional, psychological, familial, and the woman's age—relevant to the well-being of the patient. All these factors may relate to health."[51] Taking *Roe* and *Doe* together yields the conclusion that the state's right to regulate abortion in the second and third trimesters is nominal. Discretion and legal power lie completely in the hands of the physician, who can perform an abortion at any time.

Conservatives and liberals alike criticize the *Roe* and *Doe* decisions for various reasons. Conservatives challenge the court for pursuing cases that the women themselves withdrew, being personally invested in protecting women's access to abortion, misrepresenting or misunderstanding the history of abortion, shutting down a very important national conversation and debate by overriding the legal authority of states, inventing or developing a "right to privacy" doctrine which does not exist in the Constitution, inventing the trimester system and thereby legislating and not ruling, protecting the rights of doctors above all, and summarily acting by "raw judicial power." Liberals criticize *Roe* on various grounds: inventing the trimester system, going beyond the "equal protection" clause, going beyond the "right to privacy," not explicitly including the Ninth Amendment, and in some cases related to the modern feminist position, not establishing the bodily autonomy of women throughout the pregnancy.

Whatever is envisioned, it is hard to imagine that any decision would have made the American public *less* polarized on the issue of abortion. While alternative histories are hard to construct, it is very likely that the public's energy would have simply continued on in legislative battles at the state level, at a minimum. Meanwhile, doctors retained high levels of privacy in their practices as they did before *Roe*.

The conservative critique that the Constitution never upheld a "right to privacy," or one to this degree, is somewhat hard to sustain in view of

---

51. *Doe v. Bolton* (410 U.S. 179, 1973). IV.C. https://supreme.justia.com/cases/federal/us/410/179/.

conservatives' own rhetoric on other matters, along with legal history. When conservatives and liberals alike speak of government overreach in state surveillance, for instance, they speak of a "right to privacy."[52] The "right to privacy" had already been part of reflections on constitutional law, along with Supreme Court cases named in the opinion dating back to 1886. Some conservatives seeking to undermine *Roe* interpret *Griswold v. Connecticut* (1965) as allocating the right to contraception to the privacy of a married couple and not the privacy of an individual, but this is a rather forced reading. Additionally, the seven justices in *Roe* noted that the term "privacy" is equivalent to the term "liberty," which *is* in fact in the Constitution, "guaranteed by the first section of the Fourteenth Amendment," and they also cite *Meyer v. Nebraska* (1923).[53] In *Meyer*, the court established that people have "the right to marry, establish a home and bring up children," by referring to the Fourteenth Amendment.

The interaction of the Ninth Amendment with the Fourteenth is particularly relevant in this regard, as Justice White indicated in his concurrent opinion. Prior to Reconstruction, the Ninth Amendment simply meant that rights not specifically given to states were retained by the people. It reads, "The enumeration in the Constitution, of certain rights, shall not be construed to deny or disparage others retained by the people." Alexander Hamilton's *Federalist Papers*, Number 84, refers to powers not granted to the government being retained by the people,[54] which would give weight to the Ninth Amendment

---

52. Keene and Cole, "Keeping Surveillance Constitutional," subtitle their article "To preserve *privacy*, Congress must limit collection of personal communications" (italics mine). The authors say, "One of us is a past president of the National Rifle Association (NRA) and former chairman of the American Conservative Union. The other is the national legal director of the American Civil Liberties Union (ACLU). But we agree that any extension of Section 702 must include important protections to preserve privacy."

53. *Roe v. Wade* (410 U.S. 113, 1973). Section VIII. Justice White, in his concurrent opinion, included the Ninth Amendment: "This right of privacy, whether it be founded in the Fourteenth Amendment's concept of personal liberty and restrictions upon state action, as we feel it is, or, as the District Court determined, in the Ninth Amendment's reservation of rights to the people, is broad enough to encompass a woman's decision whether or not to terminate her pregnancy."

54. Hamilton et al., *Federalist Papers*, 420–21, "I go further and affirm that bills of rights, in the sense and in the extent in which they are contended for, are not only unnecessary in the proposed constitution, but would even be dangerous. They would contain various exceptions to powers which are not granted, and, on this very account, would afford a colorable pretext to claim more than were granted. For why declare that things shall not be done which there is no power to do? Why, for instance, should it be said that the liberty of the press shall not be restrained when no power is given by which restrictions may be imposed? I will not contend that such a provision would confer a regulating power; but it is evident that it would furnish, to men disposed to usurp, a plausible pretense for claiming that power."

anchoring a basic "right of privacy." The Constitution's first three words—"We the People"—affirm that the people accorded certain limited powers to the government; the remainder resided with "We the People." In 1789, this pertained indisputably to the federal government, which was of course very limited from 1789 until the Civil War. The basic idea contained here is that the people precede the government, not vice versa, so the people give *powers* to the government. The government does not give *rights* to the people.[55] Or, put simply, "rights retained by the people" can reasonably consider the common law at the time of the 1789 Constitution.

But what of the states and the various state laws regulating abortion or outlawing it? In that light, the dissenting views of Justices William Rehnquist and Byron White in the 7–2 *Roe* decision are important to consider seriously.[56] The two justices defended the right of the State of Texas to develop its own anti-abortion laws, without interference from the federal government. Justice Antonin Scalia reiterated this "states' rights" principle in *Planned Parenthood v. Casey* (1992).[57] They saw a procedural issue, centered around the rights of states. Forsythe, the most recent evangelical scholar to examine *Roe v. Wade*, argues that the "states' rights" principle would have been the correct

55. So *Chisholm v. Georgia* (2 U.S. 419, 1793), *Martin v. Hunter's Lessee* (14 U.S. 304, 1816), and *McCulloch v. Maryland* (17 U.S. 316, 1819) stated that the preamble indicates that the Constitution emanates from the people.

56. Justice Byron White "criticized the majority's arbitrary choice of a rigid framework without any constitutional or other legal foundation to support it. He believed that this aggressive use of judicial power exceeded the Court's appropriate role by taking away power that rested with state legislatures and essentially writing laws for them. White argued that the political process was the appropriate mechanism for seeking reform, rather than letting the Court decide whether and when the mother should be a higher priority than the fetus." Justice William Rehnquist "expanded on the historical elements of White's argument. He researched 19th-century laws on abortion and the status of the issue at the time of both the Founding and the Fourteenth Amendment. His originalist approach led him to conclude that state restrictions on abortion were considered valid at the time of the Fourteenth Amendment, so its drafters could not have contemplated creating rights that conflicted with it." *Roe v. Wade* (410 U.S. 113, 1973); https://supreme.justia.com/cases/federal/us/410/113/.

57. *Planned Parenthood v. Casey* (505 U.S. 83, 1992). Section IV. Scalia says: "My views on this matter are unchanged from those I set forth in my separate opinions in *Webster v. Reproductive Health Services*, and *Ohio v. Akron Center for Reproductive Health*. The States may, if they wish, permit abortion on demand, but the Constitution does not require them to do so. The permissibility of abortion, and the limitations upon it, are to be resolved like most important questions in our democracy: by citizens trying to persuade one another and then voting. As the Court acknowledges, 'where reasonable people disagree the government can adopt one position or the other.' The Court is correct in adding the qualification that this 'assumes a state of affairs in which the choice does not intrude upon a protected liberty,'—but the crucial part of that qualification is the penultimate word."

one for the court to invoke.⁵⁸ In this view, the Supreme Court should have declined to rule and pushed the case back down to the states. If federal law about the fetus and abortion were to be developed, it should have come about by people learning how the states serve as "laboratories of democracy" and then debating federal legislation in the U.S. Congress.

Factor #4: The Reconstruction Amendments and the Second Founding

The procedural, "states' rights" objection fails a basic historical test. The U.S. Constitution left open gaping holes, not simply related to slavery, but to the very definition of *citizenship*, as American Civil War and Reconstruction historian Eric Foner points out.⁵⁹ While the president had to be a "natural-born Citizen," according to the Constitution, nowhere did the Constitution specify how immigrants from abroad could become citizens. Who was a citizen? Who was eligible to become a citizen? How did one become a citizen? What rights did citizens have? Why were white women citizens and yet not eligible to vote? In our federalist framework, having changing definitions for such fundamental terms as "citizen," "life," "person," "liberty," and "privacy" can *only* be resolved on a federal level.

How might we establish legally enduring and meaningful protections for human persons when such principles varied from state to state? Unfortunately, the states were not simply "laboratories of democracy," but also laboratories of human rights and civil rights violations. Consider the parallel case when the definitions of citizenship, life, and personhood between the state and federal levels were at odds. Oregon was founded as a white supremacist haven and admitted as a state in 1859, just before the Civil War. Oregon defined citizenship as for white people only; they had a "whites only" clause in their state constitution, in fact. After Reconstruction, that clause became a violation of the U.S. Constitution's Fourteenth Amendment, which requires equal treatment under the law. The Thirteenth, Fourteenth, and Fifteenth Amendments establish the supremacy of the federal government over the states. States are required to respect the same legal rights accorded to persons by federal law. The Fifteenth Amendment, for example, requires that states extend the right to vote to *all* male citizens, notably black males, a right the Nineteenth Amendment extended to female citizens. Oregon initially ratified the Fourteenth Amendment in 1866, then *rescinded* its ratification in 1868. Despite this, it was compelled by legal and military force of the federal

58. Forsythe, *Abuse*, 12.
59. Foner, *Second Founding*, 2–8.

government to comply, making the "whites only" clause a dead letter. Oregon did not ratify the Fifteenth Amendment until 1959, and finally ratified the Fourteenth Amendment again in 1973.

Federal law and Supreme Court rulings do not simply average or aggregate existing state laws. They are their own body of laws and precedents. They often reflect, or are forced to reckon with, people's ability to physically move, commit crimes, and carry guns and birth control pills and other relevant items across state lines. They also reflect the tendency for people to have different moral frameworks and define critical legal terms differently. This is why in cases of conflicting definitions or conflicting jurisdictions, federal law must have supremacy. The relation between the individual states could not be sustained, and states did not have basic agreements about very fundamental matters. The Civil War and the Reconstruction Amendments were nothing less than a "second founding." During the Civil War, Congress passed laws related to finance, taxation, and the conscription of men for the war that were absolutely unprecedented in their scope and power. Lincoln's Emancipation Proclamation instantly destroyed "the largest concentration of property in the country (slaves as property were worth nearly four billion 1860 dollars)."[60] The fact that, after the Civil War, the federal government dictated terms to the former Confederate states and *forced* them to change their state constitutions is further evidence of this simple fact. The Southern states did not reenter the same legal and political arrangement as the one that existed before the Civil War. A new nation with a very strong central government had emerged.

The Reconstruction Amendments articulated the new reality. The Thirteenth Amendment banned slavery except penal servitude in every state, overturning state-level laws to the contrary. The Fourteenth Amendment instantly overruled the Supreme Court's decision in *Dred Scott v. Sandford* (1857) where Chief Justice Roger Taney had said that black people—free or slave—could not be citizens, bear arms, travel anywhere in the country, or enjoy freedom from legal discrimination. The Fifteenth Amendment extended voting rights into every state for every male citizen, overturning state-level laws to the contrary.

The Fourteenth Amendment is therefore the most significant touchstone for the powers of the federal government in coordination with the rights of all citizens. Congress's intention in the Fourteenth Amendment was to establish a definition of citizenship at the national level ("all persons born or naturalized in the United States") that pertained to the states ("are citizens of the United States and of the State wherein they reside"), which

---

60. Foner, *Second Founding*, 15.

included former slaves. This principle is now called "birthright citizenship." The Fourteenth Amendment has three critical clauses in section 1: the "privileges and immunities" clause; the "due process of law" clause; and the "equal protection of the laws" clause. Federal definitions of citizens' "privileges and immunities" took precedent over state ones ("No State shall make or enforce any law which shall abridge the privileges and immunities of citizens of the United States"). The Amendment strictly disallowed "any State" to "deprive any person of life, liberty, or property, without due process of law," a clause that became central to *Roe v. Wade*. The Amendment also assured citizens of "equal protection of the laws," which in this context meant laws with the whole nation in view. Sections 2 and 3 withdrew the full rights of citizenship from those who had taken part in the South's "insurrection or rebellion." Section 4 declared that the debts incurred by the Confederacy would not be recognized by the United States. Section 5 empowered Congress to enforce this amendment.

Interpreted as church history and not simply American history, *Christians* were legislating the Reconstruction Amendments to correct Christian heresies that had been woven into the foundation of the young nation from its colonial period. To say this is not to downplay the fact that American history can be told as a pitched battle *between* Christians. But it is to maintain that the Reconstruction Amendments were a victory for those Christians who wanted to defeat the colonial heresies of slavery and racism which had been institutionalized as American law. That line stretched from Roger Williams and the Moravian Brethren in colonial times; to Quaker abolitionists like John Woolman; to early black preachers like George Lisle and Sojourner Truth and all the black Catholics and Protestants who surely saw the Exodus deliverance as a sign that God would one day overturn American chattel slavery; to the half-Pequot Methodist preacher William Apess who saw that the Puritan idea of a "national covenant" was false; to Civil War–era black Christian abolitionists like Frederick Douglass, Sarah Mapps Douglass, and Harriet Tubman, and white Protestant abolitionists William Lloyd Garrison, Lewis and Arthur Tappan, Theodore Dwight Weld, Sarah and Angelina Grimke, Harriet Beecher and Calvin Ellis Stowe; to the post-Reconstruction-era black Christian legal scholars J. P. Lippincott and the Brotherhood of Liberty, who in 1889 authored *Justice and Jurisprudence: An Inquiry Concerning the Constitutional Limitations of the Thirteenth, Fourteenth, and Fifteenth Amendments*. The fiery legislator Congressman Thaddeus Stevens was not known to be a Christian during his public life, but on his tombstone, in a cemetery he selected for being racially integrated, Stevens had inscribed, "I repose in this quiet and secluded spot, not for any natural preference for solitude, but finding other cemeteries limited by charter rules as to race, I have chosen it that I might be enabled to illustrate in my death the principles which I have advocated through a long life—equality of man before his Creator." The Reconstruction Amendments reflected the fact that, finally, a sufficient number of American Christians read the Bible correctly and enacted the appropriate changes.

For a century, though, Southern lawmakers tried to circumvent and sabotage the Reconstruction Amendments. To undermine the Thirteenth Amendment or exploit the "penal servitude" loophole, Southerners used convict leasing and arbitrary criminal justice practices which criminalized black efforts to resist segregation. To resist the Fifteenth Amendment, Southerners passed Jim Crow laws to quash black citizens' right to vote at the polling booths. And to resist the Fourteenth Amendment, Southerners continued to insist on "states' rights." The North also gave up on the enforcement of Reconstruction in 1877. Clever lawyers, in *Santa Clara County v. Southern Pacific Rail Road* (1886), maneuvered corporations into the definition of "persons," which began to undermine the original purpose of the Fourteenth Amendment because it allowed corporations to discriminate and eventually wield enormous influence in political campaigns. By 1890, a former Confederate soldier "with a deep abhorrence of Reconstruction who as a young man had participated in efforts by a white paramilitary organization to overthrow Louisiana's biracial government" was placed on the Supreme Court: Edward D. White.[61] This was, unfortunately, technically legal as the Fourteenth Amendment did not forbid former Confederates from ascending to the Supreme Court, unlike other federal offices, but it certainly was against the spirit of that amendment. These political currents contributed to the notorious *Plessy v. Ferguson* (1896) decision affirming that segregation was legal, even when so legislated via a state government. The Southern states renewed their rhetoric of "states' rights," which affects us to this day.

Here we get to the crux of the abortion issue from a constitutional law standpoint. State laws on abortion, because they were varied (Texas and Georgia themselves had different laws), would not have given "equal protection of the laws" to "Jane Roe" and "Mary Doe" at once, or to their fetuses, or the doctors whose services they sought. From 1967–70, twelve states passed laws expanding the exceptions to their anti-abortion laws. In 1970, four states—Alaska, Hawaii, New York, and Washington—placed no restrictions on when a pregnancy could be terminated. From a federal perspective of common, national citizenship, this dizzying disarray of state laws posed a constitutional problem.

---

61. Foner, *Second Founding*, 130.

In light of the "second founding," the "due process" and "equal protection" clauses of the Fourteenth Amendment now protected citizens of the national body politic *from the states*, especially when combined with the Ninth Amendment, but even without it. "No State shall make or enforce any law . . . ." In 1923, the Supreme Court upheld, in *Meyer v. Nebraska*, that people had "the right to marry, establish a home and bring up children," according to the guarantees afforded by the Fourteenth Amendment.[62] In 1925, the court, in *Pierce v. Society of Sisters*, decided that a statute requiring parents to send their children exclusively to public school was unconstitutional because it unreasonably encroached on "the liberty of parents and guardians to direct the upbringing and education of children under their control."[63] In 1944, in *Prince v. Massachusetts*, this decision was strengthened using the language of privacy: "the private realm of family life which the State cannot enter."[64]

Since the federal government had not made any distinct abortion laws, the Supreme Court had to look back to the common law understanding that prevailed at the time of the Constitution and consider all that had transpired since then. For the Supreme Court to not have a previous definition available about fetal personhood and liberties for pregnant women, the first recourse for them at the federal level in *Roe* was to consider what "life" and "liberty" meant at the time of the Constitution (a la the preamble), especially for women and unborn infants, and consider whether any other constitutional amendments clarified the situation. The justices noted the legal changes:

> In 1828, New York enacted legislation that, in two respects, was to serve as a model for early anti-abortion statutes. First, while barring destruction of an unquickened fetus as well as a quick fetus, it made the former only a misdemeanor, but the latter second-degree manslaughter. Second, it incorporated a concept of therapeutic abortion by providing that an abortion was excused if it "shall have been necessary to preserve the life of such mother, or shall have been advised by two physicians to be necessary for such purpose." By 1840, when Texas had received the common law, only eight American States had statutes dealing with abortion. It was not until after the War Between the States that legislation began generally to replace the common law. Most of these initial statutes dealt severely with abortion after quickening, but were lenient with it before

62. *Meyer v. Nebraska* (262 U.S. 390, 399, 1923).
63. *Pierce v. Society of Sisters* (268 U.S. 510, 534, 1925).
64. *Prince v. Massachusetts* (321 U.S. 158, 166, 1944).

quickening. Most punished attempts equally with completed abortions. While many statutes included the exception for an abortion thought by one or more physicians to be necessary to save the mother's life, that provision soon disappeared, and the typical law required that the procedure actually be necessary for that purpose. Gradually, in the middle and late 19th century, the quickening distinction disappeared from the statutory law of most States and the degree of the offense and the penalties were increased. By the end of the 1950s, a large majority of the jurisdictions banned abortion, however and whenever performed, unless done to save or preserve the life of the mother. The exceptions, Alabama and the District of Columbia, permitted abortion to preserve the mother's health. Three States permitted abortions that were not "unlawfully" performed or that were not "without lawful justification," leaving interpretation of those standards to the courts. In the past several years, however, a trend toward liberalization of abortion statutes has resulted in adoption, by about one-third of the States, of less stringent laws, most of them patterned after the ALI Model Penal Code. It is thus apparent that, at common law, at the time of the adoption of our Constitution, and throughout the major portion of the 19th century, abortion was viewed with less disfavor than under most American statutes currently in effect. Phrasing it another way, a woman enjoyed a substantially broader right to terminate a pregnancy than she does in most States today. At least with respect to the early stage of pregnancy, and very possibly without such a limitation, the opportunity to make this choice was present in this country well into the 19th century. Even later, the law continued for some time to treat less punitively an abortion procured in early pregnancy.[65]

The seven justices chose the only *national* interpretation of this legal history. The United States, at the federal level, had never developed statutory abortion laws. Only the states had. But various states were also starting to liberalize their abortion laws; four states had even removed all restrictions entirely. What could be done? Ruth Bader Ginsburg expressed the opinion that the court should have made a decision on the "equal protection" clause of the Fourteenth Amendment.[66] On such an important matter, the right of a woman to procure an abortion could not vary so wildly from state to state. One consideration for the "equal protection" clause is political: as a more limited argument, this reasoning might not have inflamed so many pro-life

65. *Roe v. Wade* (410 U.S. 113, 1973), IV.5.
66. Zeitz, "Why Conservatives."

advocates on the national level. As a concurrent opinion, that might have added more weight to the decision, but several major questions emerge. If the states happened to be in uniform agreement, would that have rendered Roe's case moot? Can the "equal protection" clause alone, by itself, be applied on behalf of the fetus? Do we accord no rights or interests to the fetus at all on the national level? As for our political life, would Ginsburg's rationale have simply oriented the pro-life movement to state-level politics, by conceding more legitimacy to those in the "states' rights" camp? This is what happened after the Affordable Care Act was passed in 2010.

Be that as it may, in keeping with an "originalist" understanding of the Fourteenth Amendment, where federal law took supremacy over state laws, the Supreme Court majority looked back to the common law understanding of fetal life, which included "quickening" as the baseline for women's liberties (or "privacy") to abort, which prevailed at the beginning of the United States as a nation. Any state legislation, no matter how old or how recent, pertained only to that state and could not suffice for national policy. The "due process" clause now defended women from state interference with what had been the common law understanding of what she could do. If the court had explicitly invoked the "equal protection" clause and the Ninth Amendment, it would have only made their case stronger. This is not to say that federal legislation could not restrict a woman's "right" or access to an abortion; it very well could, as the meaning of "due process" includes the legislative process. The issue here is that the legislative process in question needs to be the federal one.

If only statutory laws were relevant, then in another universe, the court might have simply wiped off their books *all* state abortion restrictions, like wiping off the "whites-only" clause from Oregon's state constitution. The court might have forced the American voting public to be thrust into a spirited debate about abortion at the federal level without any framework for states to regulate doctors' activities whatsoever. That path might have been theoretically possible if only statutory law mattered, but in fact, there *had* been a law at the national level to use as a starting point: the common law. The court's deployment of the trimester system—clumsy as it was, and whatever the motivations—was an attempt to update the common law understanding in such a way as to acknowledge (or attempt to acknowledge) the interests of women, fetuses, doctors, and states, as the states developed their laws. The court thus created a baseline national framework for the states to enact further legislation to regulate abortion.

Of the two rulings, *Doe* is the more questionable and unprecedented, as it allowed doctors to perform abortions for the emotional health of the mother, which was the most expansive justification for abortions, and the one most open to abuse. *Doe* even nullified the part of *Roe* that enabled state legislatures to constrain doctors' reasons for aborting after the first trimester. Social customs and theological opinion condemned post-quickening abortions as morally wrong, and England's common law regarded it as a felony until the end of the 1500s.[67] Subsequently, until the 1800s, England considered abortion a homicide if the child was born alive and died afterwards primarily because, as Forsythe, following Dellapenna, notes, "evidentiary hurdles to confirming a pregnancy" were so high.[68] Again, a pregnant woman could deny she had felt the fetus move and would usually not willingly testify against a doctor she herself had sought, effectively making the law serve as a recourse for a woman who had been forced to abort. The leniency of the common law at the time, and the cases which did come before colonial American courts,[69] reflected the subjectivity involved with "quickening," and the difficulty with pursuing the matter in a legal setting, but not public doubt about the unborn child after "quickening." Yet in *Doe*, the court majority interpreted the English common law understanding that no law existed in the colonies in 1789 to make abortion by a physician a murder per se. "Even post-quickening abortion was never established as a common law crime."[70] From a strictly technical perspective on statutory grounds, Blackmun's reasoning might have been correct, but the court majority neglected critical aspects of social and legal history as context.

Roe eventually became much more the lightning rod of controversy. Of course, there were the stated reasons: people perceived the decision as one of a federal government overriding states, specifically of "unelected judges" overriding "the will of the people," giving pregnant women and doctors the legal basis for the murder of an unborn child who should have been regarded as a fully human person in the eyes of the law; many saw the trimester system as completely novel; etc. In *Roe*, "quickening" had returned. It was not called by that name, of course. Its time frame had even been shortened. "Quickening," the older Christian understanding tied to Exodus 21:22–25 in the Greek Septuagint version of the Bible, which Western Christians had held as a doctrine for a millennium and a half, the understanding that many Southern Protestants had preferred for years *over against* the stricter understanding Northern Protestants promoted was now given back to American Christians as a baseline policy framework for the fetus and abortion. Catholics were disappointed. Protestants became furious—in a few years.

67. Dellapenna, *Dispelling the Myths*, 57–228.
68. Forsythe, *Abuse*, 84.
69. Olasky, *Abortion Rites*, 19–108.
70. *Roe v. Wade* (410 U.S. 113, 1973), IV.3, see n. 26.

Reflection

Once again, the purpose of this chapter is not legal history for its own sake, but the use of legal history to highlight a spiritual history. The struggle over abortion policy could, and should, lead to painful, public admissions on the part of evangelicals that the U.S. Constitution was steeped in the legacy of Protestant heresies and was structured to defend them. As I explored in chapters 2 and 3, Scripture itself has critical uncertainties about how to regard the fetus and abortion, what are the other moral parameters around abortion, and perhaps who should pay the consequences for abortion. As I explored in chapters 3 and 4, it should lead Christians to at least engage with the sciences to help answer some of those questions. For various reasons, many conservative Christians today apparently believe that the answers to these questions are remarkably simple. I contend that they are not.

Unfortunately, without a long historical perspective, the politics of updating Christians' approach to abortion becomes confusing and frustrating. Aside from the circumstances of different colonial groups arriving at different times on the shores of North America, the heresies of Lockean land conquest, chattel slavery, and white supremacy played a significant role in why we have states at all, and how ridiculously difficult it is for the American people—the "we the people"—to amend the Constitution. The Constitution was designed to protect heresies and the profits that white men gained from them. As a result, the Constitution has only been amended in times of profound crisis. When, in the Civil War and Reconstruction, the federal government became overwhelmingly stronger and the individual states weaker, evangelicals held on to narratives about "states' rights" in an effort to deny the obvious legal shift. Southern evangelicals did so to maintain racial segregation and Jim Crow laws, but their Northern brethren did so to absolve themselves of any responsibility for upholding the basic constitutional rights of black citizens.

During the New Deal, evangelicals began to realize that their political narratives were unraveling when an aggressive federal government intervened in social and economic policy, but especially when the Supreme Court handed down *Brown v. Board of Education* (1954). Evangelicals largely refused to understand the Constitution in honest terms. Consequently, they assimilated the abortion debate into preexisting false narratives about "Christian America" over against "secular humanism" and "states' rights" over against "federal overreach" and "unelected judges," because the Constitution virtually requires that in order to change it, movements be built on simple-minded, mass appeals with great energy but little discernment. These movements engage in endless debates about the origin and scope of legal terms, resulting in mutual suspicion on both sides over the way people use words. It is why evangelicals turned the pro-life movement originally stewarded by Catholics into little more than a criminal justice issue, as opposed to a set of broad social and economic policies supporting the interests of children and women. To that history we now turn.

13

Abortion and the U.S. Constitution as It Could Be

Abortion Politics and Federalism

CHRISTOPHER CALDWELL, A SENIOR fellow at the Claremont Institute, makes the case in his new book, *The Age of Entitlement: America Since the Sixties*, that what roils America's politics is the liberal expansion of the federal government in the 1960s.[1] He calls the liberal, big government agenda epitomized by the Civil Rights Act of 1964 a "second constitution," an "unwritten constitution," even "a rival constitution, with which the original one was frequently incompatible." I appreciated some of Caldwell's cultural observations, especially his critique of debt-financing, which echoes my own. Although some conservatives recognized Caldwell's basic thesis was not new, and expressed other points of dissatisfaction,[2] his overall argument has been food for thought among many conservatives, like *Fox News, Washington Times*, and the Christian leadership of Hillsdale College.[3] *New York Magazine* noticed: "A New Conservative Theory of Why America Is So Polarized,"[4] read one title. Caldwell's interpretation captures some of the sentiment that many people feel—that "meritocracy" and principles of local democratic self-rule like "states' rights" have been eroded.

Caldwell's most serious problem is that the "second constitution" he refers to is in fact *written*. It is the *actual* Constitution as reflected by the *Reconstruction Amendments* which were so effectively suppressed and evaded[5]

---

1. Caldwell, *Age of Entitlement*.
2. Verbruggen, "Did Civil-Rights Laws." Chalberg, "Christopher Caldwell's."
3. Caldwell, "America's Two Constitutions." Rowe, "Review: 'The Age of Entitlement.'" Caldwell, "Roots."
4. MacDonald, "New Conservative Theory."
5. Foner, *Second Founding*, 125–67.

until black Christians and their allies reinvigorated them in the Civil Rights Movement. The difficulty for some conservatives is that the Constitution they wish for is the pre-Civil War Constitution, a Constitution *that no longer exists*. For it was indeed a "rival constitution," and it was vanquished. Yet white evangelicals like Pat Robertson, founder of the Christian television show *700 Club*, when he ran for president, continued to advocate a "states' rights" orientation. In 1986, on a *700 Club* broadcast, Robertson said that the authority of states had no legal limitations: "There is never in the Constitution at any point anything that applies to the states, none at all." In the summer of 1987, he claimed "that the Bill of Rights did not apply to the states."[6] This, despite the "privileges and immunities" clause of the Fourteenth Amendment defining national citizenship prior to state citizenship, and thus requiring states to respect the Bill of Rights. Robertson demonstrates adherence to a view of American history and the Constitution that is popular among white evangelicals, to nurture theocratic aspirations on the state level and grievance politics at the national level. He also exemplifies the investment Christian conservatives have in their own media outlets, to promote their own views about American history and law—views that are often factually inaccurate and civically dangerous because they lead to extreme forms of disappointment and/or rage. As for "meritocracy," as I have shown in previous chapters, it might have been a decent practice in limited form, where intergenerational transfers of wealth especially were limited, but the systemic racism in such fundamental sectors of the economy as housing, banking, schooling, and employment puts the lie to any claim that the U.S. has actually been a "meritocracy" for all.

For Christians, a further problem is that the legal history of the United States, including the nature of its Constitution, is the direct result of *Christian mistakes*. In particular, the U.S. has been directly shaped by John Locke's ham-handed treatment of Genesis 1 which justified theft of land, the dreadful view that the Bible endorses kidnapping and chattel slavery, a virulent racism reinforced by "the curse of Ham," among other things, and denying women the full range of Christian vocations outside of daughter, wife, and mother.[7] There are admirable, positive Christian elements to American history and the Constitution, which also have ramifications for abortion policy, as I will discuss in chapter 14. But as far as accepting the ascendancy of federal law

---

6. FitzGerald, *Evangelicals*, 386.

7. For an explanation of Christian vocations open to women and their sociological implications, as well as the Christian critique of kidnapping and chattel slavery, see chapter 5. For a critique of John Locke, see chapter 7. To see the origins of modern racism from a theological perspective, and the theological responsibility of Christians, see the beginning of chapter 8 and the footnotes there.

over state law in principle, and the importance of the Fourteenth Amendment in particular, it is hard to reach any other conclusion: the original Constitution was not only rushed, it took shape in a very unfortunate time and context, when Christians believed some aberrant and terrible things and sought to protect their ability to practice those things. In other words, one reason why national abortion policies are hard to design—aside from the inherent complexity of the issue itself—is because the Constitution and our system of federalism were designed to *protect Christian mistakes*. Failing to recognize the mistakes and the legal structures built to protect those mistakes is a failure to adequately *repent*.

Through the 1950s and 1970s, a sizable number of Southern white evangelicals resented *Brown v. Board of Education* (1954), which of course rested on the Fourteenth Amendment. Impressively, *Brown* was unanimous. While *Brown* might have been interpreted as requiring the racial integration of *housing*, it was popularly interpreted as requiring the racial integration of *public schools* via busing—the less radical of the two options. Nevertheless, Southerners viewed school desegregation as an act of Northern aggression and federal overreach. Having lost the battle over public schools, white evangelicals fought their next battle over privates. While Catholic private schools openly invited black students, white evangelicals set up "segregation academies."[8] Various leaders of Southern white evangelical churches put forward articles defending racial segregation from a "biblical" point of view.[9] In 1956, W. A. Criswell, pastor of the largest congregation in the Southern Baptist Convention at the time, First Baptist Church of Dallas, Texas, gave a "fiery sermon" admonishing his fellow Southern Baptist pastors to defend racial segregation, and in 1961 taught the "curse of Ham" theory from Genesis 9.[10] They viewed other Christians who favored integration as *heretical*: "Northern Protestants, they believed, had corrupted the pure and simple Gospel of salvation by forsaking strict

---

8. After *Brown* was decided, U.S. Senator Harry F. Byrd Sr. (D-VA) started the Byrd Organization to promote a strategy of massive resistance in Virginia. These efforts resulted in the Stanley plan adopted by the Virginia General Assembly in 1956. Virginia's voters approved an amendment to their state constitution allowing parents to opt out of desegregated schools and to send their children to a private "Christian" school of their choice, and benefit from tax-exemption status. Sociologist Jennifer Eaton Dyer, "Core Beliefs," 23, writes, "These schools included Brentwood Academy (1969), Father Ryan (1970), Franklin Road Academy (1971), or Ezell-Harding (1979), to name a few. These were the "White flight" schools where parents could send their children under the guise, conscious or unconscious, of proclaimed 'Christian' values, a safer environment, and more sound education." See also "It's Not over in the South."

9. Dupont, *Mississippi Praying*, 79–103.

10. Freeman, "'Never Had I Been,'" 1–2, 10.

biblical interpretation, discarding their zeal to save lost souls, and striving to improve conditions in the present world."[11]

After the Democratic Party embraced the Civil Rights Movement, Southern Baptist pastors, who had traditionally supported pro-segregation Southern Democrats, actively voiced support for Republicans at the national level: Goldwater, Nixon, and Reagan.[12] Southern politicians with "small government" ideology had for decades influenced Western policies and political leadership, as Heather Cox Richardson points out their economic similarities: The West depended on extractive, land-based industries like mining, cattle, and oil, just as the South depended on cotton, and prior to that, tobacco and sugar.[13] Likewise, Southern Protestant groups led the way on the ground to produce a complementary Protestant political culture. Southern Baptists, Pentecostals, Foursquare members, Church of the Nazarene adherents, Church of Christ members, and fundamentalist Baptists had also spread there, establishing Fuller Seminary, Pepperdine University, and other evangelical institutions.[14] The theological complement to accommodating white supremacy was a reduction of people down to souls and not bodies, and aversion to political action towards racial and economic justice. So it was no surprise that political figures from the West (Goldwater was a five-term Senator from Arizona; Nixon had been a U.S. Congressman and then Senator from California; Reagan had been governor of California) realigned the Republican Party away from its traditional industrial base in the North by deploying the Southern Strategy: appealing to "states' rights," anti-welfare, and other "dog-whistles" familiar to white supremacists.

In 1969, the SBC elected W. A. Criswell of First Baptist Church of Dallas to be president of the denomination; Criswell offered a statement about his updated view of race in America. He welcomed all people to his

---

11. Dupont, *Mississippi Praying*, 41 points out that two weeks after *Brown v. Board* was decided, the Southern Baptist Convention met in St. Louis, Missouri. While the majority of the Convention's ten thousand attendees celebrated the decision, whereas a minority objected, many congregants who did not attend the convention expressed intense disagreement back at home. Dupont, *Mississippi Praying*, 65–66, summarizes the situation in Mississippi, which is, at the very least, suggestive of the Deep South more broadly: "As the state actively obstructed the civil rights quest, the churches contributed considerable energy to the culture and the strategies of resistance.... Baptists, Methodists, and Presbyterians stymied integrationist arguments of religious origins by stifling, drowning out, or contravening both the national church and their local coreligionists of more moderate inclinations. They began by vigorously denouncing the denominational endorsements of desegregation."

12. Ladd, "Pastors, Not Politicians."
13. Richardson, *How the South*.
14. Dochuk, *From Bible Belt*.

church, but refused to countenance changing social and legal structures. "For Criswell, as for many other white conservative evangelicals in America, racism was limited to individual-level prejudice and discrimination. To the extent that something changed in him it was at the interpersonal level, and if all individuals were similarly to change there would be no race problem."[15] Or, Protestant ministers claimed that racial disparities would disappear if everyone became a Christian—an easily verifiable lie since most people in the South already claimed to be Christians, and considering how much resistance conservative evangelicals put up to spreading economic, educational, and political opportunities to their black counterparts, and to dismantling inequalities in the criminal justice system.

The collapse of segregated private schools brought white fundamentalists and evangelicals into politics using a strategy of invoking "religious freedom" to mask their racial segregation. In 1970, the IRS declared it would not grant tax-exempt status to private schools that practiced racial segregation. In 1971, in *Coit v. Green*, the Supreme Court affirmed the IRS's position. Battles over standards and percentages predictably ensued. In 1974, the IRS threatened to revoke the tax-exempt status of Bob Jones University for prohibiting its students from interracial dating. In 1978, President Jimmy Carter once again threatened Christian private schools with revoking their tax-exempt status if they did not take steps to racially integrate their schools. This, more than any other issue, brought Southern white evangelicals fully into the political process. Paul Weyrich was an arch-conservative Catholic who became an Eastern Rite Catholic after Vatican II, and became the intellectual leader of the new right-wing movement, cofounder of the Heritage Foundation, Moral Majority, and various other groups. He helped Jerry Falwell form the "pro-family" Moral Majority organization in 1979, and said emphatically:

> What galvanized the Christian community was not abortion, school prayer, or the ERA. I am living witness to that because I was trying to get those people interested in those issues and I utterly failed. What changed their mind was Jimmy Carter's intervention against the Christian schools, trying to deny them tax-exempt status on the basis of so-called de facto segregation.[16]

15. Freeman, "Never Had I Been," 10.

16. Martin, *With God*, 173 n. 137. Balmer, "Iowa: A Pastor's Son," recalls the 1978 election for U.S. Senate in Iowa. "Until 1978, evangelicals in Iowa were overwhelmingly indifferent about abortion as a political matter. Even after the Roe v. Wade decision of 1973, most evangelicals considered abortion a 'Catholic issue.' The Iowa race for U.S. Senate in 1978 pitted Dick Clark, the incumbent Democrat, against a Republican challenger, Roger Jepsen. All of the polling and the pundits viewed the election an

Weyrich's experience of evangelicals is far from trivial as multiple historians identify him as the thought leader behind the Republican realignment of their party. Indeed, assessments of Jerry Falwell, Southern Baptist founder of Liberty University in Lynchburg, Virginia, echo the same. Falwell campaigned against MLK and the Civil Rights Movement in the 1950s and 1960s, and founded Lynchburg Christian Academy in 1967 as a segregated school. Falwell helped organize the Moral Majority as a Catholic-Protestant political movement denouncing secular humanism as the cause of the Equal Rights Amendment, women's call for liberation, evolution, loss of patriotism, gay rights, and abortion. Falwell countered secular humanism with a "pro-family" agenda. But Paul Brown, founder of the American Life League, mocked Falwell in 1982: "Jerry Falwell couldn't spell abortion five years ago."[17] Again, this is not to say that the motivations of today's pro-life movement are purely cynical or secretly white supremacist, but it is to say that the energizing passions and ideologies share much political psychology and legal architecture in common, including the strategic appeal to "religious freedom." They continue to shape what conservative Christians believe is possible when we address the social policies that touch on abortion rates, and why pro-life advocates are willing to make political alliances with even non-Christian white nationalists and make the cause of *economic* conservatism such a high priority.

As political psychology, *Roe v. Wade* provided Christians with *two* victims of rights violations: the unborn and the Christian who stood up for them. It was therefore crucial to the formation of the Christian Right, since abortion was also used by economic conservatives to bring Christians *further* into the rights-based individualism that liberalism required. Richard A. Viguerie, a Catholic Republican and early conservative fundraising strategist in the 1970s who helped Paul Weyrich and Jerry Falwell launch the Moral Majority, explained:

> The abortion issue is the door through which many people come into conservative politics, but they don't stop there. Their convictions against abortion are like the first in a series of falling dominoes. Then we lead them to a concern about sexual ethics and standards among young people. This leads

---

easy win for Clark, who had walked across the state six years earlier in his successful effort to unseat Republican Jack Miller. In the final weekend of the 1978 campaign, however, pro-lifers (predominantly Catholic) leafleted church parking lots all over the state. Two days later, in an election with a very low turnout, Jepsen narrowly defeated Clark, thereby persuading Paul Weyrich and other architects of the Religious Right that abortion would work for them as a political issue."

17. Lepore, "Birthright," summarizing Greenhouse and Siegel, "Before *Roe*."

to opposition to secular humanism, then particularly in the schools with a purportedly decent morality we point out that secular humanism is identified as both the godfather and the royal road to socialism and communism—which points the way to minimally regulated free enterprise at home and to aggressive foreign and military policy to counter the Communist threat of Russia and its many surrogates.[18]

Viguerie confesses that abortion became the entrance into a certain worldview, morality, policy platform, and fundraising pitch. Evidently, few questioned how huge defense contracts to America's favorite corporations were compatible with "free enterprise," since "aggressive foreign and military policy" in fact required the "big government" of "corporate socialism." Regardless, the rights-oriented and justice-demanding discourse of the leftist 1960s had to be answered in like terms, and in *Roe* the right finally found it. Calling attention to the unborn because of their tremendous vulnerability was understandable, even appropriate. Surely some of these evangelicals even felt personal remorse for aborting a pregnancy. On the one hand, critiquing *Roe* accurately identified the limit of rights-based thinking: a mother and an unborn fetus, sharing one body. But on the other hand, abortion became an object lesson in the hands of Viguerie and the many others like him—a gateway drug, in fact, not to more serious reflection on Scripture or a way of relational thinking from a time before Lockean liberalism, but deeper into it. Conservatives became even more focused on *individual rights* than ever before.

Viguerie explains how conservatives portrayed the *Roe* decision as the product of heinous "secularism" or "humanism," rather than what it actually was: one more point along the way of a long, honest, Christian *and Jewish* grappling with a challenging issue, with a text inherited in two different manuscripts, where Greek scientific and medical thought went in two different directions that Christians had found reasonably acceptable in the past. Christians of old had questions: what is the proper range of views about ensoulment, and how much do challenges like poverty, prostitution, and male power factor into decisions of women who sought abortions? These conservative Christians might have said that they inherited an old Christian and Jewish question, with new scientific tools and perhaps the chance to take one more step forward. They could have even admitted that the federal-state tension in *Roe* was due in large part to painful Christian mistakes about slavery and racism, where those who constructed "whiteness" hated federal interference with their white supremacy. Now, the truth was out. They could have repented. But they much preferred not to. Such

---

18. Zeitz, "Why Conservatives."

storytelling would contribute nothing to the feelings of victimization, fear, and anger that mobilize voters. So, suddenly in 1973, that past disappeared in the blaze of a new enemy ("secular humanism") and another newly discovered righteous indignation about "rights."

Cultural and economic conservatives yoked the pro-life cause to moralistic judgments about others ("standards among young people") and economic goals that were much less moral ("free enterprise"). The conservative spokespeople positioned all this against the backdrop of an ominous foe: godlessness and "communism," embodied by "Russia and its many surrogates," made larger by the Mercatur map projection which made Russia look enormous, and made closer because Martin Luther King, Jr. was accused of being "a communist"; the black Christians of the Civil Rights Movement "were communist"; and the liberal social programs of the 1960s, which the Catholic New Deal Democrats favored, "were communist." Once upon a time, pro-life Christians believed that poverty drove abortions and that federal programs could help reduce them, but all that was forgotten because of "rights." The pro-life movement suffered because thought leaders and politicians on the right whittled the pro-life cause down to an ideology of the "right to not be killed" and a "right to punish lawbreakers," which overlapped all too well with the "right to maintain our way of life," and reinforced that sensibility rather well.

The challenge for moral conservatives who genuinely cared about the unborn was fixing their political yoke to economic conservatives and white supremacists who had many other priorities. In 1969, while the most prominent pro-life senator in the country was Democrat Ted Kennedy, Republican strategist and Nixon advisor Kevin Phillips promoted "The Emerging Republican Majority," to win Catholics and Southerners to the party and break the Democrats' long-standing New Deal coalition. In 1970, President Nixon allowed the Department of Defense to perform abortions in some cases. In 1971, Patrick Buchanan wrote to Richard Nixon suggesting that he reverse that policy and use an anti-abortion position to woo Catholic bishops and voters: "The president should publicly take his stand against abortion as offensive to his own moral principles," wrote Buchanan. The next week Nixon borrowed Catholic language at the Department of Defense when he spoke of his "personal belief in the sanctity of human life—including the life of the yet unborn."[19]

In the mid-1970s, a group of Republican strategists gathered to realign the Republican Party and to mobilize evangelical voters to their cause. Richard Viguerie and Paul Weyrich, both Catholics, approached Jerry Falwell, a

---

19. Lepore, "Birthright," summarizing Greenhouse and Siegel, "Before *Roe.*"

Southern Baptist with national political and media aspirations, in the late 1970s. In 1980, Weyrich was recorded giving a speech to fellow conservatives which is now posted on YouTube. In it, Weyrich complains that fellow Christians believe in "good government":

> Now many of our Christians have what I call the goo-goo syndrome—"good government." They want everybody to vote. I don't want everybody to vote. Elections are not won by a majority of people, they never have been from the beginning of our country and they are not now. As a matter of fact, our leverage in the elections quite candidly goes up as the voting populace goes down.[20]

Evincing early despair about democracy, Weyrich says he prefers that people not vote, and suggests that the political right use voter suppression tactics. Meanwhile, other Republican leaders manipulated the long-simmering racial resentment of whites about blacks being "undeserving" of welfare and uplift programs. Lee Atwater, for example, was a Republican campaign strategist who helped Reagan win in 1981. He discussed the Southern Strategy in an interview in 1981:

> You start out in 1954 by saying [N-word, N-word, N-word]. By 1968 you can't say [N-word]—that hurts you. Backfires. So you say stuff like forced busing, states' rights and all that stuff. You're getting so abstract now [that] you're talking about cutting taxes, and all these things you're talking about are totally economic things and a byproduct of them is [that] blacks get hurt worse than whites. And subconsciously maybe that is part of it. I'm not saying that. But I'm saying that if it is getting that abstract, and that coded, that we are doing away with the racial problem one way or the other. You follow me—because obviously sitting around saying, "We want to cut this," is much more abstract than even the busing thing, and a hell of a lot more abstract than [N-word].[21]

Others have expressed deep concern about the use of deliberately ambiguous language as "dog-whistles," and I mentioned a few examples in chapter 9. Speakers who use this style of rhetoric to communicate policy goals or a vision of society play on insider and outsider audiences. The insider hears a

20. Peoplefor, "Paul Weyrich."
21. Lamis, *Southern Politics*, 7–8. Perlstein, "Exclusive: Lee Atwater." Hinderaker, "What Did," is one person who tried to exonerate Atwater from tapping into race as the silent but guiding factor in Southern politics. Atwater, however, made a confession on his deathbed about such campaigning for Bush against Dukakis.

subtext, and the outsider does not. The speech is therefore divisive politically, and potentially even more so as outsiders understand the subtext. The speaker can always maintain her or his plausible deniability concerning racism. Mob bosses use this type of speech if they think someone else is listening in to the conversation. They can always deny that they meant what other people hear, and then blame the hearer for instigating the conflict. This is why I think Christians must critique the "myth of meritocracy" itself, as I did in chapters 7, 8, and 9, both on philosophical-theological grounds and also on historical grounds, as "meritocracy" is used to justify colonialism.

The constant stoking of anger and fear erodes the person speaking and the people delighting in hearing it and results in unsavory alliances and a vulnerability to demagoguery in the public. Kevin Phillips later regretted his role in all this, and as a disaffected Republican in 2006 authored *American Theocracy: The Peril and Politics of Radical Religion, Oil, and Borrowed Money in the 21st Century* among his other books, the same year Randall Balmer wrote *Thy Kingdom Come: How the Religious Right Distorts the Faith and Threatens America: An Evangelical's Lament*. Frank Schaeffer, son of the Christian critic of secular humanism Francis Schaeffer, wrote a memoir of regrets in 2008 called *Crazy for God: How I Grew Up as One of the Elect, Helped Found the Religious Right, and Lived to Take It All (or Almost All) of It Back*. It led to criticism of recent white evangelical political activity and alliances with fossil fuel interests and big bankers via the Council for National Policy: Frances FitzGerald discussed that in her 2017 book *The Evangelicals: The Struggle to Shape America*, and Anne Nelson devoted an entire book to it in *Shadow Network: Media, Money, and the Secret Hub of the Radical Right* in 2019. All this reinforces alarming concerns already raised by historians who have written extensively on evangelicals' approaches to politics: George Marsden, Mark A. Noll, Nathan O. Hatch, Randall Balmer, Carolyn Renee DuPont, Darren Dochuk, and Kevin Kruse. What has been missing is a sustained evaluation of Catholic and Protestant views on abortion, not just in terms of political behavior, but more foundationally, including biblical studies, church history, Christian ethics, and interaction with science. My hope is that this book takes a step in that direction.

As political and social history, then, conservative Protestants became animated by abortion policy when it was wedded to other causes. Suddenly, in the 1970s, white, conservative Protestants faced a situation where they could not break away from a larger body politic, and simultaneously felt thrust into national politics where they were outnumbered by liberal Protestants, liberal secularists, and worst of all, desegregationists. It happened at a time when deeply cherished but inaccurate *colonialist Christian* views about America were shown to be quite simply *colonialist* and racist. Just as Protestants in the mid-1800s had used two different interpretations of the fetus that were *possible* within the range of historic Christian views to serve larger political goals related to immigrants and blacks, evangelicals from the 1970s deployed the same strategy, or fell victim to it, depending on one's perspective. Once abortion became linked to "states' rights," anti-welfare, and white supremacist views of minorities, conservative Protestants bound them together and drew hard lines in the sand. But the connection was made on the level of political psychology, not Scripture or science. *Roe v. Wade* replaced *Brown v. Board* as the representation of federal encroachment against religious and local sensibilities.

Of course, resistance to second-wave feminism of the 1960s played a part. The absolute claim of a woman over the fetus on the grounds of her own bodily autonomy did not quite satisfy those who pointed out that she had bodily autonomy over her own sexual activity, so long as the pro-life advocate in question granted the standard exceptions of rape, incest, and physical health, since those experiences violated the woman's consent. "States' rights," however, was the foremost of those causes because it expressed the long-held synthesis between Protestantism, Lockean liberalism, an individualistic culture, and white supremacy. American Protestants had long habituated themselves to the assumption that they could break away from a larger church denomination if they so chose. Lockean Enlightenment liberalism held that consent was uppermost in political morality, reinforcing an economic conservatism, if not outright libertarianism. Individualism gave emotional force to the idea that "democratic self-rule" had to mean "local is better," as if a small family was more "democratic" than a large family, and as if the ability to participate at the national level was not "democratic." "Democratic" refers to a process of arriving at a group decision, not the ability to self-segregate when one dislikes the whole group. White supremacy had been tied to Enlightenment nation-state building because colonialism preceded the Enlightenment, and not just in the United States. White supremacy fueled notions of cultural elitism and self-congratulation for being "meritocratic," whereas the reality was nothing of the sort. White supremacy disguised a hidden welfare system for white people along with a brutal police state at home and militarism abroad. Within the white supremacist logic, it made emotional and political sense to tie abortion politics to a mistaken perception that liberal welfare programs were for black people who did not "deserve" it, even if the majority of welfare recipients were, and are, actually white. Protestant rhetoric was filled with the argument that taxpayers should not support people's poor sexual choices leading to children born out of wedlock or women seeking abortions, even though such rhetoric neglected the facts that (1) innocent children did not choose their parents, and (2) white supremacy itself contributed to the grinding pressures that wore down black families and contributed to the higher abortion rates of poor and/or black women.

It is significant, and telling in this case, that some conservative white evangelicals today propose stripping away the rape, incest, and mother's life exceptions, implementing death penalties for physicians and women, and pointedly ignoring the father's role even though science now allows us to include it. By going beyond anything in church history, and anything Scripture might reasonably deduce, conservative evangelicals opened the door to undisciplined and unreflective possibilities, based on "rights-based" political psychology and raw emotionalism, as opposed to a disciplined consideration of uncertainties and certainties. They yoked together an assortment of political issues with their abortion stance(s), which they believe makes an unassailably strong package of ideas. Upon closer examination, it has not the strength one might have thought.

A Constitutional Amendment?

The current pro-life movement deploys strategies that seem at odds. On the one hand, many appeal to the Constitution in an "originalist" sense. Seeking justification to overturn *Roe v. Wade*, even though *Doe v. Bolton* seems to be the weaker decision, pro-life advocates sometimes assume that a reason already exists in the Constitution. This approach is thought to justify their political approach, centered on presidential elections and then Supreme Court nominations, in the search of justices who can supposedly find that meaning in the Constitution. They hope for a Supreme Court which would not only overturn *Roe v. Wade*, but find a basis for anchoring a fetus's right to life, from conception, somewhere in the Constitution ("life, liberty, or property" in the due process clause of the Fourteenth Amendment), maybe even the Declaration of Independence ("life, liberty, and the pursuit of happiness"). If the Constitution, especially the Fourteenth Amendment, is tethered to the Declaration (which seems intentional on the part of the Amendment's authors), the interpretation of "life" would be *even weaker*. The Constitution's preamble, "We the People," did not involve various classes of people at the time it was written, including adult women in a significant sense; can it be stretched to include the unborn?

The initial responses to *Roe v. Wade* imply a willingness to admit the actual history of the U.S. Constitution. After *Roe*, pro-life activists proposed a Human Life Amendment, in various forms, as a constitutional amendment. U.S. Congressman Lawrence Hogan (R-MD) proposed a constitutional amendment one week after *Roe* was decided; Senator Jesse Helms (R-NC), a

Southern Baptist, supported it. Senator James Buckley (Conservative–NY), a Catholic, offered another; Senators Mark Hatfield (R-OR) and Harold Hughes (D-IA), evangelicals, voiced their support for that one. Various Democratic politicians who were pro-life prior to *Roe*, such as Hubert Humphrey, Sargent Shriver, and Ted Kennedy, tried to navigate the new legal terrain by putting themselves forward as being pro-life in private and pro-choice in public,[22] and in 1976, the Democratic Party adopted a constitutional amendment proposal. Eventually, though, Senate Democrats chose to not support the HLA in order to court pro-choice feminist votes.

When pro-lifers carried their hopes to the Republican Party, they found a similar ebb and flow. In 1976, the Republican Party courted the South and evangelical voters. Not only did it call for a constitutional amendment to overturn *Roe v. Wade*, it "suggested that the appointment of federal judges be conditioned on opposition to abortion."[23] In 1980, Ronald Reagan ran for president, apologizing for his previous support for "therapeutic abortions" as California governor. He declared his support for a Human Life Amendment.[24] Unfortunately, Reagan seemed to turn his back on this agenda. As FitzGerald recalls, the Reagan administration "refused to back a bill introduced by Senator Jesse Helms designed to eviscerate *Roe v. Wade* or a constitutional amendment sponsored by Senator Orrin Hatch that would have left the issue of abortion to the states. . . . When a vacancy on the Supreme Court opened in the summer of 1981, Reagan nominated Sandra Day O'Connor, an Arizona judge favored by powerful Republicans, but who, when serving in the state senate, had fought for the ERA and supported legalized abortion."[25] When George H. W. Bush ran for president in 1988, the "Christian Coalition" led by Ralph Reed had moved the Republican Party to call for an abortion ban *with no exceptions*, along with harder stances on other cultural issues like homosexuality, etc.[26] In 2012, the Republican Party proposed a platform of three constitutional amendments: one giving the fetus the rights of a person and banning abortion except in cases of rape or incest; one on marriage as a union between one man and one woman; and one to mandate a balanced budget. Only time will tell if the constitutional amendment approach will continue to be floated.

On the other hand, the Republican Party platform and other political advocacy groups recognize that a constitutional amendment is necessary

---

22. Williams, *Defenders*, 8.
23. FitzGerald, *Evangelicals*, 312.
24. FitzGerald, *Evangelicals*, 312.
25. FitzGerald, *Evangelicals*, 320.
26. FitzGerald, *Evangelicals*, 419.

because the Constitution as it stands does not have the necessary language. This approach is legislative. It indicates that the Constitution is insufficient for this purpose, as it currently stands. I suppose covering one's bases can be a pragmatic strategy, but it also nullifies the conservative intellectual critique of liberals. Today's liberals may indeed be stretching the Fourteenth Amendment beyond what it originally was intended to do, which is a separate and very worthwhile discussion. Yet many conservatives who criticize liberals as "legislating from the bench" or "exercising judicial activism" are seeking to do the very same thing. They are trying to maintain the language of the Fourteenth Amendment in a more expansive direction for "persons" to include corporations, defining "life" to include the fertilized egg, while simultaneously restricting the power of the Amendment to check racism and its effects. How long can we deny, for instance, that government programs led to a racially segregated housing market and massive wealth disparities by race and vastly unequal school systems, and that those government programs were and are violations of the Fourteenth Amendment? As a moral and intellectual strategy, this makes little to no sense, because it tries to make the Fourteenth Amendment mean something that it could not possibly have meant at the time. Advocating for a Human Life Amendment is quite harder politically, but at least it is more intellectually honest. The Personhood Initiative focuses on amending state constitutions in the hoped-for event that conservative justices like Gorsuch and Kavanaugh will overturn *Roe v. Wade*.

Most European countries make abortion legal within the first trimester, and subject to various limits afterwards, and their abortion policies are set by modifying their constitutions. In light of how intractably difficult the U.S. Constitution is to change, perhaps instead of aiming for an all or nothing solution like a Human Life Amendment, Christians and others might propose a constitutional amendment which stipulates citizens voting every four, or eight, or twelve years in a direct democracy ballot question related to abortion. For instance, I would be interested in the following questions:

> What are the legally acceptable reasons why a women can procure an abortion: none; rape; incest; risk to the life of the mother; age of the mother, mental or emotional or economic health of the mother; divorce from the father; death or desertion of the father; conceived in adultery; Down Syndrome; severe fetal deformities; etc.?
>
> Should a woman be able to legally procure an abortion for any reason? If so, until what time period: 23 days; 30 days; 60 days; 90 days; 120 days; 150 days; etc.; until birth?

> Should the biological father be identified and recorded in a health care database? Should he be financially punished in some way?

Our elected officials could then design policies to accommodate the voters' preferences.

There might be wisdom to placing the determination of the legal status of the fetus one step removed from the political party system. Abortion has been turned by Democrats and Republicans into a political football, where pro-life Democrats and especially pro-life Republicans at the national level have been forced to make strange political bedfellows in order to build coalitions with the hope of doing anything substantive. In particular, the current alliance of most pro-life advocates with the ideology of economic conservatism is deeply problematic. It is counterproductive towards the goal of bringing down abortion rates. For instance, denying women contraception and promoting abstinence-only education has been shown to *increase* abortion rates. The alliance is counterproductive towards pursuing the long-term welfare of the unborn, children, and women in general. Why only protect the unborn from abortion? What about industrial companies that place harmful chemicals into the womb? And when the unborn are born, what then? What kind of planet are we leaving our children? What economic inheritance do we envision for them? Evangelical pro-lifers might consider that their integrity, relational influence, and evangelistic effectiveness have been deeply compromised by this political alliance with economic conservatism and muted response towards other issues of great importance, like systemic racism. Perhaps that, too, makes the alliance counterproductive.

Historian Daniel K. Williams takes note of a minority of Catholic opinions published in various Catholic magazines. Those Catholics urged caution about what could be accomplished by focusing so narrowly on the passage of a constitutional amendment at the expense of economic policies and social welfare programs that Catholics traditionally supported. They also warned that the pro-life cause will become the "political tool of the right wing." This quote is worth considering:

> A few Catholics on the left worried that the bishops were making a mistake by privileging the constitutional amendment strategy over other solutions, such as social welfare legislation. If pro-life activists placed all of their emphasis on the HLA, "the anti-abortion cause will become the political tool of the right wing, of those who would resolve complex political problems with instant constitutional amendments," *Commonweal* warned in 1974. . . . "The Human Life Amendment's most dangerous

opponents are its rigoristic Catholic supporters," *America* magazine stated shortly after the cardinals' testimony on Capitol Hill. "Unwillingness to compromise could mean a total defeat instead of a partial victory."[27]

I believe these statements were prescient, and remain so. Not only for rigorist Catholics who remain committed to fetal life being regarded as more important than the mother's life, who often uphold a position against contraception even for non-Christians and for poor women, but for all moral conservatives who are willing to forsake socioeconomic and social welfare policies to accomplish more limited goals. The Republican Party stands against most of the Catholic Social Teaching. Moreover, regarding abortion, the most difficult ethical issues are systemic, having to do with any implementation of anti-abortion policies: can the health care system effectively become part of the criminal justice system? Little to no Christian ethical reflection has occurred to address that central issue. Much is unknown about how people in various roles would administer such policies, or whether an underground market in abortions would reemerge. And one very important constitutional question still needs to be addressed.

Another Constitutional and Christian Consideration: Judaism and the First Amendment

In the United States, the question of abortion also overlaps with the First Amendment, the legal basis for freedom of religious conscience. The majority of Jews hold that human personhood begins with live birth.[28] Jewish thought and tradition does not take abortion casually, but as I have explored earlier, most Jews have a different position on abortion than Christians, involving a wider set of exceptions, such as adultery. A very serious question for lawmakers, therefore, is whether Jewish parents should have greater access to an abortion if their religious tradition permits abortion for different reasons, or later in the pregnancy.

The fact that the Jewish tradition permits abortion but strongly values life is one indication that Catholic criticism of abortion after World War II did not necessarily apply to all, and that "secular humanism" was not the only consideration. After Nazi eugenics became widely understood after their defeat in 1945, Catholics equated abortion with the horrors of Auschwitz. If entire groups of people could be eliminated at the whim of the majority, this

---

27. Williams, *Defenders* 218–19.
28. *Roe v. Wade* (410 U.S. 113, 1973), IX.B.

posed a dire threat to any human beings. Why Catholics in America did not more tie their analysis of white supremacy to abortion is beyond the scope of this paper. But the Catholic argument itself was blunted, both by Jewish disapproval over the use of this comparison, Jewish moral law itself, and the Hebrew Masoretic Text of Exodus 21, the manuscript used by Jerome and the official Catholic Bible, the Vulgate.

The principle of freedom of religious conscience enshrined in the First Amendment is another faithful expression of Christian ethics. The principle is rooted in the teaching and practice of Jesus to gather disciples as a voluntary community. It was taught uniformly by early Christian leaders and teachers prior to Augustine[29] and was respected by Emperor Constantine in his Edict of Milan, which made Christian faith legal but not enforced. It stood that way until Emperor Theodosius made Nicene Christianity nominally the official religion of the Roman Empire in 395, although it was largely symbolic at the time, and simply gave him the legal basis to expel non-Nicene bishops from their seats. Unfortunately Augustine asserted that Christians should use the military power of the state to compel heretical Christians by force,[30] which gave rise to a long and storied history of Christians using force for religious persecution. Arguably, Catholic Poland from the 1300s to the 1800s practiced religious tolerance, enough so a Jewish community could flourish there. The Anabaptists and other Radical Reformers also believed in disestablishment.[31] Freedom of religious conscience was taught and practiced by the remarkable Baptist Roger Williams in Providence, Catholic Lord Baltimore in Maryland, various Native American tribes when they converted to Christian faith, Spanish Florida, and areas with no established churches (Pennsylvania, West Jersey, Delaware). It was formalized in the English Bill of Rights of 1689, which quelled the incessant fighting between Catholics and Protestants, in Thomas Jefferson's Virginia Statute of 1777, and in the U.S. Constitution's First Amendment. These Bills of Rights became the models for the rest of Europe, Canada, Australia, and other nations.

29. E.g., Tertullian, *Letter to Scapula* (AD 211–13), argues for freedom of religious conscience on Christian grounds. "However, it is a fundamental human right, a privilege of nature, that every man should worship according to his own convictions: one man's religion neither harms nor helps another man. It is assuredly no part of religion to compel religion—to which free-will and not force should lead us—the sacrificial victims even being required of a willing mind." Ambrose of Milan, *Letter 17*, para. 7, says, "You do not compel a man against his will to worship what he dislikes." The Roman emperor should not compel worship against others' free will.

30. Augustine of Hippo, *Correction of the Donatists* (ca. AD 417), attempts a theological justification for state force and even torture for religious purposes.

31. Zagorin, *Idea of Religious Toleration*.

While religious freedom is not an absolute freedom, nor is any right an absolute right for all times and places, almost no attention in the abortion debate has been given to the Christian responsibility to respect Judaism, and what that might mean for the abortion debate. Christian historians, exegetes, and ethicists have pointed out that the apostle Paul, in Romans 9–11, instructs Christians to care for those people who identify with Judaism. Christian ethicist and political theologian Oliver M. T. O'Donovan, in his life's work of surveying both Scripture and church history, writes:

> One [error] is to think that Israel is sufficiently accounted for in the church, and so to look on its continued presence as a meaningless survival, so that the church, instead of wrestling with Israel for its own fulfillment, turns its back on Israel as a displaced irrelevance.... The other [error] is that Pentecostal authorization ceases to be determinative for the church's self-understanding. It sees itself as prolonging the ancient faithfulness of Israel (or of a remnant within Israel) subject to many changes of regime. It fails to see in itself the regime that answer's Israel's hope for freedom, which was what Jesus proclaimed.[32]

In effect, O'Donovan argues, what is fundamental and constitutive of a Christian approach to politics is not a paradigm of "church and state." It must be "church, states, and Israel." Let me be clear that what is meant here by "Israel" is not the modern "State of Israel" per se, but the older use of the term by Paul in Romans 9–11: all people who subscribe to Judaism, which would today *include* the people of the modern State of Israel, but also those whom Paul knew as "diaspora Jews." If the church in Europe had taken Romans 9–11 to heart, it would not have persecuted Jews as "heretics" or "Christ-killers," nor called for pogroms and inquisitions and expulsions. Instead, Christians might have protected Jews from regimes that persecuted them, and engaged in thoughtful, humble, and loving dialogue with them with regards to Scripture and Messiah. Having learned from political pluralism with Judaism, perhaps the church might have been able to take an approach to other religions with a principled religious toleration. That might have saved Europe all the so-called "Wars of Religion."

When we put the matter in terms of American constitutional law, this dialogue between Christians and Jews over abortion policy, the legal status of the fetus, and biblical texts clearly must involve the First Amendment. The First Amendment does not simply guarantee the religious freedom of Christians. Christians cannot simply ignore Jewish scholarship and opinion about the text of Exodus 21. After all, at least some Jewish opinions also

---

32. O'Donovan, *Desire*, 162.

come from a sincere wrestling with sacred texts, too—texts which Christians share in common with Jews. Jewish opinion about abortion, and reasoning from Scripture, is a good faith argument. But it is not clear—to me, at least—how conservative Christians in the U.S. engage with this question. Instead, in order to feel intellectually "strong" against secular liberals, conservative Christians have developed what they believe is an airtight argument, not just for within the church community, but for public policy in general. In fact, sometimes the argument goes like this: "I am completely justified in being a single-issue voter; since life begins at conception, abortion is infanticide within the womb, and where else can you draw the line?" But to functionally cut ourselves off from Exodus 21—a text which *actually does suggest that a line can be drawn*—is an unacceptable theological and epistemological move. On what grounds can we ignore this text?

Ignoring the intra-Jewish debate on the subject, which also includes discussion of Exodus 21 and other biblical texts, has something in common with abandoning Christian mission towards the Jewish community because it signals that Christians are no longer connected to, and no longer respect—on this very important issue—a sacred text which we hold to be Scripture and about which we say, "All Scripture is inspired and God-breathed" (2 Tim 3:16). Religion is inextricably linked with the delineation of when a fetus can and should be treated as a full legal person. On the grounds of the First Amendment alone, conservative Christians need to stop behaving as if "secular liberals from the 1960s" or "cultural Marxists" are the only other party involved in the shaping of policy and culture.

In tactfully considering the beliefs of conservative Christians in the West, New Testament scholar N. T. Wright reminds Christians, from his exposition of Romans 9–11, of our mission to both Jews and gentiles:

> When Paul speaks of the unity of the church he means specifically a unity which crosses racial barriers. This has immediate implications for the mission which Paul envisages. The gospel is "to the Jew first and also to the Greek." I submit that if all we had to go on were the text of Romans, no-one would have dreamt for a moment that Paul was not still engaged in a mission which, though its geographical sphere was of course the gentile world, habitually embraced Jews as well as Gentiles, much on the pattern of Acts.[33]

Wright cautions us against adopting a "two-covenant" system—precisely the category popularized by the Scofield Bible and Dallas Theological Seminary, and hugely influential among conservative evangelical Protestants—whereby

33. Wright, *Climax*, 252–53.

"God has on the one hand maintained his covenant with ethnic Israel intact, and on the other hand has inaugurated the Christian 'covenant' as his regular way of saving Gentiles."[34] American Christians might adopt this "two-covenant" theology *de jure* or *de facto* to relieve themselves of any sense of humble and thoughtful mission to Jews, which would also require *making political space for them domestically and trying to discern agreeable policy positions together, not just "over there" in the State of Israel, but "right here" in the United States*. Wright's concern is primarily that we continue to hear Paul as a missionary to both Jew and gentile, as the apostle Paul was concerned about the Roman church and had to address it. Either the Roman Christians were facing the temptation of being a majority gentile church without Jewish Christians and without further loving witness to Jews; or they had some Roman Jewish Christians who were concerned that Paul's ministry and proclamation was overly "gentile" and no longer had a connection to Jews; or both. Christian mission can be related to respectful civic engagement and Christian political theology as well.[35]

To the extent that conservative Christians in America have treated Jews—either ideologically or functionally—as the other side of a "two-covenant" system, these words from Wright and O'Donovan are important. And furthermore, many evangelical Americans see the United States itself as a covenanted nation-state which has special "Christian" blessings and obligations towards God,[36] and when this plays a part in our political narrative, it is immediately problematic. We cannot inhabit a theocratic political narrative in which Christians functionally treat non Christians as villainous. Evangelism and mission are always functionally prior to political theology because respect for non-Christians is at stake. From this recognition of Jewish-Christian dialogue, we can discern more principles when advocating for, and designing, *social* policies addressing abortion.

Christians must not only explain how we come to conclusions for ourselves, but also how we would structure the interactions between religious groups in a political context and why. On any given issue, not least

---

34. Wright, *Climax*, 253.

35. Wright, *Climax*, 253 says, "The church has not become an exclusively gentile possession.... The two-covenant position says precisely what Paul here forbids the church to say, namely that Christianity is for non-Jews. To this extent, it actually agrees in form with the German Christian theology of the 1930s—while of course disagreeing in substance, because it denies that Christianity is the only way of salvation."

36. Noll, *America's God*, 3–52, discusses this and shows historically that there was no way to have a "national covenant" because unbelieving children, excommunicated people, and newcomers made a "society" different from a "church." Bellah et al., *The Good Society*, 241–43, cite Roger Williams as the earliest critic of the "national covenant." Williams said that America as a political nation "lay dead in sin."

abortion, we might swing the pendulum towards more political pluralism, which could give Judaism(s) more rights to define "life" and "human personhood" for its own community(-ies). For example, the pre-Christian Roman Empire gave Jews special privileges, as they recognized distinct peoples and allowed for some degree of self-governance. As long as Jewish men were circumcised, they could claim exemption from army service or from bowing down to the image of the Roman Emperor. That political status and exemption were probably what made physical circumcision attractive for gentile Christians to adopt (Gal 2:1–21; 5:1–12; Phil 3:2–3; Col 2:9–15), so Christians would legally be *Jews* in the eyes of the empire and would enjoy those legal exemptions, too. Today, we might consider whether to view the Jewish community's debates about abortion, and its range of options, as within the First Amendment. Possibly, Christians could propose a policy that acknowledges the Jewish community and its traditions. Christians could ask Jewish rabbinical authorities how they would certify membership in their own community.

Relatedly, Christians must consider whether to make a political and ethical distinction for Jewish people, and perhaps others, on the issue of abortion. In Matthew's Gospel, Jesus says God tolerated some undesired behaviors to some degree, like a wider range of reasons for divorce, because of humanity's "hardness of heart" prior to Jesus coming (e.g., Matt 19:3–12). Paul also attested to there being some spiritual difference between non-Christians and Christians which resulted in a morally different quality of life (e.g., Rom 7:14—8:11; Gal 5:16–24). Even traditional Catholic adherents of "natural law" have to concede that even if people have access to the same moral information (which I believe they do not, as exemplified by this very issue), they do not have access to the same moral power.

Alternatively, Christians might swing the pendulum further towards the political nation-state modality of the Enlightenment, which defines rights in a standard, uniform way for all its citizens. As with kidnapping and forced enslavement under Emperor Constantine, for instance, Christians sought to influence the entire empire. They were not content to call forced kidnapping-enslavement a sin for Christians only, or to make it a criminal act among Christians only. They believed that everyone should obey that law, and that the Roman Empire should enforce it for everyone. Not unimportantly, Christians shared this conviction with Jews, given Exodus 21:16 and Deuteronomy 24:7. Jewish communities like the Essenes at Qumran and the Therapeutae at Alexandria did not practice the servanthood of the Hebrew *ebed*, as they appear to have recognized that the practice was dependent on the family-land system of Israel before the Babylonian exile and could not even be practiced in the diaspora. This approach to abortion policy might set the First Amendment aside for all practical purposes, and place at least some Jews and some Christians in conflict.

Moreover, there is a larger missiological question at stake, extending beyond the current U.S. context but certainly including it. If "hardness of heart" is a condition that afflicts everyone, then how does that impact reproduction? Supposing that the once-universal practice of infanticide (save for ancient Egypt and ancient Judaism) was an aspect of that "hardness of heart" because disabled children were too difficult to raise, girls were less honored than boys, and poverty made welcoming another child impossible, then what kind of social and legal conditions should Christians hope to establish in order for parents to not view additional children as so burdensome? Christians should also bear in mind that sometimes, usually *male* policymakers ban abortion or promote child-bearing before or after a culture enters into a hostile or militaristic stance relative to other people groups. There are other *morally negative* concerns associated with reproduction that are not positive, and Christians must be on guard about such attitudes and political leaders who would seek to exploit them. A Christian pro-life stance can be co-opted.

There are no easy answers to these questions, even from within the fields of biblical studies and Christian ethics. Personally, in surveying all the principles on the table, and also considering Jewish-Christian history, I would be in favor of granting "freedom of religious conscience" on the fetus and abortion for the Jewish community if certain basic conditions can be met. If women and men want to procure an abortion, they should not be able to simply declare that they are Jewish the day before they find an abortion clinic. If Jewish community leaders are willing and able to set up a process to establish community membership over some period of time (at least one year, for example), and attest that they have meaningfully been involved and contributed to the community, I would find that sufficient. Curiously, to my knowledge this proposal would require that males be circumcised. Would I be worried that a more liberal abortion policy for Judaism would give people an incentive to be part of a Jewish community? In truth, I would be in favor of it for exactly that reason. This fact reminds us that Christians are not only in dialogue with "humanism" or "secular liberalism" as if the liberal political order is overwhelmingly hostile to Christians and Christians alone.[37] By reacting to "secular liberalism," Christians build a political order that is increasingly hostile to Jews and others. If other Christians want to take a different position, I maintain that they must explain how they arrive at their conclusions.

---

37. See for instance Gelernter, "Why Should."

14

Christianity and Liberalism: There Is Still Hope

Discouraged by Liberal Democracy

JUST PRIOR TO THE *Hobby Lobby* case, Catholic scholar and Notre Dame political philosopher Patrick Deneen wrote an article for *The American Conservative* entitled "Even If Hobby Lobby Wins, We Lose."[1] Voicing his support for Hobby Lobby, Deneen expressed his dissatisfaction with the Affordable Care Act's employer mandate to pay for employee contraception, under the now-standard Catholic assumption that human personhood begins at conception. Deneen correctly observes that in our late capitalist economy, social relations are now embedded within economic relations, and not vice versa as it once was in older societies. The ironic upshot of this situation is that a corporate "person" resisted a secular state on the grounds of "religious freedom." In Deneen's telling, the secular state has become so powerful that it took a multi-million-dollar, for-profit company run by Christians to challenge it.

While Deneen makes very perceptive points about liberalism, he does not often ground his arguments in the biblical narrative or Christian ethics per se. I am not sure if Deneen acknowledges that the state is *secular* first and foremost because Jesus distinguished between God and Caesar.[2] Secular *means* "temporal or worldly." The story of Jesus adds depth to what the "secular state" means: The state is "secular" in the sense that it will come to an end—for when Jesus returns to rule the earth, he will rule personally and directly, without mediation by a state. That is the conviction of Christian "eschatology"—the study of the last things. That basic, fundamental, and original distinction is why the church existed for three centuries separately from the

1. Deneen, "Even If."
2. O'Donovan, *Desire*, 146–57.

state, sometimes antithetically to the state, and then in parallel and in tension with the state in parts of Europe. Christianity thus contrasts with Islam, which started with Mohammed as both imam and caliph, resulting in the lack of distinction between mosque and state for centuries. From the Christian standpoint, therefore, the state can only exist as an institution to be partially influenced. It cannot be fully incorporated into the church and, as such, cannot ever be fully "converted" into a "Christian state."

Christianity and Democracy

In my opinion, Deneen undervalues a major Christian contribution to social and political life: separating a person from his or her role, which made it possible to love the person but impeach him or her from a leadership role. Apostles like Paul recognized that they could be removed from their role as apostles by a moral disqualification (1 Cor 9:27). While Simon Peter's disavowal and restoration was certainly possible as a precedent, Judas's betrayal and replacement also seemed to loom large in Christian memory (Acts 1:15–26). Christians were taught that church elders could be removed from their position if they did not demonstrate the moral and spiritual qualifications for their role (1 Tim 5:19–25). Within one generation of the apostles, Polycarp, bishop of Smyrna and disciple of the apostle John, applauded the Philippians for removing an elder and his wife for *greed* (Polycarp's Epistle to the Philippians 11). As a person of Japanese descent, I am frankly amazed that in the earliest Christian community, younger people could challenge their elders (1 Tim 4:11–12, 5:1–2) and even declare them no longer eligible for leadership in the church on objective grounds (1 Tim 3); the hierarchy of the family was thoroughly relativized and subordinated to a larger purpose. Christian faith led to robust organizational discipline. People could be removed from their roles based on predefined and agreed upon morality-based, character-based criterion, irrespective of age, seniority, wealth, and other traditional signs of power. People came to expect integrity from their leaders rather than simply holding to a "divine right of kings," and leadership roles came to be conditional upon character and competence. This was an early form of meritocracy. Once again, the Christian monasteries became a setting for leadership and followership to be expressed along these lines.

Historians of the Byzantine Roman Empire have argued that the emperor and the Orthodox Church had an informal balance of power,[3] but the English Magna Carta of 1215 was the first time in the West that the principle

---

3. Kaldellis, *Byzantine Republic*, helpfully reviewed by Mitchell, "Byzantine Empire." See also "Power and Authority."

was formally applied to the highest political ruler; it was drafted by the archbishop of Canterbury and was reissued at various times. Rightly or wrongly, the common people, not just the nobles, appealed to it as a guarantee of rights over against the authority of the English king. English law and custom would come to recognize "impeachment" as a formal principle, to be used against the king's ministers who were derelict or corrupt in their duties. Then the Founding Fathers of the U.S. Constitution of 1787 applied the impeachment principle to *any* high office. The separation of powers, a contractual view of political leadership, and the people's expectation that they could and should hold their leaders accountable to preestablished standards of conduct came from Judaic and Christian roots. Even an independent media was foreshadowed somewhat by the Hebrew prophets who challenged the kings, and educators teaching people the basics of law was foreshadowed by the Levitical priests. Thus, one of the foundation stones of the classical—and yes, secular—liberal order was the Christian principle that a person's identity was not their role, even their role in government, and their role was not a divine right or an entitlement, but a public trust.

When critics of the classical liberal political order—whether they be traditional Catholics like Patrick Deneen or from some other tradition—despair that secularists have departed from Christian norms and values, it troubles me that they do not seem to value democratic leadership and institutions as expressions and applications of Christian faith. Increasingly, fundamentalist Protestants and ultra-traditionalist Catholics in the U.S. seem to feel comfortable with anti-democratic tactics like voter suppression, including along racial lines.[4] In part, perhaps this attitude comes as a reaction to a secularist lie—that the Civil Rights Movement was a *secular* struggle against proper authority, instead of the black church's *Christian* struggle to bring more biblical values into a public realm influenced by heresies, and to bring the original meaning of the Thirteenth, Fourteenth, and Fifteenth Amendments back into the forefront of American law. Be that as it may, some have voiced their longing outright for a "Christendom" model of a unitary church-society-state again, with authoritarian leadership. Evangelicals and Catholics have started to embrace Bill Barr's unconstitutional theory of "the unitary executive," for example, to shield the executive from checks and balances, as if a stronger executive branch will help the Christian cause. Vice President Mike Pence, if he had become president, would have surely chosen judges from the same Federalist Society list that Donald Trump did, so the wide-ranging white evangelical support for Trump despite his very serious abuses of office can only be called anti-democratic, anti-constitutional, and authoritarian. Perhaps most surprisingly, white American evangelicals have

---

4. Reynolds, "North Carolina."

expressed a sudden admiration for Vladimir Putin and Russia, mostly because of Russia's anti-LGBTQ and anti-Muslim laws.[5]

Unfortunately, in most ways, it is hard to call Putin's Russia a more "Christian society." Would Christians really prefer Russia's social conservatism when they would have to accept Russia's endemic corruption, lack of press freedom, oligarchic economics based on fossil fuels, money laundering, disinformation campaigns against other nations, spy-killings, domestic violence, suppression of women, and startling rates of alcoholism and despair? Should Christians really prefer Russo-Eurasian geopolitics over NATO and the West? What makes Russia so much more "Christian" than the U.S. at this very moment? The U.S. is not "perfect" by any means. But it still has more fundamentally Christian elements on the institutional level and more marks of positive Christian influence than Russia or most other nations.[6] Just imagine running for public office in Russia, standing in Moscow's Red Square, and publicly accusing Putin of being corrupt, calling for his impeachment, and saying that the corporate oligarchs have preyed upon the people. In that sense, I would like to remind my fellow Christians, "There is *still* hope," in the sense that public discourse in the U.S. is still possible, and an intelligent, compassionate Christian witness is still compelling to many. After all, few on the left will deny to a fetus inheritance rights,

---

5. Graham, "Putin's Olympic Controversy," praises Putin for banning "propaganda of nontraditional sexual relations to minors." Tashman, "Religious Right," points out not only Graham's comments but also that the American Family Association's "Bryan Fischer called Putin a 'lion of Christianity' and called upon U.S. lawmakers to adopt similar speech prohibitions"; Matt Barber marveled that Putin was able to "out-Christian our once-Christian nation"; Sam Rohrer called Putin "the moral leader of the world"; Scott Lively lavished praise on Putin for "championing traditional marriage and Christian values"; and Rush Limbaugh applauded Putin for stopping "a full-frontal assault on what has always been considered normalcy." Officials with the World Congress of Families have lauded Putin as a savior of the entire world. The group organized a meeting for conservative activists at the Kremlin, which also played host to Brian Brown of the National Organization for Marriage, who traveled to Russia to defend the country's anti-LGBTQ crackdown in face of a Western "attempts to silence those of us who stand for the truth of marriage." Larsen, "At the Head," explores how "The Family," the conservative evangelical group in Washington, DC, seeking to influence policy, "helped Russian operatives attend the breakfast and connect with powerful attendees. TYT reported last month that a Seattle charity tied to the breakfast paid unspecified sums to facilitate Russian attendance. The Fellowship itself in recent years has sponsored congressional travel that included meetings with anti-LGBTQ leaders in Europe, TYT also reported." For additional reference, see Elliot, "Why Russia's Evangelicals," who describes the genuine appreciation that Christians (Orthodox and Protestant) in Russia have for Putin, based on cultural issues and antagonism towards economic-cultural globalism. These sentiments are echoed in very strong terms by Turley, "President Trump," in a Russian Orthodox media organ.

6. Dreher, "Sohrab Ahmari," highlights the same issues I am discussing here, where I believe David French's patience with liberalism is preferable. For a less kind but astute treatment of Ahmari's position, see Serwer, "Illiberal Right."

compensation for injuries done in the womb by chemicals, and even compensation for injuries done to a woman's reproductive system even before she became a mother.

Nonetheless, it is disturbing to see conservative Christians—especially white American evangelicals—praise authoritarian leaders at home and in places like Russia, Hungary,[7] Poland,[8] Brazil,[9] Bolivia,[10] etc. These conser-

---

7. Torbati, "New Trump Appointee." Merritt Corrigan is another white evangelical who praises right-wing authoritarian Viktor Orbán and Orbán's Hungary as "the shining champion of Western civilization." She criticizes liberal democracy as a "homo-empire" in the grips of "a tyrannical LGBT agenda." This posture reflects the unwillingness of many white evangelicals to recognize that "marriage" is a fundamentally religious issue, and to accept "civil unions for everyone" as I discuss in chapter 11. In a London publication called *The Conservative Woman*, Corrigan, "Home," called women to take up "the traditional roles" of mother and wife, to not compete with men and "to return to the home." Certainly there is great honor in motherhood and the marriage vow. But to restrict women to them, or to prioritize motherhood and wifehood over the full and robust vision of Christian mission, or to suggest that Christian mission is best served when women are restricted to the home, is the distortion of women's vocation that I criticize in chapter 5, and it is patriarchal even if Corrigan, as a woman, is the one voicing it. Collins, "Myth of Christian Revival," ably criticizes signs of Christian faith on the ground, in Hungary, as full of "underlying weakness . . . which is gradually degrading into a collection of shallow cultural signifiers." Collins raises the important issue that Orbán's platform of "Christian Democracy" in opposition to "Western European liberalism" is amorphous enough to be more culturally reactionary than biblically grounded.

8. Applebaum, "Warning from Europe," writes of Poland's Law and Justice party: "Law and Justice has embraced a new set of ideas, not just xenophobic and deeply suspicious of the rest of Europe but also openly authoritarian. After the party won a slim parliamentary majority in 2015, its leaders violated the constitution by appointing new judges to the constitutional court. Later, it used a similarly unconstitutional playbook to attempt to pack the Polish Supreme Court. It took over the state public broadcaster, Telewizja Polska; fired popular presenters; and began running unabashed propaganda, sprinkled with easily disprovable lies, at taxpayers' expense. The government earned international notoriety when it adopted a law curtailing public debate about the Holocaust. Although the law was eventually changed under American pressure, it enjoyed broad support by Law and Justice's ideological base—the journalists, writers, and thinkers, including some of my party guests, who believe anti-Polish forces seek to blame Poland for Auschwitz." See the links in the article for more information.

9. Sims, "Here's How Jair Bolsonaro," notes that Bolsonaro's election, which was anchored by Catholics and evangelical support, "means the decades-long effort by Brazil's indigenous populations to seek recognition and legal title to land has been foiled"; not the strengthening of an already-struggling education system across the country but an educational policy meant to remove elements of theories Bolsonaro deems "Marxist" and supportive of women's and LGBTQ rights; economic privatization of health, education and Amazonian land; and promoting private gun ownership and gun manufacturing company profits.

10. "Bolivia crisis" highlights how Evo Morales's political opponent and replacement, Jeanine Áñez, assumed the interim presidency. Áñez marched into the presidential office holding up a massive Bible. She had called indigenous Bolivians "satan

vative Christians narrowly use laws about anti-gay-marriage, gender roles, and most of all, abortion, as litmus tests to gauge how friendly regimes are to "Christianity." It is striking that those litmus tests are not often focused on, or inclusive of, respect for people of other faiths, a free press, clear limitations on political power, democratic institutions in civil society, anti-corruption measures, education for all children, ecological preservation, and labor rights compared to capital rights. For conservative Christians to have narrow preferences for laws related to sex and gender is inappropriate for a number of reasons. Those reasons are, more or less, characterized by a pseudo-theocratic vision of the nation-state which sees non-Christians fundamentally as threats, a profound neglect of 1 Corinthians,[11] and an imitation of American abortion politics.

From Colonialism to Lockean "Rights"

Perhaps Deneen tends to undervalue efforts to use liberalism to correct colonialism because he passes smoothly over the social problems that Christendom never eradicated but instead absorbed (especially anti-Semitism and patriarchy), which Christians then combined with colonialism, making them worse. This combination was imbibed by Western Christianity and the modern liberal order, creating not just a Protestant-Lockean-liberal synthesis, but a *heretical* Protestant-Lockean-liberal synthesis. For example, in his book

---

worshipers." Whereas Morales was a socialist who made evangelism a crime and upheld the land rights of the Bolivia's indigenous people, who constitute 40 percent of the population, Áñez formed a cabinet without indigenous representatives. It is notable that Áñez is backed by conservative Catholics and Protestants and was previously director of the Totalvision TV station. Blair and Bercerra, "Is Bolivia," note that as of June 1, 2020, the leadership of Áñez has been marked by brutal police repression and the killing of demonstrators (not yet investigated), the interference of the military even in the senate building and other areas of politics, the reestablishing of ties with the State of Israel, ceasing leftwing regional forms, and thirteen corruption cases in the state oil, telecom, and aviation industries. See also Phillips, "'Satan, Be Gone!'"

11. In chapter 5, I engage the issue of women's vocation, and in chapter 11, issues of politics and sexual ethics, both from the standpoint of 1 Corinthians. Paul in 1 Corinthians 6 categorizes consensual sexual sins as self-harming and not other-harming, and law has a difficult time regulating self-harm. In 1 Corinthians 7, he demonstrates that the Christian sense of vocation extends far beyond marriage and family, and in fact limits them, which has enormous implications for women in particular. Politically conservative Christians do not sufficiently ground their understanding of Christian faith and ethics in 1 Corinthians. In my assessment, this neglect makes conservative Christians reliant on the market and the criminal justice system to impose costs on unchristian behavior and to do their discipleship for them. Politically conservative Christians, it would seem, are vulnerable to being politically manipulated because of improper Christian teaching and spiritual formation.

Why Liberalism Failed, Deneen introduces John Locke as the premier theorist of liberal choice and the "state of nature," but fails to explore Locke's faulty interpretation of Genesis 1 as justifying colonizing theft of Native American land based on the notion that English people "labor" more upon the land than the Native Americans, and bring about more "progress."[12] Nor does he explore how the Judeo-Christian vision for restorative justice, where thieves give back two to five times what they stole (Exod 22:1–14; Luke 19:1–10), might be relevant to expropriated land and labor or criminal justice reform. Nor does he discuss the merits of the early British evangelical case against corporate "limited liability," which legally accommodates ongoing theft in principle and creates the political need for the regulatory state which so grieves many on the right. The legal and economic powerlessness of the average citizen against the corporation is overwhelming, almost as powerless as the individual Indian against the British East India Company.

The implications of colonialism and the heretical-Protestant-liberal synthesis are not incidental to the Hobby Lobby case, or to contraception and abortion. Jonathan Merritt points out that Hobby Lobby, the so-called "Christian company," ships products from China, with its notorious lack of religious freedom, forced abortions, high female suicide rate (56 percent of the world's female suicides), "nightmarish labor conditions, inadequate workplace regulation, and rampant child labor," where the minimum wage in Shanghai, the highest in all of mainland China, is $9.77 per day. "If you were wondering how Hobby Lobby can sell wicker baskets for next to nothing," Merritt writes, "now you know."[13] Yet Deneen accepts Hobby Lobby as a "Christian company" on the grounds of a nuance in corporate law which is itself highly dubious, and given that the Christian family who owns Hobby Lobby does not want to risk the small chance (if genuinely any) of contributing to abortions in the U.S. Meanwhile, as Hobby Lobby is implicated in abortions in China, the cost savings to the company for not providing employee contraceptive health care is strangely absent from the whole discussion, and no discussion is had about the greater *reduction* in American abortions that would almost certainly happen through contraception funding. Omissions like these are deeply problematic. Admitting to these issues weakens the case that Christians have simply been victims of the cultural shifts since the 1960s. Some Christians—not least those who own large chain stores—have been huge beneficiaries of trade deals and the erosion of the New Deal's small business-oriented legislation. Although Deneen is a Catholic, his presentation fits the pattern of evangelicals by

---

12. Deneen, *Why Liberalism*, 32–33.
13. Merritt, "Stop Calling," and Bhasin, "Christians Call Out."

using abortion as a leading issue to implicitly or explicitly argue for other policy priorities that cannot remotely be called Christian.

Some Christian thinkers on the right feel uneasy that classical liberalism cultivates a rights-based orientation to relationships and policies, whereby people question biological implications for gender and norms of reproduction. For some, like Deneen and other "Catholic integralists," the intellectual recourse was to "nature" and "natural law," and a litmus test moral issue was abortion. The argument is as follows: The nature of human beings involves reproduction, and marriage is the natural law woven by God into creation that regulated sex and promoted the best environment for children; but separating sex from marriage broke the natural law, and abortion was the cover-up, and a further denial of nature itself. Deneen says, by contrast, that in pre-liberal societies, especially under Christendom, "the dominant definition of liberty involved recognition that it required an appropriate form of self-governance."[14] Deneen's inquiry into earlier meanings of "liberty" is important, and I appreciate the sentiment, even as I grieve Christendom's anti-Semitism, patriarchy, political infighting, etc. I also concur that liberalism, by contrast, altered the meaning of liberty away from reflection on one's nature (*ontos*) and intended end (*telos*), instead directing people towards the ability to do as one wished, irrespective of any larger framework of meaning.

At times, however, Deneen seems to reduce history to philosophy, and thereby misunderstands the histories and the possibilities of both the left and the right in critical ways. Regarding the left: if the heart of colonialism, liberalism's older sibling, was a breaking of proper relations—what Ambrose of Milan and Gregory of Nyssa called *nature*—via *theft*—of other people's land, labor, spouses, children, health, development, sexual experience, reasonable self-esteem and cultural pride, and civil rights—then the real question is why traditional Christians of any stripe would resist using the liberal order, which stands as colonialism's putative successor and potentially its corrective, to undo the *theft*, at minimum. Regarding the right: Deneen does not seem willing to lay a good part of the blame for today's political culture on his fellow Catholics Viguerie and Weyrich for manipulating the political psychology of people on the right in order to reconfigure the Republican Party around the issue of abortion using the rights-based framework of liberalism. Richard Viguerie's efforts to mobilize right-wing voters *using* the issue of abortion are not incidental to the project of Western liberalism and those Christians who would despair of it.

---

14. Deneen, *Why Liberalism*, 99.

Liberalism's Denial of Relations and Jesus' Restoration of Relations

The *Curlender v. Bio-Science Laboratories* (1980) case in California publicly confirmed that Lockean liberalism is a tool of convenience, but not of fundamental truth. When a child successfully argued her *wrongful life* case that she should have never existed, the framework of consent, rights, and harm fell apart, along with its corollary, a minimal government that only enforces contracts. The *Curlender* case points out the truth: we are never asked for our consent to be brought into existence. Human life and personhood are rooted in some other mystery from beyond ourselves. In the Christian vision, we are created by, and founded upon, the love of God, which comes to us as a gift unasked-for, at once precious and terrifying, awesome and awful, at once irreversible and yet never completed because God calls for our participation in love, bound up with rights but also unending responsibilities, in response to which we cultivate feelings of joy or horror. Chief among those responsibilities is to give to others the gifts which God offers all. In the Christian vision of relations, we find not primarily an ethic of "rights" but a Christian ethic of responsibility to one's neighbor. Dr. King called it "beloved community," and Fannie Lou Hamer, "the kingdom of God."

If we approach abortion from a social policy standpoint, focusing on our *nature* and our *relatedness* to each other, we will see that our care for the unborn and children broadens out and forces us to care about a whole host of other issues. For example, it is undoubtedly true that people who care about abortion should care about criminal justice reform. Police and prosecutors should be held more accountable because when police unjustifiably kill or prosecutors excessively incarcerate, they leave behind (among others) children without fathers, and women without male partners. People who care about abortion should care about corporate law. Companies should be legally forced to internalize the costs of the "externalities" they cause, not least because birth defects in the womb make parents consider abortion (e.g., the thalidomide controversy of 1962) and imperil children's development besides. People who care about abortion should care about the structure of the economy. For what is the good in bringing a child into a nation that promises so much but delivers so little, especially according to the values for community and family we say we have? What would help parents—especially single mothers—feel less economic pressure, and less pressure to abort an unexpected pregnancy? Perhaps making women's wages equal to men's, increasing labor's share of the profits, improving corporate maternity and paternity laws, protecting the citizen producer and small businesses by actually enforcing antitrust laws, reforming finance to reduce or absolve people's indebtedness, designing multi-family housing and neighborhoods and schools with the *extended* family and the present and future labor market in mind, and publicly funding childcare would help. And how can change like that happen? Political corruption and campaign finance must be cleaned up. Corporate money, election fraud, and voter suppression cannot be tolerated, because people are tired of feeling like government works better for bankers and CEOs than for the average American.

At a minimum, it must be said that the *tools* of liberalism—however temporal and limited—have not been exhausted, even by Christians, for the purpose of properly expressing our responsibilities. There are indeed neglected civil rights, and pursuing them can still go in fruitful directions. On this diagnosis, within the liberal political order in the U.S., certain white elites, especially males, and especially Protestant, have been able to externalize the full cost of many of their choices and make other people bear them instead. This is true of abortion policies where, I would argue, the definition of "consent" and its perception have been culturally manipulated and pushed onto either the women or the doctors in question. At a minimum, conservative Christians who care about abortion must theologically and spiritually understand the Fourteenth Amendment and the Christian vision found in the Civil Rights Movement.

More substantially, the Christian vision of relations and ethic of responsibility can still be expressed with the tools of liberalism. How might Christian love and responsibility apply to public health and how to fund it? To thoughtful contraception? To Christian restoration for past home mortgage discrimination? Sadly, however, when Christians or others propose changes to this political order, not even going as far as giving restitution for past injustice, or creating more entitlement programs, but reducing or eliminating the *theft happening in the present*, focusing on *procedural justice*, they are met with stiff resistance and interpreted as "non-Christian," "secular," "Marxist," and "illiberal." If people call for men to bear more of the cost of abortions, which they cause directly via sex and indirectly when their economic activity imposes poverty on women and deformities in fetuses, then why do conservative Christians call them "leftist"? Alas, Richard Viguerie's training has worked all too well.

Why do so many white Christians resist reforms like this? When oppressed people assert that things have been variously *stolen* from them and their children, why is there so much resistance from *Christians* to acknowledging it? Is the past too painful to confront? Are the present privileges too lucrative to give up? Are other people's children simply too *other*? Have Protestants somehow lost the ability to express real penitence, believing it to be too Catholic? Does liberalism encourage people to interpret grief unasked-for as guilt, and guilt as emotional coercion? Does Protestantism? If Deneen and others feel nostalgic for "self-governance," then what is the rationale, exactly, for opposing legal changes that *deter theft*, hold men accountable, force people to pay the true cost of their actions, and develop the actual skills of "self-governance"? Why is the ideal of "self-governance" turned so easily against welfare recipients, rather than presidents who shatter the rule of law, or congresspeople who engage in insider trading, or corporate leaders who underpay their workers and poison the planet? And when Christian intellectuals like Deneen long wistfully for a time before liberalism when people lived by more principles of "self-governance," is there a selective nostalgia at work? Is it legitimate for white Catholics and evangelicals to opine for the *anti-abortion patriarchy* of "Christendom" but not the *excommunication of the usurer*, which was at times enforced by the state? Or the vision of the great fourth-century bishops for the *radical and regular redistribution of land* as an expression of *nature*?

The Cost to the Right of Commandeering and Truncating the Pro-Life Cause

Disaster struck during the COVID-19 pandemic, laying bare the fixation on negative rights by the right, not least because of how pro-life advocates cultivated in people a political psychology to accommodate the abortion issue into the camp of political and economic conservatives. During the pandemic, other developed countries notably supported their citizens through payments directly into payroll, to prevent mass unemployment and the overwhelming of the unemployment services, which was more cost-effective and led to quicker economic recoveries and less emotional anxiety.[15] The U.S. chose a different path.

Although on March 25, Congress passed a $2.2 trillion economic stimulus package which greatly benefited large corporations, few religious conservatives called for more ongoing federal support directly to citizens and small businesses, apparently unconcerned about the likely corporate consolidations that would take place, leaving small businesses to go bankrupt while large corporations got extra financing to buy up smaller ones, which would probably lead to more layoffs and lower wages overall. Conservatives did not want to spend now and tax later; they refused to spend now for a fiscal cushion to citizens and tax later the billionaires and banks to make up the deficit. Meanwhile, in April 2020, Jeff Bezos reported earning $24 billion during just the first few months of the pandemic, due to his

15. MacGillis, "How Germany."

11 percent share in Amazon, while Amazon warehouse workers were paid low wages and complained vigorously of unsafe work conditions; one of his vice presidents quit in protest over how workers were being treated.[16] Senate Republican Majority Leader Mitch McConnell (R-KY) suggested that states declare bankruptcy, probably to accomplish a long-standing Republican goal of defaulting on the pensions of teachers, police officers, firefighters, and other public employees.

Where was a more expansive vision of relations? Of substantive justice? By doubling down on economic conservatism at a time when the New Deal paradigm could have been reinvigorated, ordinary citizens were faced with levels of unemployment, financial instability, and emotional anxiety not seen since the Great Depression. Grass-roots conservatives and the Republican Party, long trained to focus on negative rights like "freedom" on the popular level, exerted that right even in the face of COVID-19. Christian ministers, who could have acted on their pro-life convictions by meeting in smaller groups for the eucharist and online for sermons, instead called together their congregations on the principle of "freedom of religion," leading to people infecting each other with the coronavirus, and not a few needless deaths. Discontented protesters of Michigan's stay-at-home order, supported by the DeVos family, marched on the Michigan State Capitol in Lansing. I support peaceful protest, but protestors did so without wearing masks and without respecting physical distance from police officers or each other, while carrying guns, which were completely unnecessary.[17] Where were the "Blue Lives Matter" advocates when police officers were put at risk of contracting the coronavirus and transmitting it to their families?

Many political conservatives spoke and acted out of a caricature of the U.S. Constitution, as if the Constitution enshrined individual freedom in some absolute sense. Only a few conservatives argued otherwise. On March 19, 2020, David Rivkin, a conservative attorney and consultant, along with Charles Stimson, a senior fellow at the Heritage Foundation, explained in the *Wall Street Journal* that governors did in fact have wide emergency powers. States possess police power and have primary responsibility for public health. Therefore, they can impose a quarantine or isolation and call in the National Guard to enforce the order. Rivkin and Stimson cited *Jacobson v. Massachusetts* (1905), when the Supreme Court ruled in a 7–2 decision that a state order to be vaccinated was constitutional and that Henning Jacobson, who refused to be vaccinated, was guilty of

---

16. Evelyn, "Amazon CEO." Rodrigo, "Amazon VP Resigns," notes that VP Tim Bray said on his way out, "Remaining an Amazon VP would have meant, in effect, signing off on actions I despised. So I resigned."

17. Gray and Egan, "Whitmer." See also Rios, "DeVos-Linked Group."

breaking state law. Justice John Marshall Harlan wrote: "The Constitution does not import an absolute right in each person to be, at all times and in all circumstances, wholly freed from restraint. . . . A community has the right to protect itself against an epidemic."[18]

Meanwhile, in the conservative intellectual Christian sphere, Rod Dreher at *The American Conservative* astutely grieved the decline of a conservative religious thought leader, the journal *First Things*.[19] Dreher narrated the gradual subservience of *First Things* to Republican Party loyalty, for example, its support of the Iraq War in 2003. Dreher also grieved statements of *First Things* editor, Catholic writer R. R. Reno. At the start of the outbreak, before anything was really known about the coronavirus, Reno simply accepted elderly deaths as the cost of capitalism during the pandemic[20] and later called people who wore medical masks according to the CDC guidelines "cowards."[21] Cowards for trying to not infect other people with a respiratory virus that you might have before you show the symptoms?

Sadly, much energy on the political right has gone into its own form of denying science. From the right came criticism and smears[22] of particular scientists, including the very reputable scientist Dr. Anthony Fauci, who regularly praised his Jesuit education,[23] who had served the country for decades as director of the National Institute of Allergy and Infectious Diseases. Dreher did not call it this, but the right has proceeded quite far into its own denial of *nature*, and *relations*, as they denied both the uncertainties about, and the biological facts of, an airborne, infectious, and deadly respiratory virus. This is ironic because conservative Catholics have long argued that those on the *left* were violating *nature* and *relations* by separating sex from marriage, and then aborting the *natural* products of those *relations*. This denial of *nature* and *relations* was supposedly the very thing Catholics believed individualistic "rights discourse" unduly promoted *from the left*. Yet "rights discourse," even on behalf of the unborn, and perhaps *especially* on behalf of the unborn, eventually led Christian conservatives to deny the reality of *nature* and *relations* during a global pandemic with a novel and deadly coronavirus. The political psychology which had cultivated a simple-minded mean-spiritedness reflected in prosecuting pregnant women who caused fetal death by attempting suicide or abusing a substance (most of

---

18. Rivkin and Stimson, "Constitutional Guide."
19. Dreher, "First Things."
20. Reno, "Say 'No.'"
21. Dreher, "First Things."
22. "Trump Retweets."
23. "Anthony Fauci." Roccasalvo, "Dr. Anthony S. Fauci."

which do not pass through the placenta), or taking away the civil rights of pregnant women in order to ensure the fetal health of those born into abject poverty reinforced individualism at a time when creative, collective actions were needed.

Scripture and Political Narratives

Above, I expressed my reservations that Deneen starts with Lockean liberalism *rather* than the biblical narrative. Scripture does not use the language of "consent" and "rights." But it is clear that Scripture does not start with the sovereign individual who consents to be part of a political order that properly respects individual rights, not least because Scripture recognizes that we all inherit a condition that we did not choose, and that a damaged nature precedes our "consent." How much more so the political order into which we were born, and about which we might be able to do very little? We were born outside of Eden, vulnerable to the fall and to the uncertainties of the creation outside the garden, through no individual fault of our own.

If we situate Christians in the literary-canonical theme of "empire" in Scripture, along with diaspora Jews in exile along with Christians, we would not simply place Christians in the "order of classical liberalism," as if Christians should feel perfectly at home in the secular liberal order. After all, the U.S. is still very much an "empire" as the Scriptures would say, or the "city of man," as Augustine suggested. Deneen, unfortunately, appears to long for a state which would be sufficiently "Christian" that it relieves Christian people of the tensions of participating in the fallen political orders that reflect the lordship of Jesus only dimly, if at all.[24] What Deneen takes from eschatology he lays upon political theology and personal Christian ethics, mourning that the containers cannot hold all he would like them to.

When Deneen voiced his support for Hobby Lobby's protest—founded in consent and negative rights—to avoid the contraception mandate of employers, I wonder if he fully acknowledged that Christians were commanded by Jesus and Paul to pay their taxes (Rom 13:1–7; Matt 22:21) despite the fact that they must have been uncomfortable with how the Roman Empire used that tax money. Rome warred against the Persians, paid salaries of soldiers who often extorted local communities, enforced cruel measures of slavery, developed warfare technology, paid for extravagant buildings, etc. Yet Jesus and Paul must have perceived some way for Christians to participate in a

---

24. Deneen, "Catholic Showdown," perceptively notes that some Catholics believe that Catholic faith is reconcilable with liberal democracy, while others do not, and places himself in the latter category. See also Deneen, *Why Liberalism*.

political order like that while still objecting to it on the personal level. This is a basic ethical point that is raised by the biblical narrative. Perhaps Jesus' love for others enabled Christians to continue on with an attitude of patience[25] and hope that Jesus' resurrection would transfigure human nature, relations, and community, something that *biological nature* by itself could not reveal. In that sense, Christians must remember, "There is still *hope*." Hope for Jesus' return is meant to play a very active part in our spiritual and emotional lives (Rom 8:18–25; 1 Cor 15). All that Jesus said he will accomplish, in which we can only participate by degree, he will accomplish. This enables us to act in ways that respect our relatedness to each other, even as we maintain a certain helpful detachment from any particular regime—any empire—even the ones that we have set up and spent all our lives investing in, because this is not yet our home.

American Evangelicals, Abortion, and Humility

I suggested in chapters 2, 3, and 4 that politically conservative Christians in the U.S. need to approach abortion with renewed humility. I made the observation that not a few conservative Christians approach abortion not just with passion but with *absolute certainty* and, at times, *single-minded and condescending arrogance*. Because deaths due to abortion outstrip deaths due to war, climate change, global starvation, COVID-19, cancer, gun violence, and lead poisoning, they believe this justifies their approach to politics. "What about the babies?" they ask. A fair question. But rather than recognizing that infanticide was universal and ancient for economic reasons, and rather than striving for a larger vision of God's gift economy for children and the future, they narrow their approach down to a criminal justice policy involving individual rights and consent in a heretical reward economy.

Many conservative evangelicals narrate their anti-abortion policy in the context of blatant historical falsehoods. "Secular humanism" is not the reason *Roe v. Wade* was decided. The true causes were the indecisive expression of the Greek Septuagint text which raised the question of when the fetus was "formed," and the historical Western Christian reliance on Aristotle as a scientific authority to answer it. This pairing happened to be *reasonable* at the time, but simply needed to be updated. As for "states' rights" being overruled by an overly strong federal government, that is another false narrative. The true cause of the growth of the federal government

---

25. Kreider, *Patient Ferment*, insightfully examines the early Christian teaching on patience as a social and political virtue, which would be an important contribution and correction to the "integralist" position.

and its interest in establishing civil rights nationally was not "Marxism" or "communism" which supposedly gave evidence of the "secular humanism" that menaced Christianity. The growth of the federal government was an after-effect of the Civil War and Reconstruction, which themselves were the result of white evangelicals believing in the heresies of sanctifying chattel slavery and white supremacy. The growth of the federal government over against the states was a *Christian* development.

Conservative white evangelicals nevertheless arranged their resistance to *Roe* to conveniently replace their prior resistance to *Brown v. Board of Education*. This correlated with evangelicals relying on false historical narratives about a once "Christian America" which had been led away by "secular liberals" and "cultural Marxists." It created intense cultural and political resentment among the evangelicals towards non-Christians, and sometimes white evangelicals against non-white evangelicals, even though it was a grievance predicated on a falsehood. American political culture also suffered, as evangelicals clamored for more of an "individual rights" framework by insisting that a fertilized egg had a legally defensible "right to life" from fertilization, because the fetus does not "consent" to its own death by abortion. The very "rights-orientation" which made intellectual conservative Christians uncomfortable was strengthened by an order of magnitude by conservatives on the ground, who thought they had found a way to outweigh the "rights" of minorities expressed in the 1960s. This political psychology makes conservative Christians unnecessarily *afraid*, and when they are *afraid*, they have a hard time being *humble*. They instead become averse to data, science, history, and Scripture itself.

I have identified some vital truths that Christians who care about reducing abortion rates need to keep in mind. What is the firm intellectual and biblical basis by which to explain why one's church tradition takes the position that it does? *There is no firm basis.* It involves looking at Exodus 21:22-25 and choosing one biblical manuscript over another, or rejecting both, which is a choice *one cannot fully justify*. It involves massaging away the Hebrew Masoretic Text's indication that human legal personhood be established at *birth*, a position for which no church today seems to argue, even though Jewish majority tradition and the State of Israel do. It involves massaging or ignoring the Greek Septuagint's view that the fetus acquires the legal status of full human person at *some point of fetal development*, which involves further interpretive decisions *which have no firm justification in the biblical text itself*. It involves an assumption that the Septuagint's marker of fetal physical development has something to do with fetal ensoulment, which is a reasonable assumption but, again, *not something stated by the biblical text itself*. Then, it involves trying to coordinate the timing of fetal ensoulment with the science of embryology, or human fetal development, which *does not strongly support the probability of ensoulment occurring at conception*. This is vital because of the high rate of non-implantation, but more importantly because of cell potency, twinning, and chimerism. It further involves recognizing that any assumption that early ensoulment establishes *legal* human personhood *sidesteps Exodus 21 altogether* and creates a gap of significant misalignment with the most important biblical text on this subject. The conservative position also ignores other biblical texts which could inform how Exodus 21 is applied, such as immoral conception, which involves more interpretive challenges *that are by no means easy*. It ignores the most relevant biblical pattern of God first building a physical *habitation* for life, then giving the *life*, which would strongly suggest a gap of time between physical formation and ensoulment.

Moreover, conservative evangelicals in particular need to recognize that their *overall* approach towards abortion policy *has no biblical precedent whatsoever*. There is no integrity in selecting the most extreme point within a range of possible legitimate positions on the fetus while portraying one's position as if it were the only biblical possibility, without also publicly acknowledging the range of possible positions and why there is poignant uncertainty about this question. For some conservative evangelicals to call for the death penalty for first-degree murder is completely without precedent, since Exodus 21:22–25 used a financial penalty and a communal process of some sort to determine the magnitude of the fine. So, too, evangelicals' failure to reflect on paternal responsibility contradicts the pattern of institutional advantages that Scripture gave to women over men. This pattern challenges the patriarchal presumption conservative Christians tend to make, that women narrow their sense of vocation to motherhood in order to bear the cost of men's choices in their bodies and livelihoods, in order for men to mature and develop a sense of responsibility. Also, evangelical acknowledgement that social conditions heavily influence abortion rates has been sorely lacking. Jewish law, by contrast, took regular structural steps to prevent Israelites from passing down disparities of wealth in land, called for regular redistribution of land through the jubilee principle, prevented people from falling into ongoing indebtedness, stopped them from stigmatizing poverty, virtually eliminated institutional incentives to turn nature into money, and greatly limited the ideology of "meritocracy," instead institutionalizing the bestowing of a gift-inheritance to children—and not just one's own children, but all of God's children. All this contributed to a social and economic safety net which encouraged childbearing and mutual responsibility towards future children. Jewish law did this without explicitly forbidding the Israelites from committing abortion.

As I explored in chapters 3, 5, and 6, evangelicals' self-imposed ignorance of early Christianity results in the lack of awareness that their approaches to Scripture, science, and poverty are without historical precedent. The early Christians engaged very deeply with the sciences of their day, even on the issue of abortion. Sadly, some political and church leaders in the Christian community use the abortion debate to negate science, rather than use science to help us understand the fetus and the ethics of abortion. Evangelicals also appear to be largely unaware that Christian leaders sympathized deeply with poverty, even to the point of excusing infanticide for impoverished parents, and were wary of the institutional power of men over women in some critical cases. Sadly, again, some evangelical leaders today isolate abortion concerns from the larger context of God's relational and social vision, using them to reinforce a patriarchal narrowing of women's vocations and using them to drive people more deeply into poverty if it could reinforce capitalism and the "myth of meritocracy" in the U.S.

The evangelicals' wresting of the pro-life cause from the Catholic New Deal Democrats via the reframing of the anti-abortion position as a criminal justice issue rather than a social welfare issue creates more problems than it solves, if it does solve anything, which is doubtful. Once a few Catholic Republicans like Paul Weyrich and Richard Viguerie drew evangelical leaders into the pro-life movement, evangelicals returned the favor by drawing more Catholics into a political and cultural realignment. The pro-life cause became a political tool to undermine the New Deal and the Great Society, promote anti-welfare legislation, and uphold economic conservatism. Just as Protestants in the mid-1800s used abortion as a tool to express anti-immigrant sentiment in the North and anti-black sentiment in the South, conservative Christians today use abortion to serve other ideological ends which are themselves *heretical*, mostly having to do with a pro-capitalist, anti-welfare stance where "the rights of the fetus" are used politically against "the rights of non-white minorities." Never mind that the majority of aborted fetuses come from non-white minorities because of capitalism and white supremacy. But the absorption of anti-abortion concerns into the framework of economic conservatism, "meritocracy," and "individual rights" was and is counterproductive on its face: economic hardship drives abortion and is not simply the result of sexual immorality; economic conservatism across generations inflicts harms onto a child because of the "sins of the parents," a principle which was roundly declared to be not a part of the new covenant (Ezek 18) and is not consistent with "meritocracy" in the slightest, even if it were true that the U.S. was a meritocratic country. The general evangelical endorsement of conservative economics and minimal government, in fact, is rooted in Protestant heresy, even if it is mislabeled as merely the neutral "political philosophy" of John Locke as if Locke were not heretical and racist as a theological ethicist. Thus, classical Lockean liberalism, inheriting and cloaking colonialism, increases abortion rates by driving so many into poverty and making the cost of childraising so high for the middle class. Some evangelicals make the problem even worse by maintaining theocratic aspirations about sex education, as if "abstinence-only education" is the only Christian option because America should be a "Christian nation."

Evangelicals also give little thought to the administration of medical and legal systems and the ethical ramifications of expressing the pro-life cause through a criminal justice paradigm rather than a pro-woman, pro-childraising, pro-future social policy. They tend to assume that health care providers can seamlessly become an arm of the criminal justice system without having unintended consequences, even though there is ample historical data that should lead us to be tentative about doing that. Evangelicals give little thought to the dangers of jeopardizing the civil rights of pregnant women. They tend to not address the problems of the vast gray market in abortion, where women who are white, and/or rich, and/or connected can find safe abortions, and differences by race, class, and connectedness make hypocrites of doctors and law enforcement. They either downplay the risk of driving women to perform self-induced abortions or procure unsafe abortions, or they view the risk as simply the moral consequence of wanting to have sex without responsibility.

It is ironic and tragic that most evangelicals feel certain that Scripture speaks with absolute clarity about the fetus, and only with ambiguity or negativity about undoing poverty and white supremacy. In truth, we do not actually know for certain from Scripture about the biological or legal status of the fetus, while we know that Jesus commands us to confront poverty and affirm our collective responsibility for all God's children to have a good inheritance. The burden of this book has been to show that we know far more about how to design economic and social welfare policies guided by Christian principles than we know about how to place abortion into a criminal justice framework. Perhaps understanding the totality of the issue might make the difference for evangelicals to humbly embrace what is uncertain and courageously commit to what is certain and doable. The future of all our children may depend on it.

Bibliography

יוחנן כהן-ישר, and Jean-Georges Kahn. "Did Philo Know Hebrew?" *Mandel Institute for Jewish Studies* 4 (1965) 337–45 (Tamuz, 5725).

"18 Profound Statistics of Rape Victims Getting Pregnant." Health Research Funding. https://healthresearchfunding.org/18-profound-statistics-rape-victims-getting-pregnant/.

"19 Shocking Post Abortion Depression Statistics." Health Research Funding. https://healthresearchfunding.org/19-shocking-post-abortion-depression-statistics/.

"20 Abstinence Only Sex Education Statistics." Health Research Funding. https://healthresearchfunding.org/20-abstinence-sex-education-statistics/.

"Abortion." United Kingdom National Health Service. https://www.nhs.uk/conditions/abortion/.

"Abortion and Judaism." https://www.myjewishlearning.com/article/abortion-in-jewish-thought/.

"Abortion or Adoption—Know the Facts before Making a Decision: Choosing the Path That's Right for You." https://www.americanadoptions.com/pregnant/deciding_between_abortion_or_adoption.

"Advocacy Group Calls Amendment 2 a 'Personhood' Measure." *Associated Press*, November 5, 2018.

Agrawal, Nina. "Abortion Rate Declines to Historic Low, with Obamacare a Likely Contributor, Study Says." *Los Angeles Times*, January 17, 2017. https://www.latimes.com/nation/la-na-us-abortion-rates-20170117-story.html.

Alexander, Michelle. *The New Jim Crow: Mass Incarceration in the Age of Colorblindness*. New York: New Press, 2011.

"All Danish Babies with Down Syndrome Aborted but 4 in 2016." *Jerome Lejeune Foundation*, December 22, 2017.

Allen, John S. "The Big Home Ownership Lie: Greed, Fear, and How the Big Banks Exploited a Human Need." *Salon*, January 10, 2016.

Alter, Robert. *The Art of Biblical Poetry*. New York: Basic, 1985.

———. *The World of Biblical Literature*. New York: Basic, 1992.

Ambrose of Milan. *Letter 17 to Emperor Valentinian II*. Translated by H. de Romestin et al. In Nicene and Post-Nicene Fathers, Second Series, edited by Philip Schaff and Henry Wace, 10:895–99. Buffalo, NY: Christian Literature, 1896.

———. *On Virgins*. Translated by H. de Romestin, E. de Romestin, and H. T. F. Duckworth. From Nicene and Post-Nicene Fathers, Second Series, edited by Philip Schaff and Henry Wace, 10:797–855. Buffalo, NY: Christian Literature, 1896.

Anderson, Michael. "Maps: Portland's 1924 Rezone Legacy Is a 'Century of Exclusion.'" *Sightline Institute*, May 25, 2018.

Angrist, Joshua D., and William N. Evans. "Schooling and Labor Market Consequences of the 1970 State Abortion Reforms." In *Research in Labor Economics*, edited by Solomon W. Polachek. Bingley, UK: Emerald Group, 2000.

"Anthony Fauci: A Goal of Service to Mankind." *NPR*, July 25, 2005.

Anum, Emmanuel A., et al. "Health Disparities in Risk for Cervical Insufficiency." *Human Reproduction* 25 (2010) 2894–2900.

Applebaum, Anne. "A Warning from Europe: The Worst Is Yet to Come." *The Atlantic*, October 2018.

Appelbaum, Yoni. "McKinney, Texas, and the Racial History of American Swimming Pools." *The Atlantic*, June 8, 2015.

The Apocalypse of Peter. Translated by Andrew Rutherfurd. In Ante-Nicene Fathers, edited by Allan Menzies, 9:298–307. Buffalo, NY: Christian Literature, 1896.

The Apostolic Constitutions. Translated by James Donaldson. In Ante-Nicene Fathers, edited by Alexander Roberts et al., 7:871–1112. Buffalo: Christian Literature, 1886.

Aquinas, Thomas. *Summa Theologica*. Translated by the Fathers of the English Dominican Province. Notre Dame, IN: Christian Classics, 1981.

Arghioroussis, Maximos. *In the Image of God: Studies in Scripture, Theology, and Community*. Brookline: Holy Cross Orthodox, 1999.

Armstrong, B. G., et al. "Cigarette, Alcohol, and Coffee Consumption and Spontaneous Abortion." *American Journal of Public Health* 82 (1992) 85–87.

Armstrong, Elizabeth, et al. "Maternal Caffeine Consumption During Pregnancy and the Risk of Miscarriage." *American Journal of Obstetrics and Gynecology* 199 (2008) E13.

Arneil, Morag Barbara. "'All the World Was America': John Locke and the American Indian." PhD diss., University College London, 1992.

Aristotle. *History of Animals*. Translated by D'Arcy Wentworth Thompson. http://classics.mit.edu/Aristotle/history_anim.html.

———. *Politics*. Translated by Benjamin Jowett. Digireads.com, 2017.

Ashton, Jerry et al. *End Medical Debt: Curing America's $1 Trillion Unpayable Healthcare Debt*. Kauai: Hoku, 2018.

Athenagoras of Athens. *A Plea for the Christians*. Translated by B. P. Pratten. In Ante-Nicene Fathers, edited by Alexander Roberts et al., 2:280–333. Buffalo, NY: Christian Literature, 1885.

Augustine of Hippo. *City of God*. Translated by H. Bettenson. Harmondsworth, UK: Penguin, 1972.

———. *Epistle 98*. Translated by J. G. Cunningham. In Nicene and Post-Nicene Fathers, First Series, edited by Philip Schaff, 1:898–904. Buffalo, NY: Christian Literature, 1887.

———. *Marriage and Concupiscence*. Translated by Peter Holmes and Robert Ernest Wallis, revised by Benjamin B. Warfield. In Nicene and Post-Nicene Fathers, First Series, edited by Philip Schaff, 5:758–885. Buffalo, NY: Christian Literature, 1887.

———. *On the Work of Monks*. Translated by H. Brown. In Nicene and Post-Nicene Fathers, First Series, edited by Philip Schaff, 3:1084–1140. Buffalo, NY: Christian Literature, 1887.

———. *Quaestiones in Heptateuchum* 2.80. Translated by John Litteral. https://sites.google.com/site/aquinasstudybible/home/exodus/questions-on-exodus-by-augustine-of-hippo.

———. *A Treatise Concerning the Correction of the Donatists*. Translated by J. R. King. In Nicene and Post-Nicene Fathers, First Series, edited by Philip Schaff, 4:1260–97. Buffalo, NY: Christian Literature, 1887.

Autor, David et al. "When Work Disappears: Manufacturing Decline and the Falling Marriage-Market Value of Young Men." *American Economic Review*. Vol.1. No.2. September 2019. 161–78.

"Average Size of US Homes, Decade by Decade." *Newser*, May 29, 2016. https://www.newser.com/story/225645/average-size-of-us-homes-decade-by-decade.html.

Avila, Charles. *Ownership: Early Christian Teaching*. Eugene: Wipf & Stock, 1983.

Badger, Emily. "Children with Married Parents Are Better Off—But Marriage Isn't the Reason Why." *Washington Post*, September 8, 2014.

Bahamondes, L., et al. "Enlarged Ovarian Follicles in Users of a Levonorgestrel-Releasing Intrauterine System and Contraceptive Implant." *Journal of Reproductive Medicine* 48 (2003) 637–40.

Baker, Kelly J. *Gospel according to the Klan: The KKK's Appeal to Protestant America, 1915–1930*. Lawrence: University of Kansas Press, 2011.

Bakke, O. M. *When Children Became People: The Birth of Childhood in Early Christianity*. Minneapolis: Fortress, 2005.

Balmer, Randall. "Iowa: A Pastor's Son Notes When Politics Came to the Pulpit." *Religion & Politics*, October 27, 2012.

———. *The Making of Evangelicalism: From Revivalism to Politics and Beyond*. Waco: Baylor University Press, 2017

———. *Mine Eyes Have Seen the Glory: A Journey into the Evangelical Subculture in America*. 4th ed. Oxford: Oxford University Press, 2014.

———. *Thy Kingdom Come: How the Religious Right Distorts the Faith and Threatens America: An Evangelical's Lament*. New York: Basic, 2006.

Basil of Caesarea. *Epistle 188*. Translated by Bromfield Jackson. In Nicene and Post-Nicene Fathers, Second Series, edited by Philip Scaff and Henry Wace, 8:649–59. Buffalo, NY: Christian Literature, 1895.

———. "Epistle 188." Translated by Andrew Radde-Gallwitz. In *The Cambridge Edition of Early Christian Writings, Volume Two: Practice*, edited by Ellen Muehlberger. Cambridge: Cambridge University Press, 2017.

———. *Epistle 217*. Translated by Bromfield Jackson. In Nicene and Post-Nicene Fathers, Second Series, edited by Philip Scaff and Henry Wace, 8:721–29. Buffalo, NY: Christian Literature, 1895.

———. *Nine Homilies of Hexaemeron*. Translated by Bromfield Jackson. In Nicene and Post-Nicene Fathers, Second Series, edited by Philip Schaff and Henry Wace, 8:251–355. Buffalo, NY: Christian Literature, 1895.

Basil the Great. *On Social Justice*. Edited and translated by C. Paul Schroeder. Yonkers, NY: St. Vladimir's Seminary Press, 2009.

Bates, Jerome E., and Edward S. Zawadski. *Criminal Abortion: A Study in Medical Sociology*. Springfield, IL: Charles C. Thomas, 1964.

Bellah, Robert N. *The Broken Covenant: American Civil Religion in Time of Trial*. 2nd ed. Chicago: University of Chicago Press, 1992.
Bellah, Robert N., et al. *The Good Society*. New York: Alfred A. Knopf, 1991.
Belluck, Pam. "Abortion Qualms on Morning-after Pill May Be Unfounded." *New York Times*, June 5, 2012.
———. "New Birth Control Label Counters Lawsuit Claim." *New York Times*, November 26, 2013.
Belsky, J. E. "Medically Indigent Women Seeking Abortion Prior to Legalization: New York City, 1969–1970." *Family Planning Perspectives* 24 (1992) 129–34.
Bergland, Christopher. "Social Disadvantage Creates Genetic Wear and Tear." *Psychology Today*, April 16, 2014.
Berman, Jillian. "Former For-Profit College Students Will Have $168 Million in Student Debt Cancelled." *MarketWatch*, June 17, 2019.
Bhasin, Kim. "Christians Call Out Hobby Lobby for Hypocrisy." *Huffington Post*, July 1, 2014.
Biggs, Antonia. "Explained: Abortion Research and Policy." *Innovating Education in Reproductive Health*, 2017.
Blachor, Devorah. "Abortion Is Immoral, Except When It Comes to My Mistresses." *McSweeney's*, July 11, 2018.
Blair, Laurence, and Cindy Jiménez Bercerra. "Is Bolivia's 'Interim' President Using the Pandemic to Outstay Her Welcome?" *The Guardian*, June 1, 2020.
Blake, John. "Return of the 'Welfare Queen.'" *CNN*, January 23, 2012.
Blakemore, Erin. "How the GI Bill's Promise Was Denied to a Million Black WWII Veterans." *History*, September 30, 2019.
Blanco-Muñoz, Julia, et al. "Exposure to Maternal and Paternal Tobacco Consumption and Risk of Spontaneous Abortion." *Public Health Reports* 124 (2009) 317–22.
Blankenburg, Stephanie, et al. "Limited Liability and the Modern Corporation in Theory and in Practice." *Cambridge Journal of Economics*, September 2010.
Block, Sharon. *Rape and Sexual Power in Early America*. Chapel Hill: University of North Carolina Press, 2006.
Bloom, Harold. *The Book of J*. Translated by David Rosenberg. New York: Vintage, 1990.
"Bolivia Crisis: Jeanine Áñez Assumes Interim Presidency." *BBC News*, November 13, 2019.
"Born Too Soon: The Global Action Report on Preterm Birth." *World Health Organization*, 2012.
Boston, Rob. "Seeking God's Law: Past Statements by Attorney General Nominee William Barr Are Cause for Concern, Americans United Says." *Americans United for Separation of Church and State*, January 2019.
Boteach, Rabbi Shmuley. "On Legalizing Gay Marriage." *Facebook*, June 30, 2015. https://www.facebook.com/RabbiShmuleyBoteach/videos/10153022077966089/.
Bottone, Angelo. "Down Syndrome and Abortion: The Facts." *Iona Institute for Religion and Society*, January 24, 2018.
Bouie, Jamelle. "The Crisis in Black Homeownership." *Slate*, July 24, 2014.
Boyer, Paul S. *The Oxford Companion to United States History*. Oxford: Oxford University Press, 2006.
Brackman, Levi, and Rivkah Lubitch. "Chief Rabbis: Fight 'Abortion Epidemic.'" *YnetNews*, December 22, 2010. http://www.ynetnews.com/articles/0,7340,L-4002145,00.html.

Brakke, David. *Athanasius and Asceticism*. Baltimore: Johns Hopkins University Press, 1998.

———. *Demons and the Making of the Monk: Spiritual Combat in Early Christianity*. Cambridge: Harvard University Press, 2006.

"Brooklyn Man Arrested for Assaulting FBI Agents and Making False Statements About His Possession and Sale of Scarce Medical Equipment." *U.S. Department of Justice*, March 30, 2020. https://www.justice.gov/usao-nj/pr/brooklyn-man-arrested-assaulting-fbi-agents-and-making-false-statements-about-his.

Brooks, David. "The Nuclear Family Was a Mistake." *The Atlantic*, March 2020.

Brotman, Barbara. "Secret Abortion Group of '60s Prepares for Return." *Chicago Tribune*, August 28, 1989.

Brown, Lauretta. "New Poll: Three Quarters of Americans Support Restrictions on Abortion." *Townhall*, January 15, 2019.

Brown, Peter. *Augustine of Hippo: A Biography*. 2nd ed. Berkeley: University of California Press, 2000.

———. *Body and Society: Men, Women, and Sexual Renunciation in Early Christianity*. New York: Columbia University Press, 1988.

Brownmiller, Susan. "Dr. Spencer, 1889–1969: Last Trip to Ashland." *The Village Voice*, January 30, 1969.

Broussard, Karlo. "Onan and Contraceptive Sin." Catholic.org, https://www.catholic.com/qa/onan-up-to-contraceptive-sin.

Bruenig, Matt. "White High School Dropouts Have More Wealth Than Black or Latino College Graduates." Demos.org, September 23, 2014.

Brueninger, Kevin. "Trump and 3M Strike Deal to Bring 166.5 Million Masks to US in Three Months to Help Coronavirus Response." *CNBC News*, April 6, 2020.

Brunet, Romain. "Abortion Laws Vary Significantly Across the EU." *France24*, May 25, 2018.

Buchmueller, Thomas, and Alan Monheit. "Employer-Sponsored Health Insurance and the Promise of Health Insurance Reform." *National Bureau of Economic Research*. 2009.

Burnard, Trevor. "Toiling in the Fields: Valuing Female Slaves in Jamaica, 1674–1788." In *Sexuality and Slavery: Reclaiming Intimate Histories in the Americas*, edited by Daina Ramey Berry and Leslie M. Harris. Athens: University of Georgia Press, 2018.

Burtchaell, James Tunstead. *Rachel Weeping: The Case Against Abortion*. San Francisco: Harper and Row, 1982.

Burton, Douglas A. "Empress Theodora: Origins of Women's Rights." Douglasaburton.com, February 5, 2020.

Calderone, Mary Steichen. *Abortion in the United States: A Conference Sponsored by the Planned Parenthood Federation of America, Inc*. Arden House and the New York Academy of Medicine. New York: Hoeder-Harper, 1958.

———. "Illegal Abortion as a Public Health Problem." *American Journal of Public Health* 50 (1960) 948–54.

Caldwell, Christopher. *The Age of Entitlement: America Since the Sixties*. New York: Simon & Schuster, 2020.

———. "America's Two Constitutions—Since the '60s, Competing Visions of a More Perfect Union." *Fox News*, January 27, 2020.

———. "The Roots of Our Partisan Divide." *Hillsdale College Imprimis*, February 2020.

Calhoun, Byron C., et al. "Cost Consequences of Induced Abortion as an Attributable Risk for Preterm Birth and Impact on Informed Consent." *Journal of Reproductive Medicine* 52 (2007) 929–37.

Calvin, John. *Commentaries on the Four Last Books of Moses.* Volume 3. Translated by Charles W. Bingham. Grand Rapids: Eerdmans, 1950.

"Cardiovascular System—Blood Development." University of New South Wales. https://embryology.med.unsw.edu.au/embryology/index.php/Cardiovascular_System_-_Blood_Development.

Cardman, Francine. "Desert Mothers." In *Encyclopedia of Monasticism*, edited by William M. Johnston, 373–75. Chicago: Fitzroy Dearborn, 2000.

"The Care of Women Requesting Induced Abortion: Evidence-Based Clinical Guideline Number 7." Royal College of Obstetricians and Gynaecologists, November 2011.

Carmon, Irin. "Texas Women Are Running Out of Options." *MSNBC*, April 25, 2014.

———. "On Eve of SCOTUS Abortion Decision, Texas Accused of Suppressing Key Data." *NBC News*, June 26, 2016.

Caron, Simone M. *Who Chooses: American Reproductive History Since 1830.* Gainesville: University Press of Florida, 2008.

Carter, Neil. "What Does the Bible Say about Abortion?" *Patheos*, October 23, 2016.

Carter, J. Kameron. *Race: A Theological Account.* Oxford: Oxford University Press, 2008.

Carter, Stephen. "'Defending' Marriage: A Modest Proposal." *Howard Law Journal* 41 (1998) 215–28.

Castillo, Michelle. "Silicon Valley Has Been 'Tone Deaf' to the Entrepreneurial Potential of Middle America: Steve Case." *CNBC*, June 1, 2017.

Cauterucci, Christina. "Russia Decriminalized Domestic Violence with Support from the Russian Orthodox Church." *Slate*, February 8, 2017.

———. "Trump's Planned Elimination of Violence Against Women Grants Is Pure Cruelty." *Slate*, January 19, 2017.

Cesaretti, Paulo. *Theodora: Empress of Byzantium.* New York: Vendome, 2004.

Chait, Jonathan. "How Conservatives Tax the Poor." *The New Republic*, April 1, 2011.

Chalberg, Chuck. "Christopher Caldwell's 'The Age of Entitlement.'" *The Imaginative Conservative*, April 1, 2020.

Chapman, Elizabeth N., et al. "Physicians and Implicit Bias: How Doctors May Unwittingly Perpetuate Health Care Disparities." *Journal of General Internal Medicine* 28 (2013) 1504–10.

"Characteristics of New Housing." United States Census Bureau. https://www.census.gov/construction/chars/.

Charles, Alan, and Susan Alexander. "Abortions for Poor and Nonwhite Women: A Denial of Equal Protection?" *Hastings Law Journal* 147 (1971).

Charles, Mark, and Soong-Chan Rah. *Unsettling Truths: The Ongoing, Dehumanizing Legacy of the Doctrine of Discovery.* Downers Grove: InterVarsity, 2019.

Charles, Vignetta E., et al. "Abortion and Long-Term Mental Health Outcomes: A Systematic Review of the Evidence." *Contraception* 78 (2008) 436–50.

Chartier, Gary. *Public Practice, Private Law: An Essay on Love, Marriage, and the State.* Cambridge: Cambridge University Press, 2016.

Chen, Cen, et al. "Electrical Stimulation as a Novel Tool for Regulating Cell Behavior in Tissue Engineering." *Biomaterials Research* 23 (2019) 25.

Cho, Timothy Isaiah. "A Tale of Two Machens: How a Christian 'Hero' Let White Privilege Color His Theology." *Faithfully Magazine*, September 8, 2018.

Chortimer, Isaac. "The Contrarian Coronavirus Theory That Informed the Trump Administration." *The New Yorker*, March 30, 2020.
Christerson, Brad. "Why Do Christians Like Trump? Evangelicals Flirt With Facism." *University of Southern California Center for Religion and Civic Culture*, February 29, 2016.
Cizik, Richard. "A History of the Public Policy Resolutions of the National Association of Evangelicals." Ibrarian.net.
Claeys, Vicky. "Abortion Legislation in Europe." International Planned Parenthood Federation European Network, 7th Congress of the ESC, April 2002.
Clapsis, Emmanuel. "St. Basil's Cosmology." *Diakonia* 27 (1982) 3.
Clark-Flory, Tracy. "Supreme Court Strikes Down Restrictive Texas Abortion Law." *Vocativ*, June 27, 2016.
Colb, Sherry F. "Withdrawing Consent during Intercourse: California's Highest Court Clarifies the Definition of Rape." *FindLaw*, January 15, 2003.
"Cold War Mobilization." https://www.encyclopedia.com/defense/energy-government-and-defense-magazines/cold-war-mobilization.
Colleges of Agriculture at the Land Grant Universities: A Profile. Washington, DC: National Academies Press, 1995. See https://www.nap.edu/read/4980/chapter/2.
Collins, Chuck. "The Wealthy Kids Are Alright." *The American Prospect*, May 28, 2013.
Collins, Will. "The Myth of a Christian Revival in Eastern Europe." *The American Conservative*, January 7, 2019.
Collins, William J., and Robert A. Margo. "Race and Home Ownership, 1900–1990." Vanderbilt University and NBER. https://www.nber.org/system/files/working_papers/w7277/w7277.pdf.
Colvin, Jill. "Trump Order Keeping Meat Packing Plants Open Worries Unions." *Associated Press*, April 29, 2020.
"Conception: How It Works." https://www.ucsfhealth.org/education/conception-how-it-works#4.
Conger, Krista. "Earlier, More Accurate Prediction of Embryo Survival Enabled by Research." *Stanford Medicine News Center*, October 3, 2010.
"Contraceptive Equity." https://blackrj.org/our-issues/contraceptive-equity/.
Cook, J. C., et al. "Analysis of the Nonsteroidal Anti-Inflammatory Drug Literature for Potential Developmental Toxicity in Rats and Rabbits." *Birth Defects Research Part B: Developmental and Reproductive Toxicology* 68 (2003) 5–26.
Cook, P. J., et al. "The Effects of Short-Term Variation in Abortion Funding on Pregnancy Outcomes." *Journal of Health Economics* 18 (1999) 241–57.
Copland, Simon. "The Many Reasons That People Are Having Less Sex." *BBC News*, May 8, 2017.
Corrigan, Merritt. "Home . . . Where Women Will Find True Liberation." *Conservative Woman*, October 16, 2019.
"COVID-19 in Racial and Ethnic Minority Groups." Centers for Disease Control and Prevention, last updated July 24, 2020. https://www.cdc.gov/coronavirus/2019-ncov/community/health-equity/race-ethnicity.html.
Cowan, Sarah K. "Secrets and Misperceptions: The Creation of Self-Fulfilling Illusions." *Sociological Science* 1 (2014) 466–92.
Coy, Peter. "The Big Reason Whites Are Richer Than Blacks in America." *Bloomberg Businessweek*, February 8, 2017.

"The Criminal Justice System: Statistics." https://www.rainn.org/statistics/criminal-justice-system.

"Crimson Contagion 2019 Functional Exercise Draft After-Action Report." U.S. Department of Health and Human Services, October 2019. https://int.nyt.com/data/documenthelper/6824-2019-10-key-findings-and-after/05bd797500ea55be0724/optimized/full.pdf.

Cross, Frank L. "Hippolytus of Rome." In *The Oxford Dictionary of the Christian Church*, edited by Frank L. Cross and E. A. Livingstone. Oxford: Oxford University Press, 2005.

Culp-Ressler, Tara. "GOP Platform Lies about Abstinence Education's Effectiveness." *Think Progress*, August 29, 2012.

———. "What Americans Have Forgotten about the Era before Roe v. Wade." *ThinkProgress*, November 19, 2014.

Daniel, Sharon, et al. "Fetal Exposure to Nonsteroidal Anti-Inflammatory Drugs and Spontaneous Abortions." *Canadian Medical Association Journal* 186 (2014) E177–82.

Daniélou, Jean. *History of Early Christian Doctrine before the Council of Nicaea*. Volume 1: "The Theology of Jewish Christianity." Translated and edited by John A. Baker. London: Dartman, Longman, and Todd, 1964.

Daniels, Kimberly, et al. "Current Contraceptive Use and Variation by Selected Characteristics among Women Aged 15–44: United States, 2011–2013." Centers for Disease Control and Prevention, National Health Statistics Reports 86 (2015).

Davis, Angela. "Racism, Birth Control, and Reproductive Rights." In *From Abortion to Reproductive Freedom: Transforming a Movement*, edited by Marlene Gerber Fried, 15–26. Boston: South End, 1990.

Davis, Stephen J. *The Cult of Saint Thecla: A Tradition of Women's Piety in Late Antiquity*. Oxford: Oxford University Press, 2001.

"Declaration on Procured Abortion." Congregation for the Doctrine of the Faith, 1974.

Dellapenna, Joseph. *Dispelling the Myths of Abortion History*. Durham, NC: Carolina Academic, 2006.

Deneen, Patrick. "A Catholic Showdown Worth Watching." *The American Conservative*, February 6, 2014.

———. "Even If Hobby Lobby Wins, We Lose." *The American Conservative*, March 25, 2014.

———. *Why Liberalism Failed*. New Haven: Yale University Press, 2018.

Denejkina, Anna. "In Russia, Feminist Memes Buy Jail Time, but Domestic Abuse Doesn't." *Foreign Policy*, November 15, 2018.

DeNoon, Daniel J. "Abortion Pill Safe as Surgical Abortion." WebMD, August 15, 2007.

DeParle, Jason. "Why Do People Who Need Help from the Government Hate It So Much?" *New York Times*, September 19, 2016.

DeParle, Jason, and Sabrina Tavernise. "For Women Under 30, Most Births Occur Outside Marriage." *New York Times*, February 17, 2012.

DePaulo, Bella. "7 Reasons Why Young People Are Having Less Sex." *Psychology Today*, November 25, 2018.

Derbyshire, Stuart W. G. "Can Fetuses Feel Pain?" *British Medical Journal* 332 (2006) 909–12.

de Rosa, Peter. *Vicars of Christ*. Dublin: Poolbeg, 2000.

Dershowitz, Alan. *The Genesis of Justice: Ten Stories of Biblical Injustice That Led to the Ten Commandments and Modern Law*. New York: Warner, 2000.

DeVega, Chauncy. "So Much for Christian Charity: Evangelicals Blame the Poor for Poverty, Which Makes Them a Lot Like Other Republicans." *Salon*, August 10, 2017.

Diamond, Dan, and Nahal Toosi. "Trump Team Failed to Follow NSC's Pandemic Playbook." *Politico*, March 25, 2020.

Didache. Translated by M. B. Riddle. In Ante-Nicene Fathers, edited by Alexander Roberts et al., 7:836–70. Buffalo, NY: Christian Literature, 1886.

Dine, Ranana. "Scarlett Letters: Getting the History of Abortion and Contraception Right." *Center for American Progress*, August 8, 2013.

Dochuk, Darren. *From Bible Belt to Sunbelt: Plain Folk Religion, Grassroots Politics, and the Rise of Evangelical Conservatism*. New York: W. W. Norton, 2011.

"Doctors and Health Care Facilities Need to Prepare as Self-Managed Abortion Increases under Restrictive Laws." https://www.ansirh.org/news/doctors-and-health-care-facilities-need-prepare-self-managed-abortion-increases-under.

Dombrowski, Daniel, and Robert Deltete. *A Brief, Liberal, Catholic Defense of Abortion*. Champaign: University of Illinois Press, 2000.

"Domestic Violence." Archived version. U.S. Department of Justice. https://web.archive.org/web/20180409111243/https://www.justice.gov/ovw/domestic-violence.

Dominguez-Salas, Paula, et al. "Maternal Nutrition at Conception Modulates DNA Methylation of Human Metastable Epialleles." *Nature Communications* 5 (2014).

Doucleff, Michaeleen. "Mom's Diet Right before Pregnancy Can Alter Baby's Genes." *NPR*, April 29, 2014.

Dougherty, Michael Brendan, and Pascal-Emmanuel Gobry. "Time to Admit It: The Church Has Always Been Right on Birth Control." *Business Insider*, February 8, 2012.

Douglas-Gabriel, Danielle. "The Courts Cleared the Way for DeVos to Grant Student Debt Relief. So Why Are 180,000 People Still Waiting for an Answer?" *Washington Post*, June 25, 2019.

———. "DeVos Reaches Settlement over Stalled Student Debt Relief Claims." *Washington Post*, April 10, 2020.

Douthat, Ross. "What Reduces Abortion Rates?" *New York Times*, February 21, 2012.

Dove, Frederick. "What's Happened to Thalidomide Babies?" *BBC*, November 3, 2011.

Dowling, M. "Welfare Encourages Polygamy in the United States." *Independent Sentinel*, October 31, 2014.

Draper, Electa. "Colorado Claims Contraceptive Program Caused Big Drop in Teen Birth Rates." *Denver Post*, July 3, 2014.

Drazin, Israel. "What Did Ruth and Boaz Do on the Threshing Floor?" *The Times of Israel*, July 21, 2017.

Dreher, Rod. "Bill Barr: Religious Liberty Warrior." *The American Conservative*, October 14, 2019.

———. "First Things and Changing Times." *The American Conservative*, May 15, 2020.

———. "Sohrab Ahmari vs. David French." *The American Conservative*, May 30, 2019.

Dupont, Carolyn Renee. *Mississippi Praying: Southern White Evangelicals and the Civil Rights Movement, 1945–1975*. New York: New York University Press, 2013.

du Preez, Ron. "The Fetus in Biblical Law." *Ministry Magazine*, September 1992.

Durant, Will. *Caesar and Christ*. New York: Simon & Schuster, 1972.

Dworkin, Elizabeth. "Coerced Abortions: A New Study Shows They're Common." *The Daily Beast*, October 8, 2010.
Dyer, Jennifer Eaton. "The Core Beliefs of Southern Evangelicals: A Psycho-Social Investigation of the Evangelical Megachurch Phenomenon." PhD diss., Vanderbilt University, 2007.
Eckholm, Erik. "A Pill Available in Mexico Is a Texas Option for Abortion." *New York Times*, July 13, 2013.
"Ectopic Pregnancy." https://americanpregnancy.org/pregnancy-complications/ectopic-pregnancy/.
Edwards, Frank et al. "Risk of Being Killed by Police Use of Force in the United States by Age, Race–Ethnicity, and Sex." *Proceedings of the National Academy of Sciences of the United States of America* 116 (2019) 16793–98.
Edwards, Jim. "Silicon Valley Is Living Inside a Bubble of Tone-Deaf Arrogance." *Business Insider*, December 15, 2013.
Eibner, Christine, and Courtney Gidengil. "What If the Supreme Court Strikes Down the ACA During the COVID-19 Pandemic?" *The Hill*, April 2, 2020.
Elliot, Larry. "Plc: The Prerogative of the Unaccountable Few: Adam Smith Argued for Free Trade and Self-Interest, But Not This Kind of Capitalism." *The Guardian*, July 9, 2007.
Elliot, Mark R. "Why Russia's Evangelicals Thank God for Putin." *Christianity Today*, January 7, 2015.
Elson, J., et al. "Expectant Management of Tubal Ectopic Pregnancy: Prediction of Successful Outcome Using Decision Tree Analysis." *Ultrasound in Obstetrics and Gynecology* 23(2004) 552–6.
Emilio, John, and Estelle B. Freedman. *Intimate Matters: A History of Sexuality in America*. New York: Harper & Row, 1988.
"The Emotional Side Effects of Abortion." https://americanpregnancy.org/unplanned-wpregnancy/abortion-emotional-effects/.
Englehardt, H. Tristam. *The Foundations of Christian Bioethics*. The Netherlands: Swets & Zeitlinger, 2000.
The Epistle of Barnabus. Translated by Alexander Roberts and James Donaldson. In Ante-Nicene Fathers, edited by Alexander Roberts et al., 1:364–403. Buffalo, NY: Christian Literature, 1885.
Ertelt, Steven. "Police Obtain DNA from Planned Parenthood in Abortion-Rape Case." *LifeNews*, September 23, 2011.
Evans, James Allan. *The Empress Theodora: Partner of Justinian*. Austin: University of Texas Press, 2002.
Evelyn, Kenya. "Amazon CEO Jeff Bezos Grows Fortune by $24bn amid Coronavirus Pandemic." *The Guardian*, April 15, 2020.
"The Facts." (n Our Own Voice: Black Women's Reproductive Justice Agenda. https://blackrj.org/the-facts/.
Fallin, Amanda, et al. "'To Quarterback behind the Scenes, Third-Party Efforts': The Tobacco Industry and the Tea Party." *Tobacco Control* 23 (2013).
Falwell, Jerry. *Listen, America!* Garden City: Doubleday, 1980.
"Family Income—Not Married Parents—More Apt to Impact Kids' Well-Being." *NBC News*, February 27, 2015.
Fang, Lee. "Key Medical Supplies Were Shipped from U.S. Manufacturers to Foreign Buyers, Records Show." *The Intercept*, April 1, 2020.

"FBI Discovers Promised Stockpile of 39 Million Masks Was a Scam." *Associated Press*, April 13, 2020.

Felitti, Vincent J., et al. "Relationship of Childhood Abuse and Household Dysfunction to Many of the Leading Causes of Death in Adults." *American Journal of Preventive Medicine* 14 (1998) 245–58.

"Felony Defendants in Large Urban Counties, 2009." 2013. https://www.bjs.gov/content/pub/pdf/fdluc09.pdf.

Fernandez, Colin. "Hundreds of Unfaithful Women Having Paternity Tests on Unborn Babies to Determine Whether to Have Abortions." *UK Daily Mail*, January 26, 2009.

Fernandez, Manny, and Abby Goodnough. "Opinion Transforms Texas' Abortion Landscape." *New York Times*, June 27, 2016.

Ferngren, Gary B. *Medicine and Health Care in Early Christianity*. Baltimore: Johns Hopkins University Press, 2016.

Fessler, Pam. "U.S. Cities Face Challenges In Reducing Homeless Population." *NPR*, December 11, 2015,

Finer, Lawrence B., and Mia R. Zolna. "Declines in Unintended Pregnancy in the United States, 2008–2011." *New England Journal of Medicine* 374 (2016) 843–52.

Finer, Lawrence B., et al. "Changes in Use of Long-Acting Contraceptive Methods in the United States, 2007–2009." *Fertility and Sterility* 98 (2012) 893–97.

———. "Reasons U.S. Women Have Abortions: Quantitative and Qualitative Perspectives." *Perspectives on Sexual and Reproductive Health* 37 (2005).

Fingleton, Eamonn. "In World's Best-Run Economy, House Prices Keep Falling—Because That's What House Prices Are Supposed to Do." *Forbes*, February 2, 2014.

FitzGerald, Frances. *The Evangelicals: The Struggle to Shape America*. New York: Simon & Schuster, 2017.

Flegenheimer, Matt, and Maggie Haberman. "Donald Trump, Abortion Foe, Eyes 'Punishment' for Women, Then Recants." *New York Times*, March 30, 2016.

Flinn, Frank K. "Abortion." In *Encyclopedia of Catholicism*, edited by J. Gordon Melton, 3–5. New York: Facts on File, 2007.

Florovsky, Georges. "St. Athanasius' Concept of Creation." In The Collected Works of Georges Florovsky 4. Belmont: Nordland, 1975.

Foner, Eric. *Reconstruction: America's Unfinished Revolution, 1863–1877*. New York: Harper, 2014.

———. *The Second Founding: How the Civil War and Reconstruction Remade the Constitution*. New York: W. W. Norton, 2019.

Ford, Matt. "Bill Barr's First Epistle to the Heathens." *The New Republic*, October 22, 2019.

Forsythe, Clarke D. *Abuse of Discretion: The Inside Story of* Roe v. Wade. New York: Encounter, 2012.

Fortenberry, Bill. "Fact Sheet on Ectopic Pregnancy." http://www.personhoodinitiative.com/fact-sheet-on-ectopic-pregnancy.html.

Foster, Diana Greene. "Unmet Need for Abortion and Woman-Centered Contraceptive Care." *The Lancet* 388 (2016) 216–17.

Foster, Thomas A. "The Sexual Abuse of Black Men under American Slavery." In *Sexuality and Slavery: Reclaiming Intimate Histories in the Americas*, edited by Daina Ramey Berry and Leslie M. Harris, 124–44. Athens: University of Georgia Press, 2018.

Fowler, C. I., et al. "Family Planning Annual Report: 2015 National Summary." *Research Triangle Park International*, July 2017.
Frangipani, Joseph Magnus. "The Cosmological Vision of St. Basil and the First Hospital." *Servant of Prayer*, April 8, 2014.
Franklin, Donna L. *Ensuring Inequality: The Structural Transformation of the African-American Family*. Oxford: Oxford University Press, 1997.
Freeman, Curtis W. "'Never Had I Been So Blind': W. A. Criswell's 'Change' on Racial Segregation." *Journal of Southern Religion* 10 (2007).
Fukuyama, Francis. *Trust: The Social Virtues and the Creation of Prosperity*. New York: Free Press, 1995.
"Funding: Tax-Funded Abortions." http://abortionincanada.ca/funding/.
Gaddis, S. Michael. "Discrimination in the Credential Society: An Audit Study of Race and College Selectivity in the Labor Market." *Oxford Academic Social Forces Journal* 93 (2015) 1451-79.
Gaines, Alexandra Cawthorne. "The Straight Facts on Women in Poverty." *Center for American Progress*, October 8, 2008.
Galen. "The Construction of the Embryo." Translated by Peter N. Singer. In *Galen: Selected Works*, 177-200. The World's Classics. Oxford: Oxford University Press, 1997.
Galli, Mark. "'When Evangelicals Were Pro-Choice'—Another Fake History." *Christianity Today*, October 31, 2012.
Gardner, Tiffany M., et al. "No Shelter from the Storm: Reclaiming the Right to Housing and Protecting the Health of Vulnerable Communities in Post-Katrina New Orleans." *Health and Human Rights Journal* (August 29, 2013).
Garratt, Canon. "On the Samaritan Text of the Pentateuch." *Journal of the Transactions*. London: Harrison & Sons, 1904.
Garrett, Laurie. "Trump Has Sabotaged America's Coronavirus Response." *Foreign Policy*, January 31, 2020.
Garrow, David. *Liberty and Sexuality: The Right to Privacy and the Making of* Roe v. Wade. New York: Open Road, 1998. Kindle ed.
Gavrilyuk, Paul. *The Suffering of the Impassible God: The Dialectics of Patristic Thought*. Oxford: Oxford University Press, 2004.
Gee, Alison. "A World without Down Syndrome." *BBC*, September 29, 2016.
Gelernter, David. "Why Should a Jew Care Whether Christianity Lives or Dies?" *First Things*, March 24, 2015.
Gemzell-Danielsson, Kristina. "Mechanism of Action of Emergency Contraception." *Contraception* 82 (2010) 404-9.
Gerdts, Caitlin, et al. "Impact of Clinic Closures on Women Obtaining Abortion Services after Implementation of a Restrictive Law in Texas." *American Journal of Public Health* 106 (2016) 857-64.
Gilens, Martin. *Why Americans Hate Welfare: Race, Media, and the Politics of Antipoverty Policy*. Chicago: University of Chicago Press, 1999.
Gleason, Fr. Joseph. "Sacred Seed, Sacred Chamber." *The Orthodox Life*, May 18, 2015.
Gold, Edwin M., et al. "Therapeutic Abortions in New York City: A 20-Year Review." *American Journal of Public Health* 55 (1965) 964-72.
Gold, Howard R. "Who's at Fault for Student-Loan Defaults?" *Chicago Booth Review*, May 13, 2019.

Gold, Jenny. "Proportion of OB-GYNs Offering Abortions May Be Lower Than Thought." *NPR*, August 22, 2011.
Gold, Rachel Benson. "Lessons from Before *Roe*: Will Past be Prologue?" Guttmacher Institute, March 1, 2003.
Goldenberg, David M. *The Curse of Ham: Race and Slavery in Early Judaism, Christianity, and Islam*. Princeton: Princeton University Press, 2003.
Goldstein, Warren. *Defending the Human Spirit: Jewish Law's Vision for a Moral Society*. New York: Feldham, 2006.
Goodwin, Doris. "The Way We Won: America's Economic Breakthrough during World War II." *American Prospect*, 1992.
Gordon, Linda. *Woman's Body, Woman's Right: Birth Control in America*. New York: Penguin, 1990.
Gould, Elise, et al. "What Is the Gender Pay Gap and Is It Real?" *Economic Policy Institute*, October 20, 2016.
Graber, Mark A. *Rethinking Abortion: Equal Choice, the Constitution, and Reproductive Politics*. Princeton: Princeton University Press, 1996.
Graham, Franklin. "Putin's Olympic Controversy." *Decision Magazine*, February 28, 2014.
Gray, Kathleen, and Paul Egan. "Whitmer Says Protests against Stay Home Order OK, but Takes a Shot at DeVos Family Involvement." *Detroit Free Press*, April 13, 2020.
Greenhouse, Linda, and Reva Siegel. "Before *Roe v. Wade*: Voices That Shaped the Abortion Debate before the Supreme Court's Ruling." Yale Law School. Public Law Working Paper No. 257, September 7, 2012.
Gregory IX, Pope. *Corpus Juris Canonici*. Vatican,
Gregory of Nyssa. *Fourth Homily on Ecclesiastes*. Translated by Stuart Gregory Hall and Rachel Moriarty, edited by Stuart Gregory Hall. Seventh International Colloquium on Gregory of Nyssa, September 5–10, 1990. Berlin: de Gruyter, 1990.
———. *On Infants' Early Deaths*. Translated by H. A. Wilson. In Nicene and Post-Nicene Fathers, Second Series, edited by Philip Schaff and Henry Wace, 5:692–708. Buffalo, NY: Christian Literature, 1893.
———. *On the Making of Man*. Translated by H. A. Wilson. In Nicene and Post-Nicene Fathers, Second Series, edited by Philip Schaff and Henry Wace, 5:714–97. Buffalo, NY: Christian Literature, 1893.
Gregory the Great. *Book of Pastoral Rule*. Translated by James Barmby. In Nicene and Post-Nicene Fathers, Second Series, edited by Philip Schaff and Henry Wace, 12:572–724. Buffalo, NY: Christian Literature, 1895.
Grenoble, Ryan. "Here's Video of Trump Trying to Explain Why He Cut the Pandemic Response Team." *Huffington Post*, March 17, 2020.
Gross, Terry. "Personhood in the Womb: A Constitutional Question." *NPR*, November 21, 2013.
Grossman, Daniel. "The Use of Public Health Evidence in *Whole Woman's Health v Hellerstedt*." *Journal of the American Medical Association Internal Medicine*. Published online: November 7, 2016.
Grossman, Daniel, et al. "Change in Abortion Services after Implementation of a Restrictive Law in Texas." *Contraception* 90 (2014) 496–501.
———. "Continuing Pregnancy after Mifepristone and 'Reversal' of First-Trimester Medical Abortion: A Systematic Review." *Contraception* 92 (2015) 206–11.

———. "Induced Abortion Provision among a National Sample of Obstetrician-Gynecologists." *Obstetrics & Gynecology* 133 (2019) 477–83.

———. "Research Brief: Knowledge, Opinion, and Experience Related to Abortion Self-Induction in Texas." *Texas Policy Evaluation Project*, November 17, 2015.

Grudem, Wayne. *Politics according to the Bible*. Grand Rapids: Zondervan, 2010.

Gruber, Jonathan, et al. "Abortion Legalization and Child Living Circumstances: Who Is the 'Marginal Child'?," *The Quarterly Journal of Economics* 114 (1999) 263–91.

Gustafson, Kaaryn S. *Cheating Welfare: Public Assistance and the Criminalization of Poverty*. New York: New York University Press, 2011.

Guttmacher, Alan, ed. *The Case for Legalized Abortion Now*. Pleasant Hill: Diablo: 1967.

———. "The Shrinking Non-Psychiatric Indications for Therapeutic Abortion." In *Therapeutic Abortion: Medical, Psychiatric, Legal, Anthropological, and Religious Considerations*, edited by Harold Rosen. Boston: Beacon: 1954.

"Guttmacher Statistic on Catholic Women's Contraceptive Use." Guttmacher Institute, February 15, 2012.

Haberkorn, Jennifer. "Abortion, Rape Shaped Key Races." *Politico*, November 6, 2012.

Hairston, James E., et al. "Water Resources in Alabama." *Encyclopedia of Alabama*, September 21, 2015. http://www.encyclopediaofalabama.org/article/h-1645.

Hall, Robert E. "Abortion in American Hospitals." *American Journal of Public Health* 57 (1967) 1933–36.

Hamilton, Alexander, et al. *The Federalist Papers*. Edited by Lawrence Goldman. Oxford: Oxford University Press, 2008.

Handlin, Oscar. "The Development of the Corporation." In *The Corporation: A Theological Inquiry*, edited by Michael Novak and John W. Cooper, 1–16. Washington DC: American Enterprise Institute for Public Policy Research, 1981.

Hanlon, Seth. "The Mortgage Interest Deduction." *Center for American Progress*, January 26, 2011.

Harding, Susan F. *The Book of Jerry Falwell: Fundamentalist Language and Politics*. Princeton: Princeton University Press, 2000.

Harrington, Rebecca, and Skye Gould. "The Number of Abortion Clinics in the US Has Plunged in the Last Decade—Here's How Many Are in Each State." *Business Insider*, February 10, 2017.

Harris, Adam. "The Lifelong Cost of Getting a For-Profit Education." *The Atlantic*, August 29, 2018.

Harris, Elizabeth A. "Judge, Citing Inequality, Orders Connecticut to Overhaul Its School System." *New York Times*, September 7, 2016.

Harris, Jonathan. "Byzantium and the Rights of Women." *Yale University Press Blog*, October 27, 2015.

Harris, Lisa H., and Daniel Grossman. "Complications of Unsafe and Self-Managed Abortion." *New England Journal of Medicine* 382 (2020) 1029–40.

Harris, Nadine Burke. "How Childhood Trauma Affects Health across a Lifetime." TED Talk, September 2014.

Hart, David Bentley. *Atheist Delusions: The Christian Revolution and Its Fashionable Enemies*. New Haven: Yale University Press, 2009.

Hasstedt, Kinsey. "The State of Sexual and Reproductive Health and Rights in the State of Texas: A Cautionary Tale." *Guttmacher Policy Review* 17 (2014) 14–21.

Hatzinikolaou, Nikolaos. "The Embryo and Its Development in Regards to Its Formation as a Complete Human Being." *Hellenic Center for Biomedical Ethics*, September 11–15, 2002.

Hays, Richard B. *The Moral Vision of the New Testament: A Contemporary Introduction to New Testament Ethics*. San Francisco: Harper San Francisco, 1996.

Healy, Melissa. "OB-GYNs Remain Conflicted about Abortion, Survey Shows, but Pills May Be Changing Attitudes." *Los Angeles Times*, February 8, 2019.

Hegewisch, Ariane, and Adiam Tesfaselassie. "The Gender Wage Gap: 2018; Earnings Differences by Gender, Race, and Ethnicity." *Institute for Women's Policy Research*, September 11, 2019.

Herrin, Judith. *Unrivalled Influence: Women and Empire in Byzantium*. Princeton: Princeton University Press, 2013.

Herron, George D. *Between Caesar and Jesus*. London: H. R. Allenson, 1899.

Heyne, Thomas. "Reconstructing the World's First Hospital: The Basiliad." *Hektoen International: A Journal of Medical Humanities*, Spring 2015. https://hekint.org/2017/02/24/reconstructing-the-worlds-first-hospital-the-basiliad/.

Hill, Catey. "6 Times It's More Expensive to Be a Woman." *MarketWatch*, April 12, 2016.

Hilton, Boyd. *The Age of Atonement: The Influence of Evangelicalism on Social and Economic Thought, 1785–1865*. Oxford: Oxford University Press, 1995.

Hinderaker, John. "What Did Lee Atwater Really Say?" *Power Line Blog*, June 9, 2013.

Hines, Darlene Clark. "Rape and the Inner Lives of Black Women in the Middle West: Preliminary Thoughts on a Culture of Dissemblance." *Signs* 14 (1989) 912–20.

Hippolytus of Rome. *Refutation of All Heresies*. Translated by J. H. MacMahon. In Ante-Nicene Fathers, edited by Alexander Roberts et al., 5:15–412. Buffalo, NY: Christian Literature, 1886.

Hochschild, Arlie Russell. *Strangers in Their Own Land: Anger and Mourning on the American Right*. New York: New Press, 2016.

Holmes, M. M., et al. "Rape-Related Pregnancy: Estimates and Descriptive Characteristics from a National Sample of Women." *American Journal of Obstetrics and Gynecology* 175 (1996) 320–4.

Holzwarth, Larry. "10 Weird Common Practices in Colonial America in the Early History." https://historycollection.co/10-weird-common-practices-in-colonial-america-in-the-early-history/8/.

Hotez, Peter J. "Neglected Parasitic Infections and Poverty in the United States." *PLOS Neglected Tropical Diseases*, September 4, 2014.

"How Many Couples Are Waiting to Adopt?" https://www.americanadoptions.com/pregnant/waiting_adoptive_families.

Howard, Kimberly, and Richard V. Reeves. "The Marriage Effect: Money or Parenting?" *Brookings Institute*, September 4, 2014.

Howley, Elaine K. "What to Know about Rising STD Rates among Seniors." *U.S. News and World Report*, December 10, 2018.

Hui, Edwin C. *At the Beginning of Life: Dilemmas in Theological Bioethics*. Downers Grove: InterVarsity, 2002.

Hylen, Susan E. *A Modest Apostle: Thecla and the History of Women in the Early Church*. Oxford: Oxford University Press, 2015.

"Ibuprofen May 'Raise Miscarriage Risk.'" United Kingdom National Health Service, September 7, 2011.

Illing, Sean. "Schools Are Segregated Because White People Want Them That Way." *Vox*, October 26, 2017.
"Induced Abortion Worldwide." Guttmacher Institute, March 2018.
Interlandi, Janeen. "The Toxins That Affected Your Great-Grandparents Could Be in Your Genes." *Smithsonian Magazine*, December 2013.
"Israel: Reproduction and Abortion: Law and Policy." *Law Library of Congress*, February 2012. https://www.loc.gov/law/help/il-reproduction-and-abortion/israel.php.
"Issues in Jewish Ethics: Abortion." https://www.jewishvirtuallibrary.org/abortion-in-judaism.
"It's Not over in the South: School Desegregation in Forty-Three Southern Cities Eighteen Years after Brown." U.S. Department of Health, Education, and Welfare, Office of Education, May 1972.
Jacobse, Father Johannes. "St. Basil the Great and Christian Philanthropy." *American Orthodox Institute USA*, December 20, 2014.
Jacobson, Louis, and Victoria Knight. "Did Donald Trump Fire Pandemic Officials, Defund CDC?" *Politifact*, February 28, 2020. https://www.politifact.com/factchecks/2020/feb/28/michael-bloomberg/did-donald-trump-fire-pandemic-officials-defund-cd/.
Jatlaoui, Tara C., et al. "Abortion Surveillance—United States, 2016 Surveillance Summaries." *Centers for Disease Control Surveillance Summaries* 68 (2019) 1–41.
Jemison, Elizabeth L. "Proslavery Christianity after the Emancipation." *Tennessee Historical Quarterly* 72 (2013) 255–68.
Jennings, Willie James. *The Christian Imagination: Theology and the Origins of Race*. New Haven: Yale University Press, 2010.
Jerome. *De Viris Illustribus*. Translated by Ernest Cushing Richardson. In Nicene and Post-Nicene Fathers, Second Series, edited by Philip Schaff and Henry Wace, 3:813–1068. Buffalo, NY: Christian Literature, 1892.
———. *Epistle 52*. Translated by W. H. Fremantle et al. In Nicene and Post-Nicene Fathers, Second Series, edited by Philip Schaff and Henry Wace, 6:243–56. Buffalo, NY: Christian Literature, 1893.
Joffe, Carole E. *Doctors of Conscience: The Struggle to Provide Abortion before and after Roe v. Wade*. Boston: Beacon, 1996.
John XXIII, Pope. *Mater et Magistra*. Vatican, 1961.
John of Damascus. *Exposition of the Orthodox Faith*. Translated by E. W. Watson and L. Pullan. In Nicene and Post-Nicene Fathers, Second Series, edited by Philip Schaff and Henry Wace, 9:541–781. Buffalo, NY: Christian Literature, 1899.
Johnson, Akila, and Talia Buford. "Early Data Shows African Americans Have Contracted and Died of Coronavirus at an Alarming Rate." *ProPublica*, April 3, 2020.
Johnson, Richard W., and Joshua M. Weiner. "A Profile of Frail Older Americans and Their Caregivers." *Urban Institute*, March 1, 2006.
Jones, Rachel K., and Jenna Jerman. "Abortion Incidence and Service Availability in the United States, 2014." *Perspectives on Sexual and Reproductive Health* 49 (2017) 17–27.
Jones, Rachel K., and K. Kooistra. "Abortion Incidence and Access to Services in the United States, 2008." *Perspectives on Sexual and Reproductive Health* 43 (2011) 41–50.

Jones, Rachel K., et al. "Abortion Incidence and Service Availability in the United States, 2017." Guttmacher Institute, September 2019.
Jones, Ryan. "Abortion in Israel on the Decline." *Israel Today*, February 7, 2011.
Josephus. *Against Apion*. Translated by William Whistleton. Project Gutenberg. January 9, 2013. http://www.gutenberg.org/files/2849/2849-h/2849-h.htm.
———. *Antiquities of the Jews*. Translated by William Whistleton. Project Gutenberg. August 9, 2017. https://gutenberg.org/files/2848/2848-h/2848-h.htm.
Joyce, Theodore J., et al. "Back to the Future? Abortion before and after *Roe*." National Bureau of Economic Research. Working Paper No. 18338, August 2012. https://www.nber.org/papers/w18338.
"Judge Says Purvi Patel Should Be Freed Immediately after Feticide Conviction Overturned." *Associated Press*, August 31, 2016.
Julian, Kate. "Why Are Young People Having So Little Sex?" *The Atlantic*, December 2018.
Justin Martyr. *First Apology*. Translated by Marcus Dods and George Reith. In Ante-Nicene Fathers, edited by Alexander Roberts et al., 1:423–501. Buffalo, NY: Christian Literature, 1885.
Justinian I. *Codex Justinianus*. Translated by S. P. Scott. Cincinnati: Central Trust Company, 1932.
———. *Novellae*. Translated by S. P. Scott. Cincinnati: Central Trust Company, 1932.
Kaldellis, Anthony. *The Byzantine Republic: People and Power in New Rome*. Cambridge: Harvard University Press, 2015.
Kanno-Youngs, Zolan, and Ana Swanson. "Wartime Production Law Has Been Used Routinely, but Not with Coronavirus." *New York Times*, March 31, 2020.
Kaplan, Laura. *The Story of Jane: The Legendary Underground Feminist Abortion Service*. Chicago: Pantheon, 1995.
Kaplan, Lawrence. *Fundamentalism in Comparative Perspective*. Amherst: University of Massachusetts Press, 1992.
Kavanaugh, Megan L., and Jenna Jerman. "Contraceptive Method Use in the United States: Trends and Characteristics Between 2008, 2012 and 2014." *Contraception Journal* 97 (2018) 14–28.
Keene, David, and David Cole. "Keeping Surveillance Constitutional." *Washington Times*, October 31, 2017.
Keirnan, John S. "Most and Least Federally Dependent States." Wallethub, March 18, 2020.
Kendi, Ibram X. *Stamped from the Beginning: The Definitive History of Racist Ideas*. New York: Nation, 2016.
Kerridge, Eric. *Usury, Interest and the Reformation*. Aldershot, UK: Ashgate, 2002.
Kertscher, Tom. "In Context: Transcript of Donald Trump on Punishing Women for Abortion." *Politifact*, March 30, 2016.
Kesling, Ben. "Veterans Affairs Hospitals Facing 'Serious' Shortage of Protective Gear, Internal Memos Show." *Wall Street Journal*, April 8, 2020.
———. "Veterans Affairs Hospitals Will Give Masks Only to Some Employees, Memos Show." *Wall Street Journal*, April 11, 2020.
Kidd, Kelley. "What White Poverty Really Looks Like in America." *Mic*, August 16, 2013.
Kiely, Eugene. "What Did Trump Say at Immigration Meeting?" *FactCheck*, January 16, 2018. https://www.factcheck.org/2018/01/trump-say-immigration-meeting/.

Kizenko, Nadieszda. "Beat Her When You Are Alone Together: Domestic Violence in the Russian Tradition, Past and Present." *Public Orthodoxy*, February 13, 2017.

Klein, Brandon. "Todd Akin and the Anti-Science House Science Committee." *Wired*, August 24, 2012.

Klippenstein, Ken. "Exclusive: The Military Knew Years Ago That a Coronavirus Was Coming." *The Nation*, April 1, 2020. Original Pentagon report now declassified and available at https://www.scribd.com/document/454422848/Pentagon-Influenza-Response.

Koopmans, M., et al. "Chimerism in Kidneys, Livers and Hearts of Normal Women: Implications for Transplantation Studies." *American Journal of Transplantation* 5 (2005) 1495–1502.

Kreeft, Peter. "Human Personhood Begins at Conception." *Medical Ethics Policy Monograph*. Virginia: Castello Institute of Stafford, 1997.

Kreider, Alan. *The Patient Ferment of the Early Church*. Grand Rapids: Baker, 2016.

Kristian, Bonnie. "Study: Federal Student Loans Increase Tuition, Not Enrollment." *The Week*, July 7, 2015.

Kruesi, Kimberlee. "Punishing Women with the Death Penalty Would Cut Abortions, Idaho Candidate Says." *Associated Press*, April 3, 2018.

Krugman, Paul. "Health Care Realities." *New York Times*, July 30, 2019.

Kruse, Kevin. "Christian America Is an Invention: Big Business, Right-Wing Politics and the Religious Lie That Still Divides Us." *Salon*, April 19, 2015.

———. *One Nation under God: How Corporate American Invented Christian America*. New York: Basic, 2015.

Kumar, Anugrah. "Are Most Single Christians in America Having Sex?" *Christian Post*, September 28, 2011.

Kurtin, Danna, et al. "Demographic Risk Factors Associated with Elevated Lead Levels in Texas Children Covered by Medicaid." *Environmental Health Perspectives* 105.1 (1997) 66–68.

Kurtzleben, Danielle. "White High School Dropouts Are Wealthier Than Black or Latino College Graduates." *Vox*, September 24, 2014.

Lactantius. *Divine Institutes*. Translated by William Fletcher. In Ante-Nicene Fathers, edited by Alexander Roberts et al., 7:12–590 Buffalo, NY: Christian Literature, 1886.

Ladd, Chris. "Pastors, Not Politicians, Turned Dixie Republican." *Forbes*, March 27, 2027.

———. "Unspeakable Realities Block Universal Health Coverage in America." *Forbes*, March 13, 2017.

Lamis, Alexander P. *Southern Politics in the 1990s*. Baton Rouge: Louisiana State University Press, 1999.

Larsen, Jonathan. "At the Head of the National Prayer Breakfast, a GOP Megadonor." *The Young Turks*, February 5, 2019.

Lascaratos, John, and Effie Poulakou-Rebelakou. "Child Sexual Abuse: Historical Cases in the Byzantine Empire (324–1453 A.D.)" *Child Abuse and Neglect* 24 (2000) 1085–90.

Lawson, Kimberly. "Men Legally Allowed to Finish Sex Even If Woman Revokes Consent, NC Law States." *Vice*, June 22, 2017.

Ledbetter, Rosanna. *History of the Malthusian League, 1877–1927*. Columbus: Ohio State University Press, 1976.

Lederer, Laura. "Examining H.R. 5411, the Trafficking Awareness Training for Health Care Act of 2014." U.S. House of Representatives, Energy and Commerce Committee, Witness Hearings, September 11, 2014.
Lederer, Laura, and Christopher A. Wetzel. "The Health Consequences of Sex Trafficking and Their Implications for Identifying Victims in Healthcare Facilities." *Annals Health* 23 (2014) 61.
Lee, Felicia R. "Doctors Who Performed Abortions." *New York Times*, October 4, 2003.
Lee, Susan J., et al. "Fetal Pain: A Systematic Multidisciplinary Review of the Evidence." *Journal of the American Medical Association* 294 (2005) 947–54.
LeMay, Michael C., ed. *Transforming America: Perspectives on U.S. Immigration*. Santa Barbara: Praeger, 2013.
Leo XIII, Pope. *Rerum Novarum*. Vatican, 1891.
Leonard, Ira M. "The Rise and Fall of the American Republican Party in New York City, 1843–1845." *New York Historical Society Quarterly* 50 (1966) 151–92.
Lepore, Jill. "Birthright." *The New Yorker*, November 14, 2011.
Levatino, Anthony. "Planned Parenthood Exposed: Examining Abortion Procedures and Medical Ethics at the Nation's Largest Abortion Provider." Testimony of Anthony Levatino, MD, JD before the Committee on the Judiciary, U.S. House of Representatives. October 8, 2015.
Levey, Noam N. "Hospitals Say Feds Are Seizing Masks and Other Coronavirus Supplies Without a Word." *Los Angeles Times*, April 7, 2020.
Levin, Matt. "Data Dig: Are Foreign Investors Driving Up Real Estate in Your California Neighborhood?" *CALMatters*, March 7, 2018.
Levine, Robert S., et al. "Racial Inequalities in Mortality from Coronavirus: The Tip of the Iceberg." *Journal of American Medicine* 9343 (2020) 30412–15.
Levitan, Dave. "Does a Fetus Feel Pain at 20 Weeks?" *FactCheck*, May 18, 2015. https://www.factcheck.org/2015/05/does-a-fetus-feel-pain-at-20-weeks/.
Lewis, Jone Johnson. "Biography of Empress Theodora, Byzantine Feminist." *ThoughtCo*, July 22, 2019.
Lewis, Robert. "World War II Manufacturing and the Postwar Southern Economy." *Journal of Southern History* (November 2007).
Li, De-Kun, et al. "Exposure to Non-Steroidal Anti-Inflammatory Drugs during Pregnancy and Risk of Miscarriage: Population Based Cohort Study." *British Medical Journal* 327 (2003) 368.
———. "Use of Nonsteroidal Antiinflammatory Drugs during Pregnancy and the Risk of Miscarriage." *American Journal of Obstetrics and Gynecology* 219 (2018) 275. e1–275.e8.
Liptak, Adam. "Supreme Court Strikes Down Texas Abortion Restrictions." *New York Times*, June 27, 2016.
Llana, Sara Miller. "In Europe, It Is Both Easier and Harder to Get an Abortion Than in US." *Christian Science Monitor*, May 24, 2018.
Locke, John. *Second Treatise of Civil Government*. Mineola, NY: Dover, 2002.
Lopez, Ashley. "For Supporters of Abortion Access, Troubling Trends in Texas." *NPR*, November 18, 2019.
Lucca, David O., et al. "Credit Supply and the Rise in College Tuition: Evidence from the Expansion in Federal Student Aid Programs." *Federal Reserve Bank of New York Staff Reports*, July 2015.
Luhby, Tami. "US Black-White Inequality in 6 Stark Charts." *CNN*, June 3, 2020.

Lupo, Philip J., et al. "Maternal Exposure to Ambient Levels of Benzene and Neural Tube Defects among Offspring: Texas, 1999–2004." *Environmental Health Perspectives* 119 (2011) 397–402.

Luthi, Susanna. "Trump Rejects Obamacare Special Enrollment Period amid Pandemic." *Politico*, March 31, 2020.

Mabus, Ray. "Moral Failure: The Incredible Cruelty of Refusing to Expand Medicaid." *Jackson Free Press*, April 23, 2020.

MacDonald, Dennis R. "Alexandria and Allegory." Bible Odyssey. https://www.bibleodyssey.org/places/related-articles/alexandria-and-allegory.

———. *Christianizing Homer: The Odyssey, Plato, and the Acts of Andrew*. Oxford: Oxford University Press, 1994.

MacDonald, Park. "A New Conservative Theory of Why America Is So Polarized." *New York Magazine*, January 21, 2020.

MacGillis, Alec. "How Germany Saved Its Workforce from Unemployment While Spending Less Per Person Than the U.S." *ProPublica*, June 3, 2020.

Mackay, Robert. "Trump Lies about Cutting White House Pandemic Team to Dodge (Checks Notes) Fox News." *The Intercept*, April 1, 2020.

Maddow, Rachel. "Barr Record of Deception for Bush Calls Credibility into Question." *The Rachel Maddow Show*, April 16, 2019.

Madrick, Jeff. "Innovation: The Government Was Crucial after All." *New York Review of Books*, April 24, 2014.

Maizes, Rachel. "Limited Liability Companies—A Critique." *St. John's Law Review* 70.3 (1996) 575–608.

Malter, Jordan. "Thank the Government for Your iPhone." *CNN*, October 24, 2013.

Mancini, Jeanne. "People with Down Syndrome Are Happy. Why Are We Trying to Eliminate Them?" *Washington Post*, August 24, 2017.

Mapping Prejudice. https://www.mappingprejudice.org/.

Maqbool, Aleem. "Colorado Birth Control Scheme Causes Drop in Teen Pregnancy." *BBC News*, August 11, 2014.

Marcus, Ruth. "I Would've Aborted a Fetus with Down Syndrome. Women Need That Right." *Washington Post*, March 9, 2018.

Marsden, George M. *Fundamentalism and American Culture*. 2nd ed. Oxford: Oxford University Press, 2006

Marsh, Frank H. "Prenatal Screening and 'Wrongful Life': Medicine's New 'Catch-22'?" *American Journal of Obstetrics and Gynecology* 143 (1982) 745–48.

Martin, Joyce A., and Michelle J. K. Osterman. "Describing the Increase in Preterm Births in the United States, 2014–2016." National Center for Health Statistics 312, June 2018.

Martin, Nina. "North Dakota Abortion Amendment Fails." *ProPublica*, November 5, 2014.

Martin, William. *With God on Our Side: The Rise of the Religious Right in America*. New York: Broadway, 1996.

Martinez, Marina Trahan, and Manny Fernandez. "Trial Opens for Former Officer Who Killed Unarmed Black Man in His Apartment." *New York Times*, September 23, 2019.

Massey, Douglas S. *American Apartheid: Segregation and the Making of the Underclass*. Cambridge: Harvard University Press, 1993.

Mattera, Philip. "The Buck Doesn't Stop Here: The Spread of Limited Liability Companies." *Corporate Research Project*, September 2002.

Matzarioti-Kostara, Sofia. "The Theology of Gender—7. The Place of Women in Byzantine Society." *Pemptousia*, April 3, 2017. https://pemptousia.com/2017/04/the-theology-of-gender-7-the-place-of-women-in-byzantine-society.

Mavrelos, D., et al. "Efficacy and Safety of a Clinical Protocol for Expectant Management of Selected Women Diagnosed with a Tubal Ectopic Pregnancy." *Ultrasound in Obstetrics and Gynecology* 42 (2013) 102–7.

Mayer, Jane. "Covert Operations." *The New Yorker*, August 23, 2010.

McCoy, James. "The Mind of a Catholic Moralist?" *Catholic World News*, March 6, 2002. https://www.catholicculture.org/news/features/index.cfm?recnum=21206.

McCrummen, Stephanie, and David A. Fahrenthold. "Akin's Congressional Legacy Small, but His Support among Christian Groups Is Big." *Washington Post*, August 22, 2012.

McGuire, Danielle L. *At the Dark End of the Street: Black Women, Rape, and Resistance —A New History of the Civil Rights Movement from Rosa Parks to the Rise of Black Power*. New York: Vintage, 2010.

McNamee, Stephen. *The Meritocracy Myth*. Lanhan: Rowman & Littlefield, 2018.

McNeil, Donald G., Jr. "U.S. Lags in Global Measure of Premature Births." *New York Times*, May 2, 2012.

McWilliams, David. "Quantitative Easing was the Father of Millennial Socialism." *Financial Times*, March 1, 2019.

Mekhilta de-Rabbi Ishmael. Translated by Jacob Z. Lauterbach and David Stern. JPS Classic Reissues. Philadelphia: JPS, 2010. muse.jhu.edu/book/1690.

Meredith, Anthony. *The Cappadocians*. Crestwood: St. Vladimir's Seminary Press, 1995.

Merritt, Jonathan. "Stop Calling Hobby Lobby a Christian Business." *The Week*, June 17, 2014.

Merritt, Keri Leigh. *Masterless Men: Poor Whites and Slavery in the Antebellum South*. Cambridge: Cambridge University Press, 2017.

Messer, Ellen, and Kathryn E. May. *Back Rooms: Voices from the Illegal Abortion Era*. New York: St. Martin's: 1988.

Mettler, Suzanne. *The Submerged State: How Invisible Government Policies Undermine American Democracy*. Chicago: University of Chicago Press, 2011.

Miller, Patricia G. *The Worst of Times*. New York: Harper Collins, 1993.

Miller, Randall M., et al., eds. *Religion and the American Civil War*. New York: Oxford University Press, 1998.

Miller, Timothy S. *The Birth of the Hospital in the Byzantine Empire*. Baltimore: Johns Hopkins University Press, 1997.

Miller, Tom. "Kill the Tax Exclusion for Health Insurance." *National Review*, August 19, 2014.

Mills, Paul, and Michael Schluter. *After Capitalism: Rethinking Economic Relationships*. London: Jubilee Centre, 2012.

Millward, Jessica. "Wombs of Liberation: Petitions, Law, and the Black Woman's Body in Maryland, 1780–1858." In *Sexuality and Slavery: Reclaiming Intimate Histories in the Americas*, edited by Daina Ramey Berry and Leslie M. Harris, 88–108. Athens: University of Georgia Press, 2018.

Minucius Felix, Marcus. *Octavius*. Translated by Robert Ernest Wallis. In Ante-Nicene Fathers, edited by Alexander Roberts et al., 4:399–460. Buffalo, NY: Christian Literature, 1885.

Mitchell, Brian Patrick. "Byzantine Empire—Or Republic?" *The American Conservative*, August 7, 2015.

Mitchell, Colter, et al. "Social Disadvantage, Genetic Sensitivity, and Children's Telomere Length." *Proceedings of the National Academy of Sciences*, April 7, 2014.

Miura, Nagamitsu. *John Locke and the Native Americans: Early English Liberalism and Its Colonial Reality*. Newcastle upon Tyne: Cambridge Scholars, 2013.

Mock, Brentin. "What New Research Says about Race and Police Shootings." *City Lab*, August 6, 2019.

Mohr, James C. *Abortion in America: The Origins and Evolution of National Policy*. Oxford: Oxford University Press, 1978.

Molynn, Mark. *It Didn't Start with You: How Inherited Family Trauma Shapes Who We Are and How to End the Cycle*. New York: Viking, 2016.

Mora, Marie T., and Alberto Dávila. "The Hispanic–White Wage Gap Has Remained Wide and Relatively Steady." *Economic Policy Institute*, July 2, 2018.

Morgan, Edmund S. *American Slavery, American Freedom: The Ordeal of Colonial Virginia*. New York: W. W. Norton, 1975.

Morrison, Tim. "No, the White House Didn't 'Dissolve' Its Pandemic Response Office. I Was There." *Washington Post*, March 16, 2020.

Munoz, Ana Patricia, et al. "The Color of Wealth in Boston." *Federal Reserve Bank of Boston*, March 25, 2015.

Murphy, Erin E. "DNA at the Fringes: Twins, Chimerism, and Synthetic DNA." *Daily Beast*, October 7, 2015.

Nagasawa, Mako A. "Slavery in Christianity, Part 1: Slavery in the Bible, Slavery Today." *Anastásis Center*, October 23, 2018.

———. "Slavery in Christianity, Part 2: Abolitionism from the First to Fifteenth Centuries." *Anastásis Center*, May 6, 2016.

Nakhai-Pour, Hamid Reza, et al. "Use of Nonaspirin Nonsteroidal Anti-Inflammatory Drugs During Pregnancy and the Risk of Spontaneous Abortion." *Canadian Medical Association Journal* 183 (2011) 1713–20.

Nanasi, Natalie. "The Trump Administration Quietly Changed the Definition of Domestic Violence and We Have No Idea What For." *Slate*, January 21, 2019.

Nasaina, Marina. "Woman's Position in Byzantine Society." *Open Journal for Studies in History* 1 (2018) 29–38.

Nash, Elizabeth, et al. "State Policy Trends 2019: A Wave of Abortion Bans, but Some States Are Fighting Back." Guttmacher Institute, December 10, 2019.

"National Crime Victimization Survey, 2010–2016." U.S. Department of Justice, 2017.

"National Youth Risk Behavior Survey: Trends in the Prevalence of Sexual Behaviors and HIV Testing: National YRBS 1991–2015." 2015. https://www.cdc.gov/healthyyouth/data/yrbs/pdf/trends/2015_us_sexual_trend_yrbs.pdf.

Natoli, Jaime L., et al. "Prenatal Diagnosis of Down Syndrome: A Systematic Review of Termination Rates (1995–2011)." *Prenatal Diagnosis*, March 14, 2012.

Nazworth, Napp. "Critics Say White House Catholic Birth Control Numbers Are Faulty." *Christian Post*, February 15, 2012.

Nelson, Anne. *Shadow Network: Media, Money, and the Secret Hub of the Radical Right*. New York: Bloomsbury, 2019.

Nesbit, Jeff. *Poison Tea: How Big Oil and Big Tobacco Invented the Tea Party and Captured the GOP*. New York: St. Martin's, 2016.

———. "The Secret Origins of the Tea Party: How Big Oil and Big Tobacco Partnered with the Koch Brothers to Take Over the GOP." *Time*, April 5, 2016.

New, Michael J. "Obamacare Not Responsible for U.S. Abortion Decline." *Catholic Vote*, January 3, 2017.

Newkirk, Vann R., II. "The Great Land Robbery." *The Atlantic*, September 2019.

Nicoll, Rachel. "Environmental Contaminants and Congenital Heart Defects: A Re-Evaluation of the Evidence." *International Journal of Environmental Research and Public Health* 15 (2018) 2096.

Nielsen, G. L., et al. "Risk of Adverse Birth Outcome and Miscarriage in Pregnant Users of Non-Steroidal Anti-Inflammatory Drugs: Population Based Observational Study and Case-Control Study." *British Medical Journal* 322 (2001) 266–70.

Nirappil, Fenit, et al. "With Focus on Testing, Maryland Buys 500,000 Coronavirus Test Kits from South Korea." *Washington Post*, April 20, 2020.

Noll, Mark A. *America's God: From Jonathan Edwards to Abraham Lincoln*. Oxford: Oxford University Press, 2002.

———. *The Civil War as a Theological Crisis*. Chapel Hill: University of North Carolina Press, 2006.

Noll, Mark A., et al. *The Search for a Christian America*. Colorado Spring: Helmers & Howard, 1983.

Noonan, John T. *Contraception: A History of Its Treatment by the Catholic Theologians and Canonists*. 2nd ed. Cambridge: Harvard University Press, 1986.

Norris, Louise. "Do ACA-Compliant Health Insurance Plans Cover Abortion?" HealthInsurance.org, January 30, 2020. https://www.healthinsurance.org/faqs/do-health-insurance-plans-in-acas-exchanges-cover-abortion/.

North, Anna. "Plenty of Conservatives Really Do Believe Women Should Be Executed for Having Abortions." *The Atlantic*, April 5, 2018.

O'Connell, T. J. "Abortion II (Moral Aspect)." In *New Catholic Encyclopedia*, 1:28–29. Washington, DC: McGraw Hill, 1967.

O'Donovan, Oliver M. T. *The Desire of the Nations: Rediscovering the Roots of Political Theology*. Cambridge: Cambridge University Press, 1996.

———. *Resurrection and Moral Order: An Outline for Evangelical Ethics*. 2nd ed. Grand Rapids: Eerdmans, 1994.

Olasky, Marvin. *Abortion Rites: A Social History of Abortion in America*. Wheaton: Crossway, 1992.

Olick, Diana. "Foreigners Snap Up Record Number of US Homes." *CNBC*, July 18, 2017.

Olson, Samantha. "Nearby Pesticides Increase Autism Risk in Mothers' Unborn Children by More Than 60%." *Medical Daily*, June 23, 2014.

———. "Pregnant Mothers: Exposure to These 2 Plastics, Found in Cosmetics and Nail Polish, Increases a Child's Asthma Risk up to 78%." *Medical Daily*, September 17, 2014.

Omondi, Sharon. "US States by Evangelical Protestant Population." *World Atlas*, March 21, 2019. https://www.worldatlas.com/articles/us-states-by-evangelical-protestant-population.html.

"One Untrue Thing." *National Review*, August 1, 2007.

Origen of Alexandria. *Song of Songs: The Commentary and Homilies*. Translated by R. P. Lawson. Westminster, Maryland: Newman, 1957.

Ortiz, Erik. "North Carolina Legal Loophole Prevents Women from Withdrawing Consent to Sex." *NBC News*, June 23, 2017.

Otis, Leah Lydia. *Prostitution in Medieval Society: The History of an Urban Institution in Languedoc*. Chicago: University of Chicago Press, 1985.

"An Overview of Consent to Reproductive Health Services by Young People." Guttmacher Institute, April 1, 2020.

Pabst, Emma, and Luke Metzger. "Illegal Air Pollution in Texas: Air Pollution from Startups, Shutdowns, Malfunctions and Maintenance at Industrial Facilities in Texas in 2018." Environment Texas Research and Policy Center, December 18, 2019.

Packer, Herbert L. *The Limits of the Criminal Sanction*. Stanford: Stanford University Press, 1968.

Padula, Amy, et al. "The Association of Ambient Air Pollution and Traffic Exposures with Selected Congenital Anomalies in the San Joaquin Valley of California." *American Journal of Epidemiology* 117 (2013) 1074–85.

Palmer, Anna, and Tarini Parti. "Akin Un-Apologizes." *Politico*, July 10, 2014.

Paltrow, Lynn, and Jeanne Flavin. "Arrests of and Forced Interventions on Pregnant Women in the United States (1973–2005): The Implications for Women's Legal Status and Public Health." *Journal of Health Politics, Policy and Law*, January 25, 2013.

Panetta, Grace. "The Trump Administration Ran a Simulation for a Virus Last Year That Revealed Many of the Failures Now Happening with the Coronavirus." *Business Insider*, March 19, 2020.

Papanikolaou, Athanasios D. "The Allegorical Exegetical Method of Origen." *Theologia* 2 (1974) 347–59.

Parazzini, F., et al. "Induced Abortions and Risk of Ectopic Pregnancy." *Human Reproduction* 10 (1995) 1841–44.

Parramore, Lynn Stuart. "What the Steve Jobs Movie Won't Tell You about Apple's Success." *TruthOut*, October 30, 2015.

Paul VI, Pope. *Humanae Vitae*. Vatican, 1968.

Paul, Maureen, et al. *Management of Unintended and Abnormal Pregnancy: Comprehensive Abortion Care*. Oxford: John Wiley & Sons, 2009.

Paul, Rand. "Government Should Get Out of the Marriage Business Altogether." *Time*, June 28, 2015.

Pearce, Matt. "U.S. Rep. Paul Broun: Evolution a Lie 'From the Pit of Hell.'" *Los Angeles Times*, October 7, 2012.

Peck, Rebecca, et al. "Does Levonorgestrel Emergency Contraceptive Have a Post-Fertilization Effect? A Review of Its Mechanism of Action." *The Linacre Quarterly: Catholic Medical Association*, February 1, 2016.

Peel, J., and M. Potts. *Textbook of Contraceptive Practice*. New York: Cambridge University Press, 1968.

Peoplefor. "Paul Weyrich—'I don't want everybody to vote' (Goo Goo)." *YouTube*, June 11, 2007. https://www.youtube.com/watch?v=8GBAsFwPglw.

Pereto, Alison. "Patients over 60? Screen for STIs." *AthenaHealth*, May 16, 2018. https://www.athenahealth.com/knowledge-hub/clinical-trends/over-60-stis-may-not-be-done-you.

Perlberg, Steven. "Texas GOP Promotes Abstinence-Only Education." *Think Progress*, June 26, 2012.

Perlstein, Rick. "Exclusive: Lee Atwater's Infamous 1981 Interview on the Southern Strategy." *The Nation*, November 13, 2012.

"Perpetrators of Sexual Violence: Statistics." https://rainn.org/statistics/perpetrators-sexual-violence.

Perrone, Lorenzo. "'The Bride at the Crossroads': Origen's Dramatic Interpretation of the Song of Songs." *Ephemerides Theologicae Lovanienses: Louvain Journal of Theology and Canon Law* 82.1 (April 2006) 69–102.

"The Personhood Movement." *ProPublica*, date unknown.

Petchesky, Rosalind Pollack. *Abortion and Woman's Choice: The State, Sexuality, and Reproductive Freedom*. Boston: Northeastern University Press, 1990.

Phillips, Kevin. *American Theocracy: The Peril and Politics of Radical Religion, Oil, and Borrowed Money in the 21st Century*. New York: Penguin, 2006.

Phillips, Tom. "'Satan, Be Gone!': Bolivian Christians Claim Credit for Ousting Evo Morales." *The Guardian*, January 27, 2020.

Philo of Alexandria. "On the Contemplative Life." In *Philo: Volume IX*, translated by F. H. Colson, 104–71. Loeb Classical Library. Cambridge, MA: Harvard University Press, 1954.

———. "On the Contemplative Life." In *The Works of Philo Judaeus*, translated by C. D. Yonge, 698–706. Peabody, MA: Hendrickson, 1993.

———. "On Special Laws." In *The Works of Philo Judaeus*, translated by C. D. Yonge, 534–639. Peabody, MA: Hendrickson, 1993.

Piaggio, Gilda, et al. "Combined Estimates of Effectiveness of Mifepristone 10 mg in Emergency Contraception." *Contraception* 68 (2003) 439–46.

Pianigiani, Gaia. "On Paper, Italy Allows Abortions, but Few Doctors Will Perform Them." *New York Times*, January 16, 2016.

Pickrell, Ryan. "Maryland Called in National Guard Troops to Defend Coronavirus Tests from South Korea Against Seizure." *Business Insider*, April 30, 2020.

Pilkington, Ed. "Hookworm, a Disease of Extreme Poverty, Is Thriving in the US South. Why?" *The Guardian*, September 5, 2017.

———. "Indiana Prosecuting Chinese Woman for Suicide Attempt That Killed Her Foetus." *The Guardian*, May 30, 2012.

Pius XI, Pope. *Casti Connubi*. Vatican, 1930.

———. *Quadragesimo Anno*. Vatican, 1931.

"Plan B Label Information." U.S. Food and Drug Administration, August 24, 2006. https://web.archive.org/web/20070124182515/https://www.fda.gov/cder/foi/label/2006/021045s011lbl.pdf.

Plato. *Republic*. Translated by Benjamin Jowett. New York: Vintage, 1991.

Polgar, S., and E. S. Fried. "The Bad Old Days: Clandestine Abortions among the Poor in New York City before Liberalization of the Abortion Law." *Family Planning Perspectives* 8 (1976) 125–27.

Pollitt, Katha. "Abortion in American History." *The Atlantic*, May 1997.

Posner, Eric. "The U.S. Constitution Is Impossible to Amend." *Slate*, May 5, 2014.

Poulakou-Rebelakou, Effie, et al. "Abortions in Byzantine Times (325–1453 AD)." *Vesalius* 2.1 (1996) 19–25.

"Power and Authority in Eastern Christian Experience: Papers of the Sophia Institute Academic Conference New York, December 2010." N.p.: Theotokos Press, 2011. https://academiccommons.columbia.edu/doi/10.7916/D86T0W0X.

Pracher, Maria. "The Marital Rape Exception." *New York University Law Review* 52 (1977) 306–23.

"Pregnancy and Chorionic Villus Sampling." *WebMD*. https://www.webmd.com/baby/chorionic-villus-sampling#1.

Qian, J., et al. "Impacts of Caffeine during Pregnancy." *Trends in Endocrinology and Metabolism* 31 (2020) 218–27.

Quiggin, John. "John Locke against Freedom." *Jacobin Magazine*, June 28, 2015.

Qur'an. Translated by Marmaduke Pickthall. New York: Dorset, 1983.

Radde-Gallwitz, Andrew. *The Cambridge Edition of Early Christian Writings*. Volume 2: "Practice." Edited by Ellen Muehlberger. Cambridge: Cambridge University Press, 2017.

Radley, David C., et al. "Aiming Higher: Results from a Scorecard on State Health System Performance, 2014." *The Commonwealth Fund*, April 30, 2014.

Rampell, Catherine. "Why the White Working Class Votes against Itself." *Washington Post*, December 22, 2016.

Rapoza, Kenneth. "These Are the Foreigners Buying Up American Real Estate." *Forbes*, July 10, 2014.

Rasmussen, Adam. "'A Vessel Divinely Molded': Basil of Caesarea on the Human Body." *North American Patristics Society*, May 25–27, 2017. https://hcommons.org/deposits/item/hc:19091/.

Raz, Raanan, et al. "Autism Spectrum Disorder and Particulate Matter Air Pollution before, during, and after Pregnancy: A Nested Case–Control Analysis within the Nurses' Health Study II Cohort." *Environmental Health Perspectives* 123 (2015) 264–70.

"Reactions to the Supreme Court Ruling on Texas' Abortion Law." *New York Times*, June 27, 2016.

Reagan, Leslie J. "When Abortion Was a Crime: Women, Medicine, and Law in the United States, 1867–1973." *The Atlantic*, May 1997.

———. *When Abortion Was a Crime: Women, Medicine, and Law in the United States, 1867–1973*. Berkeley: University Press, 1998.

"A Real-Time Look at the Impact of the Recession on Women's Family Planning and Pregnancy Decisions." Guttmacher Institute, 2009.

Ren, Sheng, et al. "Periconception Exposure to Air Pollution and Risk of Congenital Malformations." *Journal of Pediatrics* 193 (2018) 76–84.E6.

Rennie, Daniel. "How a Groundbreaking Drug Birthed a Generation of Thalidomide Babies." All That's Interesting, October 30, 2019.

Reno, R. R. "Say 'No' to Death's Dominion." *First Things*, March 23, 2020.

"Research Brief: Texas Women's Experiences Attempting Self-Induced Abortion in the Face of Dwindling Options." *Texas Policy Evaluation Project*, November 17, 2015.

Rettner, Rachael. "3 Human Chimeras That Already Exist." *Scientific American*, August 8, 2016.

Reynolds, Andrew. "North Carolina Is No Longer Classified as a Democracy." *Charlotte Observer*, December 22, 2016.

Richardson, Heather Cox. *How the South Won the Civil War: Oligarchy, Democracy, and the Continuing Fight for the Soul of America*. Oxford: Oxford University, 2020.

Richman, Sheldon. "Love, Marriage, and the State." *The American Conservative*, November 25, 2016.

Rios, Edwin. "A DeVos-Linked Group Promoted the Right-Wing 'Operation Gridlock' Tantrum in Michigan." *Mother Jones*, April 17, 2020.

Rivas, Anthony. "Air Pollution and Autism: Moms' Exposure to Fine Particulate Matter During Pregnancy Ups Risk in Kids." *Medical Daily*, December 18, 2014.
Rivkin, David B., Jr., and Charles Stimson. "A Constitutional Guide to Emergency Powers." *Wall Street Journal*, March 19, 2020.
Roberts, Dorothy. *Killing the Black Body: Race, Reproduction, and the Meaning of Liberty*. New York: Pantheon, 1997.
Robbins, Rebecca. "Churches Step In with Alternative to High-Interest, Small-Dollar Lending Industry." *Washington Post*, January 9, 2015.
Rocca, Corinne H., et al. "Women's Emotions One Week after Receiving or Being Denied an Abortion in the United States." *Perspectives on Sexual and Reproductive Health* 45 (2013) 119–75.
Roccasalvo, Sr. Joan L. "Dr. Anthony S. Fauci: A Man for Others, a Universal Treasure." *Catholic News Agency*, August 20, 2014.
Rochat, Roger W., et al. "An Epidemiological Analysis of Abortion in Georgia." *American Journal of Public Health* 61 (1971) 543–52.
Rodman, Hyman, et al. *The Abortion Question*. New York: Columbia University Press, 1987.
Rodrigo, Chris Mills. "Amazon VP Resigns after Firings of Activist Workers." *The Hill*, May 4, 2020.
"Roll Call Vote 113th Congress—1st Session." U.S. Senate, February 12, 2013. https://www.senate.gov/legislative/LIS/roll_call_lists/roll_call_vote_cfm.cfm?congress=113&session=1&vote=00019.
Rosen, Harold. "The Emotionally Sick Pregnant Patient: Psychiatric Indications and Contraindications to the Interruption of Pregnancy." In *Abortion in America: Medical, Psychiatric, Legal, Anthropological, and Religious Considerations*, edited by Harold Rosen, 219–243. Boston: Beacon: 1967.
Rosenberg, Gabe. "Ohio GOP Introduces Bill to Ban Abortion." *NPR*, March 20, 2018.
Rosenberg, Nathan, and L. E. Birdzell, Jr. *How the West Grew Rich: The Economic Transformation of the Industrial World*. New York: Basic, 1986.
Rosenblatt, Kalhan. "'Stealthing': Victims Describe Partners Removing Condoms During Sex without Consent." *NBC News*, April 29, 2017.
Rosenthal, Elisabeth. "Legal or Not, Abortion Rates Compare." *New York Times*, October 12, 2007.
Rothstein, Richard. *The Color of Law: A Forgotten History of How Our Government Segregated America*. New York: W. W. Norton, 2017.
Rovner, Julie. "Clash over Abortion Stalls Health Bill, Again." *NPR*, March 21, 2018.
———. "'Personhood' Divides Anti-Abortion Groups." *NPR*, November 9, 2011.
Rowe, Jeff. "Review: 'The Age of Entitlement' Is a Fascinating Read." *Washington Times*, January 24, 2020.
"The Rural Health Safety Net under Pressure: Rural Hospital Vulnerability." Chartis Center for Rural Health, February 2020.
Ryan, John A. *Alleged Socialism of the Church Fathers*. London: Forgotten Books, 2017.
Ryerson, A. J. "Medical Advice on Child Rearing, 1550–1990." *Harvard Educational Review* 31.302 (1961) 302–23.
"S. 47 (113th): Violence Against Women Reauthorization Act of 2013." U.S. Congress, February 28, 2013. https://www.govtrack.us/congress/votes/113-2013/h55.

"The Safety and Quality of Abortion Care in the United States." National Academies of Science, Engineering, and Medicine, 2018. https://www.nap.edu/catalog/24950/the-safety-and-quality-of-abortion-care-in-the-united-states.

Sagiv, Sharon K., et al. "Prenatal Organophosphate Pesticide Exposure and Traits Related to Autism Spectrum Disorders in a Population Living in Proximity to Agriculture." *Environmental Health Perspectives* 126 (2018) n.p.

Sailhamer, John H. *The Meaning of the Pentateuch: Revelation, Composition and Interpretation*. Downers Grove: InterVarsity, 2009.

———. *The Pentateuch as Narrative: A Biblical-Theological Commentary*. Grand Rapids: Zondervan, 1992.

"Saint Hippolytus of Rome." *Encyclopaedia Britannica*, July 20, 1998. https://www.britannica.com/biography/Saint-Hippolytus-of-Rome.

Sanders, Linly. "When Does Life Begin? Pregnant Woman's Unborn Child Counted Among 26 Killed in Texas Shooting." *Newsweek*, November 8, 2017.

Sanger, David E., et al. "Before Virus Outbreak, a Cascade of Warnings Went Unheeded." *New York Times*, March 19, 2020.

Schaeffer, Frank. *Crazy for God: How I Grew Up as One of the Elect, Helped Found the Religious Right, and Lived to Take It All (or Almost All) of It Back*. Boston: Da Capo, 2008.

Schoen, Johanna. "Reconceiving Abortion: Medical Practice, Women's Access, and Feminist Politics before and after *Roe v. Wade*." *Feminist Studies* 26 (2000) 349–76.

Scott, Dylan. "1 in 4 Rural Hospitals Is Vulnerable to Closure, a New Report Finds." *Vox*, February 18, 2020.

"Scott Peterson Fast Trial Facts." *CNN*, April 20, 2020.

Scouteris, Constantine. "The Therapeutae of Philo and the Monks." *Orthodox Research Institute*. http://www.orthodoxresearchinstitute.org/articles/patrology/scouteris_theraputae.htm.

Sedgh, Gilda, et al. "Induced Abortion: Estimated Rates and Trends Worldwide." *The Lancet* 370 (2007) 1338–45.

Servick, Kelly. "Embryo Experiments Take 'Baby Steps' Toward Growing Human Organs in Livestock." *Science Magazine*, June 26, 2019.

Serwer, Adam. "The Illiberal Right Throws a Tantrum." *The Atlantic*, June 14, 2019.

"Sexual Assault of Young Children as Reported to Law Enforcement." U.S. Department of Justice, 2000.

Shedlock, Mike. "Ben Bernanke—The Father of Extreme US Socialism." *FX Street*, March 4, 2019.

Sheets, Kayla. "Chimerism Explained: How One Person Can Unknowingly Have Two Sets of DNA." *National Society of Genetic Counselors*, January 22, 2019.

Shelton, Janie F., et al. "Neurodevelopmental Disorders and Prenatal Residential Proximity to Agricultural Pesticides: The CHARGE Study." *Environmental Health Perspectives* 122 (2014) 1103–9.

Shettles, L. "Tubal Embryo Successfully Transplanted in Utero." *American Journal of Obstetrics and Gynecology* 163 (1990) 20–26. http://www.ajog.org/article/0002-9378%2890%2990794-8/pdf.

Shin, Laura. "The Racial Wealth Gap: Why a Typical White Household Has 16 Times the Wealth of a Black One." *Forbes*, March 26, 2015.

Signorello, Lisa B., and Joseph K. McLaughlin. "Caffeine and Miscarriage: Case Closed?" *American Journal of Obstetrics and Gynecology* 199 (2018) E14–5.

Silver, Christopher. "The Racial Origins of Zoning in American Cities." In *Urban Planning and the African American Community: In the Shadows*, edited by Manning Thomas et al., 23–42. Thousand Oaks, CA: Sage, 1997.

Simermann, John. "DNA Evidence from Aborted Fetus Is Key to Aggravated Rape Conviction in New Orleans." *Times-Picayune*, August 12, 2011.

Simpson, W. J. Sparrow. *Roman Catholic Opposition to Papal Infallibility*. London: John Murray, 1909.

Sims, Shannon. "Here's How Jair Bolsonaro Wants to Transform Brazil." *The Atlantic*, January 12, 2019.

Sinclair, Upton. *The Cry for Justice: An Anthology of the Literature of Social Protest*. N.p.: Andesite, 2015.

Singer, Peter L. "Federally Supported Innovations: 22 Examples of Major Technology Advances That Stem from Federal Support." *Information Technology and Innovation Foundation*, February 2014.

Skarnulis, Leanne. "Toxins and Pregnancy." *WebMD*, October 1, 2018. https://www.webmd.com/baby/features/pregnancy-and-toxins#1.

Smith, Evan. "An Hour with Rick Perry." *Texas Tribune*, October 18, 2010.

Smith, Merril D. *Sex and Sexuality in Early America*. New York: New York University Press, 1998.

Smith, Noah. "How to Reduce the Black–White Wealth Gap." *Bloomberg*, April 23, 2018.

Smothers, Hannah. "What It Was Like to Perform Abortions before *Roe v. Wade*." *Cosmopolitan*, November 2, 2016.

Snyder, Ashley H., et al. "The Impact of the Affordable Care Act on Contraceptive Use and Costs among Privately Insured Women." *Women's Health Issues Policy Matters* 28 (2018) 219–23.

Snyder-Belousek, Darren W. *Atonement, Justice, and Peace: The Message of the Cross and the Mission of the Church*. Grand Rapids: Eerdmans, 2012.

Solomon, Richard. "Sexual Practice and Fantasy in Colonial America and the Early Republic." *Indiana University Journal of Undergraduate Research* 3 (2017) 26–36.

Sozomen. *Ecclesiastical History*. Translated by Edward Walford. London: Henry G. Bohn, 1855.

Spatig-Amerikaner, Ary. "Unequal Education: Federal Loophole Enables Lower Spending on Students of Color." *Center for American Progress*, August 2012.

Stahl, Jeremy. "DOJ: If Watergate Happened Today, We'd Block Evidence from Congress." *Slate*, October 8, 2019.

Stanger-Hall, Kathrin F., and David W. Hall. "Abstinence-Only Education and Teen Pregnancy Rates: Why We Need Comprehensive Sex Education in the U.S." *PLOS One* 6 (2011) e24658.

"State Education Budgets across the Country Are in Crisis. Here's Why." *WNYC Studios*, April 6, 2018.

"The State of the Gender Pay Gap: Executive Summary." https://www.payscale.com/data/gender-pay-gap.

Stephen, Mitchell. "Jews in Asia Minor (Antiquity)." In Encyclopaedia of the Hellenic World, December 12, 2002. http://asiaminor.ehw.gr/Forms/fLemmaBodyExtended.aspx?lemmaID=4150.

Stephens-Davidowitz, Seth. "The Return of the D.I.Y. Abortion." *New York Times*, March 5, 2016.

Stetzer, Ed. "Morning Roundup 11/5/12: Pro-Choice Evangelicals? President Obama's Faith. High Priests of Culture." *Christianity Today*, November 5, 2012.
Stewart, John W. "Higher Criticism." https://www.encyclopedia.com/philosophy-and-religion/christianity/protestant-christianity/higher-criticism.
Stoeltje, Melissa Fletcher. "Abortion Clinic Closes in Corpus Christi." *My San Antonio*, June 10, 2014. https://www.mysanantonio.com/news/local/article/Abortion-clinic-closes-in-Corpus-Christi-5543125.php.
Stoller, Matt. *Goliath: The 100-Year War Between Monopoly Power and Democracy*. New York: Simon & Schuster, 2019.
"The Story of American Poverty, as Told by One Alabama County." *PBS News Hour*, July 7, 2018.
Strain, Lisa, et al. "A True Hermaphrodite Chimera Resulting from Embryo Amalgamation after In Vitro Fertilization." *New England Journal of Medicine* 338 (1998) 166–69.
Stripling, Jack. "Trump's Liberty U. Commencement Speech Will Pair Anti-Establishment Brands." *Chronicle of Higher Education*, May 12, 2017.
Strode, Tom. "Payday Loans Targeted by ERLC, Others in Coalition." *Baptist Press*, May 15, 2015.
Stuart, Alfred W. "Overview of Religion in NC." Reprinted from Alfred W. Stuart, *The North Carolina Atlas Revisited*, 2010. NCpedia. https://www.ncpedia.org/religion/overview.
Stulberg, D. B., et al. "Ectopic Pregnancy Morbidity and Mortality in Low-Income Women, 2004–2008." *Human Reproduction* 31 (2016) 666–71.
Sullivan, Gail. "How Colorado's Teen Birthrate Dropped 40% in Four Years." *Washington Post*, August 12, 2014.
Sun, Lena H. "Bill Gates Calls on U.S. to Lead Fight against a Pandemic That Could Kill 33 Million." *Washington Post*, April 27, 2018.
———. "CDC to Cut by 80 Percent Efforts to Prevent Global Disease Outbreak." *Washington Post*, February 1, 2018.
———. "Top White House Official in Charge of Pandemic Response Exits Abruptly." *Washington Post*, May 10, 2018.
"Sweden's Prostitution Solution: Why Hasn't Anyone Tried This Before?" Women's Justice Center, 2005. http://justicewomen.com/cj_sweden.html.
Sydney, Homer, and Richard Sylla. *A History of Interest Rates*. 4th ed. Hoboken: John Wiley and Sons, 2005.
Takaki, Ronald. *Iron Cages: Race and Culture in 19th-Century America*. New York: Oxford University Press, 1979.
"Taking the Unintended out of Pregnancy: Colorado's Success with Long-Acting Reversible Contraception (LARC)." *Colorado Department of Public Health and Environment*, January 2017. https://www.colorado.gov/cdphe/cfpi-report.
Tashman, Brian. "Religious Right Hero Vladimir Putin Okays Polygamy, Sharia Law." *Right Wing Watch*, July 28, 2015.
Tatum, Carrington. "Fort Worth Police Shooting Spurs Calls for Transparency, Justice in Death of 28-Year-Old Woman." *Texas Tribune*, October 13, 2019.
Tauer, Carol A. "The Tradition of Probabilism and the Moral Status of the Early Embryo." *Theological Studies* 45 (1984) 3–33. http://cdn.theologicalstudies.net/45/45.1/45.1.1.pdf.
Tawney, R. H. *Religion and the Rise of Capitalism*. London: John Murray, 1948.

Taylor, Keeanga-Yamahtta. *Race for Profit: How Banks and the Real Estate Industry Undermined Black Homeownership*. Chapel Hill: University of North Carolina Press, 2019.

Taylor, Marisa. "Exclusive: U.S. Axed CDC Expert Job in China Months Before Virus Outbreak." *Reuters*, March 22, 2020.

Tertullian. *Apology*. Translated by S. Thelwall. In Ante-Nicene Fathers, edited by Alexander Roberts et al., 3:24–116. Buffalo, NY: Christian Literature, 1885.

———. *Letter to Scapula, Governor of Roman North Africa*. Translated by S. Thelwall. In Ante-Nicene Fathers, edited by Alexander Roberts et al., 3:215–22. Buffalo, NY: Christian Literature, 1885.

———. *On the Soul*. Translated by Peter Holmes. In Ante-Nicene Fathers, edited by Alexander Roberts et al., 3:377–496. Buffalo, NY: Christian Literature, 1885.

Tharaux-Deneux, C., et al. "Risk of Ectopic Pregnancy and Previous Induced Abortion." *American Journal of Public Health* 88 (1988) 401–5.

Theodosius I. *Codex Theodosianus*. Translated by Clyde Pharr. In *The Theodosian Code and Novels and the Sirmondian Constitutions*, 11–476. Clark, NJ: Lawbook Exchange, 2008.

Thomas, Katie. "The Story of Thalidomide in the U.S., Told through Documents." *New York Times*, March 24, 2020.

Thompson, Derek. "The Shame of the Mortgage-Interest Deduction." *The Atlantic*, May 14, 2017.

Thomson, Helen. "Study of Holocaust Survivors Finds Trauma Passed on to Children's Genes." *The Guardian*, August 21, 2015.

Thomson-DeVeaux, Amelia. "When Abortion Was Only Legal in 6 States." *FiveThirtyEight*, August 28, 2014.

Thorp, John M., Jr. "Public Health Impact of Legal Termination of Pregnancy in the US: 40 Years Later." *Scientifica*, December 13, 2012.

Thorp, John M., Jr., et al. "Long-Term Physical and Psychological Health Consequences of Induced Abortion: Review of the Evidence." *Obstetrical and Gynecological Survey* 58 (2003) 67–79.

Tighe, Mark. "Fetuses Can Feel Pain." *British Medical Journal* 332 (2006) 1036.

Toosi, Nahal, et al. "Before Trump's Inauguration, a Warning: 'The Worst Influenza Pandemic Since 1918.'" *Politico*, March 16, 2020.

Torbati, Yeganeh. "New Trump Appointee to Foreign Aid Agency Has Denounced Liberal Democracy and 'Our Homo-Empire.'" *ProPublica*, June 5, 2020.

Torbati, Yeganeh, and Isaac Arnsdorf. "How Tea Party Budget Battles Left the National Emergency Medical Stockpile Unprepared for Coronavirus." *ProPublica*, April 3, 2020.

Traub, Amy, et al. "The Racial Wealth Gap: Why Policy Matters." *Demos* and the *Brandeis University Institute for Assets and Social Policy*, June 21, 2016.

Trickey, Erick. "How Minneapolis Freed Itself from the Stranglehold of Single-Family Homes." *Politico*, July 11, 2019.

Trindel, Robin M. "Fetal Interests vs. Material Rights: Is the State Going Too Far?" *Akron Law Review* 24.3 (1991) 743–62. https://ideaexchange.uakron.edu/cgi/viewcontent.cgi?article=1618&context=akronlawreview.

Troianos, Spyros. *Chapters of Byzantine Criminal Law*. Athens: Komotini, 1996.

———. "The Embryo in Byzantine Canon Law." April 22, 2013. https://biopolitics.gr/biowp/wp-content/uploads/2013/04/VOL-III-ha-troianos.pdf.

"Trump Retweets Call to Fire Fauci after Doctor Comments on Coronavirus Response." *Associated Press*, April 13, 2020.

Turley, Steve. "President Trump and the Global Religious Right." *Katehon*, October 14, 2016.

"Turnaway Study." https://www.ansirh.org/research/turnaway-study.

"The Twinning Challenge." Personhood Initiative, http://www.personhoodinitiative.com/twinning.html.

Tyrrell, R. Emmett, Jr. "Another Peaceful Solution: Proposition 8 and How Liberals Always Go Too Far." *The American Spectator*, June 17, 2010. Page removed from site.

"UN Committee Sides against Russia in First Domestic Violence Ruling." *Moscow Times*, April 12, 2019.

"United States: Abortion." Guttmacher Institute. https://www.guttmacher.org/united-states/abortion#.

"Use of Highly Effective Contraceptives in the U.S. Continues to Rise, with Likely Implications for Declines in Unintended Pregnancy and Abortion." Guttmacher Institute, December 12, 2014.

Uyghur, Cenk. "Medical Debt Is Ravaging America." *The Young Turks*, January 4, 2019.

Valeri, Mark. "Calvin and the Social Order in Early America: Moral Ideals and Transatlantic Empire." In *John Calvin's American Legacy*, edited by Thomas J. Davis. Oxford: Oxford University Press, 2010.

Van de Weyer, Robert. *On Living Simply: The Golden Voice of John Chrysostom*. Ligouri, MO: Ligouri, 1996.

Van Dijk, B. A., et al. "Blood Group Chimerism in Human Multiple Births Is Not Rare." *American Journal of Medical Genetics* 61 (1998) 264–68.

Verbruggen, Robert. "Did Civil-Rights Laws Ruin America?" *National Review*. February 5, 2020.

Verlee, Megan. "Colorado Debates Whether IUDs Are Contraception or Abortion." *NPR*, March 5, 2015.

Voices of Choice: Physicians Who Provided Abortions before Roe v. Wade. Physicians for Reproductive Health, 2003.

Wade, Nicholas. "New Prospects for Growing Human Replacement Organs in Animals." *New York Times*, January 26, 2017.

Waldman, Paul. "Yes, Opposition to Obamacare Is Tied Up with Race." *Washington Post*, May 23, 2014.

Wallace, C. J. "Transplantations of Ectopic Pregnancy from Fallopian Tube to Cavity of Uterus." *Surgery, Gynecology, and Obstetrics* 24 (1917) 578–79.

Wamsley, Laurel. "Oregon Legislature Votes to Essentially Ban Single-Family Zoning." *NPR*, July 1, 2019.

"War Production." *PBS*, September 2007. https://www.pbs.org/thewar/at_home_war_production.htm.

Ward, Kate. "Porters, Catapults, Community, and Justice: Augustine on Wealth, Poverty, and Property." *New Theology Review*, September 2013.

Ward, Paula Reed. "Rep. Tim Murphy, Popular with Pro-Life Movement, Urged Abortion in Affair, Texts Suggest." *Pittsburgh Post-Gazette*, October 3, 2017.

Watson, Francis. *Paul and the Hermeneutics of Faith*. London: T. & T. Clark, 2016.

Watson, Stephanie. "What Are the Different Types of Abortion?" *Healthline*, August 3, 2018. https://www.healthline.com/health/types-of-abortion.

Weder, N., et al. "Child Abuse, Depression, and Methylation in Genes Involved with Stress, Neural Plasticity, and Brain Circuitry." *Journal of the American Academy of Child Adolescent Psychiatry* 53 (2014) 417–24.
Wehle, Kim. "Bill Barr's Constitution." *The Bulwark*, November 18, 2019.
Weinhold, Robert. "Environmental Factors in Birth Defects: What We Need to Know." *Environmental Health Perspectives* 117 (2009) A440–47.
Weisbord, Robert G. *Genocide? Birth Control and the Black American*. Westport: Praeger, 1975.
Weismiller, David G. "Emergency Contraception." *American Family Physician* 70 (2004) 707–14.
Weng, Xiaoping, et al. "Maternal Caffeine Consumption during Pregnancy and the Risk of Miscarriage: A Prospective Cohort Study." *American Journal of Obstetrics and Gynecology* 198 (2008) 279.e1–8.
"What Are the Tax Elements of Homeownership." *Tax Policy Center, Urban Institute and Brookings Institution*. https://www.taxpolicycenter.org/briefing-book/what-are-tax-benefits-homeownership.
"What Do Orthodox Jews Think about Abortion and Why?" *Slate*, August 25, 2000.
Whitworth, Kristina W., et al. "Childhood Lymphohematopoietic Cancer Incidence and Hazardous Air Pollutants in Southeast Texas, 1995–2004." *Environmental Health Perspectives* 116 (2018) 1576–80.
"Who Foots Bill for Polygamist Communities?" *CBS News*, April 10, 2008.
Wilcox, A., et al. "Caffeinated Beverages and Decreased Fertility." *Lancet* 2 (1988) 1453–56.
Wilkins, Alasdair. "Abortions Dropped by Half in Counties Hit Hardest by Texas Law." *Vocativ*, January 19, 2017.
Williams, Daniel K. *Defenders of the Unborn: The Pro-Life Movement Before Roe v. Wade*. Oxford: Oxford University Press, 2016.
Williams, Diana Duke. "Access to Free Birth Control Reduces Abortion Rates." Washington University School of Medicine in St. Louis, October 12, 2012.
Williams, Trina. "The Homestead Act: A Major Asset-Building Policy in American History." Washington University Open Research, July 1, 2000.
Willis, Mary, et al. "Shale Gas Development, Natural Gas Flaring, and Pediatric Asthma Hospitalizations from 2000 to 2010 in Texas, U.S.A." *ISEE Conference Abstracts*, 2018.1. https://ehp.niehs.nih.gov/doi/10.1289/isesisee.2018.P01.0600.
Wilson, Charles Reagan. *Baptized in Blood: The Religion of the Lost Cause, 1865–1920*. 2nd ed. Athens: University of Georgia Press, 2009.
Wiltse, Jeff. *Contested Waters: A Social History of Swimming Pools in America*. Chapel Hill: University of North Carolina Press, 2007.
Wise, Jacqui. "Abortion Rates Are Similar in Countries Where Procedure Is Legal or Restricted." *British Medical Journal* 360 (2018) k1308.
Wise, Lindsay. "Massive Cuts to Violence Against Women Programs Just 'Technical,' White House Says." *McClatchy DC*, May 25, 2017.
Wolinsky, Howard. "A Mythical Beast. Increased Attention Highlights the Hidden Wonders of Chimeras." *Science and Society* 8 (2007) 212–14.
"Women Who Have Abortions." https://5aa1b2xfmfh2e2mko3kk8rsx-wpengine.netdna-ssl.com/wp-content/uploads/women_who_have_abortions.pdf.
"World Abortion Policies 2013." https://www.un.org/en/development/desa/population/publications/policy/world-abortion-policies-2013.asp.

Wright, Christopher J. H. *Old Testament Ethics for the People of God.* Downers Grove: InterVarsity, 2004.
Wright, N. T. *The Climax of the Covenant: Christ and the Law in Pauline Theology.* Minneapolis: Fortress, 1991.
———. *The New Testament and the People of God.* London: SPCK, 1992.
Wu, Katherine J. "Dads Pass On More Than Genetics in Their Sperm." *Smithsonian Magazine*, July 26, 2018.
Xu, Xin, et al. "Revival of the Intrauterine Device: Increased Insertions among US Women with Employer-Sponsored Insurance, 2002–2008." *Contraception* 85 (2012) 155–59.
Yamada, Masahisa, et al. "Electrical Stimulation Modulates Fate Determination of Differentiating Embryonic Stem Cells." *Stem Cells Journals*, January 2, 2009.
Yang, Sangwon, and Mako A. Nagasawa. "How 'Race' Emerged from Colonialism: A Long Repentance Post #4." *The Anastasis Center for Christian Education and Ministry*, October 22, 2018. https://newhumanityinstitute.wordpress.com/2018/10/22/how-race-emerged-from-colonialism-a-long-repentance-post-4-new-humanity-institute-sangwon-yang-mako-nagasawa/.
Yen, Hope. "VA Says It'll Stop Almost All Use of Unproven Drug on Vets." *Associated Press*, May 28, 2020.
Yong, Ed. "Ebola Returns Just as the White House Loses Its Top Biodefense Expert." *The Atlantic*, May 11, 2018.
Zagorin, Peter. *How the Idea of Religious Toleration Came to the West.* Princeton: Princeton University Press, 2003.
Zane, Suzanne, et al. "Abortion-Related Mortality in the United States: 1998–2010." *Obstetrics–Gynecology* 126 (2015) 258–65.
Zauzmer, Julie. "Christians Are More Than Twice as Likely to Blame a Person's Poverty on Lack of Effort." *Washington Post*, August 3, 2017,
Zeitz, Joshua. "Why Conservatives Should Beware a *Roe v. Wade* Repeal." *Politico*, September 4, 2018.
Zinn, Howard. *Postwar America: 1945–1971.* Indianapolis: Bobbs-Merrill, 1973.

Author Index

כהן-ישר, יוחנן and Jean-Georges Kahn, 35n5

AbortioninCanada.ca, 223n78, 223n79
Agrawal, Nina, 200n2, 206n23, 208n31
Alexander, Michelle, 135n83
Allen, John S., 171
Alter, Robert, 235n12
americanadoptions.com, xi, xii
The American Pregnancy Association, 73n34, 118
ANSIRH, 118n17
Anderson, Michael, 166n4
Angrist, Joshua D., 145n12
Anum, Emmanuel A., 116n9
Appelbaum, Yoni, 168n12
Applebaum, Anne, 310n8
Aquinas, Thomas, 59–60
Arghioroussis, Maximos, 49n50
Armstrong, B.G., 81n57
Armstrong, Elizabeth, 65–66n10
Arneil, Morag Barbara, 148n18
Ashton, Jerry, 176n44
Autor, David, 146n15
Avila, Charles, 149n21, 149n23, 150n25, 150n27, 151

Badger, Emily, 171n22
Bahamondes, L., 74n37
Baker, Kelly J., 8n12
Bakke, O.M., 38, 40n25, 55, 56n65, 59, 104n52
Balmer, Randall, 288n16, 293

Bates, Jerome E., 127n49
Bellah, Robert N., 303n36, 240–241n21, 241n23
Belluck, Pam, 72n31
Bergland, Christopher, 183n11
Berman, Jillian, 176n41
Bhasin, Kim, 312n13
Biggs, Antonia, 118n17
Blachor, Devorah, 132
Blair, Laurence, 310–311n10
Blake, John, 189n27, 190n36
Blakemore, Erin, 187n19
Blanco-Muñoz, Julia, 81
Blankenburg, Stephanie, 222
Block, Sharon, 238n16
Bloom, Harold, 93
Boston, Rob, 95n38
Boteach, Rabbi Shmuley, 239n17
Bottone, Angelo, 76n46
Bouie, Jamelle, 170n15
Boyer, Paul S., 126n43
Brakke, David, 99n41
Brooks, David, 178
Brotman, Barbara, 130n62
Brown, Peter, 235n13
Brown, Lauretta, 224n82
Brownmiller, Susan, 126n42
Broussard, Karlo, 230n2, 232n6
Bruenig, Matt, 172n29
Brueninger, Kevin, 193n47
Brunet, Romain, 225n1
Buchmueller, Thomas, 185n14
Burnard, Trevor, 260n15

Burtchaell, James Tunstead, 127n49
Burton, Douglas A., 105n54

Calderone, Mary Steichen, 128n50, 132–33
Caldwell, Christopher, 284
Calhoun, Byron C., 116
Calvin, John, 24, 117, 159–63
Cardman, Francine, 99n42
Carmon, Irin, 206n21, 209n36, 37, 218n58
Caron, Simone M., 113, 262, 264, 265, 266, 267, 268n45–49
Carter, Neil, 13n28, 15n34
Carter, J. Kameron, 164
Carter, Stephen, 239n17
Castillo, Michelle, 189n29
Cauterucci, Christina, 94n30, 95n33
Cesaretti, Paulo, 105n54
Chait, Jonathan
Chalberg, Chuck
Chapman, Elizabeth N.
Charles, Alan, 133n74, 217n57
Charles, Mark, 147n16
Charles, Vignetta E., 118n17
Chartier, Gary, 239n17
The Chartis Group, 195–96
Chen, Cen, 68n13
Cho, Timothy Isaiah, 8n12
Chortimer, Isaac, 192n45
Christerson, Brad, 9n15
Claeys, Vicky, 137n88
Clapsis, Emmanuel, 48
Cizik, Richard, 15n35
Clark-Flory, Tracy, 211n45, 212n50
Colb, Sherry F., 89n17
Collins, Chuck, 171n20
Collins, Will, 310n7
Collins, William J., 166n7
Colvin, Jill, 194n52
Conger, Krista, 201n4
Cook, J.C., 65n8
Copland, Simon, 201n7
Corrigan, Merritt, 310n7
Cowan, Sarah K., 219n61
Coy, Peter, 172n24
Cross, Frank L., 41n29
Culp-Ressler, Tara, 138n92

Daniel, Sharon, 65n5
Daniélou, Jean, 37n13
Daniels, Kimberly, 226n85
Davis, Angela, 145
Davis, Stephen J., 99n40
De Rosa, Peter, 60n71
Dellapenna, Joseph, 281
Deltete, Robert, 6
Deneen, Patrick, 306, 308, 311, 312, 313, 316, 319
Denejkina, Anna, 94n32
DeNoon, Daniel J., 73n36
Derbyshire, Stuart W.G., 124n32
Dershowitz, Alan, 231
DeParle, Jason, 177n48
DePaulo, Bella, 201n7
DeVega, Chauncy, 145n13
Diamond, Dan, 191n39
Dine, Ranana, 257n4
Dochuk, Darren, 240n19, 287n14, 293
Dombrowski, Daniel, 6
Dominguez-Salas, Paula, 183n10
Doucleff, Michaeleen, 183n10
Dougherty, Michael Brendan, 237n15
Douglas-Gabriel, Danielle, 176n42, 176n43
Douthat, Ross, 137n88
Dowling, M., 239n18
Draper, Electa, 242n25
Drazin, Israel, 235n12
Dreher, Rod, 95n38, 309n6, 318
Dupont, Carolyn Renee, 10n17, 286n9, 287n11
du Preez, Ron, 24
Durant, Will, 41n28
Dworkin, Elizabeth, 140n98
Dyer, Jennifer Eaton, 286n8

Eckholm, Erik, 211n48
Edwards, Frank, 174n32
Edwards, Jim, 189n29
Eibner, Christine, 194n58
Elliot, Larry, 222n76
Elliot, Mark R., 309n5
Emilio, John, 238n16
Englehardt, H. Tristam, 8n13, 37, 46n40, 47n43
Ertelt, Steven, 112n1

AUTHOR INDEX

Evans, James Allan, 105n54
Evelyn, Kenya, 317n16

Fallin, Amanda, 190n34
Falwell, Jerry, 158
Fang, Lee, 193n47
Felitti, Vincent J., 183n11
Ferngren, Gary B., 108n66
Fernandez, Colin, 112n3
Fernandez, Manny, 206n19
Fessler, Pam, 145n13
Finer, Lawrence B., 143, 176, 203n11, 204n13
Fingleton, Eamonn, 174, 175n37
FitzGerald, Francis, 9n15, 10n18, 10n19, 13, 14n29, 14n32, 14n33, 15n35, 158, 240n21, 285n6, 293, 296
Flegenheimer, Matt, 119n22
Flinn, Frank K., 59n69, 59n70, 257n6
Florovsky, Georges, 48n49
Foner, Eric, 172n26, 274, 275n60, 277n61, 284n5
Forsythe, Clarke D., 116, 125–26, 129, 130, 132, 138n94, 266, 267, 273, 274n58, 281
Foster, Diana Greene, 137n86
Foster, Thomas A., 259, 260
Ford, Matt, 95–96n38
Fowler, C.I., 204n12
Frangipani, Joseph Magnus, 108n65
Franklin, Donna L., 15n37
Freeman, Curtis W., 286n10
Fukuyama, Francis, 100n44

Gaddis, S. Michael, 171n21
Gaines, Alexandra Cawthorne, 145n9, 145n10
Galli, Mark, 13n27
Garrett, Laurie, 192n43
Gardner, Tiffany M., 169n13
Garratt, Canon, 27n11
Garrow, David, 120n27, 126n43, 129
Gavrilyuk, Paul, 31n14
Gee, Alison, 76n45
Gelernter, David, 305n37
Gemzell-Danielsson, Kristina, 73n32
Gerdts, Caitlin, 211n45
Gilens, Martin, 189n26

Gleason, Fr. Joseph, 230–231n2
Goodwin, Doris, 188n24
Gold, Edwin M., 134n76, 134n78
Gold, Howard R., 175n40, 176n41
Gold, Jenny, 124n34
Gold, Rachel Benson, 133, 134n81
Goldenberg, David M., 165n3
Goldstein, Warren, 91–92
Gordon, Linda, 268n45
Gould, Elise, 144n5
Graber, Mark A., 125–29, 133–36, 139n95, 139n36, 217n56, 217n57
Graham, Franklin, 309n5
Gray, Kathleen, 317n17
Greenhouse, Linda, 289n17
Grenoble, Ryan, 192n43
Gross, Terry, 85n1
Grossman, Daniel, 73n35, 124n35, 124n37, 206n24, 208, 209n35, 210n41, 210n42, 211n43, 211n44, 220
Grudem, Wayne, 156–58
Gustafson, Kaaryn S., 189n27, 190n36
Guttmacher, Alan, 121, 127, 132

Haberkorn, Jennifer, 11n21
Hairston, James E., 187n22
Hall, Robert E., 127n47
Hamilton, Alexander, 272
Handlin, Oscar, 100n45
Hanlon, Seth, 167n10
Harding, Susan F., 15n35
Harrington, Rebecca, 208n30
Harris, Adam, 176n41
Harris, Elizabeth A., 173n31
Harris, Jonathan, 106n60
Harris, Lisa H., 220n62, 220n63, 220n64
Harris, Nadine Burke, 183n11
Hart, David Bentley, 4n2, 5n3
Hasstedt, Kinsey, 214n53, 221n66
Hatzinikolaou, Nikolaos, 46n40, 47n43
Hays, Richard B., 18, 31, 35n4, 47
Health Research Funding, 118
Healy, Melissa, 124n33, 124n37
Hegewisch, Ariane, 114n5, 114n6
Herron, George D., 150n28
Herrin, Judith, 106

Heyne, Thomas, 108n65
Hill, Catey, 144n7
Hilton, Boyd, 222n74
Hinderaker, John, 292n21
Hines, Darlene Clark, 266n42
Hochschild, Arlie Russell, 188n23
Holmes, M.M., 11n22, 74n39
Holzwarth, Larry, 238n16
Hotez, Peter J., 187
Howard, Kimberly, 171n22
Howley, Elaine K., 243n27
Hui, Edwin C., 69, 71
Hylen, Susan E., 99n40

In Our Own Voice: Black Women's Reproductive Justice Agenda, 226
Interlandi, Janeen, 183n8
Illing, Sean, 173n31

Jacobse, Father Johannes, 108n65
Jacobson, Louis, 192n43
Jatlaoui, Tara C., xii n4, 142n1, 199n1
Jemison, Elizabeth L., 8n12
Jennings, Willie James, 164n2
Jewish Virtual Library, 35
Joffe, Carole E., 120, 130, 131
Johnson, Akila, 194n55
Johnson, Richard W., 144n8
Jones, Rachel K., xii n2, 203, 213n52, 219
Jones, Ryan, 62n73
Joyce, Theodore J., 138
Julian, Kate, 201n6, 201n7
Justinian I, 103n49, 104–6, 109, 110, 162

Kaldellis, Anthony, 307n3
Kanno-Youngs, Zolan, 193n46
Kaplan, Laura, 130n62
Kaplan, Lawrence, 9n14
Kavanaugh, Megan L., 226n85
Keirnan, John S., 189n32
Keene, David, 272n52
Kendi, Ibram X., 165n3, 259n8, 259n11
Kerridge, Eric, 161n38
Kertscher, Tom, 119n22
Kesling, Ben, 194n53

Kidd, Kelley, 177n47
Kiely, Eugene, 192n41
Kizenko, Nadieszda, 94n29
Klein, Brandon, 11n23
Klippenstein, Ken, 191n39
Koopmans, M., 69n23
Kreeft, Peter, 70–71
Kreider, Alan, 320n25
Kristian, Bonnie, 175n39
Kruesi, Kimberlee, 119n23
Krugman, Paul, 189n28
Kruse, Kevin, 240n19, 293
Kumar, Anugrah, 90n18
Kurtin, Danna, 221n70
Kurtzleben, Danielle, 172n29

Ladd, Chris, 185–86, 191, 287n12
Lamis, Alexander P., 292n21
Larsen, Jonathan, 309n5
Lascaratos, John, 106n63
Lawson, Kimberly, 89
Ledbetter, Rosanna, 5n5
Lederer, Laura, 140n98
Lee, Felicia R., 125n38
Lee, Susan J., 124n31
LeMay, Michael C., 265n35
Leonard, Ira M., 264n33
Lepore, Jill, 289n17, 291n19
Levatino, Anthony, 120, 122–23
Levey, Noam N., 193n49
Levin, Matt, 171n18
Levine, Robert S., 194n57
Levitan, Dave, 124n31
Lewis, Jone Johnson, 105n55
Lewis, Robert, 188n24
Li, De-Kun, 65n6, 65n6
Liptak, Adam, 207n25
Llana, Sara Miller, 255n1
Locke, John, 147–48, 151
Lopez, Ashley, 211n47, 211n49, 213n51
Lupo, Philip J., 221n71
Luhby, Tami, 194n56
Lucca, David O., 175n39
Luthi, Susanna, 195n59

Mabus, Ray, 195–96
MacDonald, Dennis R., 234n10
MacDonald, Park, 284n4

MacGillis, Alec, 316n15
Mackay, Robert, 192n43
Maddow, Rachel, 96n39
Madrick, Jeff, 188n24
Maizes, Rachel, 222n75
Malter, Jordan, 189n31
Mancini, Jeanne, 77n49
Maqbool, Aleem, 242n24, 242n26, 244n28
Mapping Prejudice, 166n5
Marcus, Ruth, 76
Margo, Robert A., 166n7
Marsden, George M., 9n15, 240n21, 293
Marsh, Frank H., 79n56
Martin, Joyce A., 116
Martin, Nina, 87n7
Martin, William, 288n16
Martinez, Marina Trahan, 174n34
Massey, Douglas S., 166n5
Mattera, Philip, 222n75
Matzarioti-Kostara, Sofia, 106n62
Mavrelos, D., 115n7
Mayer, Jane, 190n34
McCoy, James, 64n1
McCrummen, Stephanie, 11n23
McGuire, Danielle L., 266n42
McNamee, Stephen, 173n30
McWilliams, David, 170n16
Messer, Ellen, 127n46
Meredith, Anthony, 52n58
Merritt, Jonathan, 312
Merritt, Keri Leigh, 172n25, 172n26, 266
Mettler, Suzanne, 189n26
Miller, Patricia G., 129n55, 129n56
Miller, Randall M., 8n11
Miller, Timothy S., 108
Miller, Tom, 185
Mills, Paul, 222n75
Millward, Jessica, 260
Mitchell, Brian Patrick, 307n3
Mitchell, Colter, 183n11
Miura, Nagamitsu, 148n20
Mock, Brentin, 174n32
Mohr, James C., 261–68
Molynn, Mark., 183n8
Mora, Marie T., 144n6
Morgan, Edmund S., 186n18

Morrison, Tim, 192n43
Moscow Times, 94
Munoz, Ana Patricia, 171n20
Murphy, Erin E., 69n20

Nagasawa, Mako, 103n50, 164–165n2
Nakhai-Pour, Hamid Reza, 65n4
Nanasi, Natalie, 95n37
Nasaina, Marina, 106n61
Nash, Elizabeth, 208n30
National Academies of Science, Engineering, and Medicine, 123
Natoli, Jaime L., 76n44
Nazworth, Napp, 231n3
Nelson, Anne, 240n20
New, Michael J., 206n22
Nesbit, Jeff, 190n34
Newkirk II, Vann R., 172n28
Nicoll, Rachel, 182n7
Nielsen, G.L., 65n4
Nirappil, Fenit, 193n50
Noll, Mark A., 8n11, 240–241n21, 263, 293, 303n36
Noonan, John T., 53, 93n27, 230, 231, 233, 237
Norris, Louise, 224n81
North, Anna, 119n24

O'Donovan, Oliver M.T., 247n30, 301, 303, 306n2
Olasky, Marvin, 281n69
Olson, Samantha, 183n9, 221n69, 221n73
Olick, Diana, 171n18
Otis, Leah Lydia, 101–2
Omondi, Sharon, 89n15
Ortiz, Erik, 89n12

Pabst, Emma, 221n67
Packer, Herbert L., 134
Padula, Amy, 182n5
Palmer, Anna, 11n21
Paltrow, Lynn, 86n4, 88n10
Panetta, Grace, 191n39
Papanikolaou, Athanasios D., 234n10
Parramore, Lynn Stuart, 189n31
Parazzini, F., 115n6
Paul, Maureen, 73n35

Paul, Rand, 239n17
Pearce, Matt, 10n20
Peck, Rebecca, 72n30
Peel, J., 5n6
Pereto, Alison, 243n27
Perlberg, Steven, 249n31
Perlstein, Rick, 292n21
Perrone, Lorenzo, 235n11
Personhood Initiative, 17
Petchesky, Rosalind Pollack, 268n45
Phillips, Kevin, 291, 293
Phillips, Tom, 310–311n10
Physicians for Reproductive Health, 120
Piaggio, Gilda, 73n33
Pianigiani, Gaia, 124n36
Pickrell, Ryan, 193n49, 193n51
Pilkington, Ed, 86n2, 187n21
Polgar, S., 134
Pollitt, Katha, 257n4
Pope John XXIII, 11n24
Pope Leo XIII, 11n24
Pope Paul VI, 11n24
Pope Pius XI, 11n24, 12–13
Posner, Eric, 255n2
Poulakou-Rebelakou, Effie, 106n63, 109–111
Pracher, Maria, 91n19

Qian, J., 66n11
Quiggin, John, 148n20

Radde-Gallwitz, Andrew, 43n31, 43n33
Radley, David C., 221n65
Rah, Soong-Chan, 147n16
Rampell, Catherine, 189n28
Rape, Abuse and Incest National Network, 75
Rapoza, Kenneth, 117n17
Rasmussen, Adam, 49n51, 49n52, 50n55
Raz, Raanan, 183n9, 221n68
Reagan, Leslie J., 125, 126, 264, 268n45
Ren, Sheng, 182n6
Rennie, Daniel, 182n3
Reno, R.R., 318
Rettner, Rachael, 68n17
Reynolds, Andrew, 308n4

Richardson, Heather Cox, 287
Richman, Sheldon, 239n17
Rios, Edwin, 317n17
Rivas, Anthony, 183n9, 221n68
Rivkin Jr., David B., 317–18
Roberts, Dorothy, 87, 259
Rothstein, Richard, 166n4, 166n8, 167n9
Robbins, Rebecca, 160n37
Rocca, Corinne H., 118n20
Roccasalvo, CSJ. Sr. Joan L., 318n23
Rochat, Roger W., 133n75, 134
Rodrigo, Chris Mills, 317n16
Rodman, Hyman, 133n75
Rosen, Harold, 133n75
Rosenberg, Gabe, 120n25
Rosenberg, Nathan, 100n45
Rosenblatt, Kalhan, 89n13
Rosenthal, Elisabeth, 137n85, 138n93
Rowe, Jeff, 284n3
Rovner, Julie, 87n6, 88n11, 224n80
Ryerson, A.J., 9n16

Sagiv, Sharon K., 221n69
Sailhamer, John H., 232n7
Sanders, Linly, 22n7, 78n52
Sanger, David E., 191n39
Schaeffer, Frank, 10, 293
Schoen, Johanna, 130
Scouteris, Constantine, 233–234n9
Scott, Dylan, 196n62
Sedgh, Gilda, 137n85
Servick, Kelly, 68n15
Serwer, Adam, 309n6
Shedlock, Mike, 170n16
Sheets, Kayla, 68n16
Shelton, Janie F., 183n9, 221n69
Shin, Laura, 171n20
Signorello, Lisa B., 65n10
Silver, Christopher, 166n4
Simermann, John, 112n2
Simpson, W.J. Sparrow, 4
Sims, Shannon, 310n9
Sinclair, Upton, 150n24, 150n26
Singer, Peter L., 189n30
Skarnulis, Leanne, 183n9
Smith, Evan, 249n31

Smith, Merril D., 238n16
Smith, Noah, 171n23
Smothers, Hannah, 130n61
Snyder, Ashley H., 226n85
Snyder-Belousek, Darren W., 29n12
Solomon, Richard, 238n16
Spatig-Amerikaner, Ary, 173,31
Stahl, Jeremy, 96n39
Stanger-Hall, Kathrin F., 216n55
Stephen, Mitchell, 46n41
Stephens-Davidowitz, Seth, 146n14, 209n40
Stetzer, Ed, 13n27
Stewart, John W., 5n4
Stoeltje, Melissa Fletcher, 211n46
Stoller, Matt, 176, 178n50
Strain, Lisa, 68n18
Stripling, Jack, 192n40
Strode, Tom, 160n37
Stulberg, D.B., 115n8
Stuart, Alfred W., 89n16
Sullivan, Gail, 204n15, 204n16
Sun, Lena H., 191n39, 192n42
Sydney, Homer, 162n39

Takaki, Ronald, 264n32
Tashman, Brian, 309n5
Tatum, Carrington, 174n33
Tauer, Carol A., 7, 64n1, 71
Tawney, R.H., 161n38, 162n40
Taylor, Keeanga-Yamahtta, 170
Taylor, Marisa, 192n44
Texas Policy Evaluation Project, 208–213, 219
Tharaux-Deneux, C., 115n6
Theodosius I, 103n48, 103n49, 103n51
Thompson, Derek, 167n10
Thomson, Helen, 183n8
Thomson-DeVeaux, Amelia, 138n90
Thorp Jr., John M., 116n12, 116n13
Tighe, Mark, 124n32
Toosi, Nahal, 191n39
Torbati, Yeganeh, 190n35, 310n7
Traub, Amy, 171n21, 171n22, 172n24
Trickey, Erick, 166n6
Troianos, Spyros, 19n4, 41–42, 45n38, 53, 106n62

Turley, Steve, 309n5
Tyrrell Jr., R. Emmett, 239n17

Uyghur, Cenk, 176n44

Valeri, Mark, 162n41, 162n42
Van de Weyer, Robert, 150n25
Van Dijk, B.A., 69n22
Verbruggen, Robert, 284n2
Verlee, Megan, 200n3, 205n17, 205n18
Virginia Slave Act of December 1662, 258n7
Virginia Slave Law of 1682, 259n9
Virginia Slave Codes/Law of 1705, 186, 259n9

Wade, Nicholas, 68n14
Waldman, Paul, 189n33
Wallace, C.J., 115n7
Wamsley, Laurel, 166n6
Ward, Kate, 150n26
Ward, Paula Reed, 131n67, 132n68
Watson, Francis, 232n7
Watson, Stephanie, 224n83
Weder, N., 183n11
Wehle, Kim, 96n39
Weinhold, Robert, 182n4
Weisbord, Robert G., 134n80
Weismiller, David G., 73n32
Weng, X., 65–66n10
Whitworth, Kristina W., 221n71
Wilcox, A., 65n9
Wilkins, Alasdair, 209n38, 209n39
Williams, Daniel K., xiii n5, 12n25, 13n26, 14n30, 14n31, 15n36, 127n44, 127n47, 181n1, 181n2, 255n3, 296n22, 299n27
Williams, Diana Duke, 226n86
Williams, Trina, 172n26
Willis, Mary, 221n72
Wilson, Charles Reagan, 8n12, 241n22
Wiltse, Jeff, 168n12
Wise, Jacqui, 137n85
Wise, Lindsay, 95n33
Wolinsky, Howard, 68n19, 69n25
Wright, Christopher J.H., 152

Wright, N.T., 36n9, 302n33, 303n34, 303n35
Wu, Katherine J., 183n8

Xu, Xin, 202n8

Yong, Ed, 192n43
Yang, Sangwon, 164–165n2

Yamada, Masahisa, 68n13
Yen, Hope, 194n54

Zauzmer, Julie, 145n13
Zinn, Howard, 188n24
Zagorin, Peter, 300n31
Zeitz, Joshua, 114, 279n66, 290n18
Zane, Suzanne, 209n34

Subject Index

abolition of slavery, 8, 101, 276
abortion rates, Germany, 175
abortion rates, U.S., xi–xii, 12, 15, 125–39, 142–47, 198–216, 219, 225–26, 262–63, 267–68
abortion rates, U.S. and marital status, 142
abortion rates, U.S. and poverty, 143–45
abortion rates, U.S. and racial/ethnic identity, 133–34, 142, 145, 209, 210
abstinence-only education, 216, 242, 248–49, 298, 324
adoption, xi xii
Affordable Care Act, 186, 189, 190, 191, 194–97, 202, 205, 225, 280, 306
Akin, Congressman Todd, 11
Akiva, Rabbi, 56
Alabama, 87, 95, 187, 196, 265, 279
Alexander the Great, 20, 30
American Bible League, 8
American College of Obstetricians and Gynecologists, 220
American Medical Association, 220, 263
Anselm of Canterbury, 59, 257
anti-welfare, 145–46, 157–59, 185–97
Aquila of Sinope, 56
Aristotle, 4, 30, 33–34, 37, 55, 57, 58, 59, 60, 63, 104, 179, 257, 269, 320
asthma, 182, 221, 222
Augustine of Hippo, 19n4, 42, 54–58, 63, 69, 100, 101, 150, 235n13, 251, 257, 300, 319

Autism, 182, 183n9, 221–22

Barnett, Ruth, 129–30, 133
Barr, William, 95–96, 308
Basil of Caesarea, 42, 43–53, 54, 55, 57, 58, 63, 99, 107–9, 111, 148–49
Beck, Glenn, 189
Bergstreser v. Mitchell (1978), 79
biblical infallibility, 8
birth defects, 75–79, 181–84, 198, 221–22, 314
blastocyst, 65–66
brain damage, 182, 222
breakdown of the family, 15, 94, 98 101, 105–7, 146, 171–74, 176–80, 250–51
Brotherhood of Liberty, 276
Broun, Paul, 10, 16
Brown v. Board of Education, 15, 282, 286, 287n11, 294, 321
Bryan, William Jennings, 9
Buckley, Senator James, 296
Burnell v. Hobby Lobby (2014), 226–27, 306–7, 312–13, 319

caffeine, 65–66, 229
California, 78, 79, 89, 128, 182, 189n29, 199, 265, 287, 296, 314
Calvin, John, 24, 117, 159–63, 164, 176
cell potency, 67–72, 81, 200, 228, 322
Centers for Disease Control (CDC), 133, 142, 192, 199, 200, 201n5, 205, 212, 214, 318

Chalcedonian Creed, 47
Charlemagne, 106–7, 162
Carter, Jimmy, 288
chiasm, 26–28
child sacrifice, 177
chimerism, 67–72, 81, 200, 229, 322
Chisholm v. Georgia (1793), 273n55
Christendom, 95, 237–41, 247, 250–51, 269, 308, 311–13, 316
Christian libertarianism, 8n12, 179, 240, 247n30, 294
Christianity Today, 12, 14
Civil War, U.S., 8, 263, 266, 270, 273–76, 282, 285, 321
classical liberalism, 117, 308, 313, 319. See also John Locke.
Clean Air Act, 221
Cohen v. State of Israel (1981), 90–91
Colorado Family Planning Initiative, 204–5, 214–15, 242–44, 250
Colorado Right to Life, 242, 244
communist, accusation of being, 179, 240, 290, 291
Comstock Act, 9–10, 268
Comstock, Anthony, 9–10
Connecticut, 10, 138, 148n20, 261, 262, 268, 272
Constantine, 59, 101, 103–4, 300, 304
contraception, 5, 9–10, 11n24, 12–13, 60, 62, 66, 72–75, 89, 115, 125, 137n85, 184, 195, 198–229, 230–51, 267, 268, 272, 298, 299, 306, 312, 315, 319
Costello, Catherine, 263
Council of Ancyra, 43, 44, 45, 111
Council of Arles, 161
Council of Carthage, 161
Council of Elvira, 42, 43, 102, 111
Council of Laodicea, 161
Council of Nicea, 162
Council of Troullos, 52, 111
COVID-19 pandemic, 183, 190–97
Criswell, W.A., 15, 286–88
Curlender v. Bio-Science Laboratories (1980), 79, 314
curse of Ham, 164–65, 285–86

Darwin, Charles, 5, 8, 10, 192–193n45, 242
Dead Sea Scrolls, 20n5, 21, 31–32
debt, home mortgage, 144, 160, 164, 166–75
debt, medical, 175–76
debt, student loan, 175–76
Delaware, 300
Democratic Party/Democrats, xii–xiii, 11, 15, 146, 179, 186, 187n19, 195, 202, 224, 256, 287, 288, 291, 296, 298, 323
deterrence, 126, 135, 137, 210, 216, 220, 316
Didache, 38–39, 41, 46, 53–54, 99
dilation and curettage, 127, 130
dilation and evacuation, 122, 123
DNA, 68–69, 112, 224
DNA test, 112, 224
Doctrine of Discovery, 147
Doe v. Bolton (1973), xi, 121, 271, 277, 280–81, 295
Down Syndrome, 75–77, 297
du Preez, Ron, 24–25

Eastern Orthodox Christians, 4, 16, 21, 32, 37, 41n28, 42, 43–53, 55, 63, 82, 94, 107–111, 151, 230, 231, 233, 238, 307, 309n5
ectopic pregnancy, 73, 74, 115, 269
Edwards, Shannon, 131–32
Eisenhower, Dwight, 240
embryo, 6, 10, 16, 19n4, 34n3, 42n30, 44, 45n38, 49–50, 51–52n57, 60, 65, 67–75, 81, 109, 110, 200, 257, 269, 322
Emden, Jacob, 61
Emergency Contraceptive Pills (ECPs), 66, 72
Enlightenment, 5, 147, 179, 243, 294, 304
ensoulment, 3, 6–8, 30, 33, 34, 49, 50, 51, 56–60, 63, 66, 67, 69, 70–72, 81, 200, 228, 257, 290, 321–22. See also quickening.
equal choice, 135–39, 217n56
equal protection, 125–26, 135–39, 217, 271, 276–80

SUBJECT INDEX

Eternity magazine, 14
evangelical. *See* Protestant evangelical.
evolution, 9, 10, 48, 242, 248, 289
expositio (exposure of infants), 34, 38

Falwell, Jerry, 158, 288–89, 291
Falwell Jr., Jerry, 192
feminism, 5, 15, 94, 107, 130, 271, 294, 296
fertilization, 3, 6–8, 18, 65–77, 79, 85, 140, 200–201, 214, 228–29, 297, 321
fetal rights, 78–80
feticide charge, 37, 85–86
Fifield Jr., James W., 240
Finkbine, Sherri, 181
First Amendment, 100, 239, 299–305
Fitkin Memorial Hospital v. Anderson (1964), 78
Florida, 86, 192–193n45, 300
Focus on the Family, 242, 249–50
foetus animatus/inanimatus, 257–58. *See also* ensoulment.
Food and Drug Administration (FDA), 72, 194, 225
formed/unformed, 3, 18, 30, 38, 43–60, 257
Fourteenth Amendment, 79, 135, 136, 173n31, 217, 270, 272–80, 285–86, 295, 297, 315

Galileo, Galilei, 5
Gates, Bill, 190
Georgia (U.S. State), 10, 16, 133, 134, 196, 265, 271, 273n55, 277
G.I. Bill of 1944, 187
Gingrich, Newt, 190
Ginsburg, Justice Ruth Bader, 279
Goldwater, Barry, 287
Gosnell, Kermit, 120, 207, 218
gray (or underground) market for abortion, 128, 134n76, 136, 141, 299, 324
Graham, Billy, 15, 240
Graham, Franklin, 309n5
Great Depression, 15, 130, 134, 146, 317

Greek Septuagint (LXX), 7, 19–32, 35–38, 40, 46, 47, 50, 53–59, 60–61, 63–64, 80, 257, 281, 320
Gregory of Nazianzus, 52n58, 57
Gregory of Nyssa, 49–52, 57, 99, 109, 149, 151, 234, 235, 313
Grudem, Wayne, 157–58
Guttmacher Institute, xii, 118, 137, 142, 199, 200, 213n51, 219

Hale, Dr. Edwin M., 263
Hanson, Dr. Mildred S., 124–25
Hatfield, Senator Mark, 296
higher criticism, 5, 9
Health and Human Services (U.S. Department of), 223
Hebrew Masoretic (MT), 7, 19–24, 26, 28, 30–32, 35–38, 40, 46, 47, 50, 52, 57–58, 60–62, 63–64, 80, 266, 300, 321
Helms, Senator Jesse, 295–96
HIPAA laws, 113, 224
Hippocrates, 4, 34, 58, 63, 109
Hippocratic Oath, 45, 52, 108, 109, 261
Hodgson, Dr. Jane, 130–31
Hogan, Governor Larry, 193
Hogan, Congressman Lawrence, 295
Holcombe, Crystal, 78
Homestead Acts, 172
housing prices, 166–69
Hughes, Hubert, 296

Illinois, 130, 138, 261
implantation/non-implantation, 65–66, 72–74, 81, 200–201, 214, 228–29, 322
In re Jamaica Hospital (1985), 78
Indiana, 85, 86, 138, 268
individual rights, 15, 290, 319–23
infanticide, 33, 39, 40, 41, 45, 59, 97, 103, 104, 108, 109, 163, 238, 266, 302, 205, 320, 323
Intra-Uterine Devices (IUDs), 66, 72, 73, 74, 75, 115, 195, 200–205, 214, 225, 226, 228, 242
Internal Revenue Code of 1954, 185
Internal Revenue Service (IRS), 176, 288

Jane (organization), 130, 133
Jehovah's Witness, 78
Jerome, 54–58, 63, 235n13, 300
Jewish ethics, 7, 19n4, 23, 35–38, 61–62
Jim Crow, 187n19, 196, 266, 268, 277, 282
John Chrysostom, 100, 150, 162
Johnson, Jennifer Clarise, 86–87
Jorgensen v. Meade Johnson Laboratories, Inc. (1973), 79
Justinian, 101, 103n49, 104–7, 109, 110, 162

Keegan, Karen, 68–69
Kelley, Devin Patrick, 78
Kennedy, Justice Anthony, 208
Kennedy, Senator Ted, 291, 296
Kentucky, 192–193n45, 266
King Solomon, 26, 161
Know-Nothings (political party), 263, 265
Koch brothers, 190

land grant colleges, 172
long-acting reversible contraception (LARC) devices, 203, 204, 214, 225
leukemia, 182, 221
Levatino, Dr. Anthony, 120
levonorgestrel, 72–73, 202, 226, 228
libertarianism, 8n12, 179, 189, 240, 247n30, 294
Limbaugh, Rush, 189
limited liability law, 222
Lindsell, Harold, 13
Lippincott, J.P., 276
Locke, John, 117, 147–48, 151, 157, 163, 164, 165n3, 195, 196, 282, 285, 290, 294, 311–12, 314, 319, 324
Lockean philosophy. *See* John Locke *and* classical liberalism.
Lost Cause ideology, 241
Louisiana, 188n23, 208, 266n39, 277
low infant birth weight, 116

Maine, 138
Malthus, Thomas, 5
Martin v. Hunter's Lessee (1816), 273n55

Maryland, 121, 133n75, 193, 199, 238, 259, 260, 273n55, 300
Massachusetts, 138, 261, 264, 265, 278, 317
maternal mortality rate, 134, 138, 207
Maxwell, Mrs. W.H., 263
McCulloch v. Maryland (1819), 273n55
McClesky v. Kemp (1987), 135, 217
Medicaid, 115, 189, 194, 195–96, 214, 223
menopause, 81, 236
mental and emotional health, 14, 45, 74, 77, 89, 95, 102, 112, 113, 118–19, 123, 127, 271, 280, 297
meritocracy, 146, 147–59, 173, 177, 181–96, 198, 284–85, 293, 307, 322, 323
Meyer v. Nebraska (1923), 272, 278
Michigan, 138, 173–174n31, 194n55, 317
Ministry Magazine, 24
miscarriage, 4, 18, 19, 21–25, 26–29, 35, 36, 38, 52, 57, 58, 65, 79, 81, 113, 115, 123, 182, 207, 220, 229, 257, 262
Mississippi, 10, 17, 87, 187, 195, 208, 265, 286n9, 287n11
Missouri, 11, 196, 208, 226, 261
monasticism, monasteries, 99–100
moral injury, 120, 122, 124
moral probability, 6–8, 67, 71, 81, 200
morning after pill. *See* Plan B pill.
Mulvaney, Mick, 95
Murphy, Tim, 131

National Advocates for Pregnant Women, 86, 137
National Association of Evangelicals, 15
National Health Service U.K., 65, 197, 223
natural law, 245–48
New Deal, xii, 11, 15, 141, 146, 178, 179, 187, 240, 282
New Hampshire, 138, 199
New Jersey, 78, 138
New York City, 127, 133, 134, 263, 264
New York State, 78, 128, 138, 259, 261, 265, 267–268n44, 277, 278

SUBJECT INDEX

Newton, Sir Isaac, 5
Nixon, Richard, 204, 287, 291
non-steroidal anti-inflammatory drugs (NSAIDs), 65
North Carolina, 88–89, 90, 133, 237, 259, 265, 308n4
North Dakota, 87, 208
nursing homes, 243

Obama, Barack, 95
Ockenga, Harold, 13
Onanism, 230–38
Oregon, 129–30, 138, 166n4, 166n6, 274–275, 280
O'Reilly, Bill, 189
Origen, 48, 52, 56, 99, 234–35
Origen's Hexapla, 56

Patel, Purvi, 86
People v. John Z (2003), 89
Perry, Rick, 249
personhood amendments, 17, 87
Personhood Initiative, 17, 297
Personhood USA 85, 112
Peter of Spain, 60
Peterson, Scott (and wife Laci, son Connor), 78
Pew Jr., J. Howard, 240
Pharaoh, 25–26
Pierce v. Society of Sisters (1925), 278
placenta, 67, 73, 116, 228, 319
placenta previa, 116
Plan B pill, 11, 72, 73n32, 214, 226
Planned Parenthood v. Casey (1992), 256, 273
pluripotency, 67–70, 228
Pope Gregory I (the Great), 150, 236
Pope Gregory VI, 59
Pope Gregory XIII, 60
Pope Gregory XIV, 60
Pope John XXI, 60
Pope John XXIII, 11n24
Pope Leo III, 106–7
Pope Sixtus, 60
poverty, xii–xiii, 12, 15, 16, 32, 45–46, 59, 79, 93, 103, 111, 114, 137, 143–46, 151, 156, 163, 171n22, 176–78, 183, 187, 188n23, 194, 195, 197, 214, 216, 221, 225, 290, 291, 305, 315, 319, 322, 323, 324
pregnancy, unintended, 74, 96, 113, 125, 127, 138, 143, 144, 145, 176, 184, 197, 203, 204, 209, 219, 220, 226, 242, 243
pregnant women's civil rights, 85–88, 113, 319, 324
premature/preterm birth, 19–25
Prince v. Massachusetts (1944), 278
Prohibition, 126, 136, 219, 264
prostitution, 101–3
Protestant evangelical, xii, xiii, 4, 8n12, 8n13, 9–16, 62, 69, 89, 90, 107, 145–48, 157–59, 162 (including "John Calvin and his theological heirs"), 191, 195, 222, 226, 228, 238, 240–241n21, 242, 246n29, 250, 256–57, 263, 273, 282–83, 284–99, 302, 303, 308–310, 312, 316, 320–24
Protestant fundamentalist, 4, 5, 8, 9, 10, 287, 288, 308
Protestant-individualist synthesis, 179, 311, 312
Ptolemy, 30
Pulcheria, 104
Puritans, 8, 60, 162, 165n3, 238, 240, 257–58, 276
Putin, Vladimir, 94
Pythagoras, 34, 58

quickening, 3, 5, 45, 46, 55, 60, 63, 257, 258, 261, 262, 265–68, 278–81
Quinisext Council. *See* Council of Troullos.

Rankin, John, 187
rape, 11, 72, 74–75, 89, 96–97, 105, 112, 125, 127, 238, 248, 266
rape, marital, 91–94, 237
rape exemption in abortion law, 12, 14, 62, 81, 128, 132n68, 223, 224, 241, 249, 294, 295, 296, 297
Reagan, Ronald, 10, 169, 176, 189, 264, 287, 292, 296

Reconstruction, 172, 265, 272, 274, 276, 277, 282
Reconstruction Amendments, 270, 274, 275–77, 284, 321
religious freedom, 15, 78, 288, 289, 301, 306, 312
Renslow v. Mennonite Hospital (1977), 79
Republican Party/Republicans, xii–xiii, 3, 10, 12, 15, 87, 119, 189n33, 190, 192, 193, 195, 202, 205, 206, 224, 256, 264, 287, 288n16, 289, 291, 292, 293, 296, 298, 299, 313, 317, 318, 323
restorative justice, 29, 30, 160, 247n30, 312
retributive justice, 29, 30, 148, 165, 247n30, 251
Rhode Island, 138
Roe v. Wade (1973), xi, xiii, 3, 15, 17, 76, 87, 120, 121, 124, 125, 126, 128, 130, 132, 136, 138, 139, 217, 255–57, 267, 270–81
Roman Catholic Church on abortion, xii, 3–5, 6–7, 11–13, 14, 16, 32, 42, 47, 53, 54–60, 63, 64n1, 70–71, 72, 82, 90, 95n38
Roman Catholic Congregation for the Doctrine of the Faith, 6
Roman Catholic Declaration on Procured Abortion, 6
Roman Catholic doctors/physicians, 12, 127, 146
Roman Catholic immigration, 9–10, 263–68, 294, 323
Roman Catholic New Deal Democrats, xii, xiii, 11, 15, 141, 146, 179, 291, 323
Roman Catholic orders, 100
Roman Catholic papal infallibility, 4, 6, 8, 269
Roman Catholic Vatican I, 4, 269
Roman Catholic Vatican II, 12, 14, 288
Roman Empire (pagan), 34, 36, 42, 58, 110, 304, 319
Roman Empire (Christian), 104, 304
Roman Empire (Byzantine Christian), 19n4, 41, 52, 105–111, 162, 238, 300, 307
Romney, Mitt, 190
Roosevelt, Franklin Delano, 11, 166, 240
Roosevelt, Theodore, 268
RU-486 pill, 73, 75, 136, 209, 211, 220
Russian Orthodox Church, 94, 309n5

Samaritan Pentateuch, 21, 27n11, 31
Santorum, Rick 190
Scalia, Justice Antonin, 273
Sessions, Jeff, 95
Seventh Day Adventist, 24
sex before marriage, 90
sexual freedom, 15, 133, 177
Shriver, Sargent, 296
Shuai, Bei Bei, 85
single parent, xii, 15, 77, 142, 171n22, 175
Smith, Adam, 222
Smith v. Brennan (1960), 78
South Carolina, 87, 95, 265, 266n39
South Dakota, 208
Southern Baptist Convention, 14–15, 286, 287n11
Southern Baptists, 14, 89, 286, 287, 289, 292, 296
Spencer, Dr. Robert Douglas, 126, 129
spina bifida, 182, 221
State of Florida v. Johnson (1989), 86–87
State of Israel, 62, 91, 131, 301, 303, 310–311n10, 321
Storer, Dr. Horatio Robinson, 263–64
Symmachus, 56
Synod of Pavia, 162
Syriac/Syrian Christianity, 38, 41, 42, 53–54, 58, 63

targeted restrictive abortion provider (TRAP) laws, 136, 208, 210, 215–16, 218, 219, 220, 225
Tay-Sachs Disease, 79, 182
Tertullian of Carthage, 19n4, 40, 46
Texas, 15, 78, 136, 183, 196, 202, 206–249, 270, 273, 277, 278, 286
Texas House Bill 2, 206

Texas Policy Evaluation Project, 208–213
thalidomide, 181
Theodora (Empress, wife of Emperor Justinian I), 101, 104–6, 110
Theodotion, 56
Thomas Aquinas, 59, 151, 257
tobacco, 81, 182, 190, 197, 229
Todd, John, 264
totipotency, 67–68, 228
Trump, Donald, 94–95
twinning, 67–68, 71, 81, 200, 228, 322

Unborn Victims of Violence Act of 2004, 22, 78
undocumented status, 79–80
Uziel, Rabbi Benzion, 61

vasectomy, 66, 81, 140, 230, 243, 268
Vereide, Abraham, 240
Vermont, 138
Violence Against Women Act, 94

Virginia, 186, 238, 239, 258, 259, 260, 286n8, 289, 300
Virginia Slave Act of December 1662, 258n7
Virginia Slave Law of 1682, 259n9
Virginia Slave Codes/Law of 1705, 186, 259n9
Vulgate Bible, 56, 300

Waltke, Bruce, 13
Washington, DC, 95n38, 129, 138, 199, 250, 268, 309n5
white supremacy, 8, 107, 164, 166, 170, 177, 196, 198, 282, 287, 290, 294, 300, 321, 323, 324
White, Justice Edward D., 277
Whole Woman's Health v. Hellerstedt (2016), 206
Williams, Roger, 240
Winthrop, John, 240

Yick Wo v. Hopkins (1886), 135, 217
young earth theory, 8, 248

Ancient Near Eastern Documents Index

Old Testament/Hebrew Bible

Genesis

1	25, 47, 147–51, 154, 163, 196, 234, 245, 248, 285, 312
1:1–2:3	50
1:26–28	91, 151
2	91, 245, 248
2:1–3	26
2:4–4:26	51
2:4–25	51
2:7	50, 72
2:10–14	151
2:15	151
2:18–25	151
2:21–22	72
2:22	50
2:24	154, 244
3:20–24	30
4	21
9	286
9:5–6	21
9:6	241
9:20–29	231, 248
9:25–27	165n3
10	151
16	248
17–18	248
18:12	236
19:5	248
19:30–38	248
27:45	24n10
29–30	231
29:20	26
29:30	26
31:38	24n10
38	230–38
38:8–9	248
38:24–26	248
42:36	24n10
43:14	24n10
46:20–22	20n5
47:12	153
47:24	153

Exodus

1:5	20n5
1:8–14	26
1:15–22	26
8:2	24
12:23	24
15:26	108
12:27	24
14	25
15:26	108
16:18	156
20:4–6	30
20:5–6	153
20:13	18
20:15	25
20:16	217

Exodus (continued)

21	13, 18, 23, 25, 32, 35, 38, 40, 46, 47, 52, 56, 57-58, 62, 63, 80, 81, 300, 301, 302, 322
21:2–23:33	25
21:2–36	26–27
21:2–6	25
21:2	161
21:10	92
21:12–14	26
21:13	22
21:16	25, 103, 304
21:18–21	26, 29
21:18–19	28
21:22–27	26
21:22–25	3, 17, 18, 19, 26, 28, 29, 36, 37n12, 52, 54, 60, 61, 63, 64, 113, 200 257, 266, 281, 321, 322
21:22–23	40n24, 54, 55
21:22	19, 23, 24n10, 28, 64
21:23–25	21, 29
21:28–31	22, 29
21:32	29
21:35	24
22:1–23:33	26
22:1–14	30, 312
22:26–27	160
23:8	135
23:26	24n10
25:40	234
32	25
32:35	24
33–34	25
35–Lev 27	25
40:34–38	72

Leviticus

13–15	157
13	233
15:1–15	233
15:16–18	233
15:19–33	233
17:11	49
18	248
19:17–18	29
19:22	135, 217
20	248
20:11	231
24:17–22	29
25	152, 153, 158
25:1–55	217
25:1–7	153
25:10–15	153
25:10	159
25:23	157
25:25–27	153
25:35–38	160
25:39–41	161
25:40–41	155
25:54–55	161
25:55	152
26:17	24
26:22	24n10

Numbers

5	62, 96
5:11–31	61
14:42	24
27:8–11	157
35:11–24	157
36	231

Deuteronomy

1:42	24
4:5–8	153
5:17	18
6:10–11	72
10:16	247
11	152
14:17–22	157
14:22–29	157
14:28–29	157
15:1–17	155, 157, 160, 217
15:3	160
15:8	161
16:19	135
17:6	96

17:12	23
19:1–13	22
19:15–21	29
21:15–17	231
22	62
22:13–30	61
22:13–19	61
22:25–27	96
23:19	160
24	152
24:1–4	93n27, 154
24:1	93
24:6–15	157
24:7	103
24:10–24	160
24:17–22	157
24:10–22	217
24:19–22	159
25:5–10	231
25	232
25:9	230–231n2, 232
25:11–12	22, 28
27–28	30
27:25	135
28:7	24
30:6	247
32:8	151
32:9–10	31–32n18
32:37–43	31–32n18
32:43	20n5
35:11–24	157

Judges

4–5	98, 100
11	98

1 Samuel

1–2	98
8:10–18	158
14:41	31n18

2 Samuel

11–12	248
12:1–15	239
12:5–6	30

1 Kings

8:10–11	72
9:15	26
9:19	26
9:21	26
9:24	26
21	153

2 Kings

22	98
22:14–20	100

Isaiah

1–5	153
1:23	135
5:23	135
7:14	20n5
33:15	135
58–59	153
58:1–14	217
58:6	160
59:20	20n5
61:1	20n5

Ezekiel

16	153
18:10–18	161
22	153
22:12	135, 161, 217
40–47	152
46:18	157

Hosea

9:14	24n10

Amos

5:12	135

Micah

4:1–5	153
6:8	153
7:3	135

Habakkuk

2:6–7	161

Job

10:18	17
21:10	24n10
29:12	153
29:17	153

Psalms

1	153
15	153
15:5	135, 161
16:6	159
22:16	31n18
37	153
40:6	20n5
72:1–13	158
112	153
119	153
139:15–16	17–18

Proverbs

1:8	152, 159
5	97
5:19	235, 248
5:20	248
10:4	158
17:23	135
19:14	157
23:10–11	159
28:3	158
28:7–9	159, 161
28:15–16	158
29:14	158
31	100
31:11	233

Ruth

3:2–12	153
3:12–4:15	231
4:1–6	153

Song of Songs

1:1–3:5	235
2:7	235
2:16	233
3:5	235
4:12–16	235
5:2	235
5:11	248
5:16	248
8:4	235

Ezra

	98

Nehemiah

5:1–15	161
6	98

Daniel

4:27	154
7:13–14	154n32

2 Chronicles

19:6–9	135
36:20–21	153

New Testament

Matthew

3:13–17	161
5:27–30	93
5:31–32	93
5:42	161
6:14	161
6:19–34	155
6:25–34	155
7:12	135
9:18	23
14:1–5	239
15:18–20	154
16:12–15	155
18:21–35	161
19:3–12	154

19:4	154	17:20–24	161
19:5	154	20:22	72
19:7	154		
19:8	154	## Acts	
19:12	90, 98, 100		
19:13–30	154	1:1–10	154–155n33
19:14	18	2:41–45	217
19:27–29	155	4:31–34	217
19:28	154	7:14	20n5
24:15	154n32	13:1–3	98
24:27	154n32	16:14	100
24:30	154n32	17:26–27	151
24:39	154n32	18	246n29
25:31	154n32	19–20	246n29
26:26–29	155	21:9	98
26:64	154n32		
27:27–37	154–155n33	## Romans	
28:16–20	154, 155		
28:18–20	161	1:21–32	247
		2:1–4	247
		2:12–16	247
## Mark		2:28–29	247
		6:6	247
10:12	93	7:14–25	247
10:13–31	154	8:3	247
		8:18–25	153
## Luke		11:26	20n5
		12:17–21	241
1:44	47–50	13:1–7	241
4:18	20n5	16:1–2	98–99
6:21–49	154	16:3	98
7:36–50	161	16:7	98
8:41	23		
11:9–13	161	## 1 Corinthians	
12:13–34	217		
14:7–35	154	1:11	98
14:12–25	217	2:9	161
15:1–32	154	5:1–7:39	244
16:19–31	154, 217	5:1–13	245
18:15–19:10	154, 217	6–7	247n29
18:15–30	154	6	311n11
18:15	18	6:10	103
19:1–10	312	6:12–20	245
24:13–30	154	6:16	244
		6:13	244
## John		6:14	244
		6:15	244
1:12	156	6:17	244
3:16–21	156	6:18	241, 244
4:39–42	98		

1 Corinthians (continued)

6:19–20	245
6:19	244
6:20	245
7	98, 100, 311n11
7:1–7	93–94
7:1–6	245
7:1–5	90
7:7–9	245
7:17–20	245
7:21–23	245
7:25–40	245
7:36–39	245
7:39	89
9:27	307
10:1–13	234
11:2–16	98, 246n29
11:2	246n29
11:16	246n29
11:17–24	154, 156
11:28–32	42
15	320
15:12–58	244
15:22	50, 245
15:45	50, 245
16:8–9	246n29
16:9	98

2 Corinthians

8–9	217
8:9	156
8:10–15	156
8:13–15	156

Galatians

4:21–31	234
5:20	18

Ephesians

	246
1:22–23	246n29
3:20	161
4:15–16	246n29
4:28	156
5–6	246n29
5:22–6:9	246n29
5:22–33	247n29
6:1–4	246n29
6:5–9	247n29
6:9	247n29

Philippians

3:2–3	304
4:2–3	98

Colossians

	246
4:15	98

2 Thessalonians

3:10–13	156

1 Timothy

1:10	103
4:13	248
5:3–22	98, 100, 104
6:1–2	104

2 Timothy

3:16	248

Titus

3:5	154n31, 154–155n33

Hebrews

1:6	20n5
7–11	233
10:5	20n5

1 Peter

	247n29
3:18–20	232
4:6	232
4:17	96

James

5:1–6   217

1 John

3:16–18   217

Pseudepigrapha

Letter of Aristeas

20

Dead Sea Scrolls

4Q22   31
4Q44   32n18

Rabbinic Writings

Josephus, *Against Apion*

2.202   36

Josephus, *Antiquities of the Jews*

4.33   36

Makot

1:1   29

Mekhilta de Rabbi Ishmael

37n12

Midrash Nidpas

37

Mishnah Arakhin

61

Philo of Alexandria, *On Special Laws*

3.108–9   35n4

Responsa Maharit

1:5   92

Sanhedrin

57b   37n12

Sanhedrin

84b   37n12

Talmud Bava Kamma

83b–84a   29

Talmud Eiruvin

100b   92

Talmud Niddah

44b   37n12

Tosefta Sanhedrin

59a   37

Yevamot

37

Greco-Roman Writings

Aristotle, *History of Animals*

7.3   30, 33, 34

Aristotle, *Politics*

7.16   33n2

Plato, *Republic*

5.460b-c	33n1
5.460e-461c	33n1

Galen, *The Construction of the Embryo*

	49n51

Papyrus Oxyrrhynchus 744

	34–35

Early Christian Writings

Acts of Paul and Thecla

	99

Ambrose of Milan, *Letters*

17:7	300n29

Apocalypse of Peter

	41
8	39, 40

Apostolic Constitutions

	42, 44, 53–54, 57, 58
7.3	53
Canon 85	41n28

Athenagoras of Athens, *Plea for the Christians*

	46
35	39–40

Augustine of Hippo, *Epistles*

98:6	54n62
121	55n63, 56n65

Augustine of Hippo, *Expositions on the Psalms*

	150

Augustine of Hippo, *City of Man*

66.3	69

Augustine of Hippo, *Correction of the Donatists*

	300

Augustine of Hippo, *Marriage and Concupiscence*

1.15–17	235

Augustine of Hippo, *Questions on Exodus*

2.80	55

Augustine of Hippo, *On the Work of Monks*

	100

Basil of Caesarea, *Epistles*

188	53
188:1	44
188:2	43, 46
188:8	53
217:52	45–46

Basil of Caesarea, *Hexaemeron*

	47–51
1:2–4	48
1:3	48
1:10	50n55

5:10	48n45	2:2	38–39
8:1	48n45	5:2	38–39
9:2	48n45		
9:3	50n53		

Ecloga

19n4

Basil of Caesarea, *Homilia in illud, Attende tibi ipsi*

7   48–49

Epistle of Barnabus

19:5   39, 46 / 39

Basil of Caesarea, *Homilia in sanctam Christi generationem*

4   49

Gregory of Nyssa, *Fourth Homily on Ecclesiastes*

149

Basil of Caesarea, *On Social Justice*

69–70   149

Gregory of Nyssa, *Making of Man*

29.1   50–51 / 51n56

Clement of Alexandria, *Eclogae Propheticae*

41   40

Gregory of Nyssa, *On Infants' Early Deaths*

51–52

Council of Ancyra

     43–45, 53, 111
Canon 21   43
Canon 22   43

Hippolytus of Rome, *Refutation of All Heresies*

9.7   40–41

Council of Elvira

     42–43, 102, 111
Canon 22   43
Canons 47–48   42–43
Canon 63   42–43

Jerome, *De Viris Illustribus*

117   57n66
128   57n66

Council of Troullos

     52–53

Jerome, *Epistles*

52:8   57n66

Didache

     38–39, 41, 46, 53–54, 99

John of Damascus, *Exposition of the Orthodox Faith*

4.17   41

Justin Martyr, *First Apology*

27	39, 46
	39

Lactantius, *Divine Institutes*

6.20	59

Marcus Minucius Felix, *Octavius*

30–31	41

Origen, *Hexapla*

	56

Origen, *Song of Songs: The Commentary and Homilies*

1	235n11

Philocalia

	52n58

Tertullian of Carthage, *Apology*

9:8	40

Tertullian of Carthage, *Letter to Scapula*

	300n29

Tertullian of Carthage, *On the Soul*

37	40

www.ingramcontent.com/pod-product-compliance
Lightning Source LLC
Chambersburg PA
CBHW050611300426
44112CB00012B/1457